The Threefold Struggle

SUNY series in American Philosophy and Cultural Thought

Randall E. Auxier and John R. Shook, editors

The Threefold Struggle

Pursuing Ecological, Social, and Personal Wellbeing in the Spirit of Daniel Quinn

Andrew Frederick Smith

Cover art: Daniel Quinn, Ishmael.org

Chapter 4: Excerpt from *The Holy*. Copyright © 2006 by Daniel Quinn. Reprinted with permission from Steerforth Press.

Chapter 8: Selection adapted from Andrew F. Smith, "Surviving Sustainability: Degrowth, Environmental Justice, and Support for the Chronically Ill," *Journal of Philosophy of Disability* 1(1) (2021), pp. 175–199; https://doi.org/10.5840/jpd20217263.

Chapter 8: Selection adapted from Andrew F. Smith, "Symbioculture: A Kinship-Based Conception of Sustaiable Food Systems," *Environmental Philosophy* 18(2) (2021), pp. 190–225; https://doi.org/10.5840/envirophil202179108.

Chapter 10: Selection adapted from "Intended and Unintended Successes," in *The Ethics of Homelessness*, 2e, ed. G. J. M. Abbarno. Copyright © 2020 by Andrew F. Smith. Adapted with permission from Steerforth Press.

Published by State University of New York Press, Albany

Printed in the United States of America

For information, contact State University of New York Press, Albany, NY
www.sunypress.edu

Library of Congress Cataloging-in-Publication Data

Name: Smith, Andrew F., 1972– author.
Title: The threefold struggle : pursuing ecological, social, and personal wellbeing in the spirit of Daniel Quinn / Andrew Frederick Smith.
Description: Albany : State University of New York Press, [2022] | Series: SUNY series in American philosophy and cultural thought | Includes bibliographical references and index.
Identifiers: LCCN 2022005556 | ISBN 9781438488714 (hardcover : alk. paper) | ISBN 9781438488738 (ebook)
Subjects: LCSH: Quinn, Daniel—Philosophy. | Quinn, Daniel—Political and social views. | Quinn, Daniel—Criticism and interpretation. | Well-being. | LCGFT: Literary criticism.
Classification: LCC PS3567.U338 Z87 2022 | DDC 813/.54—dc23/eng/20220217
LC record available at https://lccn.loc.gov/2022005556

10 9 8 7 6 5 4 3 2 1

For Daniel—and anyone
"who wants more from life than just a chance to
feed at the trough where the world is being devoured"

Contents

Preface

If asked to sum up this book in one sentence, I'd say that it's about convincing fellow members of settler colonial culture that we benefit immensely from decolonizing our minds, our practices, and (ultimately) the lands we occupy. It's aimed at convincing those of us who comprise the latest iteration of a long Taker lineage, to use Daniel Quinn's terminology, that we deserve better than being captive to a culture in which we're compelled to destroy the world, one another of the living community, and even ourselves. Every last person on this planet, colonizers and colonized alike, is worthy of living otherwise. And we all stand to gain from decolonization if we're willing to struggle on its behalf.

What exactly this means and what it entails will take some time to unpack, but let me offer just a few orienting comments.

I'm not an acolyte of Quinn; he wouldn't want me to be even if this were my inclination. But I am an appreciator of his wide-ranging ideas. I've spent the bulk of my life formally and informally trying to create a vision of a world that I could tolerate living in. This enterprise has kept me going in all but my darkest of days. The relationships I've formed along the way, including with Daniel, kept me going when my "vision quest" couldn't.

This book is one manifestation of my attempt to uncover criteria not merely of tolerability but of wellbeing. And what I've found is that wellbeing involves fostering relations of responsibility, particularly with the human and other than-human beings and entities who comprise one's ecology. Even under ideal conditions, acting responsibly is a heavy lift for us colonizers. This isn't because we're evil or immoral. It has more to do with the vast majority of us being well trained to be both cannibals and zombies—unthinking, largely unperceptive devourers of others' lives.

Again, not a condemnation. Instead, a condition to recognize, understand, and resist.

"I'm exhausted by a heartbreak that never seems to stop," Michelle Obama proclaimed in the wake of George Floyd's murder by Minneapolis police in 2020. Indigenous peoples across the globe—particularly those subject to settler colonialism—know unending heartbreak at least as well. At the same time, countless black and brown persons persistently, doggedly struggle against the breakers of hearts. Indigenous peoples in particular fight tooth and nail to maintain relationships with and responsibilities to their ecologies. Their responsibilities aren't mine; I've got responsibilities of my own. But mine and theirs interweave and overlap in what Quinn refers to as the web endlessly woven.

"We're on dangerous ground now, because of our secrets and our lies," Valery Legasov states in the miniseries *Chernobyl*. "They're practically what define us. When the truth offends, we lie and lie until we can no longer remember it is even there. But it is still there. Every lie we tell incurs a debt to the truth. Sooner or later the debt is paid."

Legasov, a nuclear scientist, discovered the depths of his own naiveté regarding the appeal of truth late in life. He failed, he states, "to consider how few actually want us to find it. But it is always there, whether we see it or not, whether we choose to or not. The truth doesn't care about our needs or wants, it doesn't care about our governments, our ideologies, our religions. It will lie in wait for all time. And this, at last, is the gift of Chernobyl, that I once would fear the cost of truth, now I only ask: What is the cost of lies?"

This question wends through what I call the threefold struggle: the struggle for ecological, social, and personal wellbeing. It motivates my ongoing attempt to enact a new story, as Quinn puts it, in concert with others who want more from life than just a chance to feed at the trough where the world is being devoured. If you too want more than this, this book is for you. Read whatever parts of it suit your fancy. Let me know what you think. More importantly, let's talk further about how we can escape our captivity. We deserve it, every last one of us.

Acknowledgments

When a book takes a decade (from conception to publication) to produce, one ends up having many people to thank. I've done my level best to keep track of all those who deserve thanks. I apologize to those who I've overlooked.

First, I must thank Doug Anderson for introducing me and my project to series editors Randy Auxier and John Shook. Doug's friendship and mentorship are priceless. And Randy and John's strong recommendation of the project sent it on its way with SUNY Press. I also thank Michael Rinella, Senior Acquisitions Editor at SUNY Press, for ably shuttling the project through proper channels. Diane Ganeles, Senior Production Editor, ably guided the project through the production process. Two anonymous reviewers provided invaluable feedback.

Abioseh Porter and Donna Murasko afforded me much-appreciated release time in the project's early stages. They also supported a much-needed sabbatical.

Countless students have given me welcome feedback. I owe a huge debt of gratitude to Ian Bowen and Mackenzie Grapes who independently urged me to read *Ishmael* and *The Story of B* in the first place. Sarah Griggs and Rachael Wilson offered crucial organizational support as Humanities Fellows in 2013 and 2016, respectively. Thanks as well to Oli Glass, Maddie Worth, Mia Bevilacqua, Jessica Kunadia, Suguna Chaganti, Ananya Yalamanchi, Trisha Menon, Abim Sharpe, Melissa Duong, Andrew Rindlist, Francis Rosato, Caiti McCormick, Eric Petsopoulos, Kevin Biallis, Robert Keyser, Sabrina Ahmed, Zachary Norton, Kelechi Chukwueke, Jackie Garcia, Laura Somogie, Atiq Rahman, Lia Domico, Kerry David, Evan Baum, Bennett Furman, Annie Haftl, Cece Cirne, Abby Wagner, Lauren Lowe, Morgan Sarao, Maz Mazokowski, and Jessica Hervey.

Huge thanks to Gwen Ottinger, friend and colleague, who read and commented on several chapters and offered incredible feedback on the book proposal. I must acknowledge the members of Making Meaningful Connections—Sarah Wirth, Seona Boyle, Dane Ward, Sherry Brandt-Rauf, Steve Dolph, and Carrie Hutnick—for providing friendship and emotional support. Thanks as well to Ali Kenner, Kristy Birchard, Ian Werkheiser, Emily Holmes, Mark Ranalli, Amanda Corris, Ghadi Tayeh, Trevor Smith, Lisa Schwartzman, Sarah Clarke Miller, Gaile Pohlhaus, and John Hacker-Wright.

Members of my outpatient support group helped save my life. Thank you Mary Therese Kelly, Marni Drames, Steve Greene, Max Lawrence, Nancy Tallis, Ron Snell, Bill Shane, and John Branton.

Childhood friends have provided more inspiration than they can possibly know. In particular, I must acknowledge David Horn and Stephen McLaughry.

Indigenous philosophers have offered both key support and critical feedback, if often indirectly. Thanks especially to Andrea Sullivan-Clarke, Kyle Whyte, Brian Burkhart, Shay Welch, and Shelbi Nahwilet Meissner.

Former student and current friend Jay Jolles is an inspiration and a fellow traveler of a road to nowhere. We need more like you in the world.

I benefited greatly from participation in a 2016 National Endowment of the Humanities Summer Institute, headed by Joan McGregor and Dan Shilling. Research support also came from the Drexel Office of the Provost via a 2017 Faculty Scholarly and Creative Activity Award.

Finally, all love to my immediate family. The six of us are home, wherever we may be. Thank you Sherrilyn for, well, every minute of every day I've had the privilege of sharing with you. And endless chin scratches and belly rubs for Celie, Hugo, Sasha, and The Do.

List of Abbreviations for Quinn's Texts

A list of mentioned characters, with their descriptions, can be found on page 297.

AD	*After Dachau*
AW	*At Woomeroo*
B	*The Story of B*
BC	*Beyond Civilization*
BD	*Book of the Damned*
D	*Dreamer*
H	*The Holy*
I	*Ishmael*
IS	*The Invisibility of Success*
MI	*My Ishmael*
MGY	*The Man Who Grew Young*
NGA	*A Newcomer's Guide to the Afterlife*
P	*Providence*
Q&A	Ishmael.org Questions and Answers
TA	*Tales of Adam*
WS	*If They Give You Lined Paper, Write Sideways*
WWW	*Work, Work, Work*

Prologue

The Threefold Struggle for Ecological, Social, and Personal Wellbeing

In his autobiography, Daniel Quinn remarks that every time he says something like, " 'It was my good fortune at this point that . . .' or, 'As luck would have it . . .' or, 'If this had happened just one week earlier . . .' or words to that effect" (P, 114), we can assume he's talking about Providence. Providence, it's something like divine inspiration or guidance, right? This is how the term is commonly conceptualized, and while Quinn intentionally leaves it undefined he does have something like this in mind. As we'll see, though, we need to be very clear that we're on the same page when we're discussing what he means by divinity, inspiration, and guidance. The devil—or, the Antisavior, as it were—is in the details.

But let's not get ahead of ourselves. For the moment permit me simply to say a few words about the rationale for this book, which I can't help but think of as a work of Providence in its own right. Despite the popularity of Quinn's best-selling novel *Ishmael* and its follow up *The Story of B*, published in 1992 and 1996, respectively, I'd not heard of him until a decade ago. It was my good fortune that Quinn's work found me when I was ready to give it the sustained philosophical attention it deserves and hasn't yet received.[1] As luck would have it, I also was ready to see my crippling alcoholism as a manifestation of our cultural pathology. I needed to see this in order to get and stay sober. And we need to see why our culture, which Quinn calls Taker culture—settler colonial culture is its most recent manifestation—works neither for the planet nor for people.

Captivity

I started drinking in my mid-teens and regularly binged over the next couple decades. But after a devastating experience centered on my professional life, I began hitting the bottle really hard. For five years, I downed nearly a fifth of bourbon a day.

I guess I was what's called a functional alcoholic, although the term is really a misnomer. I got drunk, really drunk, almost every night. But with a pot or two of coffee each morning I was able to make it through the next day before coming home and doing the whole thing over again. I taught my classes, managed to write a book and several articles, somehow landed a tenure-track job, and otherwise got done what I needed to do. Yet I lived in a perpetual fog, hung over during the day and pretty much inert at night—with "night" coming earlier and earlier as the years progressed.

Henry David Thoreau asserts in *Walden* that most people of our culture aren't quite awake. We sleepwalk through life, able to engage in the daily essentials and perhaps a few distractions but not much else that we would deem genuinely worthwhile. I see how this description applied to me, but Julie's way of expressing it in *My Ishmael* comes closer to what I remember of my day-to-day experiences as an alcoholic. "Do you know what I say to myself all the time?" she says to Ishmael. "I mean *all* the time—twenty times a day. I say to myself, 'I've got to get out of here.' . . . I'll be taking a shower or washing the dishes or waiting for the bus, and that's what'll pop into my head: 'I've got to get out of here' " (MI, 17). And I would, disappearing into the bottom of a bottle.

In time, though, I began to notice that my disappearing act wasn't working as well as I once thought it had. The more I chased numbness, the harder it became to achieve. In common parlance, my tolerance for the drink increased. But there was something else going on, too. I was becoming aware that getting out of here each evening was constantly just out of my reach—and actually always had been. It was always one more drink away. Along with beginning to experience the breakdown of my blood platelets, this awareness turned out to be a key factor for getting me into rehab. And the fuller understanding I now have of what led me to drink in the first place, what I desperately wanted to escape, has helped me to feel far more compassion than I thought possible for the person (or quasi-person; more later) I was.

Particularly in the United States, we tend to view addiction in two competing ways, neither of which is all that helpful. Organizations such as Alcoholics Anonymous support the widespread belief that addiction results from abiding moral defects. The medical community views addiction primarily through a pharmacological lens, as the routine abuse of dangerous substances that, in due time, alter one's neurobiology in ways that create and strengthen reliance. Both parties, though, depict addiction as irrational. No one of sound mind willfully chooses to become an addict. One becomes an addict because one's mind becomes warped. Or, in more clinical terms, destructive habits reinforce adverse modifications to one's neurobiology.

Yet, I've come to think of my alcoholism instead as a manifestation of what I can only call a *rational dysfunction.* It's a fucked-up practice that nevertheless makes sense to engage in, given one's prevailing options. No, I didn't want to become a drunk per se. But why I abused alcohol certainly makes sense to me, and it's reducible neither to moral deficiency nor to pharmacology.[2]

What exactly was the *here* I urgently needed to get out of? What was I trying to escape by drinking myself into oblivion? My demons past, present, and (presumably) future, for sure. But there was something else, too, something far uglier that I couldn't identify until I first cracked open *Ishmael.*

"My subject is: *captivity,*" Ishmael tells his new pupil, Alan Lomax (I, 24). Alan doesn't know quite what to make of this. But when I first read this line I felt as if I'd been struck by a thunderbolt. We Takers are captives of a culture that compels us to destroy the world. This isn't our path of least resistance. *There's no other path within our cultural confines.* Traveling it is required of us to live and make a living. In order to get by, we're compelled to engage in behaviors that are profoundly damaging—to the planet, to others, and to ourselves. This too is a rational dysfunction. It's also ugliness incarnate.

In a culture that only compounds our demons with the inability to escape being both damaging and damaged, even self-destructive relief had erstwhile advantages. Comedian Russell Brand states in jest that "drugs and alcohol are not my problem. Reality is my problem. Drugs and alcohol are my solution" (2013). They're a terrible solution, yes, but for an even more terrible reality.

I still want to get out of here, mind you. But the *here* that I want out of, I now see, isn't my body or my life. I want out of Taker culture so that I can more deeply embody my life. What I was missing during my foggy years that I now have isn't yet a path in view free from cultural captivity—a means to live and make a living in a manner that works for the planet and for people. But I do have the rough sense of a path. And it begins by embracing what, inspired by Quinn, I call the *threefold struggle.*

The Threefold Struggle

At the core of Quinn's philosophy is an abiding focus on the *interweaving roots of ecological, social, and personal wellbeing.* These three forms of wellbeing are co-implicated, not compartmentalized. We can't enjoy one without equally enjoying the others; they're a package deal. What works for people individually and collectively works for the planet, and vice versa. This is the core proposition of the threefold struggle, which Quinn defends with a level of clarity and narrative force I find in no other author's work.[3] Its implications are breathtaking, potentially chain breaking.

"All that you touch you change. All that you change changes you," writes Octavia Butler (1993, 3). Our everyday practices and the larger systems in which we live both shape and are shaped by one another, often imperceptibly. Even caring for ourselves "is not self-indulgence, it is self-preservation, and that is an act of political warfare," Audre Lorde proclaims (2017, 130; see also Q&A, 588). More to the point, reclaiming our lives and bodies and revitalizing our human and more-than-human communities are acts of resistance against our "culture of maximum harm" (BC, 109).[4]

Resistance is rarely effortless. It's often unsuccessful. To be shapers of the systems that shape us doesn't imply that we can transform them at will. Entrenched institutions that operate according to even more entrenched axioms have made it incredibly difficult for Takers not just to find the key to our cell door but to fully grasp the extent of our captivity. These axioms have an ambient quality. They're "like the sound of blood rushing through your veins," Quinn contends (P, 89; see also BD, 7, and I, 36). They're etched onto our subconscious. Indeed, neither you nor I necessarily avow the Taker axioms. We may even reject them outright. But we nevertheless *enact a story*—carry out a vision of ourselves and our place in the order of things (I, 41)—that's guided by them. In other words, they're part of our cultural inheritance: unstated, implicit, background assumptions that shape how we live and make a living.

Let's look briefly at three of these axioms. For starters, one belongs to Taker culture if one regards as pro forma keeping food under lock and key. It's impossible to understate how significant this seemingly simple practice has been for the emergence and perpetuation of our culture. The second axiom, Quinn states, is "as important as the ones Copernicus and Darwin overturned" (Q&A, 257; see also BD, 11ff.). Namely, "The people of our culture are what humanity was *meant* to become" (ibid.). The way Takers live, as intensive agriculturalists and aggressive builders of hierarchically organized societies, is how humans are intended to live. Third, we're insatiable devourers of the earth's biomass and unrestrained disseminators of pollutants in such massive quantities that we've triggered a sixth mass extinction (IS, 10; see also Kolbert 2014) because we're inherently flawed.

That these axioms, particularly the latter two, don't cohere is of scant consequence, Quinn contends (Q&A, 577), and not just because their ambient quality renders them nearly invisible to us. Even if we do register their dissonance, we tend to rationalize it anyway. At most, we tinker around the edges of our worldview until things fit together a bit more comfortably.

But tinkering will do us no good, Quinn insists. Taker culture doesn't work and can't be made to work—not because of how we're constituted but because of how we live. Intensive agriculture, or what Quinn calls *totalitarian agriculture,* and the *hierarchalism* at the root of our socioeconomic structures must be abandoned if we're to enact a story that works for people and for the planet. No elaborate arguments are required to make this clear, Quinn adds. Rather, we can look to myriad examples of people not of our culture who enact workable stories—Leaver peoples, as Quinn calls them, or members of Indigenous communities and those who acquire food nonintensively and largely live nonhierarchically.

In this context, William Ross McCluney remarks, "'What works' means what is sustainable, fits well into the overall web of life" (2004, 191). It represents a means of living and making a living that's robust (resistant to internal failure), adaptable (responsive to changes such that overall functionality is maintained), and resilient (able to withstand and/or bounce back quickly from disruption). This applies ecologically, socially, and personally, although the interweaving roots of these three forms of wellbeing aren't always easy to see.

"The dancer's admonition is *Never let them see you sweat,*" Quinn exhorts. "When it comes to the laws of the universe, the admonition is *Never let them see you at all: make them deduce your existence. . . .* What works in the living community is similarly cloaked by its success" (BC, 11). Great dancers' flawless performances belie years of effort. The elaborate and intricate interactions between ecosystems, species, and individual organisms that make up the living community—which is a community of communities, really—are no different.[5] These interactions function smoothly only after eons of evolutionary trial and error. Their very seamlessness makes them largely invisible to us even though we depend on a healthy and vibrant world to survive and thrive.

The ways turtles live works, the ways ferns live works, the ways phytoplankton live works. These claims aren't subject to question. The ways *some* humans live works, too, despite widespread skepticism among Takers. For Takers, our workaday experience is of cultural pathology, which we translate as human pathology. But, taking an extended and expanded view, our culture is an anomaly. Otherwise, our species would have gone extinct long ago.

Rejecting Environmentalism in Favor of Saving the World

Permit me now to offer some context for the threefold struggle. Quinn is well aware of the accelerating rate of habitat destruction; massive biodiversity loss and the impending collapse of marine and terrestrial food webs; widespread soil salinization and erosion; the global dependence on nonrenewable fuels; the loss of fresh, potable water; toxic chemical proliferation; the devastation of ecosystems by invasive species; the greenhouse effect; explosive human population growth; and the increasing per capita ecological impact of the people of our culture. Any one of these phenomena threatens our existence, yet they're *all* occurring.[6] As Aric McBay puts it, "These crises are not 'possible' or 'impending'—they are well underway and will continue to worsen. The only uncertainty is how fast, and thus how long our window for action is" (2011a, 49).

But this doesn't mean they're best treated as "environmental problems," Quinn avers. Indeed, environmentalism as a theoretical category is poorly conceived. It "reinforces the idea that there is an 'us' and an 'it'—two separate things—when in fact what we have here is a single community" (WS, 81–82). "The environment" isn't out in the woods, the sea, or the desert sands. "There is no 'it' out there," Quinn declares ("EcoGeek"). There's not even an *out there.* What needs to be sustained, restored, and cared for is *right here,* wherein we're one another's habitats. "We are all in this together. There are no two sides. We cannot survive as a species somehow separate from the rest of the living community" (ibid.; see also Kimmerer 2013, 103).

Quinn's rejection of environmentalism has two important implications. First, we can dispense with the idea that we must either be "for the environment" or "for people" (IS, 99)—for spotted owls, say, or for loggers' jobs. The health and wellbeing of the former's habitat is intimately connected to the health and wellbeing of the latter's habitat. And the forms of socioeconomic organization that lead to the destruction of the former also undermine the latter. Clashes between organisms occur, of course, routinely. Colliding agendas are inevitable (Hall 2011, 163). But zero-sum games aren't.

Second, while global climate summits get lots of media attention, the governmental and large-scale nongovernmental organizations (NGOs) that feature at them focus almost no direct attention on the needs of the living community.[7] Governments and NGOs tend to frame their advocacy in terms of protecting the environment. "But I refuse to accept 'protecting the environment' as a meaningful description of our problem," Quinn asserts, "In fact, I think it's a lousy description" (IS, 36; see also Kingsnorth 2010). This frame highlights effects rather than causes. Shielding the planet from abuse is prioritized over preventing abuse in the first place.

Forms of resistance that are intended to protect ecosystems, watersheds, and sacred lands are critically important, particularly in the face of imminent destruction. But most contemporary environmental organizations, at least in their institutionalized form, aren't intimately involved in such enterprises. Nor are they concerned with Quinn's primary objective: facilitating a broad cultural transformation that makes protection unnecessary.

Indeed, those concerned with "protecting the environment" tend to misidentify cultural shortcomings as governmental shortcomings (IS, 36; see also Kingsnorth and Hine 2009, 14, and Boyle 2017). They assume that we need politicians and bureaucrats to take the lead for change to occur. Yet even when government officials aren't beholden to our culture's agents of maximum harm, they overwhelmingly remain under the thrall of "essentially reactionary, essentially defensive" (IS, 38) strategies for fostering sustainability. Political leaders aren't leaders at all. Across the board, they're cultural acolytes.

For these reasons, and for all its grandiose connotations, Quinn regards *saving the world* as a more fitting subject of our concern. Leave "protecting the environment" to governments and NGOs. "Saving the world is for upstarts and lovers," he quips. "Saving the world is for the rest of us" (ibid.).

Upstarts and lovers? We'll get to this in due course.

❧

I recall a commercial running during my alcoholic days that opens with a man languidly singing the following line (in a poor imitation of the blues): "Today, the world is pretty sad." But we learn this can't be so as the commercial progresses, since the world is home to the wonderful product being peddled—in this case, an automobile. Most of us don't buy it: either the car or the claim. With respect to the latter, there's something so obviously wrong with the world. With so much pain, suffering, anger, and hatred, the world really is a sad place. For too many people (both human and other-than-human), it's cruel, harsh, and unforgiving.

Quinn disagrees, not with the proposition that there's untold suffering in the world but instead that it's something about the world itself that's creating this situation. There's no more anything wrong with the world than there's anything wrong with humanity. "Assuming that by 'the world' you mean the world of life . . . it's a self-perpetuating, self-renewing organism that has been functioning flawlessly for four billion years or so—and is still functioning flawlessly today" ("Dialogue on *Beyond Civilization*").[8]

Saving the world doesn't mean somehow fixing it, then. Rather, the world needs to be rid of a culture whose inhabitants are well trained to think nothing of destroying and devouring it in ever-increasing quantities. And jettisoning this culture also means saving ourselves, since this culture encourages us to think nothing of destroying and devouring ourselves and one another. These aren't two separate propositions for Quinn. *Saving the world means saving ourselves. Saving ourselves means saving the world.* They're two sides of the same coin (MI, 193f.). So it shouldn't be surprising that ecological, social, and personal wellbeing are intimately connected.

Quinn does state elsewhere that the world to be saved is "something that would be better described as 'the sphere of human material activity' " (B, 48). What's in need of saving is "a *human habitat,*" a Goldilocks zone for human life (P, 6; see also "Dialogue on *Beyond Civilization*"). While this might sound anthropocentric to the core, this isn't the case. Yes, we humans matter. But if saving the world and saving ourselves are interchangeable propositions, then Quinn can't be suggesting that we *alone* matter. We must foster conditions that are conducive to our survival and capacity to thrive over the long term, which means we must give up the benighted idea that we can ruin our home while expecting it to go on sheltering and supporting us.[9] Our home is populated by living communities, of which we, too, are full-fledged members. Again, we're one another's habitats. For this reason, saving the world as a human habitat "will mean (*must* mean) saving the world as a habitat for as many other species as possible. We can *only* save the world as a human habitat if we stop our catastrophic onslaught on the community of life, for we depend on that community for our very lives" (P, 6; see also MI, 193f.).

How We'll Proceed

Throughout his corpus, Quinn presents his considerations by means of what he describes as the construction of a mosaic. Topics are covered not at random but also not in a preestablished order. His intention is to permit the proverbial image the mosaic embodies—ultimately, of why and (broadly) how to exit Taker culture in favor of a culture that works for the planet and for people—to emerge no matter where one begins one's study of it. Yet after teaching Quinn's books in numerous courses and discussing his work informally with lay readers and fellow scholars in the humanities and social sciences, I've found that analyzing and assessing his ideas systematically helps to clarify how different conceptual tiles of the mosaic connect. I also draw extensively on the work of scholars both inside and outside academia to further illuminate, elaborate on, and sometimes challenge his considerations.

Broadly speaking, the first part of the book focuses on Taker culture, hence on what *doesn't* work for the planet and for people. We begin in chapter 1 by looking more closely at Quinn's specific approach to cultural criticism. John Meyer notes that social and cultural critics have traditionally sought to take the position of the "moralistic outsider" (2015, 7), relying on independently justified standards to challenge problematic institutions and practices. This ostensibly permits them to "escape the assumptions and biases" (ibid.) of the society or culture that's the subject of their attention.

Meyer instead favors a form of internal critique, accepting one's position as an insider who nevertheless can assume a degree of critical distance from the status quo. Internal critics meet their audience halfway by engaging with familiar, everyday experiences. Their goal is to show that the way their audience tends to live is inadequate by the lights of their own avowed needs, interests, and desires. As a result, internal critics make the familiar strange, often by looking at it from a new and unfamiliar angle.

Quinn self-identifies as a cultural critic (Q&A, 498, and "*Diminuendo*"), and his approach to this enterprise operates similarly. Integral to the narrative structure of his novels is the interplay between insiders and quasi-outsiders whose dialogue creates a reflective tension for readers. This supports Quinn's uncanny ability to decenter the Taker frame, revealing the familiar not merely as strange but as *lethal*. Indeed, he makes the incult, blasphemous, and benighted appealing, apposite, and even essential to our engagement in the threefold struggle. This proves particularly useful as we take a deeper dive in chapter 2 into the Taker axioms. We'll see how they support the problematic proposition that engaging in intensive and highly destructive forms of food production supported by hierarchical forms of socioeconomic organization represent the one right way for human beings to live. We'll also explore in greater depth why enacting a story based on the Taker axioms doesn't work and can't be made to work. Quinn's approach to cultural criticism also proves invaluable in chapter 3, as we assess the most common way that Takers have sought to alleviate enduring anguish: namely, via organized religion. Since it's a vestige of Taker culture it doesn't work either, Quinn contends. Nor does it provide a suitable or satisfying pathway for engaging in the threefold struggle. Matters are rather more complicated than he suggests, but I'll leave it at that for now.

In the second part of the book, we examine the philosophical underpinnings of Leaver culture, a culture that has stood the test of time because it supports human and more-than-human life and wellbeing. Quinn's intent isn't, *per impossibile,* to convince Takers to become Leavers. Nor should Takers view Leavers as our cultural life coaches. Both ideas are vestiges of settler colonial culture (again, the latest iteration of Taker culture); they're forms of plastic shamanism and cultural appropriation. Shifting from an assessment of Quinn's cultural criticism to his contributions as a "world philosopher" ("*Diminuendo*"), we focus firmly on the theoretical underpinnings of the threefold struggle.

We proceed from the more general to the more specific: from a focus on the core characteristics of life to humanity to personhood. In chapter 4, I examine what makes embracing our membership in the living community an evolutionary lesson in success. This involves developing a better understanding of the interplay of biological diversity and biological interdependence at the heart of what Quinn calls the *fire of life* and how it's manifest in the *Law of Life*. In chapter 5, I explore how *Homo sapiens* emerged, or how we became human. This can permit us Takers to set ourselves on a path to remembering (yes, most of us have forgotten) how to be human. At our core, we're beings who are capable of acquiring "gifts of wisdom" that permit us to appreciate the sacredness of that which promotes our full-spectrum wellbeing. I then rely on the work of North American Indigenous philosophers in chapter 6 to adumbrate the attributes of personhood and how personhood is connected with our specifiable relationships with and responsibilities to the living community and the land. We learn that personhood—and also peoplehood—is a decolonial kinship-based concept with a more-than-human scope rather than an attribution of specifiable (human) traits or capacities.

In part three, I offer some examples of what *can* work as we members of settler culture explore how to enact a new story. Consider this where we look at putting theory into practice. Quinn devotes attention to quintessential Leaver means of making a living that persist in (and largely in spite of) Taker culture, insisting that they offer examples of how to circumvent subjection to hierarchical institutions. But he rarely connects the dots, leaving it to readers to consider how to operationalize these examples. So in chapter 7, I assess specifically how and whether worker cooperatives offer a model for making a living that can help facilitate the demise of heirarchalism. In chapter 8, I turn my sights to food systems. I explore how longstanding and successful Indigenous alimentary practices might provide means to unlock food—via both decolonizing land and foodways and decommodifying food, traditional food-based knowledge, and food labor—by altering how we relate to the beings who we eat and also to the land.

Chapter 9 tackles the difficult topic of human population. It's here that I'm most critical of Quinn. He offers a systems approach to understanding human population growth, which I too favor. Yet, in assessing specifically why exponential growth is damaging to the planet and to people, he betrays this approach in a manner that prevents him from envisioning how an equitable and incremental reduction in our numbers can take place. Chapter 10, on education, hits particularly close to home. I here present how schooling at every level undermines learning in favor of the creation of pliant workers fit for use by prospective employers. I also wrestle with my complicity in this process and how I can better respect my students' sacredness as well as my own.

While this is a work of scholarship, my focus at times is intensely personal. You've already had a taste of this. As a storyteller and memoirist,

I'm very much the amateur. The broad scope of Quinn's considerations has pushed me to be more eclectic in my research, too. Neither amateurism nor eclecticism (nor dilettantism, I guess) is generally regarded as a sign of good scholarship. Meyer suggests, though, that both are necessary if we're intent on effectively exploring the human experience. When it comes to such an undertaking, he remarks, "The alternative is not to do so as a professional but rather not to do so at all" (2015, 11; see also Stengers 2018, 8f.). I'll take him at his word.

Three More Things to Note

First, you already may have noticed that I'm using a rather peculiar citation style. Abbreviations refer to Quinn's texts, a list of which can be found on page xiii. When I refer to Quinn's speeches, parables, and the like—nearly all of which can be found on his website, ishmael.org—I cite an abbreviated title. References to works by other authors and works by Quinn found in anthologies are in the familiar author-date style.

Second, many of Quinn's texts are novels, so they contain dialogue between characters. I typically refer to these characters by name when I quote their dialogue. But I reserve details about them for the list of mentioned characters, starting on page 297.

Third, you won't always find gender-neutral references in Quinn's novels. He offers the following explanation for this:

> *Ishmael* is not an essay written for an academic journal but rather a work of fiction, specifically a novel. In a novel, characters speak in accordance with their individual backgrounds and experiences, not in accordance with some committee's manifesto. Thus, in a novel, a 12-year-old crack dealer doesn't talk like a middle-aged librarian, and an ambassador doesn't talk like a stevedore. In *The Story of B*, the narrator is a parish priest—someone who is used to being constantly judged by his language—and so, by habit, he's pretty consistently PC in his language. But when it comes to *Ishmael*, it would make no better sense for the narrator and his gorilla teacher to speak the language of political correctness than it would for them to speak the language of gangsta rap. (Q&A, 29)

I find this explanation underwhelming and off-putting, but I leave gendered language unchanged when quoting Quinn's work. Otherwise, I choose to employ gender-neutral language myself. Suffice it to say that I agree with Quinn's own lament that "the English has no genderless personal pronoun" (P, 141).

PART I

TAKER CULTURE: FASHIONING A MOSAIC

Chapter 1

The "Quinn Method" of Cultural Criticism

Memes, Martian Anthropology, and Maieutics

I mentioned in the prologue that Quinn constructs a mosaic the image of which is intended to help us see axioms such as the following for the dubious claims they are: putting food under lock and key reflects the one right way to live; the people of our culture are what humanity was meant to become; there's such a thing as "the environment" that's somewhere *out there*; and we humans are inherently flawed. Other such claims emerge in this chapter and the next. Were Quinn a professional philosopher, perhaps he'd prosaically but methodically give reasons to reject these claims. Taken together, his reasons presumably would constitute a well-developed justification of his position. His argument would be subject to its fair share of criticism, of course. Being able to stand up to scrutiny is a necessary condition for justificatory success. Assuming that his reasons and the way they support the construction of his mosaic hold up, the "force of the better argument" would be in a position to win the day. Ideally, the strength of Quinn's argument would leave many readers itching to do their part to save the world.

If only it were so straightforward. Argumentation can be quite an effective tool when the stakes of acceptance or rejection of the conclusion on offer are relatively low.[1] But saving the world—a high-stakes affair if there ever was one—requires enacting a new story, living according to a different vision of ourselves and our place in the order of things (I, 41). We must undergo a sweeping change of mind. Argumentation alone isn't typically a powerful enough tool for the task at hand, Quinn contends (Q&A, 600, 629, and 650; see also Powers 2018, 336). Changing minds requires a fuller repertoire of strategies.

I begin by exploring in greater depth what Quinn means by having a changed mind and why it's vital for playing a salient role in saving the world. Next, I discuss Martian anthropology, a key (if oddly labeled) part of Quinn's method for identifying questionable background assumptions that serve to perpetuate Taker culture. I then focus on Quinn's use of maieutics, a specifiable form of dialogue among characters in several of his novels. Quinn regards maieutics as a particularly important narrative tool for cultural criticism. It's intended to help bring to full consciousness ideas about which readers are only dimly aware. This permits us to better understand how we're prevented from living well on our own considered terms and why enacting a new story can alleviate this state of affairs. Lastly, I address Quinn's call to become someone who can awaken others to the axioms we live by. This is key to the threefold struggle. If the world is to be saved, minds must change. If minds are to change, we must become invested in stories that work for people and the planet. Capable teachers—in all walks of life—play a critical role in this process.

From Old Minds to New

Perhaps the best place to start to explain more fully the character and importance of a changed mind is to draw on Quinn's discussion of *memes,* a term coined by Richard Dawkins in *The Selfish Gene* that has since taken on a life of its own in social media. This will give us a better sense of the difference between what Quinn calls *old minds* and *new minds* and why, on his account, having a new mind is the most powerful weapon not just to hasten the collapse of Taker culture but also to help facilitate the emergence of a culture that works in its wake.

Memes

According to Dawkins, a meme is "a unit of cultural transmission, or a unit of *imitation*" (1989, 192). The term derives from *mimesis,* or more specifically from *mimeme,* Greek for imitation and imitated thing, respectively. Memes operate as replicators, something they have in common with genes. Genes replicate hereditary data, which are transmitted from body to body over generations via sexual reproduction. Memes replicate ideas and are transmitted from mind to mind both within and across generations via linguistic communication.

Dawkins provides the following example to illustrate how the transmission of memes works:

> If a scientist hears, or reads about, a good idea, he passes it on to his colleagues and students. He mentions it in his articles and his lectures. If the idea catches on, it can be said to propagate itself, spreading from brain to brain. . . . When you plant a fertile meme in my mind you literally parasitize my brain, turning it into a vehicle for the meme's propagation in just the way that a virus may parasitize the genetic mechanism of a host cell. (Ibid.)[2]

Not all memes go viral, of course. Most don't possess the requite infectiveness, contagiousness, communicability, or what Malcolm Gladwell calls "stickiness" (2000, 25) to trigger an outbreak. For this to happen, a meme must transfix us. It must dominate our attention and overshadow rival memes.

This is an especially difficult task when it comes to the dissemination of new memes, since the meme pool that constitutes the whole of a culture "comes to have the attributes of an evolutionarily stable set," states Dawkins (1989, 199). Established memes have inertia, or the force of habit, behind them. So the new memes must be of such "great psychological appeal" (ibid., 193) that established memes by which we're currently parasitized pale in comparison.

Concerns and Qualifications

A number of scholars question whether memetics has the explanatory or predictive power we've come to expect of genetics, hence whether the analogy Dawkins offers is sufficiently salient. Others suggest that memetics is little more than a poor knockoff of semiotics, the study of signs and symbols and their communicative function, dressed up in the language of genetics to look more reputable. Tim Lewens offers a version of both criticisms, focusing the bulk of his attention on the first.

Lewens notes that while genes make copies of themselves, memes don't. People certainly do influence one another, but there's no clear evidence to support that this is caused by identifiable idea-replicators reproducing themselves in a new host (2007, 206f.; see also Hull 2001, 98). Moreover, the spread of a gene through a population occurs because it confers reproductive success on its bearers. This may happen with memes, but it also may not. A tune may catch on simply because its producers or distributors are "powerful enough to make it ubiquitous" (ibid., 208), not because it does much of anything for its hosts. Lastly, Lewens highlights that the way memeticists tend to describe the operation of memes conflates concepts that geneticists hold separate. Memes are said to function like genotypes (that which is replicated) *and also* like phenotypes (the composite of an organism's physical characteristics, that which experiences selection pressure). This would be quite a feat of self-transformation, were it possible. The weight of the evidence suggests that it's not.

Mary Midgley expresses dissatisfaction with two further characteristics of memes, particularly as Dawkins describes them. First, she contends that Dawkins thinks of memes as "fixed, distinct natural units" (2003, 93). They're the ultimate particles of thought and culture. So a proper understanding of culture involves viewing it as divisible into discrete parts, and a proper understanding of thought involves viewing it as atomistic in function. Second, Midgley alleges that Dawkins regards memes as having a life of their own beyond what you or I or any individual can control, so they function as "alien puppet-masters previously hidden from us but revealed now as the true causes ruling our life" (ibid., 70). This invites fatalism, since it insinuates that we're unable to change the way we think.

Quinn's appeal to memetics takes place in *Beyond Civilization,* which was published during the height of scholarly interest in the subject—roughly, the mid-1990s through the early 2000s. On reflection, I suspect he'd find Lewens's challenge compelling. It's likely, too, that he'd partially agree with Midgley. But this doesn't mean we need to give up on memes altogether.

Midgley describes customs and norms as "organic parts of human life, constantly growing, developing, changing, and sometimes decaying like every other living thing. Much of this change, too, is due to our own action, to our deliberately working to change them" (2003, 66). Quinn would agree (as do I). So, rather than being discrete units, let memes serve as proxies for *patterns of movement* in thought, much like roughly discernible ocean currents. We'll see in due order that this fits well with other aspects of Quinn's philosophy. Quinn would hold the line, though, against Midgley's assertion that the "true causes" of our destructive tendencies aren't memes but "conflicting motives" or "warring parts of ourselves" that arise from the "human tendency to self-destructiveness" (ibid., 72). This is simply another way of proposing that we're inherently flawed.

In reply to Lewens, it's worth noting that memes have a folkloric component that can be retained even if we abandon the gene analogy

(Oring 2014a and 2014b). Folklorists attend to the ways in which customs, traditions, stories, and artistic practices are passed from one person to another and from one generation to the next. The study of folklore in particular focuses on how communities both retain and also subtly transform what's passed on.[3] So why not go ahead and think of memes as patterns of folkloric movement? Or, for our purposes, they can be patterns of formation, perpetuation, and transformation of the stories we enact.

Lethal Memes

We Takers, particularly in commercialistic societies, perceive our own culture as dynamic because we encounter numerous memes that are highly volatile. Fashion and music (and scholarly) trends come and go with amazing regularity. New diet fads emerge and disappear every few months, it seems. What's the "new black" today? We can barely keep up. "Nonetheless," Quinn notes, "there is a central core of culturally fundamental memes that we've been transmitting with total fidelity from the foundation of our culture ten [actually twelve] thousand years ago to the present moment" (BC, 32). Much like alcoholism, some of these memes are lethal for us—not instantly, no, but eventually (B, 154)—including each of the axioms we've already identified. They precipitate our extinction and the extinction of millions of fellow species.

Memes don't disappear just because they're lethal. Indeed, their lethality has taken twelve millennia to become fully evident. They're at the core of our culture because they've proven to be particularly sticky. Part of what makes them sticky is that there are all sorts of institutions at work, personified by what Quinn calls *Mother Culture* (WS, 67), that prevent us from seeing them as lethal, if we see them at all.

Every culture has its own set of mechanisms that nurture and sustain the story the people of that culture enact, Ishmael tells Julie (MI, 28). What's unique about *our* Mother Culture is that she nurtures and sustains a message that's not just lethal for our culture—this has happened before—but lethal for much of life on Earth.[4] Also unique, Quinn contends, is the extent to which her message has been absorbed and internalized not just by those who overtly benefit (for now) from exploiting the planet and other people but also by many Takers who are exploited. Takers both with and without socioeconomic status take most or all of Mother Culture's message at face value, as the "way things are" (I, 218, and MI, 172). Furthermore, as odd as it may seem, the memes that Quinn identifies as lethal are precisely those that people without changed minds construe as what make human beings so special and our culture so remarkable. This is what makes them so dangerous.

Belief in Mother Culture's messaging isn't required. Even if you or I or anyone in particular rejects the ideas we live by, we must still live within such a cultural nexus if we're to be fed. How, then, does one play a role in killing a lethal meme? Quinn expands on Dawkins's contention that meme killers champion competing memes that have greater psychological appeal than at least some of the memes that constitute one's current set. He emphasizes that this is most readily possible when people are looking for or are open to a better story (Q&A, 161). Rather than simply working to reveal how and why the way we currently live doesn't work, offering such a story is necessary to change minds.

Note that for a culture (or a subculture, as suggested by the following quote) to collapse and for another to emerge in its place, not all of its core memes must be replaced simultaneously. As Quinn asserts, "To produce the Renaissance, it wasn't necessary to change out ninety percent of the memes of the Middle Ages—or eighty or sixty or thirty or even twenty. And the new memes didn't have to come into play all at once. Indeed, they *couldn't* have to come into play all at once" (BC, 23; see also Brown 2017, 20ff.).[5] New means of living and making a living are composed bit by bit, meme change by meme change. Seemingly insignificant modifications, especially as they accumulate, can turn out to have significant effects (WS, 95).

This suggests that any one of us can spark the sort of viral outbreak that facilitates cultural collapse (IS, 45, and WS, 180). As anthropologist Robert Kelly remarks, "in any given culture, at any given time, each individual represents slight variations on a cultural theme. . . . Culture change is change in the frequency of these variants" (2013, 37). This doesn't mean, though, that it takes only one person to make a change, particularly when it comes to something as colossal as enacting a new story. Ta-Nehisi Coates rightly identifies this is yet one more lethal meme (2015, 96f.), and Quinn agrees. Anyone may transform the meme pool. But major obstacles confront us. This is why Coates defends the proposition that those committed to enacting a story that works are called to *struggle*—his term for engaging in the process of changing minds—not because we're assured of being difference makers but because it can help to keep us sane and resilient under adverse, even oppressive, conditions. This, I dare say, is required to see lethal memes for what they are and to search for ways to make them less sticky.

The Difference between Old and New Minds

According to Quinn, old minds are minds that replicate the lethal memes specifically of our culture. New minds reflect the replacement of these memes with ones that foster enacting a story that facilitates ecological, social, and personal wellbeing.[6] Consider these contrasts:

> Old minds think: *How do we solve these problems?*
>
> New minds think: *How do we make happen what we want to happen?* (BC, 187–88)
>
> Old minds think: *How do we stop these things from happening*?
>
> New minds think: *How do we make things the way we want them to be*? (Ibid., 8)
>
> Old minds think: *If it didn't work last year, let's do MORE of it this year.*
>
> New minds think: *If it didn't work last year, let's do something ELSE this year.* (Ibid., 9)

Notice that old minds—shorthand for *people* with old minds—tend to get stuck in a pattern of trying to deal with issues as they arise. Their priority is putting out fires. New minds are more proactive. They concentrate on developing ways of thinking and acting that work well in general and on the whole without having to need to worry so much about putting out fires.

Seeing and understanding the difficulties we face here and now is hardly immaterial. Accounting for these difficulties is a necessary condition for making happen what we want to happen. But Doug Brown emphasizes that to change minds, "critical awareness is not enough, because although people see what's wrong, if they don't have a realistic vision of what can replace it, then they are subject to demobilization—despair, cynicism, resignation" (2009, 130). From Quinn's perspective, this is precisely why the revolutionary spirit of the 1960s fizzled.

Programs and Visions

"If there are still people here in two hundred years, they won't be *thinking* the way we do," Quinn states WS, 172–73; see also Scranton 2015,

19). Their lives and livelihoods will reflect a new vision—a new story. So must ours, in short order, if we're to find ways to mitigate accelerating ecocide.

If old minds countenance the prospect of our imminent extinction at all, they assume that we can prevent it through the implementation of new programs. But so long as we maintain our current vision, all the new programs in the world can't save us (B, 48, 51, and 91). This is because programs function *within* a vision. They're the product of visions. So we can't expect them to be sufficiently transformative. No, we need a vision that "works so well that programs are superfluous," Quinn asserts. Such a vision "works so well that it never occurs to anyone to create programs to make it work" (BC, 10).[7]

Policies to address global climate change—pricing carbon and taxing emissions, funding renewable energy sources, and setting automobile fuel efficiency standards—are programs. Recycling is a program. So is bioengineering microbes to eat into oceanic garbage patches. This by no means entails that they're useless or shouldn't be pursued, Quinn insists. His point instead is that they aren't sufficient to save the world, even taken together:

> There are many programs in place today that are staving off our death—programs to protect the environment from becoming even more degraded than it is. Like the first aid in [an] ambulance, these programs are essential but ultimately inadequate. They're ultimately inadequate because they're essentially reactive. Like the medics in the ambulance, they can't make good things happen, they only make bad things less bad. They don't bring into being something good, they only drag their feet against something bad. If there's no hospital at the end of the road, the patient in the ambulance will die, because first aid (useful as it is) just doesn't have the capacity to keep him alive indefinitely. If there's no new vision for us at the end of the road, then we too are going to die, because programs (useful as they are) just don't have the capacity to keep us alive indefinitely. (BC, 18)

Again, that programs are essentially reactive doesn't make them worthy of rejection. But it does mean "that they always follow, never lead (because they only react to something else)" (B, 51). There would be no need for them otherwise. And when they fail to do anything more than serve as Band-Aids old minds pin the blame on "poor design, lack of funds and staff, bad management, and inadequate training" (BC, 9)—namely, anything other than the vision from which they arise.

"By contrast," Quinn continues, "vision doesn't wait for something to happen, it pursues something desirable. Vision doesn't oppose, it proposes. It doesn't have to stave off defeat, it opens the way for success" (ibid., 52). Visions thus are self-sustaining. They take no effort on our part to perpetuate. Isolation coupled with the illusion of self-reliance—a separate home or flat for each nuclear family with locks on doors; having no need or desire to rely on or even know one's neighbors (McKibben 2010a, 133); "bowling alone," to use Robert Putnam's (2000) catch-all term for our withdrawal from collective forms of engagement—is a product of our culture's vision. So is the Industrial Revolution. "No one had to 'take action' to make it happen—no one had to pass laws requiring people to be inventive" (WS, 135).

So whereas a vision is like a river, programs are like sticks driven into the riverbed that are meant to impede or channel its flow (B, 49). The vision underlying Taker culture, its direction of flow, is toward catastrophe. Indeed, it's been catastrophic since its inception, Quinn insists, in terms of its ongoing ill effects on the planet and people. This is why a new direction of flow is required. "With the river moving in a new direction, people wouldn't have to devise programs to impede the flow, and all the programs presently in place would be left standing in the mud, unneeded and useless" (B, 52; see also BC, 8).

Is Changing Minds Enough?

Sure, you may reply, changing minds is all well and good. But it can't possibly be sufficient to save the world. Quinn agrees, but he regards this sort of challenge as shortsighted. "This is rather like saying that getting elected president is not enough. Changing minds (and getting elected) is where it *begins*. The fact that it isn't where it *ends* doesn't make it inadequate" (Q&A, 548).

But maybe what you want from Quinn is a definitive plan of action. He refuses, though, to offer anything that looks like a step-by step primer for how to succeed in facilitating the emergence of a new vision (WS, 178). Social change in frequently unpredictable. Those who claim to have a clear-cut blueprint for it are rarely worth listening to, he contends. They're engaging in prophecy, which tends to be attractive to old minds but is basically useless for developing new ones (I, 85f., P, 160f., and BC, 116).

For Quinn, then, there can be no set of instructions for how to get from *here* to *there* if we don't yet have a clear sense of what *there* looks like. All we can do is start *here* and see what works to give us a chance to have a *there*. This is Quinn's concern: not what *there* must be or how we're to arrive at it but how we can foster a *here* that makes possible coming up with a story that facilitates a *there*.

At the same time, Quinn asserts that we shouldn't overlook "that changing minds *is* a 'real plan'—and the only plan we are going to have" (Q&A, 64; see also B, 77, WS, 180, and "Just Talk"). It "may not seem like a very dramatic or exciting challenge, but it's the challenge that the human future depends on" (WS, 180). Discussion and deliberation certainly have their place ("Thoughts on Dialogue"). Along with lecturing, these are often what come to mind when we consider what it means to *teach*, Quinn's go-to term for engaging in the enterprise of changing minds. Indirect forms of resistance may work. More direct forms of resistance against those who currently benefit most from the perpetuation of our culture can count as teaching moments, too.

But one aspect of Quinn's position is in need of immediate correction, or at least clarification. "*What people THINK is what they DO*," he declares. "*To change what people DO, change what they THINK*" (IS, 44; see also McCluney 2004, 285). The first statement strikes me as correct. Thought and action typically coincide. This doesn't mean that people are always completely aware of why they do what they do. The point instead is that people's actions can be taken to be reflective of their background assumptions.

What about the second claim? To change what people do, change what they think. Alter people's background assumptions, and how they act is transformed. Sure, this happens. But is it not also the case that changing what people do can change their background assumptions? Can't we change how people think by changing what they do? I think so, because I'm a case in point. Many recovering alcoholics I know have some sort of epiphany that leads them to seek recovery. We see ourselves and our actions differently and seek help as a result. A new action follows from a new insight. So far, so good for Quinn's claim.

But once in recovery things work very differently. The achievement of long-term sobriety starts with changing entrenched habits: whom one associates with, where one goes and doesn't go, what one spends one's evenings and weekends doing, and so forth. All we can do at first is to alter our actions so that we don't put ourselves in situations in which we can act on what our minds insist that we do, which is to have that drink. With time and effort, our actions develop into habits. What we think catches up with what we do. Our brains develop new neural pathways that support our new habits, which makes staying sober easier. We're no longer constantly battling with ourselves.

Why is this important? If it's the case that the relationship between changed minds and changed actions is unidirectional (a change of mind changes actions, but not the opposite), then we shouldn't expect that *living differently* before we're fully committed to living differently can change minds. This strikes me as limiting, and it doesn't fit well with other aspects of Quinn's philosophy. I think it's best to acknowledge that how minds change is subject to great variety. That they must change is the main point. It's necessary for the success of the threefold struggle.

What about Those Who Aren't Convinced?

How easy or hard it is to change people's minds is largely beside the point, Quinn contends. The relevant metric for us is instead whether or not people are open to and ready for a new story. "If people aren't ready for it, then no power on earth can make a new idea catch on" (IS, 44; see also B, 50f.). Obviously, not everyone is ready at the same time. Many Takers, perhaps most, never are. Even Takers who find new ideas appealing may not be willing to figure out what to do with them ("Uru in the Valley of the Sleepers"). Maybe they find it hard to get past thinking about what they must give up, particularly when it comes to enacting a new story. Or maybe the prospect of enacting a new story is so overwhelming—and the forces dead set against it so daunting—that they don't know where to begin.

Quinn provides a compelling reply to those in the first situation. He doesn't take the complaint of people in the second situation as seriously as he should. But let's assume that the vast majority of the people in situations such as these never end up changing their minds. Let's assume that they turn out to be unreachable. Saving the world doesn't depend on changing everyone's mind. As it goes with memes, in terms of triggering cultural transformation, so it goes with minds. Namely, it may not require changing many minds at all to initiate significant changes ("EcoGeek" and Q&A, 392). Try all kinds of strategies to kill the lethal memes that are the focus of others' attention. But don't admit defeat if others—even *many* others—fail to agree with you.

Martian Anthropology

The process of enculturation fits us with a set of eyeglasses that are all but undetectable, Derrick Jensen proclaims. "People believe they are perceiving the world as it is, without the distorting lens of culture." But my eyeglasses largely determine "what will be in focus, what will be a blur, what gives me a headache, and what I cannot see."[8] It's the same for us all. But, with effort, our worldview is defeasible. It's possible to remove our cultural eyeglasses "or at least to grind the lenses to make our focus broader, clearer" (2000, 40). We shouldn't be taken aback, Jensen adds, when new insights are met with anger and derision. From his perspective, this is because manipulators of enculturative eyeglasses have done the equivalent of cursing God. Similarly, for Quinn's character B, they've committed *blasphemy* (B, 32) by beginning to develop a new story to *be* in.

We've talked a bit about the relationship between thought and action. What, then, about the relationship between thought and perception? How about this: to change how we think, we must hone our ability to change how we see. We must perceive ourselves and the world anew. I don't mean to suggest that we must learn to see the *really* real behind what's deemed real according to our culture. When we remove our enculturative eyeglasses, we invariably replace them with another pair. We trade one vision for another.

Indeed, there's no Archimedean point, no view from nowhere, no perspective from which we can observe the world as if from the outside. Cultural criticism doesn't work this way. But via internal critique we can improve our ability to detect lethal memes, train ourselves to see more clearly what works and what doesn't, and get better at cutting through cultural bullshit. We can *get real,* in the idiomatic sense. It's with these endeavors that Martian anthropology comes in particularly handy.

Bombed Back to the Stone Age

Quinn spent years, decades, painstakingly altering his enculturative eyeglasses. The first such adjustment began when a familiar meme suddenly struck him as nonsensical. The meme is this: *victims of nuclear holocaust would be "bombed back to the Stone Age."* No one who says this means it literally. Obviously, it's nonsense to suggest that the detonation of a nuclear arsenal would somehow transport people back in time. But this isn't what bothered Quinn. What struck him was what this meme says about a common view—a "general, cultural impression" (WS, 9)—maintained by Takers about our distant ancestors.

The common view is this. Because they didn't have access to any of the amenities that make our lives comfortable and secure, our Stone Age predecessors lived in perpetual misery and on a knife's edge of survival (I, 220). Notice how nicely this dovetails with the idea that Takers are what humanity was meant to be. Notice also that it's rubbish, Quinn asserts:

> Stone Age peoples had all the tools they needed to support themselves in a comfortable lifestyle—not a lifestyle that you or I might find comfortable but one that *they* found comfortable. They had not only the tools—hundreds of them—but the knowledge of how to *make* the tools. Whereas you and I, along with 99.99 percent of our population, have none of this knowledge. I myself couldn't even make a piece of string from scratch. (WS, 8; see also Zerzan 1994, 16, Zerzan 2002, 69, and Brown et al. 2012)

If our ancestors didn't have these skills, we wouldn't be here. We're products of their success just as they were products of the success of those who came before them. On due reflection, this is eminently clear. But why is reflection required? What does the meme we Takers perpetuate about Stone Age peoples say about us?[9]

The "Quinn Method"

Discerning the nonsense embodied by this meme "awakened the Martian anthropologist in me," states Quinn. "It was just a loose thread, but pulling on it began to unravel the fabric of our culture's received wisdom" (WS, 10). This didn't require discovering a new set of facts about our culture but a new way of looking at the facts at hand, a new way to perceive them ("IndieBound").

Such an awakening might suggest that Quinn wishes to assume an outsider's role. How much more outside can one get than going extraterrestrial? But this isn't exactly what Quinn has in mind. In a conversation with Quinn, his interlocutor Elaine describes the means by which we can gain this new perspective as "Backing off. Trying to get a higher, wider view of the terrain" (WS, 147; see also Meadows 2008, 164). This is the essence of what assuming the position of the Martian anthropologist involves. Operationalizing it—using what Quinn off-handedly and cheekily calls the "Quinn method" (WS, 115)—is a five-step process that requires the sort of interplay between insiders and quasi-outsiders I commented on in the prologue.

Step 1: Hone "alertness to nonsense" (WS, 115; my emphasis). This involves looking for two things. First, keep an eye out for what Robert Talisse calls *halo terms* and *smear terms.* Halo terms connote a positive moral judgment. Smear terms do the opposite. Both are intended to be "handy instruments for evading controversy and building consensus," Talisse states (2012, 3). They function as rhetorical devices that signal what we should see as worthy of endorsement or condemnation without calling on us to give any thought to why we should do so. *Cult* and *gang* are quintessential smear terms; joining the latter involves being *brainwashed,* while joining the former makes one a *thug* (MI, 221 and 224). *Civilization* is a halo term; no one wants to be identified as *primitive* (except, I suppose, anarcho-primitivists), right? Both *thug* and *primitive* are also racialized terms. The former refers, at least in the United States, to black and brown men who refuse to live by the standards of those who valorize whiteness. They're outlaws within Taker culture. The latter are Indigenous peoples who refuse to bow to Taker culture. They're outlaws from without.

On their own, halo and smear terms aren't forms of nonsense. They do help us to chart the patterns of our enculturation, though, which can make it easier to see absurdities that we otherwise take for granted. This task is supported by a second practice within step 1: namely, considering common tropes that are meant "to reassure us that everything we're doing is okay" (WS, 67).

Oddly, the proposition that humans are inherently flawed is one such trope. Renée Lertzman (2008) suggests, for example, that most people aren't apathetic about global climate change. Rather, we care *too much* about the wellbeing of the earth *and* our way of life. This creates a conflict that's too painful for us to bear, which leads us to shut down psychically. We can't endure the truth that what we love is the cause of unimaginable devastation to what we also love. Daniel Gilbert (2010) proposes in turn that our inaction is due in part to how the human brain functions. We easily perceive rapid climatological and ecological shifts, but we have great difficulty grasping the full magnitude of gradual changes. We don't easily register phenomena such as the greenhouse effect or biodiversity loss, for example, in part because we're influenced by shifting baseline syndrome.

This helps to explain why we're reticent to make major life changes to respond to climate change and widespread ecological devastation.

I'm not qualified to say that either Lertzman or Gilbert is wrong. But the implicit message contained in each of these propositions is that we humans are powerless, or all but powerless, to change course. This incapacity is baked in to our very being. It renders questionable whether we have any sort of responsibility to enact a new story or even engage in more modest reforms. This, I dare say, is nonsense.

Step 2: Develop a clearer sense of the assumptions that support identified nonsense. Quinn once found himself listening to a radio talk show on which the subject of the day was the protection of endangered species. The host was unconvinced that anything needed to be done to prevent their extinction. "Personally," Quinn recalls him saying, "I can do without songbirds" (WS, 112).

The assumptions the host makes go something like this. Songbirds exist to entertain us. (Nonsense.) But being entertained by them is unnecessary, which means *they're* unnecessary. (Nonsense.) So the protection of endangered species like songbirds is a waste of time, energy, and money. (Nonsense on stilts.)

Step 3: Connect these assumptions to more general ones that go to the core of the story we enact. At the root of the radio host's comment is the presumption that humans are separate from the rest of the community of life. We don't have habitats, even if every other living organism does. Songbirds can lose their habitats, which is the primary factor that contributes to their endangerment. But this doesn't affect us, because their habitats are *out there*, away from where we live. Our lives will go on largely unchanged with or without them . . . or so the Taker story goes.

Step 4: Consider what other notions these assumptions generate or what actions they engender. If humans are separate from the rest of the living community, we can do whatever we please to it without repercussion. Maybe we lose songbirds. But the economic returns, which are what really matter, outweigh whatever entertainment these species might provide for us (WS, 116). Indeed, we're better off without them if they're getting in the way of our material progress. Their loss is our gain. Once they're gone, resource extraction from their former habitats can proceed without interference or distraction . . . or, again, so the Taker story goes.

Step 5: Specify what makes these notions lethal. Humans are full-fledged members of the living community. The evolutionary success of our species depended on it. And our continued existence requires that we stop endangering ourselves by endangering fellow species. Songbirds may entertain us, yes. But they don't exist for our pleasure. No member of the living community does. Indeed, their wellbeing and ours are ineliminably linked. To go on believing otherwise will be the death of us.

The radio host's comment isn't necessarily indicative of some moral deficiency on his part, mind you. As Peter Senge points out, structure strongly influences behavior. "When placed in the same system, people, however different, tend to produce the same results" (1990, 42). This doesn't necessitate that we're inevitably powerless to change how we think and act, but adjusting our enculturative eyeglasses is rarely easy. "In fact, we usually don't see the structures [that influence us] at play much at all. Rather, *we just find ourselves feeling compelled to act in certain ways*" (ibid., 44). This is precisely what the use of Quinn's method is intended to disrupt.

"Tackling a difficult problem is often a matter of seeing where the high leverage lies, a change which—with a minimum of effort—would lead to lasting, significant improvement," Senge continues. "The only problem is that high-leverage changes are usually highly *nonobvious* to most participants in the system" (ibid., 64). Making them more obvious thus involves transitioning "from seeing parts to seeing wholes, from seeing people as helpless reactors to seeing them as active participants in shaping their reality, from reacting to the present to creating the future" (ibid., 69).

Maieutics

Etymologically, *mosaic* comes from the Greek term *mouseion,* of the muses. It's indicative of an inspirational experience. In medieval Latin, the term morphed into *musaicus* or *mosaicus,* which connotes having a different state of mind. This is fitting.

In the process of engaging in mosaic construction, Quinn relies on an array of narrative techniques: metaphor (angel dust in "The Great Awakening" in *The Story of B,* the dancers of Terpischore in *My Ishmael*), parable (the jellyfish story and the ABCs of ecology in *Ishmael,* "The Story of Uru"), aphorism (*Beyond Civilization,* "The B Attitudes"), redescription (the Genesis story in *Ishmael*), dream sequence (the beetle in *Providence*, Tim in Rome in *The Holy*), proceeding backward in time (*The Man Who Grew Young*), genealogy ("The Boiling Frog" in *The Story of B*), and straight-up exegesis (once Shirin becomes B). But the technique that Quinn finds most worthy of attention is maieutics. He singles it out for discussion in the books in which it's used, which isn't the case with any other of his techniques. For it permits him perhaps most easily to reveal that which is familiar and commonplace to Takers to be lethal by placing cultural insiders in sustained dialogue with quasi-outsiders.

Giving Birth to Ideas

Maieutics is a pedagogical technique that's intended to help pupils become aware of ideas and insights that they may not realize they accept or are even familiar with. The most well-known practitioner of maieutics is Socrates as he's depicted in Plato's dialogues. Socrates asks probing questions that encourage his interlocutors to give birth, as it were, to ah-hah moments (the term derives from the Greek *maieuesthai,* to act as a midwife; B, 70, and MI, 16). In contrast to passive forms of instruction like lecturing, in which the teacher's goal is—according to received wisdom—to fill students' previously empty minds with newfound knowledge, maieutics supports students playing an active role in making explicit that about which they're only nascently aware. It can't be a one-way dictation from teacher to student. It must be interactive, for it's the give and take between teacher and student that facilitates the birthing process.

But the tone Quinn's maieutic teachers use differs markedly from Socrates's tone. Socrates often treats his pupils as adversaries, even if his language is amicable. This is because he sets out to show them that they don't know what they think they do. His immediate goal is to expose the weakness of their claims and the fragility of the grounds for their beliefs. In his hands, maieutics is thus a prototypical ground-clearing exercise. He's often at least as interested in showing pupils that they don't know what they think they know as he is in assisting them with birthing new ideas.

Yes, Ishmael and Charles do get frustrated with their pupils. But their message is consistently nonantagonistic, states C. A. Hilgartner. " 'You know this material,' " they implore. " 'Mother Culture has been whispering it into your ear during practically every waking moment of your life. You know it—*dig*.' Again and again, the pupil denies knowing it, then digs, and comes up with the treasure" (1998, 172).

Even so, Quinn's message isn't that maieutics is the best teaching method that he's identified. Ishmael himself admits when telling Julie about a previous student of his (Charles) who became an "itinerant lecturer or preacher," that "Each must do what is within his or her compass. . . . I know only how to bring people along in *this* context—through dialogue.

I simply can't imagine doing it in a lecture hall. My deficiency, not his" (MI, 44; see also P, 103). It's striking, for example, how differently Charles (as B) and Shirin (as B) engage with Jared in *The Story of B*. Charles shines light on the core of Taker culture by leading Jared back in time to its founding. Shirin proceeds forward in time, taking Jared across the threshold of what makes us human in order to highlight the contours of a story that's worked for people and the planet for as long as humans have inhabited Earth (B, 128).

But the difference between Shirin's and Charles's respective teaching styles is more pronounced than this. It highlights why maieutics isn't, and needn't be, for everyone. As do some of my own students, Shirin finds maieutics "too cerebral and too circuitous" (B, 122). As she states:

> Charles didn't want to carry you across the gap, Jared. He wanted you to leap across it yourself, that's why he proceeded as he did. . . . Every sentence he spoke was designed to extend the road for you by a centimeter. He was closing the gap pebble by pebble, hoping you'd eventually make the leap by yourself. . . . I don't have the patience to follow that procedure, Jared—the patience or the time. I'm going to throw you across the gap. I'm going to start with the conclusion. (Ibid., 122–23)

No two approaches to constructing, or reconstructing, a mosaic are alike, Ishmael acknowledges, "because no two pupils are ever alike" (MI, 44). This is also true of teachers. Pay close attention to what you and those with whom you engage need. "And don't flinch from looking with wide-open eyes at the things people *show you* they want" (ibid., 225). If killing lethal memes, changing minds, and enacting a new story that works for people and the planet require taking a circuitous route, so be it. If a straightforward path reveals itself, get moving. There's no one right way to proceed.

Description Versus Prescription

It's not always easy to distinguish between when Quinn is offering descriptions and when he's offering prescriptions. Quinn himself acknowledges experiencing the "anthropologist's dilemma": "If I *describe* something, simply doing my job as an anthropologist, it's often assumed that I must also be *prescribing* something" (WS, 30). Indeed, descriptions are largely what he provides, intentionally leaving it up to readers to figure out how his descriptions can inform the development of a new vision.

On the other hand, when he refers to Jean Liedloff's reports of child-rearing among tribal peoples in *The Continuum Concept*, Quinn remarks that "you can't automatically dismiss the utility of turning a description into a prescription" (WS, 40). A good deal of what Liedloff depicts is worth putting into practice by us, he contends. The same at least provisionally may be said of Quinn's ideas, which leaves me wondering whether this actually is what he intends.

"All descriptions carry with them weighty presumptions of value," Jensen proclaims (2006a, 10). So perhaps we do well neither to take Quinn's descriptions at face value nor to assume out of hand that they're really prescriptions. Instead, consider the presumptions of value that are operative in his descriptions. What does he want to convey to us, what can we learn, how does this fit into the larger mosaic he's constructing, and how can we build on it?

You Are Needed

Among the interesting narrative twists in *Ishmael* is the increasing irritation that Ishmael displays in his interactions with Alan. Some students of mine find Ishmael condescending and unlikable. Others find Alan unbearably dimwitted. Whatever the case may be, Alan tells us that he's finally found in Ishmael what he's long desired: someone who can be a teacher for life (I, 122). Alan feels depressed and rejected when Ishmael sends him away to spend some time trying to work out on his own what laws are operative in the community of life. Nor can he bear the thought that each insight rendered through his maieutic lessons brings him one step closer to the end of his relationship with Ishmael. Even upon having a fairly complete sense of why being a Taker doesn't work and can't be made to work for people or the planet, Alan still displays a thoroughgoing Taker mentality when he tries to purchase Ishmael from the menagerie owner. The message is clear: Alan's intent is to possess and control the gorilla.

More significantly, Alan's desire to be a lifelong student signals that he's unwilling to be a teacher himself, to engage in struggle. This betrays that he may not have the earnest desire to save the world that Ishmael's newspaper ad requests. (At least this seems so until, in a final plot twist, he gets up the nerve to write the manuscript that becomes *Ishmael.*) Part of what holds Alan back is his refusal to accept that Ishmael isn't holding out on him. Ishmael never intended to lay out every contour of a new story to enact and how to enact it. Ishmael couldn't do so even if he wanted to. Alan wants a quick fix and assumes that, in due time, Ishmael will provide it.

But this is an old mind at work, which is why Ishmael implores Alan to do what the people of our culture take ourselves to do exceptionally well: "invent" (I, 250). It's why Ishmael emphasizes to Julie that each of his students encodes and transmits his message differently, which improves the prospects of its dissemination (MI, 68). And it's why Quinn is insistent that each of us has the capacity to be a lethal meme killer because each of us can affect—if subtly and imperceptibly—the shape of our culture ("Who *Is* the Awakener?").

So why not simply try this, he requests: "Be outrageous with me. . . . Be ridiculous. . . . Be totally absurd. . . . Be preposterous. . . . Stretch yourself" (BD, 35–37). Let the contagion spread. No one of us can save the world on our own. But who ever said we had to? And don't assume that we'll know immediately and with perfect clarity what the spreading contagion looks like.

Finally, it's important that we attend to our needs. But it's equally important to seek out where we're needed. Yes, each of us is needed. Where and how isn't for Quinn to say. He has his beetle encounter—his breakthrough epiphany (P, 16ff.). Jared has his (B, 142ff.). So does Tim (H, 375). Pay attention, Quinn implies. Keep your eyes peeled. Your beetle encounter will come, if it hasn't already.

Chapter 2

Axiomatic Lies

Totalitarian Agriculture and The Great Forgetting

Before I got sober, I recall visiting a psychiatrist to deal with some issues I was having with my antidepressant medication. I haven't had good luck with psychiatrists. While they may know their craft, the way they relate to patients tends to be pretty atrocious. The situation with this particular shrink was no different.

Prior to this visit, I'd been silent with my doctors about how much I drank. I'm not sure what compelled me to be somewhat more honest on this occasion. So even before we talked meds, he asked me if I was doing anything to get my drinking under control.

"I'm working on it," I lied.

"Are you?" he responded with a sneer.

Well, no, but he didn't have to be such an asshole about it, I thought.

Still, I'm lucky I saw him. He told me about a rehab option about which I was unaware. It's called an intensive outpatient program (IOP), and it sounded way more appealing than going inpatient. Inpatient programs seem sort of like prison lite. They also tend to be an expensive waste of time, as they have a poor track record for actually helping clients to stay sober (Fletcher 2013). Choosing an IOP permitted me to tell myself that I could bail out if I didn't like the process or didn't see it working for me. Besides, I wasn't really convinced at that point that I had enough of a drinking problem to go to *any* form of rehab, so I thought I might as well look into an option that allowed me to live at home between therapy sessions.

I'm not sure exactly how long it was between learning about IOPs and actually doing an intake eval, but once I finally considered getting sober I found a local option that got decent reviews. During my first session, I admitted how much I drank . . . and quickly learned from the shocked reactions of fellow addicts in my group (this IOP was premised entirely on group therapy during the early stages) that, yes, it seems I was indeed an alcoholic. The breakdown of my blood platelets indicated to me that things with my body were bad. Not being able to drink my demons away no matter how much I imbibed eventually indicated to me that my supposed solution had run its course. But that I was an alcoholic? No, this I didn't accept, until that first session.

Along with attending five extended group sessions per week, we were strongly encouraged to find Alcoholics Anonymous (AA) meetings that worked for us, too. Early on during IOP, I tagged along to a few with people from my group. And I can say unequivocally that no part of the process of getting sober was more miserable than those meetings. AA may work for other "Friends of Bill W.," although the organization has never made an effort to quantify its success. It didn't work at all for me. Indeed, I was so strongly triggered (my desire to drink was so overwhelming) after a meeting perhaps a month into my IOP that I gave up on AA entirely.

In no other forum was the cultural pathology of alcoholism clearer. The wider set of issues that made my drinking a rational dysfunction were irrelevant, I was told. Suggesting, tentatively, that drinking might be even minimally rational was met with open derision (despite standing prohibitions against judgmental crosstalk). Indeed, failure on my part to willingly embrace the one-size-fits-all approach to sobriety AA offers was evidence that I was damaged goods, fundamentally morally defective. Freedom through submission—to the process and to a higher power—was my only option.

But freedom is relative in this case, for one can never abandon AA without putting one's sobriety at severe risk, or so the creed goes. Freedom through *perpetual* submission, then. Freedom, yes, through accepting permanent captivity.

I'm forever grateful to my IOP therapist for recognizing this wasn't my path. She told me plainly that she was defying professional custom by giving me a pass on AA. It's no stretch to conclude that she helped save my life by doing so.

❧

"It's valid to say there are two fundamentally different human cultures," states Ishmael. "It's also valid to say there are thousands of human cultures"

(MI, 39). We're perfectly comfortable acknowledging the latter claim. Forms of dress, cuisine, and mannerism; marriage and funeral customs; observed holidays; and religious rituals differ greatly the world over. By contrast, the former claim may give us pause. But Quinn insists that observed differences such as those listed here are actually relatively superficial. The majority of people alive today—Takers—enact the same story, which tells them what to expect and unthinkingly accept about "the most fundamental thing of all, getting the food they need to stay alive" (P, 5).

They are *we:* probably you and definitely me. We Takers enact a story whereby we expect food to be locked away. "It's all owned and if you want some, you'll have to buy it," Ishmael emphasizes (MI, 40). Worse still, food not produced with poisons generally costs us more. In essence, the people of our culture must pay to live and pay more to live more healthily—and we accept this with relatively few reservations.

The other culture, Leaver culture, is far older than our own.[1] While our story has been enacted for about twelve millennia, the Leaver story "began to be enacted some two or three million years ago . . . and is still enacted today, as successfully as ever," Ishmael adds (I, 41). Takers typically fail to see this because we tend to assume that our culture represents a second, distinctive chapter in human history—a step forward in human social evolution (MI, 49). In essence, though, two human experiments are now running concurrently. One set of experimenters have endeavored to *take our lives into our own hands.* The other are content to *leave their lives in the hands of the gods.*[2] What exactly these descriptions mean will become clearer later on. But the monikers are meant to be neutral, Quinn insists.[3] It's not that Takers take from the world without giving back, nor that Leavers leave the world as it is. Leavers and Takers both must take from and give back to the world, as must all living organisms, and no one can leave an ever-changing Earth untouched. But these two cultures do result in the development of drastically different forms of social, political, and economic organization (BC, 58). They're the basis of quite divergent visions.

It's hardly uncommon for people of our culture to think of Leavers strictly as gatherer-hunters and Takers as sustained by agriculture, including domesticated animal farming. (Takers also tend to think that all gatherer-hunter peoples garner their food in pretty much the same way, which is far from true.) But this isn't quite right. Leavers practice agriculture—and pastoralism (Q&A, 123)—as well, although not as Takers do. And the different approaches the former take compared to the latter—in particular, how the people of each respective culture relate to the beings who they make their food—have dramatic ripple effects.

In this chapter, we look more closely at the characteristics specifically of Taker culture. We begin by getting clearer on our cultural mythology, which is reflected not just in the story we enact but also in the cluster of lethal memes on which our story is predicated.[4] Critical to our cultural mythology is the *Great Forgetting*, which is primarily a product of the ongoing work of Taker philosophers, historians, and theologians. As strange as it may seem, they serve as protectors not of our cultural memory but of our distinctive lack of such a memory. Even though more iconoclastic researchers across academia have thoroughly debunked core elements of our cultural mythology, the Great Forgetting continues to hold Takers in its thrall.

This is due in large part to the overwhelming (if unseen) significance among the people of our culture of what Quinn calls *totalitarian agriculture*. Totalitarian agriculture is the primary spreading mechanism for Taker culture (I, 153). Assessing both how it functions and its abiding legacy will permit us to see more clearly why Taker culture works neither for people nor for the planet.

The Taker Story

The Taker story is "about the conquest of the world," Quinn proclaims. "It's about man gaining control over his environment. It's about man rising above nature and mastering it as a workman masters a tool. It's about man reshaping the earth for his own purposes" (BD, 4). We're captives of this story, and this compels us to destroy the world as we seek to become its master. Indeed, we're compelled to be destructive even if we reject mastery.

Each of us faces enormous, unending pressure to play our role in this story. To do otherwise is all but inconceivable for most of us. For, Ishmael states, to depart or diverge from it "is to venture into oblivion. Your place is *here*, participating in this story, putting your shoulder to the wheel, and as a reward, being fed" (I, 37). Even those who benefit most from our captivity, who oversee those shouldering the wheel (as well as those who oversee the overseers), are inmates in our cultural prison. Privileged inmates, yes, but inmates nonetheless. "For all their power and privilege—for all that they lord it over everyone else in the prison—not one of them has a key to unlock the gate" (ibid., 252; see also McBay 2011a, 51). So we go on enacting our story whether or not we can convince ourselves of its value. What else can we possibly do?

For starters, Quinn contends, we can work on identifying the bars of our cell and the character of the lock on our cell door. His reconstruction of the Taker story is meant to be part of this enterprise. It's a first, necessary step toward developing a viable exit strategy.

The Basic Plotline

Humans began to fulfill our destiny, so the Taker narrative goes, upon initiating the Agricultural Revolution and the incumbent advent of civilization. Before that, nothing much happened that was worth noting. Humans certainly weren't worth God's attention. Genus *Homo* is some three million years old. "But he wasn't too bright back then; he didn't know he could control the environment. So he had to live pretty much like an animal, just taking whatever came to hand" (BD, 5). *Homo sapiens* may be more intelligent than our evolutionary predecessors, but it took two hundred thousand years even for members of our species to attempt to gain mastery over the world. "God knows why. Probably didn't occur to him" (ibid.). Instead, our early ancestors frittered away their days "getting nowhere and doing nothing" (I, 68).

But the light bulb in *Homo sapiens'* brains finally flickered to life. *Homo sapiens* chose to "settle down in one place where he could get to work, so to speak" (ibid.). This is the point at which humans started stamping our authority on the world. People were never intended to live like animals, to be confined "by the limits that apply to other, lesser creatures," as Paul Kingsnorth and Dougald Hine quip (2009, 18). They finally were proving it.

Most significantly, people learned to manipulate the land "so that it produced *more human food*" (I, 68). This gave them command over their food supply. They were no longer at the whim of what could be found at hand:

> That was the beginning of everything. Mastery over food supply was the key that unlocked the box of keys. It was the mastery that made all the other masteries possible. Mastery over food supply meant that man need no longer follow the game as a

> nomadic hunter-gatherer. He could settle down in one place. He could build. He could invent. He could think. Mastery over food supply meant that man was free. Free to conquer the world. Free to reshape the world to his liking. (BD, 5–6)

With settlement came division of labor. With division of labor came technology, trade, and commerce, which in turn gave rise to mathematics, literacy, and the arts. And here we are, enjoying all sorts of accommodations that are so integrated into our lives that we can't rightly count them as luxuries.

The world, originally in a state of "primeval anarchy," has been "put in order," Alan proclaims (I, 71). True, the world didn't "meekly submit" (ibid., 73). But submission was inevitable, since the hierarchical socioeconomic form of organization we call civilization is "the ultimate home of man." We're the world's rulers by right. And "an everlasting future of richness, grandeur, enlightenment, and unimaginable accomplishment" is our destiny (BD, 6). Sure, there still may be pockets of Leavers scattered here and there. But "these are anachronisms, fossils—people living in the past, people who just don't realize that their chapter of human history is over" (I, 42).

Admittedly, our pursuit of world mastery isn't going exactly as planned. As we struggle for order, we can't seem to put an end to our destructive ways (ibid., 80). All we can do, though, is continue on as we have with more earnest resolve. If we double down, do what we're doing right now *even better,* and "finally manage to make ourselves the absolute rulers of the world—then nothing can stop us" (ibid., 81).

Up until perhaps a half-century ago, it would've been unthinkable to most Takers that we might not be able to fulfill our destiny. But the spell was broken, according to Quinn, by the publication of Rachel Carson's *Silent Spring* (IS, 22; see also Taylor 2016, 283). Today, legions of Takers know that somewhere along the way we screwed up. How did this occur? One common refrain of old has taken on new life. "It's because there's something fundamentally *wrong* with humans," Alan asserts. "Of course," Ishmael responds. "Everyone in your culture knows this. Man was born to turn the world into a paradise, but tragically he was born flawed. And so this paradise has always been spoiled by stupidity, greed, destructiveness, and shortsightedness" (I, 83).

So, according to the basic Taker plotline, conquest is possible. Yet because of humanity's compromised nature it's impossible *for us* to get it right. We've come awfully close, but we can't quite get there. We're the pinnacle of life on Earth. And without a fix for our flaws, we're screwed. All we can do is just ride high on the civilizational wave until it crashes ("Dialogue on *Beyond Civilization*"). Like Achilles's, ours will be "a brief life of glory," but it sure beats "a long uneventful life of obscurity" (ibid., 75).

Again, Quinn isn't claiming that all of us Takers accept this story. His point instead is that your rejection of it and mine don't change that we continue to enact it day after day, week after week, and year after year. Because it's what permits us to get fed. Quinn also isn't claiming that this is how it must be. Saving the world depends on breaking free from this dynamic. It helps, though, to figure out how to get where we want to go if we have a clear sense of where we are now. That little "You Are Here" arrow on the map is invaluable.

The Great Forgetting

Now let's focus on a particularly odd twist to the Taker story. Only a few thousand years after the inception of our culture, our cultural progenitors came to take for granted that humans originated as agriculturalists and civilization builders. "As they saw it," states B, "agriculture and civilization were just as innately human as thought or speech. Our hunting-gathering past was not just forgotten, it was unimaginable" (B, 243–44; see also BD, 12, and MI, 114). B labels this phenomenon the *Great Forgetting*. It continues to this day to frame the story we enact. It operates at the core of our cultural vision.

How can this be? It's the result of "one of the most amazing occurrences in all of human history," B continues. "When the thinkers of the eighteenth, nineteenth, and twentieth centuries were finally compelled to admit that the entire structure of thought in our culture had been built on a profoundly important error, *absolutely nothing happened*" (B, 245). No thinker—or no thinker considered to be worth listening to—pondered how new scientific findings should influence the way we view ourselves and our story. Apparently, there was no appetite to face "the truth about our origins. I fear the truth is that they wanted to leave things as they were. They wanted to go on forgetting . . . and that's exactly what they did" (ibid., 245–46).[5]

But thinkers couldn't just pretend that nothing had changed. In order for the Great Forgetting to pass intellectual muster, some sort of justification was required. This justification has three components. First, the myth of the Agricultural Revolution was developed. Second, thinkers needed an explanation for why they chose to presume that nothing happened prior to the Agricultural Revolution. Third, they determined that even if humans weren't born as agriculturalists and civilization builders, it was inevitable that this was what we'd become.

The Myth of the Agricultural Revolution

"In a nutshell," B asserts, "the central idea of the Agricultural Revolution is this, that about ten [no, twelve] thousand years ago, people began to abandon the foraging life in favor of agriculture" (B, 247). Simple, right? Perhaps, but it also represents "slovenly thinking at its worst" (ibid., 246). It misleads in two ways: "first, by implying that agriculture is basically just one thing (the way that foraging is basically just one thing), and second, by implying that this one thing was embraced by people everywhere at more or less the same time" (ibid., 247).

As for the first component of the myth, we can distinguish between two broad kinds of agriculture. The first kind, intensive—totalitarian—agriculture is practiced by exactly one culture: ours. Intensive agriculture involves aggressively clearing the land, manipulating the flow of available water sources, and exploiting topsoil. Stable, mature ecosystems are sacrificed for the sake of short-term fertility. "Crops are raised," Jared Diamond remarks, "not only for eating by those who cultivate them, but for sale, which means that people can live in larger groups, with a division of labor between those who do the growing and those who buy or trade for the produce" (2005, 47). Food is locked away, and those who control its distribution gain significant power over those who must purchase it. As a result, societies in which intensive agriculture is practiced tend to be socioeconomically stratified.

The second kind of agriculture, horticulture, isn't intensive. Crops are cultivated in ways that don't cause long-term damage to the land (ibid., 46). Tillage is kept to a minimum, as is manipulation of waterways. Horticulturalists may be sedentary, but also may live in small groups that make seasonal rounds (relocating by season in a relatively fixed pattern), rather than permanently clustering in villages or towns. Many Leaver peoples have practiced, and still practice, horticulture (Mohawk 2008 and Kimmerer 2013). Horticulture long predates when the Agricultural Revolution supposedly took place.

With respect to the second component of the myth of the Agricultural Revolution, *people everywhere* didn't abandon gathering-hunting to take up farming twelve thousand years ago. The practice of totalitarian agriculture is a cultural phenomenon, not a human phenomenon. Until about five hundred years ago, some three-quarters of the planet was still occupied by peoples who engaged in gathering and hunting, often in combination with some degree of horticulture (WS, 11). Leavers across the globe continue to resist totalitarian agriculture to this day. So if we must call it a revolution, we should at least jettison the illusion that it's over. No, the spread of intensive agriculture continues unabated.

Nothing Happened

We might not have been born intensive agriculturalists and civilization builders. But this needn't be of any consequence for Takers if nothing worth noting happened before we became intensive agriculturalists and civilization builders. Whatever came before this is *prehistory,* so the "intellectual guardians of our culture—the historians, the philosophers, the theologians" (B, 246; see also P, 137ff.)—don't need to bother accounting for it.

Some claim it can't easily be studied because prehistoric people left no written record. But then why call it *pre*history? Why not, if we must, *preliterate* history or *precivilizational* history? Because our intellectual guardians are content to perpetuate the Great Forgetting.

Taker intellectuals didn't "mislay" more than 99 percent of the time human life has existed on Earth. They just defined history "so as to begin at a certain arbitrary point, and what came before isn't defined in its own terms but only in terms of its beforeness" (P, 129). The story of humankind is the story of us. "It's the story of mankind as told by *Homo magister*—Man the Ruler, Man the Master." And why not? "He's the hero of the story. That's easy to see. In his telling of it, the action only begins when *he* arrives on the scene" (BD, 8).

As It Was Always Meant to Be

Once upon a time, human beings were at the center of all creation. The earth marked the center of the universe, and all of life existed for the purpose of serving us. For many centuries, astronomers dutifully corroborated this vision of our place in the cosmos and were held in high esteem for it. This made the Copernican revolution an especially heavy blow to the Taker psyche. So it took some time for our intellectual guardians to abandon the Ptolemaic cosmology.

Still, if Takers were born (intensive) agriculturalists and civilization builders, then we were at the center of life on Earth. All other life "was man's food preserve, to be used as suited him. It had no other reason for being there, except to support man's life" (BD, 12). The people of Africa and the Americas could be used as Takers saw fit as well, since they effectively lived like animals (ibid., 13). Taker women counted as human, but they were too delicate in constitution to rule. Mastery wasn't for them. So they could be regarded as qualified chattel. Takers, particularly white men, might not reside at the physical center of the universe. But this didn't matter. As model humans, they were "the end product of creation, the creature for whom all the rest was made" (ibid.).

Then, paleontologists and biologists, including Darwin, burst this bubble, too. Humans hadn't come into being at a separate order from the rest of life on Earth. Indeed, Takers shared a biological heritage with the people who our ancestors systematically enslaved and exploited and who continue to be enslaved and exploited today. This couldn't be ignored, since, like the astronomers, Taker intellectuals took the paleontologists and biologists seriously. But these intellectuals could do the next best thing, Quinn notes. They could regard the paleontologists' and biologists' findings as meaningless for understanding the story that humans are meant to enact.

Whatever our prehistoric forebears were up to, it still wasn't very important. Why? Because "they weren't *fully* human," which is corroborated by their unwillingness or inability to seek mastery over Earth (BD, 15; see also WS, 19).

What does this mean in practical terms? Being (intensive) agriculturalists and civilization builders was our destiny after all. Why else would God wait for Takers to come along to take any interest in human endeavors? "He was waiting for someone worth talking to. Someone fully human. Someone smart enough to recognize the destiny He had set for man. Someone who could appreciate him. Someone civilized" (ibid., 15–16). Whatever came before can be "discarded as a mere prelude" (B, 247; see also P, 138).

The Taker Axioms

We've already seen a number of the lethal memes at work in Taker culture. Permit me now to present them and some others in a more structured manner. (I reserve fuller discussion of locking up the food for later, since it deserves extended consideration.) Ishmael uses the term *axiom* to demarcate these assumptions, as have I (I, 90ff.). I find the term fitting, since an axiom—a postulate, premise, starting point of reasoning—is classically conceived as a proposition that's accepted without definition, reservation, controversy, or proof.[6]

Throughout his corpus, Quinn focuses most attention on the following six axioms:

- Takers are what humanity was meant to be. There's only one right way to live: our way.
- "*Humans belong to an order that is separate from the rest of the living community.* There's us and then there's Nature. There's humans and then there's the human environment" (WS, 174).
- The world was made for humans (by God). It belongs to us to exploit for whatever purposes we see fit. It's "endlessly and infinitely resilient," as Jensen puts it (2006a, 299), so we can have it all and never pay a price.
- Even though the world was made for humans (by God), it doesn't fit us. So we need to fix it by conquering it—which we were made (by God) to do.
- Success with this enterprise isn't possible because we're inherently flawed.
- Surely, someone must know how to overcome our flawed nature. The best thing to do is wait for this person's arrival.

Let's look at each axiom more closely.

Takers are what humanity was meant to be: Only the people of our culture are fully, genuinely human because only we are civilized intensive agriculturalists. The most civilized among us are to be venerated above all others, for civilization is as good as it gets. Those who persist in their disagreement must be either killed or assimilated, particularly if civilization is enhanced by acquiring their land. It's also entirely fitting and proper to put food under lock and key. This is the cornerstone of our economy, and we "imagine that nothing could possibly make better sense" (MI, 40).

"*Humans belong to an order that is separate from the rest of the living community*": This meme is especially harmful. It inspires taking the ongoing extinction of species after species in stride. What may harm the rest of the living community generally doesn't harm us. "The environment is *out there,* suffering, while we're *in here,* safe and sound" (WS, 175). We're biological beings, yes, but we're not subject to biological pressures.

The world was made for humans (by God): According to Aristotle, "All animals exist for the sake of man" (1984, I.3.1256b21–25). Since all plants exist for the sake of animals, they're ours to do with, too. For René Descartes, we can use the knowledge of Earth and the heavens "for all the purposes for which it is appropriate, and thus make ourselves, as it were, the lords and masters of nature" (1985, 142–43). Francis Bacon's "only earthly wish is . . . to stretch the deplorably narrow limits of man's domination over the universe to their promised bounds" (cited in Farrington 1964, 62; see also Bacon 1768, 44). And here's theoretical physicist Gerard J. Milburn: "The aim of modern science is to reach an understanding of the world, not merely for purely aesthetic reasons, but that it may be ordered to our purpose" (cited in Jensen 2000, 20).

Perhaps we can liberate ourselves from nature and hereby stop damaging it (Asafu-Adjaye et al. 2015; see also Brand 2009 and Lynas 2011).[7] Maybe we can shed our bodies and merge with machines to create a new superspecies, suggests futurist Ray Kurzweil (2005), proponent of the *singularity*. Maybe even death itself can be overcome.

True, *Silent Spring* changed many people's view of the earth's resiliency. We have a much clearer sense of the damage we do. Moreover, people rarely use the harsh and not-so-vaguely misogynistic language today that our cultural forebears so freely employed when defending the pursuit of planetary mastery (Merchant 2006). We may even have lost faith in the proposition that God is an unwavering supporter of our cultural vision (B, 282). But our actions speak louder than our words. "These people merely articulated, brilliantly, urges that are woven together throughout our culture like rivulets in sand," Jensen contends (2000, 20).

Even though the world was made for humans (by God), it doesn't fit us: Despite nature coming into being red in tooth and claw, it was never supposed to stay that way. To master Earth and all that it contains is our destiny. Per the basic Taker plotline, we're "uniquely fitted to rule it" ("Dialogue on *Beyond Civilization*"). But somehow we and the planet just don't quite click. We're a match made in heaven, but our courtship is a rocky one.

Success with this enterprise isn't possible because we're inherently flawed: Thus far, our attempts to conquer the world have only imperiled our survival. The only way to avoid being further imperiled is to dig in and succeed at conquering the world—nonsensically, "even if it kills us" (WS, 190). We face an insurmountable hurdle, though. There's something fundamentally wrong with us. "And that's why we don't work," Julie states (MI, 34).

What exactly is our problem? It's not that we're civilized (intensive) agriculturalists. Goodness, no. Rather, "We're not civilized enough" (ibid.). Or we're both too intelligent and not intelligent enough: too intelligent in comparison with other creatures, not intelligent enough when measured against the divine order. "We're in an awkward stage," as Julie puts it. "We were all right when we were *less* than human and we'll be all right when we're *more* than human, but we're washouts as we are right now. Humans are just no good" (ibid., 35).

Surely someone must know how to overcome our flawed nature: Our defect is that we don't know and can't figure out how to conquer and rule the world without destroying it. But *someone*—a prophet, a notable public figure, a politician, a visionary technocrat, the entire human race meditating or praying or engaging in consciousness raising or doing whatever we must to "Evolve to some new plane of existence" (B, 283; see also BC, 171)—must come along eventually to tell us what to do in order to succeed. Or maybe instead it's not someone but *something* we need to do that we haven't yet done: elect the right party or politician; get rid of a particular politician; fix public schools; privatize schooling; leverage technology; put an end to "out-of-control technological advancement, out-of-control industrial greed, out-of-control government expansion" (ibid., 74); attend the church of our choice; abolish religion; write stricter laws; confine or kill our enemies; for God's sake, "kill somebody" (ibid., 283).

Totalitarian Agriculture

Agriculture per se isn't lethal to our species, Quinn emphasizes (Q&A, 123 and 612). Contrary to geneticist and anthropologist Spencer Wells's (2010, 90) suggestion, agriculture per se isn't fundamentally mismatched with our biology. Contrary to what conservation researcher John Feeney (2010) contends, it isn't inherently unsustainable either.

Totalitarian agriculture—the emergence of which marked the founding of Taker culture—is a different matter entirely. It ushered in a new mode of food production predicated on the unprecedented notion that all food on the planet belongs exclusively to Takers (Q&A, 48). This notion directly reflects the view that the world is made for us to do with as we will. From such a vantage point, totalitarian agriculture is regarded as an inevitable step forward for the human race, a step that has made life far more comfortable and secure.

Three Associated Practices

Among all members of the living community, Takers alone employ three related practices, states Alan; "these are all fundamental to their [*our*] civilizational system" (I, 126). First, food that's dedicated to Taker use is denied to all others, both human and other-than-human. Taken to its limit, our policy is this: "Every square foot of this planet belongs to us, so if we put it all under cultivation, then all our competitors are just plain out of luck" (ibid., 127–28; see also ibid., 259f.). Second, other-than-human competitors for Taker food may be exterminated at will, and human competitors may be contained or also killed if they refuse conversion to our ways. Third, food that Takers don't designate as ours but that's needed by others is destroyed at will to make room to produce Taker food. "That's the whole point of totalitarian agriculture," B proclaims. "We hunt our competitors down, we destroy their food, and we deny them access to food. That's what makes it totalitarian" (B, 154; see also "*Diminuendo*").

Ecological Mercenaries, Cultural Missionaries

The practice of totalitarian agriculture has progressively and quite effectively destroyed countless ecosystems. In order to support the expansion of a subset of a single species, Takers have greatly diminished biodiversity. More and more other-than-human biomass continues to be converted into human mass.

This process is designed to support unlimited growth (I, 134). Its success has given rise to the idea that to be human is to be insatiable, that there are no limits to what we can have and what we can accomplish (see Brown 2002, 26). Infinite growth, expansion without limits even out into the cosmos, isn't just possible. It's an imperative. And to support unlimited growth, the rest of the community of life must be our private food preserve (BD, 28).

Totalitarian agriculture is thus monocultural in two senses. It supports the elimination of biodiversity for the express purpose of allowing

Takers to produce greater and greater quantities of staple crops. It also facilitates the assimilation and destruction of Leaver peoples, reducing the multiplicity of stories enacted on Earth to just one: "the best story, the real story, the most advanced story, the most developed story," Jensen saltily states (2006a, 23; see also Davis 2002).

In due course, we'll focus on how biodiversity and cultural diversity are mutually reinforcing—mutually necessary for ecological, social, and personal wellbeing (BD, 37). For now, we can note that these two forms of monoculture reinforce one another, too, in ways that do untold harm. "Totalitarian agriculture gave us fabulous food surpluses," states B, "which are the foundation of every military and economic expansion. No one was able to stand against us anywhere in the world, because no one had a food-producing machine as powerful as ours" (B, 84; see also B, 156, I, 167, and MI, 63). At the same time, military and economic successes ostensibly confirm that Takers are living the one right way for humans to live, that what we do is what everyone should do.

We have here "a sort of rough-and-ready empiricism," B remarks (B, 156). Food surpluses plus the conquest they facilitate yields proof of hegemony. When we add to this dynamic a third essential ingredient, the Great Forgetting, we Takers succumb to the illusion that we're not only justified in devouring lives and lands planetwide but are also destined to do so.

Discomfort and Insecurity

To be clear, B states, totalitarian agriculture wasn't adopted because people are cruel or sadistic or evil. "It was adopted because, by its very nature, it's more productive than any other style (and there are many other styles). Totalitarian agriculture represents productivity *to the max,* as Americans like to say. It represents productivity in a form that literally cannot be exceeded" (B, 260). But despite conventional Taker wisdom, maximal surpluses don't convert to maximal comfort and security. The story we enact fails us on its own terms.

Brick by Brick

Here's a nice little parable from Quinn. In it he sums up quite well the ecocidal character of Taker culture. The intrepid explorer Uru comes across a tower that's tall beyond compare. Its residents live in a penthouse at its peak. Each day, the residents set off one or two explosions on lower floors. None of these explosions is strong enough on its own to bring down the tower. But, Uru informs the residents, "every single blow out necessarily reduces the integrity of the entire structure, and eventually all the weaknesses you've introduced must combine dynamically to bring about its downfall" ("Uru and the Tower").

The implication is clear. The people of our culture, the proverbial residents of the penthouse, can't go on indefinitely destroying the biotic and abiotic bases of our existence. Our vaunted tower, the biospheric preconditions for the perpetuation of our species, can tolerate precious few additional explosions before it comes crashing down.

Another telling of the parable focuses on how we're compelled to devour the living world—to convert other-than-human biomass into human mass. On this telling, the tower residents maintain the walls of their penthouse by descending to lower floors each day and knocking out some two hundred bricks to bring back upstairs for their own use. Again, the writing is on the wall. The tower eventually will topple. And when that day comes that they fall, the residents of the penthouse may try to cushion themselves on the bodies below. But it won't save them. They still have the longest fall and the hardest impact when they hit the ground.

Quinn chooses two hundred for the number of bricks removed because it reflects that, statistically speaking, as many as two hundred species are going extinct every day (WS, 61, Q&A, 747, and Pimm et al. 2014). This is some one thousand times faster than the background rate (De Vos et al. 2014). If we desire, we also can account for our ongoing excavation of the tower's underground supports via our consumption of the long dead, now embodied in coal, oil, and natural gas.[8] But let's stick with Quinn's telling, which is worth citing at length:

> It would be different, of course, if two hundred extinctions a day were just a temporary thing. It's not. And the reason it's not is that, clever as we are, we can't increase the amount of biomass that exists on this planet. We can't increase the amount of land and water that supports life, and we can't increase the amount of sunlight that falls on the land and water. We can *decrease* the amount of biomass that exists on this planet—for example, by making the land sterile or by poisoning the water—but we can't increase it.

> All we can do is shift that biomass from one bunch of species to another bunch—and that's what we're doing. We're systematically shifting the biomass of species we *don't* care about into the biomass of species we *do* care about: into cows, chickens, corn, beans, tomatoes, and so on. We're systematically destroying the biodiversity of the living community to support ourselves, which is to say that we're systematically destroying the infrastructure that keeps us alive. (WS, 176–77; see also Heinberg 2005b, 123)[9]

It's folly to think that this is occurring by accident. It's a product of cultural design. "This does not preclude consuming [the biosphere] 'wisely' or consuming it as slowly as possible," Quinn adds ("On Investments"). Scientists may throw their support behind *ecosystem management,* theologians may preach about the merits of *good stewardship,* and a small handful of economists may favor *sustainable development.* Those who defend such approaches mean well, of course. But they nevertheless reinforce our current practices, if with a slightly lighter touch. For *management, stewardship,* and *development* all presuppose that, ultimately, we're in control of earthly matters.

In C. A. Hilgarnter's words, "By enacting the story we enact, we commit our full forces, as individuals and as a culture or a collection of cultures, to the pursuit of species suicide and extinction. Whether we say we do so or not" (1998, 170). "The uniquely calamitous feature of this culture," adds Daniel Wildcat, "is that we are killing ourselves by ending the lives of many of our other-than-human relatives on which our own lives depend" (2009, 39). As such, Jensen may be right that Taker culture is the expression of nothing short of a "death urge" (2000, 20).

Dismissing Jensen's declaration as hyperbolic doesn't make him wrong; believing otherwise doesn't eliminate this as a genuine possibility. "I also know," he continues, "that the nature of physical reality is not determined by popular vote. Many people sharing the same delusion does not make the delusion true" (ibid., 65). Indeed, states Quinn, our crisis "will continue to deepen for as long as people would rather endure any catastrophe than give up the right to live catastrophically" ("On Investments").[10]

Perhaps, though, Quinn is being alarmist. Can't we solve our ecological and climatological woes with technological advances? With ingenuity and initiative isn't it possible to wean ourselves off fossil fuels and make our use of nonrenewable resources so efficient that people can continue to live basically like we do for many generations to come? No, this isn't possible, for reason that we'll explore later. For now, suffice to say that this is program thinking in its most crystalized form.

But haven't lots of people assumed before that they were living in end times? We'll discuss in chapter 6 that we do both Leavers and ourselves a disservice if we suppose that what we face is entirely unprecedented. Still, ecosystem after ecosystem is collapsing. We've hit anthro-historically extreme atmospheric carbon and methane concentrations that threaten to raise global temperatures beyond what large mammals and most other life forms can sustain (Hartmann 2013 and Spratt and Dunlop 2018).[11] Both airborne and marine oxygen levels are in decline (Ward 2007 and Breitburg et al. 2018). We're bumping up against the limits of the photosynthetic ceiling, the ultimate limiter of ongoing population growth (Sanderson et al. 2002 and Diamond 2005, 491). And we're witnessing precipitating levels of biodiversity loss and crop yield decline, both of which herald the imminent collapse of both marine and terrestrial food webs (McCauley et al. 2015 and Diaz et al. 2019).

Okay, but does it really matter whether our current actions eventuate catastrophe? We'll almost certainly be dead and gone before things really fall apart anyway. One implication here is that the wellbeing (let alone the existence) of future generations doesn't matter. Quinn suggests, though, that we have good reason to enact a story whereby we remain here—transformed but nevertheless among the living—even after death. We thus have reasons related to our own future wellbeing to avoid unendurable experiences for (much of) life on Earth. I save discussion of this issue for chapter 4.[12]

Somatic Rebellion

We Takers are a people, we're routinely reminded, who can't abide living with limits. No people can, from our vantage point. So even if our tower does come toppling down, people will rise from its detritus to do what we've done all over again (BD, 9). They won't be able to help themselves.

In *This Changes Everything*, Naomi Klein puts this idea another way and then dismantles it. "Contemporary humans are too self-centered, too addicted to gratification to live without the full freedom to satisfy our every whim—or so our culture tells us every day." And yet we routinely make both individual and collective sacrifices "in the name of an abstract greater good all the time" (2014, 17). We're forced, she states, to give up pensions, decent jobs, and hard-won labor rights. We send our children to schools with overcrowded classrooms, stripped-down and cookie-cutter curricula, and harried teachers. We consign ourselves to dirty air and water for the sake of destructive energy sources and industrial products we don't need and must be convinced we want. And we put up with crumbling infrastructures and failing services, university educations that result in a lifetime's worth of debt, and a middling healthcare system that can bankrupt even the financially secure. It's clear Klein primarily has the American middle class, among the world's leading purveyors of maximum harm, in mind here.

With respect specifically to employment, we tend to privilege having any job whatsoever, no matter how miserable and degrading, over having no job at all (Boyle 2010). We value productivity, no matter what's being produced, over wellbeing ("Indiebound"). Paul Eppinger, the model for the story about Jeffrey in *My Ishmael* (MI, 196ff.), puts it this way in his journal, published shortly after his suicide: "I thought of what some of my friends were doing that summer. Building cardboard boxes or shaving poodles or maybe even being the Head Pickler at Burger King. Shit, I got pretty angry thinking of all the fresh young energy being wasted. Folks just getting stiffer and staler every day" (Eppinger and Eppinger 1994, 12). We reward what we value, Jensen notes in turn. "All fancy philosophy aside, we value asking someone if they would like fries with their burger more than we value a rich and healthy emotional and spiritual life and a vital community" (2000, 328).

Stark socioeconomic stratification, common throughout Taker culture, damages those not just at the bottom of the hierarchy but those at the top (and everyone in between), too. According to Richard Wilkinson and Kate Pickett, "Individual psychology and societal inequality relate to each other like lock and key" (2009, 33). Rooted deep in human evolutionary development is a sensitivity to stark differences in social status. This helps to explain why "The scale of income difference has a powerful effect on how we relate to each other" (ibid., 4–5). It turns out that health and social problems are decidedly worse for *everyone* in more unequal societies. Socioeconomic inequality strongly correlates across all social classes with lower life expectancy; increased mental health issues and addiction; lower rates of literacy and competence with math; higher rates of infant mortality, teenage births, homicide, suicide, and imprisonment; eroded social trust; and reduced social mobility (ibid., 18ff.).

Even what qualify as decent ways to make a living have become increasingly immiserating and alienating, Bruce Levine asserts. Getting fed "means more degrees, compliance, ass-kissing, shit-eating, and inauthenticity." We want better but see no salient options; we may even want out altogether but see no exits. We feel helpless and hopeless. "So, many of us . . . rebel by what is commonly called mental illness" (2013).

Words like *illness, disease, and disorder* typically indicate that our focus should be on individuals who are in need of treatment, Levine asserts, "not on a troubled society in need of restructuring" (2001, 3). But anxiety, depression, addiction, and other such maladies are better characterized as commonsense reactions against a culture that's antithetical to:

> (1) *autonomy*—self-direction, experience of potency, and capacity and ability to self-govern; (2) *community*—strong bonds among small groups that provide for economic security and emotional satisfaction; and (3) *humanity*—the variety of ways of being human, the variety of satisfactions, and the variety of negative reactions to feeling controlled rather than understood. (Ibid., 4)

A culture that's hostile to autonomy, community, and humanity perpetuates itself via a specifiable form of institutionalization, Levine adds, one that proliferates "large, bland, standardized, hierarchical, bureaucratic, authoritarian, coercive, manipulative, expansionistic, and impersonal entities" (ibid., 6; see also WS, 28). It also identifies, and urges us to self-identify, our adverse reactions to institutionalization as malingering or signs that we simply can't cope. AA, of course, is just one such institution.

Levine contends instead that these reactions are evidence of a somatic rebellion against systemic cultural deformities. They're neuro-corporeal refusals fully to comply. Even as we rebel, we remain largely disempowered. But we're nevertheless increasingly checked out: looking for means to psychically absent ourselves from reality or fleetingly to alter it (I, 44, MI, 115f., and Jensen 2000, 59).

Both individually and collectively, somatic rebellion is scattershot, inchoate, and unstructured. We also mischaracterize it as our minds and bodies betraying us when what they're doing is demanding our undivided attention. They're signaling that—for the sake of our wellbeing, if not our very lives—we must heed our unease rather than changing the channel, explaining it away, or repressing our misery while telling ourselves ad infinitum that we nevertheless live as humans are meant to live.

"Deep down," Jensen states, "our needs are very simple: apart from food, shelter, and clothing there are the need to love and be loved, for community, to be open to the world at large and for it to be open to us, to affect and be affected, to understand and be understood, to hear and be heard, to accept and be accepted" (2000, 328). As water is to fish, though, and air is to birds, coercion is to us (ibid., 244). And what we're often coerced to do is to ignore our most basic needs. To get fed, often we have no choice but to accede, which triggers even more visceral forms of somatic dissent.

Over time, though, our minds and bodies get beaten down. Captivity, invariably accompanied (at the very least) by persistent low-level trauma, takes its toll. Jensen contends that this leads many of us to become zombies of a sort. We "waste away, shrivel, and die as from hunger and thirst. We die, but we go on surviving" (ibid., 328). Trauma specialist Judith Herman notes in turn that perception, emotion, experience, empathy, and the capacity to resist coercion atrophy, particularly when we're "rendered helpless by overwhelming force" (1997, 3). Our sense of connection—to ourselves, to others, to the world at large—breaks down, and we come to "belong more to the dead than the living" (ibid., 52).[13]

Experiencing routine intimidation, humiliation, and disrespect, all of which often accompany coercion in Taker culture, also can lead people to commit aggravated forms of harm both to themselves and to others. In the process, somatic rebellion inverts and ends up exacerbating our systematic cultural deformities. Jack Forbes appropriates the Cree term *wétiko*—cannibal—to denote what he describes as a "genuine, very real epidemic sickness" (2008, xviii). Those afflicted commit wanton acts of murder, brutality, and deceit. They cannibalize others' lives and lands, sometimes in short order and sometimes over the span of many years. "*Cannibalism,*" as Forbes defines it, "*is the consuming of another's life for one's own private purpose or profit*" (ibid., 24). As such, it's a "sickness of exploitation" (ibid., xix) or, as Quinn puts it in a related context, a "madness" that turns one into a "murderer of all life" (TA, 14). But because *wétiko* also breeds dementia, the afflicted tend to view their acts as benign or even virtuous. They have great difficulty perceiving their cannibalistic behavior as destructive. This is due in part, as Levine alludes, to the fact that their actions are condoned and supported by a litany of formal and informal institutions within our culture.

The term *wétiko* is closely associated with the Ojibwe term *Windigo,* which may have derived from *ween dagoh,* "solely for self," or from *weenin n'd'igooh,* "excess" (Levy 2013, 34). Windigo is the name attributed to a fabled diabolical being whom the Ojibwe feared beyond all else (Mowat 2005, 253). Whether it's encountered in the form of a spirit or a human person (it can take either form), Windigo is a destroyer par excellence of social cohesion and ecological integrity (Simpson 2017, 77).

According to traditional tales, states Robin Kimmerer, Windigo is most closely associated with the "ever-present fear of winter famine," during which time "the icy hunger and gaping maw" of the beast can undermine entire communities (2013, 304). Windigo cares more for its own satisfaction than anything else. But its satisfaction can never be achieved, for it "suffers the eternal pain of need, its essence is a hunger that will never be sated. The more a Windigo eats, the more ravenous it becomes" (ibid., 305).

Takers are prototypical carriers of *wétiko,* which comes in degrees, Forbes contends. Some of us are full-on cannibals, who Forbes calls Big *Wétikos* (2008, 116ff.; see also Levy 2013, 53f.). Others, completely cannibalized, still identify at least in part with the *wétiko* ethos. Most of us fall somewhere in between, which means we both invidiously consume others and are invidiously consumed. The rape of women, of workers, of the land, of a people, of a river, of a forest, of the air, of competitors for food: they're all of a piece. The lives of the cannibalized are devoured not symbolically or metaphorically but literally, Forbes asserts. At root, this is the most visceral legacy of the Taker axioms. "And as unchecked by most vaccines [*wétiko*] tends to become worse rather than better with time. More and more people catch it, in more and more places, and they become the true teachers of the young" (ibid., xix). This makes it extremely difficult to uproot once it takes hold within a culture.[14] It becomes normal to reward those who cannibalize and delegitimize those on whom they prey. No wonder, to paraphrase Richard Powers (2018, 20), Taker history is the story of increasingly disoriented hunger.

Of course, we would face no such problems if we lived otherwise. Indeed, considering doing so—most notably by shedding our Taker ways for another story to be in—may have its allure. Yet, ambient in our culture is the assumption that, ultimately "you're really going to hate it. It's going to be painful" (MI, 189). Living otherwise will involve the loss of so much that we love and can't do without; "giving up *anything* would necessarily represent a step backward in human development" (ibid., 190; see also BD, 8f.). Would you prefer to be "shitting in bushes? You wouldn't like that, would you? No bathrooms, no electric blankets, no television, no governments, no churches, no theaters, no museums, no penitentiaries, no schools. No nothing" (BD, 8–9). Just a Stone Age existence, living on a knife's edge of survival.

Domination Systems

Takers are hereby taught to normalize living in and with what Raine Eisler calls *domination systems*. Domination systems are premised on rigid top-down control. They drive socioeconomic inequality, foster high levels of abuse and violence, and are typically starkly heteropatriarchal, Eisler contends (2007, 97). Unsurprisingly, their proponents regard hierarchalism as both inevitable and moral. Takers may struggle, often unwittingly, against the bars of our cultural cage. But constantly impressed upon us is the idea that these bars are nevertheless in place for our own protection.

Domination systems enforce control in part by presupposing that people must be kept on a tight leash because (1) the scarcity of the goods we need to survive and thrive is inevitable and (2) humans are inherently greedy. We humans have unlimited wants but limited means to satisfy them. This is part of what fuels our axiomatic drive for conquest.

Even for the most committed, though, the pursuit of conquest comes with an immediate downside. As John Gowdy states, "Every act of consumption is . . . also an act of denial, resulting ultimately in deprivation" (1998, xv). The best we can hope for as economic beings is to maximize enjoyment of the relatively few things we're able to acquire. And since acquisition inherently involves competition, it requires that we either find ways to dominate others, exploiting them in ways that permit us to extract wealth from our interactions (often through fear and force), or that we submit to domination ourselves and get what we can from being just another economic input—human capital, a unit of productivity.

Within domination systems, trust is understandably scarce and tension runs high, Eisler remarks (2007, 30). Satisfaction is commodified and invariably fleeting. Taker culture—specifically, the economic systems that it fosters—thus both ostensibly provides the only means to enjoy comfort and security and ensures that they can't be had. Seeking wellbeing is a self-defeating exercise (ibid., 33; see also Sahlins 1972, 4, and Kimmerer 2013, 111). One of our primary goals in life, to satisfy our wants and needs, is structurally *unachievable* ("Dialogue on *Beyond Civilization*").

Thunderbolt in Freefall

For generation after generation, the Taker axioms have represented "the simple truth" for the people of our culture, Julie states (MI, 189). Rarely are they stated as baldly as presented here. Still, they're familiar to us and are still widely accepted.

But what if they're components instead of a "simple lie" (ibid.), as Ishmael describes them? What then?

Upon his first visit to Ishmael, a poster with this message catches Alan's eye:

WITH MAN GONE,
WILL THERE
BE HOPE
FOR GORILLA?

It's a koan that can be read in two straightforward but contradictory ways, Alan suggests. Hope for gorilla(s) lies in the *extinction* of the human race. Or hope for gorilla(s) lies in the *survival* of the human race.

I think there's another, more speculative interpretation as well. Takers aren't humanity, Ishmael and B emphasize, so maybe we're not "man" in the poster. Rather, like Ishmael at the menagerie, we're captives. We're the proverbial "gorilla." Perhaps, then, the questions before us are *can we Takers survive the loss of our humanity*—to ongoing zombification and cannibalization? Or, alternatively, *is hope for Takers to be found in rediscovering our humanity?*

The second of these questions is particularly compelling. It coheres with Ishmael's specification of the root sense of the term *wealth. Wealth* isn't synonymous with money, he states, but instead with *wellness:*

> In terms of products, you [Takers] are of course fabulously wealthy, but in terms of human wealth, you are pathetically poor. In terms of human wealth, you are the wretched of the earth. And this is why you shouldn't focus on giving up things. How can you expect the wretched of the earth to give up *anything*? That's impossible. On the contrary, you must absolutely concentrate on *getting* things—but not more toasters, Julie. . . . Not more playthings. You must concentrate on getting the things you desperately need *as human beings*. At the moment you've given up on all those things, you've decided they can't be had. (MI, 191; see also I, 203, and "Investments")

As with an aircraft with a fatally compromised design, the "Taker Thunderbolt" (I, 107; see also Q&A, 749) doesn't work and can't be made to work. Ersatz aeronauts who push their plane, which defies the laws of aerodynamics, off a high cliff face imminent freefall. The people of a culture that defies what Ishmael calls the Law of Life face freefall, too. Risks abide should we prepare to bail out from our "Civilizational flight" (ibid.). But, Quinn avers, these risks may appear less ominous, less salient, less worthy of our time and attention as we see more clearly wherein human wealth lies.

Before we get to this, though, we must look more closely at the most common institutional means Takers have relied on to seek escape from our suffering.

Chapter 3

Egress Regress

The Antisavior's Devotional

Soteriology derives from the Greek term *sōtēria,* salvation. It involves the study of religious theories and doctrines of redemption, liberation, and deliverance—most frequently from that which causes human suffering and woe. While their forms vary, soteriologies play a central role in every major Taker religion. Across the board, Quinn contends, they amplify the core Taker axioms more powerfully than any other institution of our culture. The Taker soteriologies are also quintessential examples of *cruel optimism* (Berlant 2011). They promise relief from suffering while instead reinforcing its cultural causes.

This wasn't always Quinn's considered opinion. From an early age, he was obsessed with Christian soteriology. This impelled him to attempt in his late teens to join the Trappist order at the Abbey of Our Lady of Gethsemani in Kentucky. The Trappists had never given up the medieval Catholic view that the earth is "the prize contested by cosmic forces of good and evil," Quinn states (P, 36). As such, the monastery at Gethsemani wasn't a refuge. It was instead "the first line of defense against the almost overwhelming power of Satan." To join the order would mean becoming a warrior in one of God's "strongholds, bastions, citadels" (ibid., 37). As a young man, that's what it meant to Quinn to be engaged in saving the world.

A profound experience he had at Gethsemani led him decades later to radically alter his view of what saving the world entails. His obsession with the task didn't wane, but his view of the merits of Taker soteriologies did. Indeed, he became something of an "Antisavior" (B, 324), not in the sense that he was intent on precipitating people's damnation or its non-Christian equivalent. Rather, he maintains that the manner in which salvation is typically understood by Takers is *antithetical* to saving the world, hence to saving ourselves. The pursuit of salvation as we typically understand it thus systematically undermines the pursuit of ecological, social, and personal wellbeing. It's a positive hindrance to the threefold struggle, according to Quinn.

Does this mean that for the world to be saved Taker religions must go? This question is more difficult to answer than Quinn lets on, I think, but we'll get to that in due course. Let's first consider the world-historical events depicted in the first few chapters of the biblical Book of Genesis, the significance of which transcends the Jewish and Christian traditions with which they're now associated. Are you familiar with the stories of Adam and Eve in the Garden of Eden? What about Cain and Abel? These tales are generally taken to represent a spiritual catastrophe the implications of which haunt humanity to this day. This is true, Quinn avers. But the character of this spiritual catastrophe is radically different than biblical scholars and theologians typically assume. For the Genesis stories actually come from *Leaver peoples* who bore witness to the initial geographical expansion of Taker culture. What we see through their eyes isn't the Fall, embodied by a rift between God and humanity *writ large*. No, we witness transgressions specifically against a god of the land by practitioners of totalitarian agriculture. These transgressions serve as seeds for the discomfort and insecurity endemic to Taker culture today.

Switching perspectives, we then examine the salvific imperative itself. In one way or another, Quinn asserts, every Taker soteriology supports the idea that our highest calling is to achieve either otherworldly relief from an earthly existence marked by ongoing misery or the wholesale transformation of our earthly existence into a state free from all causes of misery. The concerns of the wider community of life either count for very little or nothing at all. Indeed, while a quick survey of Christianity, Judaism, Islam, Hinduism, Buddhism, Daoism, and Confucianism shows that each may be at least partially supportive doctrinally of doing well by the living community, it's less clear whether the needs and interests of other-than-human beings are much of priority in the workaday practice among most adherents of Taker religions. What role these religions might play in recovering from the spiritual catastrophe Takers have faced remains an open question.

Spiritual Catastrophe

Biblical scholars and theologians commonly accept that three separate documents from three different sources were brought together to comprise the Book of Genesis. In fact, Genesis begins with two entirely different creation stories. The first is newer; it likely was crafted centuries or even millennia after the second. Because the source of the first creation story is presumed to be of the Israelite priestly class, that source is called P.

Written during or just after the Babylonian exile of the Israelites, or somewhere between 600–540 BCE, the first creation story describes the six-day process of creation: of light; the heavens and waters; land and vegetation; astral bodies; the creatures of heaven and the waters; and terrestrial animals, including humans. God—called Elohim by P in the original Hebrew—declares each creation good, particularly the last. Throughout the creation process, Elohim remains an isolated and unique presence, outside of and generally distant from that which is created (Sarna 1966, 10). All of creation is utterly subordinate. Elohim "has simply to speak and his words articulate the formless waste of chaos, giving it grammar, shape, and form," Karen Armstrong remarks (1996, 9).[1]

The second, older creation story was written by J, the Jahwist. J refers to God as Yahweh (*Jahve* in German, the nationality of the scholars who proposed this abbreviation), or, frequently, Yahweh Elohim, "Lord God." While this story first may have been written down in the form presented in Genesis in the fifth century BCE, it was commonly known in Israel at least from the tenth century BCE. It has roots as part of an oral tradition, though, that may date back as far as the Chalcolithic Age, or 4000–3150 BCE (Broadt 1984, 30).

Narratively speaking, J is much more grounded than P. Earth and heaven refer to land and sky. Living beings are created not by pronouncement but by combining earth and breath. And Yahweh is quite present, walking amidst and freely interacting with his creations. His most notable companions are man and woman, the human protagonists in the Garden of Eden tale, which constitutes the first part of J's fuller story.

The Garden of Eden

In the Garden of Eden, Yahweh makes grow every sort of plant and tree that's pleasant to the eye and good for food.[2] Two special trees are planted here: the tree of life and the tree of knowledge of good and evil. The former is referred to in many oral traditions the world over. It's assumed by numerous biblical scholars and theologians to confer immortality (Armstrong 1996, 33). Incredibly, the latter has no parallel outside the story of the Garden of Eden, despite being the tree around which the narrative revolves (Sarna 1966, 26, and Broadt 1984, 119).

After creating the man, who's yet to be named, Yahweh places him in Eden "to till and keep it" (Gen. 2:15) and issues his first commandment: "You may freely eat of every tree of the garden; but of the tree of knowledge of good and evil you shall not eat, for in the day that you eat of it you shall die" (Gen. 2:15–16). Robert Alter (2004, 21) notes that the original Hebrew conveys that the man is actually "doomed to die" should he eat the forbidden fruit. So immediate death isn't entailed. "The fruit is not cyanide," j. Snodgrass comments, "it's more like 'Angel Dust,' confusing the user's understanding of physical limitations as they endanger themselves" (2011, 47).

After issuing this commandment, Yahweh recognizes that the man deserves to have a helpmate or helper fit for him. This being isn't to be a maid or servant, a subordinate. The original Hebrew indicates that this being is a supporter of the man, yes, but in the sense of being a compatible counterweight of equal strength and worth (Freedman 1983). Yahweh thus creates every manner of bird and beast, bringing them to the man to be named. Whether these naming rights are intended to give the man power over the birds and beasts isn't clear. Nothing in the story suggests that these acts of naming confer power over the named (Pedersen 1926, 108).[3] The main takeaway is that none of these creatures is a fit counterweight for the man.

So Yahweh puts the man into a deep sleep and creates a woman from one of his ribs. (Why a rib? Because the word for *rib* in ancient Sumerian also means *life*.) Yahweh then issues a second commandment: that upon marrying, a man leaves his parents and joins his wife's family, whereby "they become one flesh" (Gen 2:24). This is generally taken to imply sexual intimacy, but whatever the case may be both husband and wife are naked and unashamed.

The plot now thickens. The serpent, "more subtle than any other wild creature that the Lord God had made" (Gen. 3:1), asks the woman if Yahweh has declared any food in Eden to be off limits to her and the man. This is a jarring transition from the tranquil scene earlier depicted. It's not clear whether the serpent is part of the original story or was introduced sometime after the Babylonian exile, around the time that the notion of a supernatural adversary was appropriated from Persian religious ideas (Asimov 1968, 31).[4] But a serpent may have been chosen to play the role of the mischief maker because this creature served as an ancient symbol for a Canaanite goddess who presumably competes with Yahweh for the woman's affections (Charlesworth 2010, 323).

Whatever the case may be, the woman replies to the serpent that she and the man are prohibited only from eating the fruit of the tree "which is in the midst of the garden" (Gen. 3:2). She doesn't refer to the tree by name, but the context makes clear that she's speaking about the tree of knowledge of good and evil. She adds that they would die should they partake. The serpent, however, tells her that this isn't so. "For God knows that when you eat of it your eyes will be opened, and you will be like God, knowing good and evil" (Gen. 3:5).

Now comes the first of two critical moments comprising the Fall. The woman eats the forbidden fruit, also giving it to the man who eats along with her. They defy Yahweh's first commandment. But why exactly does Yahweh prohibit the man and woman from eating of the tree of knowledge of good and evil in the first place? This has been a source of unending speculation among the people of our culture. Here's an incomplete list of suggestions based on my limited review of the voluminous literature on the subject:

1. Eating the forbidden fruit is proscribed simply as a demand for obedience by Yahweh (Buber 1986 and Kidner 2008).

2. It confers a loss of innocence, specifically via either the emergence of sexual consciousness *simpliciter* (Eiselen 1910, Gordis 1957, and Aron 2005) or the tendency to succumb to our own desires at the expense of heeding Yahweh's dictates (Broadt 1984).

3. It enables the man and the woman to make moral distinctions (Gordon 1907, Stern 1958, and Armstrong 1996) or to judge right and wrong for themselves, particularly in relation to their own interests and concerns (Callicott 1994).

4. It enables the woman and the man to free themselves from dependence on guidance by Yahweh, since knowledge of good and evil is actually an idiom for omniscience, knowledge of everything (Engnell 1955, Brueggemann 1970, and Buchanan 1976).

5. As in the *Midrash*, eating the forbidden fruit prevents any of the other creatures of Eden from gaining rule over the woman and man (Ginzberg 1956).

6. And since the terms *good* and *evil* are better translated, respectively, as *nurture* and *destroy* (von Rad 1962, 89), the fruit of the tree of knowledge of good and evil is forbidden because only Yahweh has rightful power over what's nurtured and what's destroyed.

We'll see moving forward that Baird Callicott and Gerhard von Rad are both on to something.

Transgression completed, the woman's and man's eyes open, and the first thing they recognize is that they're naked. After covering themselves, they hide upon hearing Yahweh walking around Eden in the cool of the day. When Yahweh calls out to them and asks where they are, the man comes out of hiding. He's afraid, he admits, hiding "because I was naked" (Gen. 3:10). Yahweh asks how he knows this and, given this knowledge, if he and the woman have broken the first commandment. The man responds that he received the forbidden fruit from the woman but implies that the decision to eat it was his. The woman then confesses as well, telling Yahweh that the serpent beguiled her into transgressing.

Here then is the second of the critical moments comprising the Fall. Yahweh curses each of the three protagonists (and the prose here takes a liturgical form, as if it's a public pronouncement). The serpent is cursed, among other things, to be perpetually at enmity with the woman, as will be the serpent's offspring and her offspring. The woman's curse is twofold. Her pain in childbearing is greatly multiplied, and her husband shall henceforth rule over her. So she goes from being an equal partner to a servant. She's the first earthly victim of hierarchalism. Adam's curse—yes, the man finally gets a name—is perpetual toil. He's exiled from Eden along with his wife and condemned to cultivate and "eat the plants of the field," which will produce no shortage of "thorns and thistles" in the process (Gen. 3:18). The return on investment for his labor shall not be great.

Upon being cursed, Adam designates his wife as Eve, "because she is the mother of all living" (Gen. 3:20). (*Adamah* means dirt or earth in Hebrew, so Adam's name is essentially *earthling*; Eve, or *hawah* in Hebrew, means life.) Yahweh then makes an important pronouncement. "Behold, the man [and presumably the woman, too] has become like one of us, knowing good and evil; and lest he put forth his hand and take also of the tree of life, and eat, and live forever . . ." (Gen. 3:22). Inexplicably, the text trails off here, as if there's more to the story. Perhaps something's missing or isn't being divulged by J. Perhaps J assumes that we've gotten the gist and can move on. Or maybe material was later excised. Whatever the case may be, Adam and Eve are officially cast out of Eden, and cherubim, Yahweh's deific subordinates, are placed at its entrance "to guard the way to the tree of life" (Gen. 3:24).

This passage is odd, though. J's syntax suggests that Adam and Eve's exile from Eden is intended in part to prevent them from eating of the tree of life. Why else place cherubim to bar their way to it? But nowhere does Yahweh forbid Adam and Eve from eating the fruit of this tree. What's going on?

Here's Quinn's take. Adam and Eve must now be barred from eating the fruit of the tree of life only because they ate from the tree of knowledge of good and evil. Spit out the fruit of the latter and the former would be freely available to them again. I know this sounds rather obtuse, but bear with me. It will make more sense as we proceed.

Before we move on, though, permit me to comment on God's name. Elohim, the name P uses, is actually the plural of *eloah*. So perhaps P isn't referring to a singular God but to a pantheon; maybe P actually embraces polytheism. There's evidence after all that the God of the Israelites had a female partner at some point (2 Kings 23:6, Jer. 44:17–19, and Prov. 8:22–31). But most biblical scholars assume that the use of the plural Elohim is instead intended to be an honorific. It's the "we" that monarchs use to refer to themselves when conveying that they're a living embodiment of the entire realm under their rule.[5]

More pertinent for our purposes is the shift in names between P and J. Yahweh is the God of the nation of Israel. P may well use the name Elohim, though, because the first creation story was written during or just after the Babylonian exile, "when a more *universal* view of God's blessing was needed—one that was not tied so closely to the land and that did not make God quite so 'human' and available as J did," states Lawrence Broadt (1984, 113–14). If so, Yahweh Elohim, "Lord God," in J probably doesn't mean: Yahweh, one of many Elohim. Instead, J is pronouncing that the God of Israel is also the universal God. But this isn't what matters for us. Note, rather, the shift from a distant God in P to a personal and familiar God in J. This trajectory reverses itself as Genesis unfolds, and this is significant.

Cain and Abel

The first thing we learn after Adam and Eve are cast out of Eden is that Eve gives birth to a son, whom she names Cain. Cain's name may derive from the Hebrew term *qanah,* or acquisition, since Eve declares that "I have gotten a man with the help of the Lord" (Gen. 4:1). Yahweh may have cursed them, but they aren't abandoned by him. Alternatively, Cain's name may come from *qáyin,* for craftsman, foreshadowing what becomes of him. Eve also gives birth to Abel (perhaps from *hebel,* breath).[6] We learn that Abel is a herder and Cain a farmer.

Cain brings an offering of what he's produced to Yahweh. Abel does, too, giving "of the firstlings of his flock and of their fat portions" (Gen. 4:4). Yahweh approves of Abel's offering but rejects Cain's. Is Yahweh's rejection due to the quality of Cain's and Abel's respective offerings? The text suggests this. But Joel Lohr (2009) indicates that the differentiation of the quality of their offerings was introduced into the text by a Greek translator. The original Hebrew is silent on the matter. Maybe instead Yahweh's actions are the result of the brothers' respective demeanors when presenting their offerings, but no such information is provided. Of course, it also may have to do with the fact that Abel is a herder and Cain a farmer. Why this should lead to differential treatment by Yahweh isn't stated either, though. All we know for sure is that the rejection of his offering angers Cain greatly.

When they're both out in the fields, Cain rises up against Abel and kills him. Shortly after, Yahweh asks Cain where his sibling is. Cain says he doesn't know, asking, snarkily, "Am I my brother's keeper?" (Gen. 4:9). But Yahweh knows the truth, saying that Abel's voice is crying out from the earth. Yahweh tells Cain that he's "cursed from the ground" (Gen. 4:11). In other words, Yahweh isn't cursing Cain, *the land itself is.* And the land accepts Abel's blood and body for good measure. As a result, Yahweh tells Cain, "it will no longer yield to you its strength" (Gen. 4:12). Note that the land is an active agent here, expressing that Cain's farming days are over, at least in *this place.* Cain is now to be a fugitive and a "restless wanderer" (Gen. 4:14) of the earth. The land of *this place* rejects him.

Now note this. In responding to Yahweh that this punishment is more than he can bear, Cain declares that it's Yahweh who has driven him from the land, as if he's being subject to divine retribution after all. Cain adds, seemingly as a result, that he'll be hidden from Yahweh's face. It's not clear whether he's implying that the land *is* Yahweh, but the context suggests that this reading is plausible. Cain's relationship with both the land and the god—with the Land/God, really—is severed.[7]

Being a fugitive and restless wanderer, Cain worries that he'll be killed by whomever finds him.[8] So Yahweh places a mark on Cain, which is to serve as a warning to anyone who should attempt to kill him that vengeance will fall on them sevenfold. Cain then departs from Yahweh, the Land/God, dwelling in Nod (Hebrew for *wanderer*), east of Eden. He gets married and his wife bears a son, Enoch, whose name Cain chooses for the city he builds, the first city ever built. Yes, the seeds of civilization are the handiwork (*qáyin,* craftsman) of a murderer, of one who commits fratricide no less.

Narrative Appropriation

So Cain, the farmer/craftsman, waters the fields with the blood of Abel the herder. But this isn't a one-off incident being described, Ishmael tells Alan. It's a description of "what has always happened along the borders of Taker expansion: the Leavers were being killed off so that more land could be put under cultivation" (I, 173). The peoples of the world who don't practice totalitarian agriculture are under threat of death when they encounter those who do.[9]

Quinn classifies Abel as a representative of the Semitic peoples and Cain as a representative of the Caucasians, the people of the Caucasus. If he's correct, the Caucasians descended from the north into the Levant as they sought to put more land to the plow (I, 170ff., and WS, 124). There are good reasons to question whether Quinn is correct that the invaders depicted in this tale came from the Caucasus. Evidence instead points to Northern Syria and Southeast Turkey as the point of origin of totalitarian agriculture in the Fertile Crescent (Bar-Yosef 1998). This doesn't negate the dynamic that he illustrates, though. J is portraying a people behaving destructively. Their arrival heralds ecological catastrophe for the land, cultural catastrophe for the people represented by Abel, and, most notably for present purposes, spiritual catastrophe for the people represented by Cain. Yes, the Fall occurred, Quinn contends, and it did mark a spiritual rupture—but not between God and humanity. No, the rupture was between the Land/God of a specifiable place and a people who gave birth to Taker culture (B, 256, and P, 151).

When Curses Should Be Blessings

Did you notice a key oddity in J's tales? In both, Yahweh curses the protagonists for engaging in practices that Takers otherwise valorize. In the opening pages of a text that's a critical source of support for Taker culture, Taker practices are condemned and their practitioners are harshly punished. Why?

It's clear, Ishmael states. These stories must have "originated among the *enemies* of your cultural ancestors" (I, 174). They're actually written from a Leaver point of view.

If the story of the Garden of Eden had been written by Takers, Ishmael continues, "the knowledge of good and evil wouldn't have been forbidden to Adam, it would have been *thrust* upon him. . . . And if the people of your cultural persuasion had authored it, this event wouldn't be called the Fall, it would be called the Ascent" (ibid., 166). Consider again the suggestions offered by biblical scholars and theologians for why Yahweh forbids eating the fruit of the tree of knowledge of good and evil. If he's simply demanding obedience, why do so in this arbitrary way? Moreover, it makes no sense to prohibit Adam and Eve from gaining the knowledge they need to become conquerors and masters of the world. Indeed, gaining this knowledge wouldn't entail a loss of innocence. Yahweh would welcome it as a sign of maturity, a necessary condition for taking our lives into our own hands. The same can be said of the capacity to make moral distinctions, gain omniscience, and prevent other earthly creatures from acquiring the capacity to rule over us. Even possessing the power over what's nurtured and what's destroyed is a critical component of the Taker lifestyle. But each is depicted by biblical scholars and theologians as something that Yahweh doesn't want for us.[10]

Furthermore, the invention and spread of totalitarian agriculture is, for Takers, "humanity's greatest blessing" (WS, 123). But J's description suggests that becoming a totalitarian agriculturalist—utterly toilsome and nutritionally unrewarding—is the greatest punishment Yahweh can confer upon Adam:

> It was literally inconceivable to the authors of these stories that anyone would *prefer* to live by the sweat of his brow. So the question they ask themselves was not, "Why did these people adopt this toilsome lifestyle?" It was, "What terrible misdeed did these people commit to deserve such a punish-

> ment? What have they done to make the gods withhold from them the bounty that enables the rest of us to live carefree lives?" (I, 178)

In short, what got these people ejected from Eden?

Eve's curse was even more damning. She goes from being Adam's equal to being "his slave and incubator," Snodgrass bluntly states (2011, 58). Moreover, childbirth became the hardest of hard labor. Does this suggest that the original authors of what became J prized equality of the sexes? It certainly seems so. It also indicates shock at the level of death in labor among female practitioners of totalitarian agriculture, owing, perhaps, to widespread malnutrition among early adopters.

As for the story of Cain and Abel, Yahweh likely would have shown favor to Cain for his offering and rejected Abel's had it been written by Takers. From a Taker viewpoint, Cain's actions shouldn't condemn him to be a fugitive and restless wanderer. They should be rewarded. But no, the Land/God exiles Cain from his presence. Civilization is born beyond that presence, and only later does Elohim (first, and then Yahweh) shine light upon it.

Abel's Explanation

"What sort of story would the Leaver people tell about the appearance of the Takers in the world?" Ishmael asks Alan (I, 155). How would Abel explain Cain's behavior if he was given a voice? For an answer, we do well to begin by looking at what the Takers are doing and saying. Let's make our analysis, speculative though it must be, from the point of view of the people represented by Abel.

It's clear that these invaders aren't a mere raiding party. They're annihilators. We're familiar with tillers of the soil of the horticultural sort that Adam embodies in Eden. But the form of tilling that these invaders do is destructive beyond anything we've seen or could imagine:

> Our brothers from the north are saying that we've got to die. They're saying that Abel has to be wiped out. They're saying we're not to be allowed to live. Now that's something new, and we don't get it. Why can't they live up there and be farmers and let us live down here and be herders? Why do they have to murder us? (I, 176)

> They're not just saying that *we* have to die. They're saying that *everything* has to die. They're not just killing us, they're killing *everything*. They're saying, "Okay lions, you're dead, we've had it with you." They're saying, "Okay wolves, we've had it with you too. You're out of here." They're saying . . . "Nobody eats but us. All this food belongs to us and no one else can have any without our permission." They're saying, "What we want to live lives and what we want to die dies." (Ibid., 177; see also B, 96)

"Something really weird must have happened up there to turn these people into murderers. What could it have been? . . . Look at the way these people live. Nobody has ever lived this way before" (ibid., 176). These people must somehow have come to believe that they're gods! For they act as if they have the supreme right to determine who lives and who dies.

Our people have been familiar with the vaunted tree of life since time immemorial. Its fruit gives us the strength we need to work and run and play and sing and dance (MGY, 65). Eating of the tree of life symbolizes not that any individual among us becomes divinely immortal but, rather, that we're living in the hands of the gods. We're living a lifestyle that's commensurate with the perpetuation of our people, both human and other-than-human (I, 161).

But given this unprecedented invasion, we can't help but think that there must be another tree in our midst as well, which we'll call the tree of knowledge of good and evil. This tree flourishes wherever life flourishes, but its fruit is strictly for the gods. They walk among us and must be nourished, too. This tree gives the gods the wisdom they need to sustain Eden.

Why is this wisdom from the tree that's forbidden to us about good and evil? What does this have to do with life and death? This is what an extended prequel that Ishmael provides to the Genesis stories is about (I, 156ff.). From the perspective of the gods, there's a special form of wisdom that one must have in order to foster life (B, 138). Since the experience of death is often unwelcome it may be considered evil, while being able to go on living by being nourished by the lives of others is typically considered good. Hence, the connection between good and evil and life and death (P, 151; see also I, 165, and WS, 124f.).

In the hands of the gods, biodiversity flourishes (MGY, 65). But to our horror, these invaders now assume that they have wisdom that only the gods can have. They're acting as the arbiters of life and death. "Yes, that's it. That's what must have happened up there. These people found the gods' own tree of wisdom and stole some of its fruit" (I, 177). Conveniently, they have determined that all the food fit for human consumption should be exclusively for them. So it's not exactly that they're destroying everything. The beings who become their food are permitted to live . . . at least until it's time for them to end up in the invaders' bellies. This the invaders call good. The living beings who aren't fit for human consumption or who compete with them for their food sources must be stamped out, for the invaders regard them as evil. This includes us, of course. It's why they're "watering the soil with our blood" (ibid.).

It's one thing to regard fellow members of the living community, whether human or other than human, as pernicious or dangerous. But among the most lethal memes propagated by these invaders is that the gods filled the world with lots of superfluous creatures that are better off being exterminated to put more and more land to the plow (WS, 186f.). This fuels the invaders' presumption that the world is made exclusively for them.

So we have a fuller picture now of what's going on here. The invaders are attacking and killing us because their ancestors ate the forbidden fruit. The fruit poisoned their ancestors, and the poison passed to them. Theirs is a unique malady; it's made them delusional (MGY, 65; see also WS, 187). We're in danger because they imagine they possess Yahweh's wisdom and have become power-crazed as a result (I, 161f.). Failing to see that they can't possibly see as Yahweh does, they call good whatever they can justify to themselves as being in their interest and evil whatever isn't. Actually, it's worse than this. What they believe to be good is to be able to grow and expand without limit, for being limited is evil (ibid., 163). And they're willing to kill anyone who they see as a threat to this undertaking.

This is all "arrogant foolishness," of course (ibid., 162). These people surely are cursed, and their progeny will pay for it. Because we're all paying for it. The gods have made clear that it's still possible for the invaders to spit out the forbidden fruit. Their path to the tree of life isn't permanently barred. But they must abandon the crazy notion that they're better off taking their lives into their own hands. What has this gotten them? They're fugitives now, restless wanderers.

But Why?

One glaring questions remains, though. Why would Takers appropriate these stories? They're "war propaganda" (I, 174) directed at our ancestors that our ancestors nevertheless saw fit to take as their own. Perhaps their appropriation marks a rejection of the toilsome life of the totalitarian agriculturalist and a yearning for a mythic, idyllic past that lingered on in Takers' oral histories. Ishmael seems to have something like this in mind. Because the Takers "couldn't work up any enthusiasm for the peasant lifestyle," he states, the stories were preserved even if not fully understood (I, 175; see also Asimov 1968, 32).

But these stories can be interpreted to support the Taker vision, too. From the Leaver vantage point, the Taker invasion was a spiritual catastrophe. The people represented by Cain were rejected by Yahweh, the Land/God, because of their destructive behavior. But then Elohim—as he's called by E, the Elohist, whose writings begin when Abraham becomes a central figure in Genesis 12—definitively switches teams to become the Takers' God. What was thus needed from a Taker point of view was an explanation for how this God remained true to them despite their repeated transgressions. For surely he would stay true to a people living the one right way to live.

The stories of Adam and Eve and Cain and Abel both fit within a clear pattern. People transgress, God punishes, and then God forgives, establishing a covenant that confers ongoing protection and support. The point is that God remains faithful to the Israelites even when they stray. As Broadt puts it, "The sin in the human heart has unleashed on the world an ever growing round of murder, war, and hatred, robbed us of life and brought frustration and pain to our labors. But over and over, the theme of God's mercy to a sinful world can be heard in the background" (1984, 112; see also Sarna 1966, 8). We see it again with the flood story and God's subsequent covenant with Noah in Genesis 6. And it culminates with the story of the flight from exile in Egypt and the establishment of the Mosaic covenant, which loomed large in the founding myth of the Israelites (Meyers 2005, 5).

So the tales of the Garden of Eden and Cain and Abel may not have come from Takers, but our cultural forebears nevertheless found creative ways to reinterpret them. It's fascinating, though, that so much of the original Leaver imprint remains—assuming that Quinn's theory holds up. J surely could have done more to massage the narrative. Did J consciously choose not to?

The Salvific Imperative

It's unsurprising that the spread of Taker culture is treated as a spiritual catastrophe by Leavers. But it has not been all wine and roses from a

Taker viewpoint either. Salvation from everyday existence takes center stage in the Taker religions after all. Let's now examine how this came to be, on Quinn's telling.

The Boiling Frog

Drop a frog into a pot of boiling water, and "it will of course frantically try to clamber out," B states (B, 258). But place it in a pot of water that's at a comfortable temperature and it will stay put even as the water is heated, so long as the temperature increase is so gradual as to be barely perceptible. Eventually, "the frog will sink into a tranquil stupor, exactly like one of us in a hot bath, and before long, with a smile on its face, it will unresistingly allow itself to be boiled to death" (ibid.).

It turns out that this isn't true. Neither can frogs hop out of boiling hot water (the protein in their legs coagulates too quickly for them to do so) nor would they remain in gradually heating water past the point of toleration (Kruszelnicki 2011). But this is no matter. B's example is part of a just-so story. Just-so stories are sometimes maligned by philosophers for being unverifiable explanations for how specifiable practices, traits, or behaviors emerged. But the story B tells has a genealogical quality in Friedrich Nietzsche's sense of the term.[11] It's meant to help us understand how changes so subtle that they barely registered to those experiencing them might have occurred among Takers—in this case, how the salvific imperative emerged.

On B's telling, a far as I can tell, the frog represents Taker culture, the water is the people of our culture, the cauldron constitutes the Taker axioms, the fire is food, and the burning wood is totalitarian agriculture. Taker culture first emerged several millennia before the stories J transcribes were first told. Its emergence occurred when our earliest cultural progenitors adopted a nascent version of totalitarian agriculture. In the Fertile Crescent, as with elsewhere, it was initially the experiment of a single people—or, perhaps, of several disparate peoples. Why they continued to practice totalitarian agriculture despite its toilsome characteristics we'll explore later. For now, we can note that the first people of Taker culture stayed put. They might have pushed at their boundaries with surrounding peoples but not yet with overwhelming force. Indeed, the water temperature (Taker people) remained fairly temperate for almost half of the history of our culture, B notes. Over those first six thousand years or so, "signs of distress are almost nonexistence. The technological innovations of this period bespeak a quiet life, centered around hearth and village—sun-dried brick, kiln-fired pottery, woven cloth, the potter's wheel, and so on" (B, 259).

But the fire burning under the cauldron slowly but steadily got hotter. The frog wasn't yet boiling. Not even close. But the water temperature slowly but surely became less comfortable because the fire was growing in intensity. Totalitarian agriculture (the firewood) produced food surpluses (a hotter fire), which led to population expansion (heating water). And to support the fire's ever-growing intensity (more food for an enlarging population), more wood had to be added to the fire. Totalitarian agriculture expanded; more land was put to the plow.

Human population doubled during the first three thousand years of Taker culture and then doubled again in just two thousand years. "In an eye blink of time on the geologic scale, the human population jumped from ten million to fifty million—probably eighty percent of them being practitioners of totalitarian agriculture: members of our culture, East and West" (ibid., 262). It's at this point, around 5000 BCE, that signs of distress we now regard as normal aspects of civilizational living first emerged.

The first city-states, political entities with codified laws, starkly hierarchical governing structures, and a firm division of labor, emerged around 3800 BCE. With hindsight, Takers assume this is because people were becoming more technologically and culturally sophisticated. But B attributes it to the pressure felt by those with the keys to the storehouse to (1) control internal strife—namely, crime and insurrection, which were entirely new phenomena—and (2) organize for external strife—war.[12] "From this point on," B remarks, "the frequency and severity of wars will serve as one measure of how hot the water is getting around our smiling frog" (ibid., 264). In other words, population expansion led to all manner of social tensions, even if Takers now insist they were signs of advancement rather than trouble.

Times of food shortage are known to Leavers, of course (TA, 7ff.). But famine, which originally resulted from catastrophic crop failure in monocultures but now more routinely occurs due to disastrous political decisions, isn't. Takers became increasingly well acquainted with it starting roughly 2,500 years ago, by which time the human population had risen to around 250 million people, far larger than the population of five to ten million in 8000 BCE (Wecskaop Project 2011). By 400 BCE, plague, which is symptomatic of overcrowding and poor sanitation, was also "a regular feature of life all over the civilized world" (B, 266). Slavery emerged as "a huge international business, and of course would remain one down to the present moment" (ibid.). Political corruption and economic instability became common features of our culture, too.

At this point, most Takers were accustomed to being overworked, subject to poor living conditions in cities, and faced with the ongoing struggle to maintain yields on overtaxed land (ibid., 270). People didn't walk away, but they weren't satisfied either. And now they began to wonder, with apologies to Peggy Lee, *Is this really all there is to life?*

The idea of salvation—that this isn't all there is—probably had been in the wind for some time. But a critical mass of Takers was now ready to accept it. Around two thousand years ago, it went viral. It didn't take hold among Takers all at once, of course, and it never took hold among everyone in our culture. But a new and powerful meme emerged. My God, people were saying, there's a problem here. It's us! What we're seeing are signs of human evil and deficiency. We're damaged goods. So we have only ourselves to blame for our suffering.

This meme is accompanied by another, according to which there's a way to alleviate suffering. The conditions in which we're forced to live may be beyond our control, but the state of our souls isn't. Our souls can be saved, no matter how uncomfortable our bodies become. "Forget the boiling. Forget the pain" (B, 269). They can be endured, and they aren't ultimately all that important anyway. And for God's sake, don't walk away. Again with apologies to Ms. Lee, *let's keep dancing.* Let's codify our dances into "a framework of universal laws and moral account-keeping" (Kingsnorth and Hine 2009, 18) that lays out clearly how we can achieve salvation. Yes, this is the right way to live.

The core tenets of the Taker soteriologies now began to emerge. To ease human suffering either in this world or the next, people must fix what's broken. And what's broken is us. Most notably, we fail to heed God's dictates or routinely fall out of step with the order of the cosmos.[13] Moreover, Quinn emphasizes, "All the major world religions (excluding animism, of course), are founded on these notions: that man and man alone was the desired object of creation, that man occupies a preeminent place in the order of creation, that man has a value in God's eyes that is transcendentally greater than that of all other creatures, that this world of matter is illusory, transitory, and worthless" (P, 168). Taken as a whole, the Taker religions share "a single, central vision: Whether it's release from the endless round of death and rebirth or blissful union with God in heaven, salvation is the highest goal of human life, unimaginably beyond any other, such as wealth, happiness, honor, or fame" (B, 323).

It's almost as if the Taker religions have made a virtue of displacement from the land and remoteness from the divine. They also handily serve to institutionalize social control. Across the board, Jensen states, they:

> naturalize the oppressiveness of the culture—get people (victims) to believe that their enslavement is not just cultural but a necessary part of existence to which they have been "condemned" . . . and then to point people away from their awful (civilized) existence and toward "liberation" in some illusory better place (or even more abstractly, no place at all!). How very convenient for those in power. How very convenient for those who enslave humans and nonhumans alike. These are religions of the powerless. These are religions to *keep* people powerless. (2006a, 285–86)

In certain respects, this is what Taker religions are designed to do, Jensen adds. What better way to keep people from overthrowing you than to have them blame themselves for their misery? If they aren't being goaded by demagogues and dictators into scapegoating others, of course.

Consider, for example, that the religions of our culture are forever trying to improve us, to turn our attention to higher, nobler things. Perhaps they do so by demanding that we internalize guilt, cultivate willpower in the face of temptations of the flesh, feel ashamed for our baser instincts, hold ourselves accountable for each act of wrongdoing, or fix our attention on eternal rewards for good behavior in the hereafter. What matters is that we not only achieve self-discipline but that we become and remain its enforcers (Eisenstein 2007, 284). This is a respect in which the religions of our culture are "the highest expression of our cultural vision," B states (B, 145). They're designed to get us to focus on perfecting ourselves so that we can get on with the hallowed business of perfecting the world—unless, of course, we just jettison the whole enterprise and set our sights on the afterlife.

Indeed, B remarks, we can even see something of this dynamic at work in the most basic of religious practices. Here's one from Christianity: "The pious don't go to church every Sunday because they've forgotten that Jesus loves them but rather because they've *not* forgotten that Jesus loves them. They want to hear it again and again and again. In some sense or other, they *need* to hear it again and again and again and again" (ibid., 240). Why? Maybe because, for Takers, if something doesn't work, one should do more of it—as opposed, say, to doing something else.

Muddying the Waters

Those among you who are adherents of a Taker religion assuredly have your hackles up by this point, particularly if you think Quinn offers a simplistic and one-sided view of your faith. Charles and Shirin are especially worthy of indictment in this respect.

The religious traditions of the people of our culture aren't monolithic, and they aren't fixed entities. They're continually evolving and even intermingling, including with folk practices. The issue gets more complicated when we look at the ongoing debates among denominations and schools of thought within individual religions. It should go without saying that there are complex differences and forms of hybridity both within and across the world's major faiths (Tucker 2017, 33f.).

Moreover, while proponents of what Bron Taylor (2016, 293f.) calls the *greening of religion hypothesis* acknowledge that the Taker religions haven't typically made ecological wellbeing a priority, times are changing. The faithful are becoming increasingly ecologically aware. So while there are certainly prominent forms of support among each of the Taker religions for the idea that humans maintain dominion over the earth—Callicott (1994) calls this the *despotic interpretation*—other views are now coming to the fore. What Callicott calls the *stewardship interpretation,* the idea that we're caretakers of creation and maintain a special responsibility to do well by it, is now prominent. To a lesser extent, a *citizenship interpretation* is gaining increasing attention among the faithful, too. Those who endorse it abandon the heavy-handed anthropocentrism of despotism as well as the more modest anthropocentrism of stewardship in favor of something much closer to biocentrism or ecocentrism.

Quinn is nonetheless skeptical of attempts by proponents of the greening of religion hypothesis to "rewrite their prophets' lines to give them an environmental spin" (P, 169). They're welcome to engage in as much eisegesis, selective reading, as they want. But if, for the Taker religions, the world is "theoretically beyond redemption," as Vine Deloria puts it (1973, 95), and life itself is judged by their wisest sages to be "*no good,*" as Nietzsche claims is the case (see Hatab 2008, 17), then they have no salient role to play in the threefold struggle.

Indeed, states B (B, 145), the Abrahamic religions are openly channeling, not impeding, the flow of the river toward ecocide that Taker culture embodies. The same holds for Taker religions of the East, despite what Emerson and Thoreau suggest about Hinduism, Lynn White (1967) and Gary Snyder (1969) proclaim about Buddhism, Dolores LaChapelle

(1978) alleges of Daoism, and Weiming Tu and Mary Evelyn Tucker (2003) assert about Confucianism. In this respect, once again, "East and West are twins" (B, 248).

Let's see how this all plays out within each of these religions. You'll notice a pattern in the way I present the material. I start by focusing on their respective soteriologies, look next at their otherworldly or even world-denying aspects, and then present their this-worldly tendencies for good measure. We can use this material to assess Quinn's claim that as things go with Taker culture, so they go with the Taker religions.

Christianity

I start with Christianity because it's the religion on which Quinn primarily focuses. He has most to say about it, in all likelihood, because of his own life history (Q&A, 668). And, of course, Christianity has played a key supporting role in global colonization and the spread of Taker culture (I, 182).

The basic problem for Christians is our sinful nature. Sin is universal (John 8:34 and Romans 5:12). In no other religion has personal salvation—via achievement of a place for one's soul in a heavenly paradise—been pushed as much to the forefront. The soul is pure spirit untainted by materiality, individual to each human being, and immortal.[14] The path to salvation is through acceptance of the incarnation and sacrifice of God, via Jesus Christ. Christ's death on the cross has provides a singular path to atonement for humanity.[15]

We're all prone to stray from the path of righteousness, principally because we so easily succumb to earthly temptations. For this reason, more than adherents of any other Taker religion, Christians have been prone to despise the world. As Quinn points out, Jesus himself is adamant that his kingdom " 'is not of this world' [John 8:23], and for two thousand years everybody knew that he meant exactly what he said. . . . Christ never made anything clearer than the fact that . . . he belonged to the world *above*" (P, 78). " 'Anyone who loves the world is a stranger to the Father's love,' " Quinn adds, quoting John the Evangelist. " 'The whole world lies in the power of the evil one' " (ibid., 168–69; see also B, 325, James 4:4, and Marrow 2002).

This certainly makes it easier to regard the earth as, at best, a "testing-ground" (Deloria 1973, 171) on the way to our true home in heaven. Upon death, the body perishes, but the soul, which is our the most essential component of selfhood, is called home. This makes us "strangers and exiles" here (Heb. 11:13). "Our citizenship is in heaven" (Phil. 3:20). Surely, these sorts of ideas have made the proposition that the earth is ours to subdue easier to accept. God didn't "give his only begotten son for anything in the world but the people in it. Christ very definitely did not come to save the whales," Quinn emphasizes (P, 168–69).

Yet numerous scholars of Christianity reject these views. Ecologically minded reformers acknowledge that there's obvious textual support for Christianity's world-denying tendencies. But the Bible is a mixed bag. Just look at the differences between P and J. What's required is the reconstruction of Christian doctrine to emphasize themes that support not just saving souls but also saving the world (Wirzba 2003, Wallace 2005, and McFague 2008). Apologists, moreover, argue that, properly understood, Christian doctrine is actually far more supportive of ecological sustainability than is typically assumed. Pope Francis's encyclical *Laudato Si'* is an example of this approach.

The pope appeals to his namesake St. Francis of Assisi, who defends the equality of all God's creatures in his canticle, "Brother Sun, Sister Moon." Because the earth is designed for the glorification of God it must be respected and cared for. The pope thus rejects the despotic interpretation of Christian doctrine in favor of stewardship. Humans have a special place in creation, yes, but this confers on us responsibilities to act as the earth's caretakers (Pope Francis 2016, 90f. and 161). All of creation has intrinsic value (ibid., 14, 43, 50). Even the desacralization of the earth, somehow, bolsters the pope's case (ibid., 57).

Judaism

Stephen Prothero (2010, 253) highlights that the central problem on which adherents of Judaism focus is exile, both in terms of the global diaspora and the spiritual distance of people from God. Redemption is achieved by means of return: to God and to Israel, the true and enduring father and home, respectively, of the community of the faithful. Although they reject the doctrine of original sin, Jews do place a high value on individual morality. Final redemption, embodied by a world free from war and suffering and in which all are united under the fatherhood of God, marks the spiritual regeneration of humanity. Redemption is thus largely a communal reward. *My* redemption is a function of *our* redemption. But being redeemed still depends on each individual doing their part. As such, those of the Jewish faith are a chosen people not because they're deserving of special privileges from God but because they're charged by God with showing all people the way to redemption by both precept and example (Erlewine 2010, 172).[16]

Otherworldly tendencies in Judaism are hereby muted compared to those of Christianity. Quinn himself remarks that Judaism is the "least otherworldly" of the Abrahamic religions. "Its mystical tradition recognizes the need to 'leave room'—for one's spouse, for one's children, and, by easy extension, for all living creatures" (P, 168). Moreover, considerable ambivalence and debate over whether there's an afterlife continues to this day ("Ask the Rabbis" 2011). This may be because the locus of concern in Judaism is a people as a whole and Israel as a spiritual homeland. Callicott notes that "An individual person may have a *nefesh,* or soul—an older version of the hylozoistic breath of life—but a people as a whole does not. And while individuals are born, live, and die, the nation enjoys, if not eternal life on earth, at least indefinite life on earth—a life that may endure, as have the Jews themselves, for millennia" (1994, 32).

Ecological wisdom may be mediated by sacred texts such as the Torah that convey God's revelations and commands. But putting God at the center of our concerns nevertheless helps us to see the world as a source of awe that mustn't be treated merely as a resource for our use, let alone abuse. And because God himself has absolute ownership over Creation (Ps. 24:1, and I Chron. 29:10–16), Judaism's worldview is more theocentric than anthropocentric. This implies that the proscription against abuse of creation stems from the fact that, strictly speaking, it's not ours to do with as we will in the first place (Tirosh-Samuelson 2019).[17]

Islam

Islam emerged in the seventh century CE, built on the mythic and historical bases of both Judaism and Christianity. Mohammad regarded himself as a prophet of the same God, in the same prophetic tradition as Jesus, Moses, and Abraham. So Islamic soteriology is influenced by both of the other Abrahamic faiths.

According to Muslims, everyone is responsible for their own actions. Even though Adam and Eve, the proverbial parents of humanity, committed a sin by eating the forbidden fruit, we, their descendants, aren't held responsible for this. As with Judaism, we aren't subject to original sin. "Every human being is born with an inclination toward God and the good," states Prothero. But the basic problem we face is hubris, "acting as if you can get along without God" (2010, 31–32). The solution, the basic means for salvation, is complete submission to God. This is achieved via the embrace of *Tawhid,* acknowledgment of the indivisibility and singularity of God. God alone is self-sufficient, and the wellbeing of our souls depends on surrender to no being other than God. Mohammed, for example, is worthy of veneration for his sage prophecies. But he's no savior (Ansary 2009, 351).

In line with Christianity, Islam emphasizes the importance of personal salvation. But again as with Judaism, Islamic doctrine also supports the creation of a perfect earthly community. Each person must repeatedly and routinely repent for their acts of hubris if they're to be in a position for God to grant them salvation. Salvation, though, isn't just about winning entrance into heaven, as important as this is. It's also about becoming servants in this life within a community of fellow devotees joined together in obedience to God (ibid., 166).

In terms of its otherworldly tendencies, Muslims do hold that the earth is but "a temporary abode for man," Callicott states (1994, 33). This supports the despotic interpretation. All other-than-human beings are simply goods at our waystation, explicitly created by God for the sake, use, and benefit of humans. The earth "exists for man to exploit for his own ends," Fazlur Raman asserts. "The utility, serviceability, and exploitability of nature are spoken of in many verses" (2009, 79; see also *Qu'ran* 14:32, 16:12, 22:65, 29:61, 31:20, 35:13, 39:5, 43:12, and 45:12).

A robust strain of stewardship pervades Islam, too, however. Appealing to J, Muslims who challenge the despotic interpretation underscore that human beings, like all terrestrial creatures, are made of earth (*adamah,* remember?). While we may be exalted, we thus maintain a kind of fellowship with our fellow earthly inhabitants. Adam was God's original *khalifa*—viceroy or, yes, steward—and we're charged with following in Adam's footsteps. Even if we have dominion here on Earth, Callicott hereby states, our actions "must be benign, rather than wantonly destructive" (1994, 31; see also *Qu'ran* 2:60, 2:284, 6:165, 7:31, 16:65, and 22:87). Defacing and defiling the earth is impious, even blasphemous. Earthly creatures deserve to be valued intrinsically rather than instrumentally (Foltz 2006, 3f., and *Qu'ran* 6:38).

Hinduism

"Hinduism is so varied, both classically and in its eventual modern forms, that it resists facile doctrinal definition," Callicott observes (1994, 44). The term *Hinduism* itself was coined by Westerners as a means to compartmentalize a constellation of different paths to *moksha* (liberation or release) from *samsāra* (the painful cycle of birth, death, rebirth, and redeath) outlined in the Vedas (Noss and Grangaard 2011, 70f.). For Hindus, states Prothero, "this world is a veil of tears, and whatever happiness we might cobble together here is transitory and impermanent" (2010, 136). Definitive release from *samsāra* is achieved through transitioning from selfishness to oneness with all beings through union with *Brahman,* or the Supreme Being (Dallmayr 2011, 143). *Moksha* is achievable through righteous conduct and, depending on one's tradition, devotion to one or more deities. So *Brahman,* more like the impersonal order of the cosmos than the personal deity of the Abrahamic faiths, isn't the only god in the Hindu pantheon. And each of us is responsible for our *karma,* or the sum total of our thoughts, words, and deeds in this and previous lives. We must resolve all harms that we have caused throughout *samsāra* to be released from it.

The Vedanta, the concluding portion of the Vedas, focuses among other themes on speculation about an inner, invisible, spiritual reality (which itself is a manifestation of *Brahman*) underlying the phenomenal world—the world of everyday experience. This led to the emergence of an ascetic tradition focused on discipline, contemplation, and withdrawal, with the goal of fully experiencing and understanding this reality. It's connected with the concept of *ātman,* of a person's inner self, and the presumption that the spiritual realm is superior to our earthly existence. "A better and holier life could thus be attained by abandoning the body and freeing the soul," Callicott remarks (1994, 46). By breaking the cycle of suffering embodied by *samsāra,* one escapes the phenomenal world and unites fully and eternally with *Brahman.*

While Hinduism's ascetic tradition tends to be world-denying, it also encourages minimal consumption. The journey toward liberation from *samsāra* progresses from selfishness toward the realization that we're one with all beings. With liberation, we're no longer caught up in the world because we're no longer preoccupied with egoistic attachments.[18]

The emergence of a devotional tradition that broke with asceticism has taken the this-worldly concerns of Hinduism a step further. Adherents of the devotional tradition don't see the world as phenomenal (hence, derivative). The world instead is replete with sacred spaces and features: rivers (including the Ganges), trees, mountains, and so forth (Narayanan 2001 and Haberman 2017). And in the *Bhagavad Gita,* the universe as a whole is declared a divine manifestation; it's the body of Krishna. A divine body surely mustn't be defaced and defiled.

Buddhism

Within Buddhism—which took hold in other lands after "dying out in its mother country, the valley of the Ganges" (Callicott 1994, 57)—the central difficulty we face is, again, the recalcitrant cycle of suffering emblemized by *samsāra* resulting from *karma*. *Moksha*, liberation, is achieved by reaching *nirvana*. *Nirvana* is a transcendent state in which there's neither suffering nor desire nor even a sense of self. Its achievement marks a permanent release from *samsāra*. Most Buddhists hereby "see the end of suffering in soteriological terms," Susan Darlington remarks, "as humans perfect themselves until they are no longer reborn" (2019, 24).

The Four Noble Truths prescribe the path out of *samsāra*. First is *dukkha*, suffering itself. Change, impermanence, is distressing. Because life is defined by change, it's invariably marked by distress. Second is *samudaya*, that suffering is caused by desire, particularly for permanence and control. Third, *nirodha*, is the truth that the cessation of suffering requires the elimination of all desire, including for liberation. Since nothing is permanent, there's no enduring self, no soul-like entity. Fourth, *magga*, is the truth that *nirvana* is achieved only when one can live as non-self, or *anātman*. The discipline required to achieve *nirvana* comes from following the Eightfold Path: practicing right view, right resolve, right speech, right conduct, right livelihood, right effort, right mindfulness, and right stillness in presence.

The two major schools of Buddhism, Theravāda and Mahāyāna, demarcate its migration from the subcontinent. Theravāda migrated south to Sri Lanka and southeast to Myanmar, Thailand, Laos, and Cambodia. Mahāyāna is dominant in China, Japan, Taiwan, Tibet, Nepal, Mongolia, Korea, and most of Vietnam.[19] The key distinction between the two schools is the manner in which they regard how *anātman* is realized. In Theravāda, it involves the rejection of both a theoretical belief in self and, with increasing enlightenment, the ability to let go of a phenomenology of self. Mahāyāna carries the realization of *anātman* further, beyond the absence of a phenomenology of self to the experience (if we can call it that) of the emptiness or formlessness of everything in the world. In the case of both Theravāda and Mahāyāna, though, realization of *anātman* is necessary for the achievement of *nirvana*, hence for breaking free of the cycle of suffering.

It's impossible to ignore the centrality of suffering for Buddhists. Quinn is right about this (Q&A, 100). But we should be careful about how we stipulate exactly what the first truth, *dukkha*, is meant to convey. In consonance with the ascetic tradition in Hinduism, in Theravāda suffering is self-imposed because of our tendency to be self-centered and fixated on material things (Collins 1990, 82f.). And while the idea that the world itself is invidiously ensnaring is prominent in early Buddhism, it largely drops out of the picture in modern Buddhism, particularly in Mahāyāna. As a result, liberation from *samsāra* is seen today less as an escape from the world than as "living an awakened life in the midst of the world," David McMahan comments (2008, 158). The realization of *anātman* thus involves freedom from enslavement to our delusional belief that our worth as human beings is measured by "wealth and achievements, credentials of one sort or another. This to the Buddhists is the essence of ignorance," Wade Davis contends (2009, 183).

Even more noteworthy is the attribution, most notably in Zen Buddhism (a branch of Mahāyāna), of the soteriological significance to earthly manifestations (Callicott 1994, 93). All living beings have Buddhahood, as do specifiable features of the land (Shoson 1961).[20] So transcending egoism can be regarded as coextensive with attuning ourselves to our membership in the living community (Macy 1990). These ideas are supported as well by the notion of *dependent origination,* according to which all beings and doings intermingle. While early practitioners of Buddhism focused on freeing themselves from this entanglement, dependent origination now serves to valorize a relational sense of lived experience (Kaza 1993).

Daoism

Much like Hinduism, the term *Daoism* was developed by scholars to compartmentalize a multitude of self-cultivation practices found throughout China. The word *Dao* itself means (right) *way, road,* or *path*. For Daoists, the main problem we face in life is that we let it slip away without noticing, "either by not living fully or by not living for long," Prothero states (2010, 285). We should strive instead to live a life of enjoyment and vitality by attuning ourselves to an order of things that's tranquil and serene (Dallmayr 2011, 152). This order is the *Dao,* "which at any given moment we can work with or against" (Prothero 2010, 288). The best way to heed the *Dao* is to return to the rhythms of the country, beyond "the artificial syncopations of civilization" (ibid., 293–94). Heeding the *Dao* leads not to liberation. Daoists are far less overtly concerned with soteriology than devotees of the other Taker religions, save for Confucianism. But the goal of Daoist practices is, in part, to live a simple life in harmony with nature.

The dynamics of nature are orderly, and order is emergent, not designed. It's a manifestation of the mutual adjustment of the myriad beings who compose the living community.

Given our typical rat race lives, harmonizing with nature takes "great mental and physical discipline," Mary Pat Fisher remarks (2014, 193). As Laozi teaches in the *Dao de Jing,* experiencing attunement of this kind involves realizing "the transcendent unity of all things, rather than separation," which "can only be attained when one ceases to feel any personal preferences" (ibid., 195). Yet, Daoists also acknowledge the uniqueness and worth of every living being. This highlights, note Richard Sylvan and David Bennett, that "a high level of ecological consciousness is built into [Daoism], and it provides a practical basis for a way of life whose main tenet is 'Follow Nature'" (1988, 148). The key to following nature is *wu-wei,* or a mode of interaction with fellow beings that's neither coercive nor assertive. As far as possible, the needs and interests of others are acknowledged and accommodated. This represents a rejection of *yu-wei,* "the exploitative, coercive, destructive relationship of agricultural-industrial civilization with the natural environment" (Callicott 1994, 74).

Confucianism

Social chaos and strife are the central problems for Confucians. The achievement of social harmony through civility and propriety, which are cultivated by the pursuit of personal perfection, offers the solution. While there's no overt concept of salvation for Confucians, overcoming disharmony via self-elevation is key. We should aim to live a good life not just for our own sake but to facilitate the same for all the world's inhabitants. As with Daoism, this is achieved by aligning our actions with the "great harmony" (Dallmayr 2011, 152) of the *Dao.*

This act of alignment is conceived strictly in this-worldly terms. The secular itself is sacred (Fingarette 1972). This is particularly true of human relationships. Confucius sought to remind us that the otherwise mundane ideals associated with friendship and filial piety aren't trivial. Too often we just go through the motions when it comes to engaging with others. We're so preoccupied with workaday concerns that we fail to give our full attention to the abiding value of our connections with others.[21] Perfectibility is hereby embodied by being the very best friend, parent, daughter, son, and so forth, that's humanly possible (Callicott 1994, 77).

Confucianism seems on its face to be thoroughly anthropocentric in its orientation. But this may not be so. Exhibiting *jen,* the virtue of humaneness, is paramount and is perhaps most appropriately construed non-anthropocentrically (Yao 2014). This is because it involves the recognition that all of creation is one and that we're part of this unity (Cheng and Cheng 1988, 15, Taylor 2009, 97, and Huang 2017). Once again, selfish desires are what block us from perceiving ourselves as such.

Distinguishing Theory from Practice

I trust it's clear by now that the Taker religions offer more than "environmental spin" (P, 169). There's abundant material here to support saving the world. Look at how frequently concern over self-centeredness and the ills associated with fixating on material accumulation come up. Notice how often the interdependence of all living beings is emphasized. Ideas such as these surely promote enacting a story that works for both the planet and for people.

But there's a key qualifier, voiced by Jensen, that supports Quinn's overarching concerns about the ecological friendliness of the Taker religions. As Jensen states:

> we have to ask ourselves how these religions are expressed *on the ground, in the real world*—I mean both of these literally—how they play out in the lives of living, breathing human beings and others. What have been the effects of Christianity on the health of landbases? Has biodiversity thrived on the arrival of the cross? How has the arrival of Christianity affected the status of women? How has it affected the Indigenous peoples it has encountered? We can and should ask the same question of Buddhism, science, capitalism, and every other aspect of our or any other culture. Not how they play out theoretically, and not how their rhetoric plays out, not how we wish they would play out, not how they *could* play out under some imaginary ideal circumstances, but how they *have* played out. (2006a, 288)

Even defenders of the greening of religion hypothesis admit that there's a sizable "disjunction between principles and practices" (Tucker and Grim 2017, 7).

Increasing appeals by Christians in particular to stewardship haven't yet translated into a significant shift in behavior, largely due to the fact that care for the earth isn't regarded as a religious priority (Johnson 2013, 107ff., and Veldman 2016). Indeed, appeals to stewardship have faced a substantial backlash from evangelicals, who worry that it puts concern for creation before the Creator and challenges the all-controlling sovereignty of God, or the idea, as Donna Haraway puts it, that "God will come to the rescue of his disobedient but ever hopeful children (2016, 8; see also Q&A, 655, Zaleha and Szasz 2014, and Taylor 2016, 289).

A similar gap between word and deed abides in the Eastern religions as well. Take Buddhism, for example. Textual evidence supports not merely indifference toward the concerns of the living community but even open hostility to raising such concerns (Harris 1995). The "Japanese love of nature," for example, tends to bleed into a "Japanese love of cultural transformations and purifications of a world which, if left alone, simply decays," Allan Grapard maintains (1985, 243).[22] This is evident as well with the tendency among Daoists to praise rural life not in spite but *because* of the transformative capacities of totalitarian agriculture (Guha 1989). Just looking at the environmental histories of Asian societies renders questionable the proposition that Eastern religions are somehow greener than their Western counterparts. Whatever sway adherents of Eastern religions who favor saving the world have is minimal. Neither Eastern nor Western Taker religions have an advantage in this respect (Kellert 1995).

To what extent are adherents of Taker religions who are moved to engage in the threefold struggle thwarted by their religions, and to what extent are they, like nonadherents, blocked by a wider array of hierarchistic social, political, and economic institutions? It's difficult to say. I'm not convinced by Quinn's assertion that these religions will disappear with cultural collapse (Q&A, 594). It's hard to imagine, though, that any of them can survive such a transition without undergoing significant doctrinal changes.

Antisalvation

What, finally, are we to make of the idea of an "Antisavior" (B, 234), a description that applies most specifically to B?[23] What does this have to do with enacting a story that works? Despite Jared's initial resistance to B being an Antisavior (ibid., 59), he comes to accept that B's preoccupation is to divert the flow of our cultural vision away from ongoing catastrophe—ecological, cultural, and spiritual. In contrast to many adherents of Taker faiths, saving the world for B just is a matter of saving ourselves, and vice versa. Refashioning, reforming, and reconciling Taker faiths may have their place. But can these faiths survive if *human* salvation, redemption, deliverance, liberation, release, harmonization, or whatever other soteriological label we apply loses top billing? Both Shirin and Charles express their doubts. I've expressed my doubts about doubts like theirs, but I get their point.

I wonder what the Taker religions would look like stripped not just of despotic tendencies but characteristics that support stewardship as well. Consider this statement from *Laudato Si'*:

> A misguided anthropocentrism need not necessarily yield to "biocentrism," for that would entail adding yet another imbalance, failing to solve present problems and adding new ones. Human beings cannot be expected to feel responsibility for the world unless, at the same time, their unique capacities of knowledge, will, freedom and responsibility are recognized and valued. (Pope Francis 2016, 88)

I take it that no Leavers were consulted before the encyclical was released. Of course we human beings matter. As we'll see starting in the next chapter, we're here because we're manifestations of the sacred—but neither exclusively nor preeminently. Does this somehow undercut our responsibility to fellow members of the living community? I don't see how.

The use of branding letters wasn't Hawthorne's invention, Charles remarks. "If you met someone branded with the letter *B*, you knew that his sin was *blasphemy*" (B, 32). This is the sin that Shirin, too, commits when she declares that we must remember who we are—one species among millions, all equally belonging to the world (ibid., 324f.). This is one aspect of a *kincentric* view, as I suggest in chapter 6, which exhibits similarities with biocentrism. While kincentrism marks but one path to living and making a living in a way that works for the planet and for people, I suspect that it has distinctive advantages for reversing the spiritual catastrophe recorded in the opening chapters of Genesis. In both of J's stories, the human protagonists experience a devastating loss of intimacy with God and/as the land. God becomes a distant figure.

Armstrong suggests that Elohim's relative remoteness in P is actually positive and redemptive (1996, 23).[24] The same perhaps can be said of the stories transcribed by E, wherein the gulf between the divine and the mundane is expansive. Yet this again seems to be a case of grasping at straws. It has all the hallmarks of spiritual catastrophe rather than a divine gift.

If, at the end of the day, devastation is all there is to Taker culture, then it's high time we quit the damn dance (MI, 51ff.). Throw J's stories into reverse, Ishmael tells Alan:

> First, Cain must stop murdering Abel. This is essential if you are to survive. The Leavers are the endangered species most critical to the world—not because they're humans but because they alone can show the destroyers of the world that there is no *one right way* to live. And then, of course, you must spit out the fruit of that forbidden tree. You must absolutely and forever relinquish the idea that you know who should live and who should die on this planet. (I, 248; see also ibid., 168, and MGY, 72)

Leavers don't exist to help us Takers save ourselves, of course. This, too, is a common Taker trope that we must abandon—for Leavers' sake and for our own. Let's consider, though, what spitting out the forbidden fruit looks like. This is the subject of Part II.

A Certain Road

The Road. It "dominates the geography of the Afterlife, if only because it seems central to all our goings-on," states the phantom author of *The Newcomers Guide to the Afterlife* (47). Leavers see no sharp distinction between life and the afterlife, the author implies, which suggests that the Road is also a manifestation of life, even if Takers fail to appreciate it.

One of the main characters in *The Holy*, David Kennesey, was lucky enough briefly to encounter it, fatefully realizing when out for a nighttime drive with friend Gil Bingham:

> how deeply satisfying it would be to stay on this road forever, to never turn back—to renounce achievement and the self-imposed pressure to achieve, to abandon the thrust to go somewhere. To purify himself of the very concept of *destination*. No, not exactly that. To seek an uncommon destination: A road. A

> certain road. A road that doesn't lead to just another road, just another town, just another house, just another shop, just another factory. *A road to nowhere.* (H, 176–77)

Takers tend to assume that living otherwise than we do "leads to nowhere," Alan declares (I, 219). To struggle against taking one's place in Taker culture makes one's life "devoid of meaning," even "stupid, empty, and worthless" (ibid., 216). David knew otherwise. It was on this drive that he first caught sight of Andrea, standing on the crest of a bank silhouetted against the moon. David, driving, skidded to a stop. To Gil's shock he flung open his door and jumped out. Andrea descended the far side of the bank. David followed, despite Gil's attempts to restrain him, and caught sight of her again upon reaching the crest. She stood motionless, waiting, before disappearing over another crest. It was the last young David saw of her. He searched for an hour or so before finally returning to the car, telling Gil, curtly, that he "lost her" (H, 180).

David also lost all track of the Road and of himself under the typical pressure to perform his expected role as just one other collector of precious achievements. "*Of course I betrayed myself,*" he admitted two decades later. "*I was sure I wouldn't, but of course I have. For comforts, for pleasant companionship, for acceptance, for respectability, for security. For the sake of appearing a sensible, mature fellow. I thought I could get away with it, but of course I didn't, no one can*" (ibid., 112).

Is this true? Is no captive of Taker culture able to *go nowhere*—to live otherwise than we currently do? Maybe David's is an old mind at work. So maybe we instead should ask: *How do we make things the way we want them to be? How do we make happen what we want to happen?* Before we do so, though, let's do our level best to remember who we are—as living beings, humans, and (potentially) as persons.

PART II

LEAVER CULTURE: CHARTING A CERTAIN ROAD

Chapter 4

Lessons in Success

Fire of Life, Law of Life, Community of Life

A few months after Quinn walked on (in 2018), a colleague asked me how the book was progressing. I told him about Quinn's passing, adding that because I was still in mourning my work had dramatically slowed.

He smiled broadly. "But that's great!" he replied. "Now you're able to take more authorial license."

I was at a loss for words, dumbstruck by his callousness. It wasn't just Quinn's passing that gutted me. It was also the knowledge that he'd never read any of this material, save for an early draft of the prologue I shared with him.

I'm particularly sad not to be able to show him this chapter. I here cover some of Quinn's most eloquent writing. Hermeneutically, it's also quite complex, so it's taken some effort to disentangle. But rather than taking authorial license, I've made every effort to stay true to Quinn's philosophy, even if my intent is to present it more systematically. I've learned much in the process, for which I'm grateful.

As the first of the chapters primarily on Leaver culture, we focus here on what we can call lessons of success. "Success is our study," Ishmael tells Alan (I, 126). Namely, their discussions are aimed at highlighting what makes the Leaver story successful and the Taker story unsuccessful in the sense that enacting the former works for people and the planet while the latter doesn't. This is the conceptual framework within which Quinn operates. And the signs of success with which he's primarily concerned are those that have to do with the *perpetuation of life.*

Philosophically, how should we approach our study of the quintessential form of success that we call life? Recall Quinn's assertion, mentioned in the prologue, that what works for people and the planet is cloaked by its success (BC, 11). It's hidden in plain view—"so evident as to be unseeable" (IS, 1).[1] The perpetuation of life, in general and on the whole, is evidence that something works. So our task in this chapter is to make explicit what we otherwise take for granted about the character of life itself.

We proceed by working out an apparent contradiction at the heart of Quinn's characterization of life. He suggests that all living beings are ultimately one thing. He also contends that no two living beings in the whole of the universe are alike. How can it be that no two organisms are alike *and* are simultaneously all one thing? I have an answer. To get at it, I explore Quinn's discussion of three key manifestations: the fire of life, the Law of Life, and the community of life.

The *fire of life* isn't life's essence, nor is it an animating force that's somehow distinct from the biochemical qualities of life. Quinn is no proponent of vitalism. Rather, the fire of life is the most intimate and powerful expression of life. Moreover, it's at the heart of the most important hour of Quinn's life (P, 64). This makes it fitting to investigate first. The intimacy and power expressed by the fire of life can be viewed, in turn, as a function of two factors: biological diversity and biological interdependence (Brown 2009, 14). Quinn highlights the significance of biological diversity in his far-flung discussion of the *Law of Life*. Its basic workings are readily apparent for those with "eyes that see." This is because it's "written in the very fabric of the living community" (BD, 44; see also B, 179). The significance of biological interdependence is given pride of place in Quinn's discussion of the *community of life*. And it's time once and for all to shatter the illusion that we're of a separate order from the manifold beings with whom we share this planet.

What does this all have to do with the apparent contradiction Quinn offers us? Here's a hint. The trajectory of the chapter will help us to see that its resolution can be expressed by the Latin phrase, *ex uno plures*: out of one, many.

The Fire of Life

According to David Abram, "Nothing is more common to the diverse Indigenous cultures of the earth than a recognition of the air, the wind, and the breath, as aspects of a singular sacred power" (1996, 226). Air is an unseen medium "that enlivens the visible world" (ibid., 249). It flows around, in, and through our bodies, connecting us with our world, hence with one another.

Abram relays how the ancient Greeks, the progenitors of Western philosophy, transformed the psyche from a phenomenon associated with the act of breathing into the immaterial entity that we now think of as the mind. In the process, the locus of human awareness, intellect, and consciousness became internalized, "trapped, as it were, within the human body" (ibid., 255). These capacities were no longer thought of as being shared with and made possible by our embeddedness in the world. The sacred character of air was forgotten. Its role as a common medium became privatized as Western philosophers did their level best to support the presumption of human separateness from the rest of the community of life.

Abram is at pains to help us "reacquaint ourselves with our breathing bodies" (ibid., 63), to remind us that human awareness, intellect, and consciousness are dependent on and inextricably connected with our *respiratory* capacities. (Note, for example, the dual meaning of "inspiration.") That's his story to tell, not mine. I mention it because the elemental role that air plays in Abram's story and the stories enacted by numerous Indigenous peoples is filled by *fire*—of a sort—for Quinn. But he too is aware of the significance of air and its intimate connection with fire. This connection plays a pivotal role in Quinn's description of the most important hour of his life.

Gethsemani

This hour took place while Quinn was a postulant at Gethsemani. A postulant, he states, is "someone on probation, someone asking for admittance" (P, 51) into the corps of novices training to become monks.[2] At a crucial moment during his time at Gethsemani, he was given permission to go outside with the novices:

> I went last, stepped over the threshold, turned around to close the door, then turned back to face the sunshine.
>
> And the god spoke.
>
> There are no words for it.
>
> I turned and faced the sunshine, and the breath went out of me. I could say that the world was transformed before my very eyes, but that wasn't it—and I knew that that wasn't it. The world hadn't been transformed at all; I was simply being

> allowed to see it the way it is *all the time.* I, not the world, had been transformed.
>
> Everything was on fire. Everything was *burning. From within,* everything was burning. Every blade of grass, every single leaf of every single tree was radiant, was blazing—incandescent with a raging power that was unmistakably divine.
>
> I was overwhelmed. In a single second of this, of seeing this truth, tears flooded my eyes and poured down my face as I walked along behind the novices. It was strange to see fence posts sitting dead and silent and cold in the midst of this tremendous, thrumming effulgence.
>
> You know the sparklers they sell around July 4th. The world was ablaze with sparklers. Every blade of grass, every leaf of every tree was *charged* with energy—packed, jammed, evanescent with energy, which radiated forth into the air irresistibly. The whole landscape pulsed, breathed, moved, was made iridescent with this energy.
>
> No, no, I wasn't in a trance. I wasn't in anything remotely *like* a trance. I was gathering kindling, for God's sake!
>
> It lasted for about an hour. The radiance just faded away, gradually subsided, and the world resumed its normal appearance. The rest of the crew came along, and we loaded up the kindling and headed back. (P, 62–66)[3]

Tim has the same sort of experience in *The Holy,* although, unlike Quinn, he struggles with its achievement. "Let me show you something," Pablo says to him. "What do you think of that?" (H, 359):

> The boy blinked at it. It was a slender, sickly-looking cholla cactus about ten inches high, listing to one side as if it were about to expire from sunstroke.
>
> Tim looked at Pablo doubtfully. "Do you mean the cactus?"
>
> Pablo shook his head. "It's not a cactus. Spend some time in its company. Get to know it well—so well that you forget its name. On the day you can look at it without thinking *This is a cactus,* it will speak to you. It will tell you a secret forgotten among most of your kind for thousands of years." (Ibid.)

This secret would permanently change how Tim sees the world, Pablo tells him (just as working out the Taker and Leaver cultural mythologies would permanently change Alan, according to Ishmael). Tim's struggles with his assignment are typical of the people of our culture. He consults Dudley, who tells him to make himself a stranger to the cholla cactus. Tim initially thinks this is the opposite of the instructions Pablo has given him. But Dudley clarifies: "*To get to know it at all, you have to begin by meeting it as a stranger. You're still thinking, 'This is a cactus, just another cactus.' When you see it and don't know what in the world it is, then you can begin to know it*" (ibid., 372).

Returning later to the cactus, Tim falls asleep and has a momentous dream. Upon awakening:

> He opened his eyes and found an alien creature towering over him—a visitor from the stars, bristling with silver spikes and armored in glossy green. In the tenth of a second during which Tim's mind struggled to reimpose order and sense on the world, he saw that the creature meant him no harm—accepted him as an equal, seemed to enfold him in its own aura of vibrant power and dignity, as if to say, "It's all right. I see that you too are alive. No more is required. We are comrades."
>
> The surface of the creature's armor suddenly began to cloud, pearling with a liquid iridescence that moved across it like a melting rainbow—and involuntarily Tim sucked in a breath that was almost a sob: never, never had he witnessed anything so majestically lovely as this. It was vastly more than a visual experience of beauty; in an act of unimaginable generosity, the creature was revealing to him the very nature and substance of its life. The iridescence flowing across its surface wasn't a color, wasn't the reflection of light. It was a vibrant, sublime energy emanating from within, pulsing inexhaustibly from each atom—a conflagration almost beyond control, surging irresistibly outward, so that the tip of each of its spines was a glittering fountain of energy.
>
> Tears were coursing down Tim's cheeks in a flood, and he made no effort to check them. Astounded, awed, and humbled, Tim was weeping for sheer joy, dragging each breath up from the depth of his bowels.

> He had of course long ago realized that what was before him was the cactus he'd spent so many hours with. Recognizing it now made no difference, because now he was recognizing it for what it truly was: not "just a cactus"—indeed not a cactus at all—but rather a unique, unclassifiable individual whose moment in the thundering, never-ending drama of creation would never be repeated here or anywhere else in the universe.
>
> Standing up to look around, Tim saw that the world was everywhere ablaze with the same thrumming effulgence that shook the cactus. Each dry, gray chamisa, each stunted piñon, each blade of grass, each scruffy weed was crackling and trembling and all but exploding with the awesome power that animated it. Hungry to see more, he climbed to the crest of the hill and looked down into the valley of the Rio Grande, already resplendently green. If it had been a sound instead of a sight, it would have been a jubilant roar of a million voices. Every leaf of every tree was radiant, lustrous—incandescent with a power that was unmistakably divine.
>
> A truck chugged uphill along the highway beside the river, a lump of dead matter—a black hole of lifelessness in a landscape scintillant and effervescent with glorious vitality—and Tim thought, "Oh, you poor things. If you could only *see.*" (H, 378–79)

Soon, the effervescence waned, and Tim's vision returned to its typical state. But he knew "without the slightest doubt that—ecstasy notwithstanding—he was merely seeing what's always there to be seen." Moreover, although he could no longer see it, "that joyous bonfire was still blazing all around him and would blaze for as long as there was life on this planet" (ibid., 379). Of this he was certain.

"What Did It Mean?"

This is the question Quinn poses—or, rather, that's posed to him by his phantom inquisitor in *Providence*—after describing his experience at Gethsemani. Specifically, what does Quinn mean when he says, "And the god spoke"? This is the same as asking what the experience itself means, he notes, since it turns out that what he experienced *just is* the god speaking. So let's start with another crucial question: Who or what is the god?

Quinn refers to "the god" in the singular in this passage while referring to "the gods" in the plural elsewhere. Is he sending us some sort of mixed message? No. B explains:

> The number of the gods is written nowhere in the universe, Jared, so there's really no way to decide whether that number is zero (as atheists believe) or one (as monotheists believe) or many (as polytheists believe). The matter is one of complete indifference to me. I don't care whether the number of the gods is one, zero, or nine billion. If it turned out that the number of gods is zero, this wouldn't cause me to alter a single syllable of what I've said to you. (B, 134; see also P, 139 and 141, and Q&A, 538 and 724)

For Takers, this is a bizarre thing to say. The people of our culture are preoccupied with whether the god (or God, actually) exists.[4] Like B, Quinn isn't.

Indeed, when Quinn speaks of the god(s), we can just as easily substitute the term *life* in its place. I think Quinn chooses to use the term *god(s)* in part to highlight the sacredness of life.[5] Enacting a story in which *life is the god* works.

How many gods are there? Who cares? What matters is the story we enact. Where are the gods? This matters, too, B states, for "the great secret of the animist life" (B, 159)—of the Leaver approach to the sacred—is that "The gods are *here.*" More to the point, *this place, every place,* "is a sacred place, like no other in the world" (B, 160).[6] The god who spoke to Quinn isn't in or at the place where Gethsemani stands. The god is *this place,* its life (P, 181, and TA, 14). It's the animating fire of the community of life that embodies *this place.* And it just so happens that *fire breathes.*

Look back at the above passages. Do you notice how many times Quinn refers to breath? When Quinn turned and faced the sunshine upon stepping outside at the abbey, the breath was knocked out of him. In awe of what he was witnessing, Tim had to drag each breath from his innermost recesses. The very landscape that both Quinn and Tim saw before them breathed with raging, incandescent energy. In an act of unimaginable generosity, Quinn adds, "the god let me watch it *breathing* that place" (P, 141).

In the process, the god said "something like this: *I am the fire of life that animates the world. I am not to be found in the sky, not to be found in some remote heaven. I live in your midst, and all that lives lives in the midst of me. I am HERE and I am never absent*" (ibid., 140). The gods aren't transcendent. They aren't a higher power residing somehow beyond this world, and they care nothing about adjudicating our salvation. This is a Taker way of conceptualizing God. The god that animates this place is *right here.* The god is the kindler and rekindler of the fire that burns in every member of the community of life that inhabits *this place.* Each of us is kindled with the fire of life at birth. We're ablaze with it over the course of our lifetime. And in death we pass it on to others of the living community to be rekindled in turn. The same fire that is "life itself, the life of this universe, of this galaxy, of this planet, of this place and every place" (ibid., 181) courses—no, *rages*—through us.

Remember, we aren't *on* fire. Again, all living creatures are ablaze *from within.* And the raging quality of the fire of life isn't violent. It doesn't embody malice. It's *exuberant.* It's the most intimate and also the most powerful expression of life because, for those with eyes that see, a phrase whose full meaning we'll cover in the next chapter, it conveys with utmost force "the overwhelming preciousness of life and the laughable insignificance of the things we [Takers] puff ourselves up over" (ibid., 142).

The fence posts in Quinn's description and the truck in Tim's are but two examples of our puffery: the one a sign of private property (as if the land isn't shared) and the other of hypermobility (as if our very *displacement* is a virtue). But there the fence posts stand, "dead and silent and cold" (ibid., 64–65). There chugs the truck, "a black hole of lifelessness in a landscape scintillant and effervescent with glorious vitality." The poor thing, thinks Tim. "If only you could *see*" (H, 379).

One Thing and No Two Things Alike

"In this vast, scintillating clarity," Quinn remarks, he could "distinguish with absolute clarity each leaf, each blade of grass—no two alike anywhere" (P, 65). The cactus before Tim was "not 'just a cactus'—indeed not a cactus at all—but rather a unique, unclassifiable individual." Like all of us, the cactus plays out its role "in the thundering, never-ending drama of creation," and this role, this individual life, this specific agglomeration of atoms and molecules, "would never be repeated here or anywhere else in the universe" (H, 378–79). Our paths in life may cross, coincide, and intermesh. But your path and mine are nevertheless unique.

At the same time, though, Quinn emphasizes that we're *one thing.* The fire of life is a fountain of energy that extends through the entire living community and, to one extent or another, unites us all (I, 162f.). Karlak tells Adam in *The Man Who Grew Young* that they're both bison. "It's all one thing, you see. One thing: man and bison. One thing: grass and grasshopper. One thing: grasshopper and sparrow. One thing: sparrow and fox. One thing: fox and vulture. One thing . . . and its name is . . . *fire.* All together, we're the fire of this place. Indistinguishable from one another, intermingling in the flow of fire" (MGY, 86). B says the same. "One thing, Jared . . . burning today as a stalk in the field, tomorrow as a rabbit in its burrow, and the next day as an eleven-year-old girl named Shirin" (B, 187).

The Law of Life

According to Quinn, the term *Law of Life* was coined by the Ihalmiut, a people who inhabit the Barrens in northern Canada.[7] According to Farley Mowat, the Law of Life applies to the actions of both the Ihalmiut and the gods. It is a "code of behavior" (2005, 180) that fosters social stability by keeping Windigo at bay. Most basically, this involves pooling food, possessions, and labor, especially during trying times. Otherwise, people are left to their own business so long as they don't adversely affect the wellbeing of others or the community at large. Spiritually, the Law of Life embodies such elemental forces as wind, water, and the passage of seasons (ibid., 250ff.). Each of these forces plays a critical role in the interactions between the Ihalmiut and their primary food source: the caribou, or deer, who once thundered in massive herds through their lands.

From Quinn's perspective, that a people actually employs the term *Law of Life* "sounds almost too good to be true" (BD, 46). While Mowat doesn't say whether the Ihalmiut assume that it applies to other-than-human members of the living community (they likely do), Quinn is adamant that every living creature is subject to it. The community of life has the shape and character it has because this is so. Indeed, the community of life *exists* because this is so. It's written into the fabric of our being.

Not quite as overt is that Quinn appropriates the bimodal view of the Law of Life maintained by the Ihalmiut. For Quinn, too, it applies both to the behavior of us members of the community of life and to the behavior of the gods. Moreover, how it applies to us members of the living community differs based on whether we're dealing with constituents of other species or our own.

Signs of Success

We'll see as we proceed that the Law of Life has "sublime" (BD, 46) qualities. But strictly from a biological standpoint, B tells Jared, "what I'm calling the Law of Life is just a collection of evolutionarily stable strategies—the universal set of such strategies, in fact" (B, 151).[8] A strategy is a "behavioral policy." The evolutionary stability of any such policy entails that "The normal process of evolution, natural selection, doesn't eliminate it" (ibid., 152). B adds that behavioral policies that aren't eliminated via natural selection "can't be improved on by any alternative strategy" (ibid., 151; see also MI, 74). This doesn't mean that they can't destabilize when ecological or climatological conditions change (BC, 185). Of course this happens. Quinn is simply highlighting that less workable behavioral policies tend in due course to be eliminated by evolutionary processes, while more workable ones tend to perpetuate and spread throughout the population of the species that employs them (IS, 56ff.). The latter occurrence is a quintessential sign of success with respect to the Law of Life.

"Evolution brings forth what works," Ishmael informs Julie (MI, 79). The community of life isn't just a "random collection" of species. "It's a collection of *successes*. It's the remainder that is left over when the failures have disappeared" (ibid., 70). What look to our eyes like the strangest and most awkward creatures—the emu, the sloth, the tardigrade, the blobfish—all exist today because their progenitors maintained evolutionarily stable strategies. Our progenitors lived in accordance with the Law of Life, too, Jared remarks. We can be certain of this since we "wouldn't be here at all" (B, 149; see also I, 238) were it not so. This is yet another way of pointing out that we humans can't possibly be inherently flawed. One subset of our species may eliminate humanity and countless fellow members of the living community by failing to accede to the Law of Life. But it doesn't take much of an intellectual leap to see, as Julie puts it, that "No species comes into existence by failing. That's simply unthinkable" (MI, 71).

Regarded in this light, we also should see straightaway why totalitarian agriculture and the lifestyle it supports exemplify evolutionarily *unstable* strategies. At root, totalitarian agriculture requires that we Takers deny competitors access to food that we regard as exclusively ours. It also requires that we destroy their habitats to grow more food for ourselves. In essence, biodiversity must be eliminated to produce ever-greater quantities of staple crops. (And cultural diversity must be eliminated to produce more and more Takers.) What makes these practices evolutionarily unstable is that, by engaging in them, "we're fundamentally attacking the very ecological systems that keep us alive," B declares (B, 154). We need our competitors and their habitats to flourish insofar as we need the ecosystems on which we both depend to remain healthy. Our success and the success of our competitors go hand in hand.[9] Indeed, this is a core feature of the threefold struggle.

So the Law of Life "protects" (I, 118) the members of the living community. It "fosters" (B, 138) life for all those who heed it. Evolutionarily stable strategies tend to proliferate, while evolutionarily unstable strategies disappear. The intransigent "outlaw" (BD, 48, P, 174, and B, 254)—one who "exempts" (I, 133 and 143) themselves from the Law of Life, who refuses to be "in compliance" (I, 104) with it, who "flouts" it (I, 149) by taking their life into their own hands—inevitably ends up on the vast cutting room floor of evolution. They're excised from the community of life by natural selection. The perpetuation of life wouldn't be possible otherwise (BD, 47).

But can one really be an outlaw with respect to the Law of Life? Can we actually defy it? The way Quinn refers to it sometimes gives this impression. He states on several occasions that members of the community of life "follow" the Law of Life (BD, 44ff., I, 118, and TA, 17).[10] He remarks at least once that it's "obeyed" (BD, 44). This makes it seem as if we have an element of choice in the matter when this can't possibly be so. We don't follow or obey the Law of Life any more than we follow or obey the laws of gravity or aerodynamics.

For this reason, I'm partial to a turn of phrase Ishmael uses when he discusses human settlement with Alan. Settlement isn't somehow *against* the Law of Life, Ishmael insists. No, it's "*subject* to" it (I, 135). It can't be otherwise. And an outlaw with respect to the Law of Life is someone who persists in vain trying to defy what they can't possibly defy. (Do you recall the erstwhile aeronauts from chapter 2?) They may "imagine" (BD, 48) that they can enact a story that operationalizes evolutionarily unstable strategies without paying any price. But failure is inevitable, not necessarily immediately but eventually.

Here's another way to think about what it means to be subject to the Law of Life. In *Tales of Adam*, Adam tells Abel the following: "There is almost always a way to move alongside the power of the elements. Never oppose them directly as though they were enemies to be overcome. If you do, you'll be crushed like an egg under a boulder" (TA, 38–39). Outlaws treat life as if it's an enemy to be conquered. They (futilely) oppose how life operates. This is yet another way to understand what it means to take one's life into one's own hands.

To leave one's life in the hands of the gods, then, is to pay close attention to and move with the rhythms of life. This doesn't mean "turning your life over to them like a leaf in the wind," Adam adds. "It doesn't mean collapsing helplessly and letting the elements do what they will to you" (ibid., 61). It means cultivating your ability not just to survive but also to flourish by working with rather than against "the power of the elements"—just as the protagonists of every other evolutionary success story do.

The Sublimity of the Law

Part of what makes the Law of Life sublime is that natural selection itself is such an "elegant concept," as Jared puts it (B, 152), when it comes to explaining how life is perpetuated.[11] But there's more to its sublimity than this. Recall, with respect to the views of the Ihalmiut, that the Law of Life is bimodal. It applies both to the gods and to the living community. In being guided by this view, Quinn describes the behavior specifically of the gods in sublime terms.

The Emergence of Diversity

Quinn opens *Tales of Adam* with the following statement:

> When the gods set out to make the universe, they said to themselves, "Let us make of it a manifestation of our unending abundance and a sign to be read by those who shall have eyes to read. Let us lavish care without stint on every thing: no less upon the most fragile blade of grass than upon the mightiest stars, no less upon the gnat that sings for an hour than upon the mountain that stands for a millennium, no less upon the flake of mica than upon a river of gold. Let us make no two leaves the same from one branch to the next, no two branches the same from one tree to the next, no two trees the same from one land to the next, no two lands the same from one

> world to the next, no two worlds the same from one star to the next. In this way the Law of Life will be plain to all who shall have eyes to read: the rabbit that creeps out to feed, the fox that lies in wait, the eagle that circles above, and the man who bends his bow to the sky. (TA, 3–4; see also B, 161f.)

Permit me to elaborate on three crucial points. (1) The gods facilitate abundance. They also can be regarded *as* abundance itself. And abundance is "life's very secret of success on this planet," states B (B, 143; see also TA, 7). This is because it's a manifestation of the gods (2) making no two things alike in the whole of the universe, and (3) lavishing care without stint on each and every living being.

The gods facilitate abundance. B informs Jared that the Law of Life can in fact be summed up by this single word. The proliferation of diverse genotypes in particular is the secret of life's success here on Earth. It's essential for the functional integrity of ecosystems—for their robustness (resistance to internal failure), adaptability (responsiveness to changes such that overall functionality is maintained), and resilience (ability to withstand and/or bounce back quickly from disruption).

As Stephen Buhner states:

> The larger the number of plants with diverse chemistries that occupy the largest number of ecosystem functional categories, the more vital and healthier the ecosystem. This is because no year is ever the same as the previous year; environmental conditions are always different. Local habitats are always shifting in response to changing conditions. A plant producing major contributions to habitat need one year may not play the same role when environmental factors change. This is why a large range of plants in a local community is necessary: to give the system maximal response ability. (2002, 185)

The same applies to animal populations, of course. It's no different with evolutionarily stable strategies either. The wider the array of successful behavioral policies within a given ecosystem, the more robust, adaptable, and resilient it is. Without genetic diversity and a wide array of evolutionarily stable strategies, the community of life would be "highly vulnerable. Any change at all in the existing conditions, and the whole thing would collapse" (I, 129–30).

No two things alike. It would seem, then, that the gods "love diversity," Quinn declares (BD, 42). You might say that it's a particular obsession of theirs. You also might say that they're unceasingly creative. No two galaxies, no two planets, no two places on Earth, and not even any two of the (seemingly) humblest of living creatures—the mouse, the burying beetle, the phoretic mite—is exactly the same (B, 141ff. and 161ff., BD, 42 and 46f., P, 65 and 181, and TA, 16).

Lavishing care without stint. But the gods don't just love diversity in the abstract. That no two things are alike is itself a sign of the care the gods lavish without stint on every living being. Look, for instance, at the phoretic mite. If we think of it at all, we can't help but regard it as "such an inconsiderable creature," living as it does on the burying beetle. But B tells Jared that if he were to examine the mite under a microscope, he would see that it's "a work of so much delicacy, perfection, and complexity that it makes a digital computer look like a pair of pliers" (B, 143). Phoretic mites aren't "stamped out in a mold." No creature is. This is because the gods "care for *everything*" in equal measure (BD, 36; see also B, 162). Not a single organism is "made with any less care than any other" (B, 161; see also TA, 4). Indeed, B adds, "The brain in that precious human head of yours is not more wonderful than one of those mites" (B, 162). Nor is a fly's egg any less wondrous than the eye of Michelangelo.

So the secret of the success of life on Earth is genetic abundance—the proliferation of diverse genotypes. Behavioral abundance in the form of diverse evolutionarily stable strategies greatly matters, too. The gods bringing forth/embodying abundance creatively and caringly is itself an evolutionarily stable strategy from the perspective of the gods (TA, 3ff.). This is their pivotal contribution to the success generated by the Law of Life.

More on Creativity and Care

Stuart Kauffman sees God—his preferred term—as creativity itself. Creativity is a real property of the universe, he contends. It's on clearest display with respect to the development and perpetuation of life, which is both "partially lawless" and "ceaselessly creative" (2008, xi). Another way to put this is that biological evolution is "partially indescribable" by physical laws. The diversity of ecosystems is expanded via the use of available sunlight and nutrient sources. Increased diversity magnifies the possible directions their development can take. And how they develop can't be precisely determined before the fact (Kelso 1995).

Quinn nowhere endorses the idea that life is partially lawless. It's not clear that the way Kauffman defends this claim even holds up (Bugbee 2007). But this isn't the only way for creativity to be a real property of the universe. What if physical laws permit some wiggle room, as it were, with respect to the behavior of the phenomena they facilitate? Doug Anderson notes, for example, that "a law may determine that something of a certain kind will occur, but it offers a continuous range of ways in which it might occur" (1995, 60). This doesn't mean that statistically reliable knowledge is unattainable. But it does mean that "Margins of error and deviations from exact continuities are always encountered and are expected; indeed, they are even factored into calculations of what is supposed to happen lawfully. The best that observations show is that there is some regularity in nature. Irregularities and minor (and sometimes major) deviations are pervasive" (Anderson 1992, 198–99; see also Kronz and McLaughlin 2007, 191).

These ineliminable irregularities can be viewed as indicators of ceaseless creativity. Whether or not the universe is fully lawful or partially lawless, creativity is real. And it plays an essential role in no two things being alike.

Think about it this way. Creativity, which is akin to what Peirce calls *spontaneity*, can't facilitate evolution on its own. Evolution would lack all order. But evolution also can't be fully regimented, since the reality of creativity provides arguably the best explanation for the proliferation of life's diversity (CP, 6.24).[12] Evolution thus occurs in systems in which order and disorder are in dynamic tension (Q&A, 682). Only in such systems can new genetic mutations and recombinations not only emerge (via spontaneity) but also be retained (via order) when they support the enactment of evolutionarily stable strategies.

Like Kauffman's take on creativity, Peirce hereby views spontaneity as a real property of the universe. Also like Kauffman, Peirce views God as "living spontaneity" (CP, 6.553). But Peirce goes two steps further. He views physical laws as themselves "enabling" and "empowering" rather than as constraining (ibid., 6.288). And he suggests that God, as living spontaneity, actually fosters diversity and complexity (hence bringing forth and embodying abundance in Quinn's terminology) without determining the shape and composition of the community of life in advance.

A parent's love for their child is made evident in part by helping their child develop the skills and capabilities the child needs to succeed in life. Likewise, God—the gods, the god, life in abundance—expresses what Peirce calls "evolutionary love" for every member of the community of life. Each of us is crafted uniquely and delicately. Moreover, cooperation and care among members of the living community are themselves vital drivers of evolutionary development (ibid., 6.288). I'll say more about the last point momentarily. I simply want to acknowledge here that this complements Quinn's way of describing what it means for the gods to lavish care without stint on every thing. And it adds an interesting dimension to his claim that the Law of Life fosters the living community.

Quinn is thus a holist. The community of life isn't merely the sum of its parts any more than we're merely the sum of our cells (Hookway 2000, 162). But since the community of life can only exist because no two things are alike (Brown 2009, 15), and, furthermore, no two things are alike because the gods lavish care without stint on every thing, the gods surely value every thing along with the community of life as a whole. This makes Quinn a *differentiated holist.* As Fred Evans puts it, "Everything is intrinsically related to everything else and yet each preserves its integrity. Thus, 'integrity, stability, and beauty' or, to pick other terms, 'diversity, fecundity, and spontaneity,' can be affirmed of any animate or inanimate part of the whole as well as of the whole itself" (2008, 277–78; see also Deloria 1999, 34). How we constituents of the living community fare really matters, and how the entire community of life fares really matters, too. Why else would Quinn bother emphasizing that what works for the planet also works for people?

I noted back in the prologue that saving the world is for upstarts and lovers, according to Quinn. We've now seen something of the lovers. And we shouldn't be surprised that their role has to do with facilitating abundance.

Displays of Evolutionary Stability

Let's now expand on the idea that evolutionarily stable strategies are preserved by natural selection. Another way to put this is that evolutionarily stable strategies tend to promote reproductive success. In the long run and on the whole, those whose behavioral policies work for the planet and for people "become better represented in the gene pool" than those whose behavioral policies don't (B, 139; see also MI, 72ff.).

Darwin states forthrightly in *The Descent of Man* that natural selection can also be called "survival of the fittest" (1981, 152 and 163). Contrary to the common belief, at least among Takers, this isn't primarily a function of physical strength (including the ability to muster it on one's behalf), ruthless cunning, or the capacity to dominate others. Such a view arises from the presumption that, particularly among the beasts of the wild, the world is "a place of lawless chaos and savage, relentless competition, where every creature goes in terror of its life" (I, 117; see also I, 145f., and B, 252). But this isn't the case. Life in "the wild" (itself a misnomer) is anarchic, yes, in the sense of being self-organizing.[13] Again, we wouldn't be here otherwise.

I don't mean to suggest that kindness, compassion, or altruism is necessarily evolutionarily stable. The Law of Life favors representation in the gene pool over kindness if the two are in conflict, B emphasizes (B, 139f.). But thinking in these terms isn't particularly helpful anyway. It opens the door for the useless debate over whether kindness, compassion, and altruism are "really" forms of selfishness, hence manifestations of cunning after all. Thankfully, Quinn avoids getting mired in this debate by describing evolutionary stability in terms of the interplay of cooperation and competition among members of the community of life. How these two modes of behavior are manifest differs based on whether we're examining relations within or between species. It also bears on how we're to engage in the threefold struggle.

Interspecies Strategies

For cases in which it applies to interspecies interactions, Ishmael calls the Law of Life the *law of limited competition.* He also refers to it as the *peacekeeping law.* Here's the way B specifies it: "You may compete to the full extent of your capabilities, but you may not hunt down your competitors or destroy their food or deny them access to food. In other words, you may compete but you may not wage war on your competitors" (B, 252; see also I, 129, and MI, 76). She elaborates as follows:

> In the miscalled "natural" community (meaning the nonhuman community), you'll find competitors killing each other when the opportunity presents itself, but you won't find them *creating* opportunities to kill each other. You won't find them hunting each other the way they hunt their prey; to do so would not be evolutionarily stable. Hyenas just don't have the energy to hunt lions—calories gained by eliminating these competitors wouldn't equal the calories spent eliminating them—and attacking lions is not exactly a risk-free venture. In the same

> way, in the "natural" community, you won't find competitors destroying their competitors' food—the payoff just isn't big enough to make it worthwhile. (Ibid., 153)

This isn't to say that such behavior can't happen among hyenas or anyone else within the living community, B adds. The point is that we don't see it today among members of species other than our own. Takers account for this by appealing to our specialness. But it's possible members of species other than ours have behaved this way in the past and, inevitably, have failed. So they're no longer with us.

What exactly makes the law of limited competition a peacekeeping law? Why not instead regard it as condoning something like just war? Think about it this way. The evolutionary development of every species that exists today is the product of two strategies that only appear to contradict one another. Every individual living being competes with other living beings for food, yes, but this competition takes place within a wider *cooperative framework.* Lynn Margulis and Dorion Sagan (1995) go so far as to assert that a key mechanism driving the evolution of early life on Earth was two or more species initially collaborating and then permanently joining together as a single, more complex life form.[14] So this cooperative framework is life-enhancing even if the process of competition between individuals involves taking life.

Consider the bacteria populating your digestive system. Their evolutionary development has coincided with ours. Yes, this relationship is partially competitive. Our immune system has evolved to prevent them from eating us or monopolizing the food we ingest. This explains why antimicrobial acids are secreted in our stomachs. At the same time, though, the bacteria facilitate the production of digestive enzymes that break down our food for ready absorption in the lower digestive tract—which is where our gut flora reside. They feed on these "enzymic digestive products" (Keith 2009, 96) and, in the process, make them easier for us to digest.

Mahlon Hoagland insists, in turn, that all of us actually "exist as 'corporate elaborations'—composite communities of cells built out of the accomplishments of our one-celled forebears" (1995, 2).[15] We're what Donna Haraway calls "multispecies muddles," products of "*sympoesis*" (2016, 31 and 58, respectively). As Charles Eisenstein relays:

> Not just our intestines, but all of our mucosa, skin, and even eyelashes are host to bacteria, yeasts, and microscopic insects that are not competitors drawing down our resources, but

> partners in health. Since we are partly or even wholly dependent upon them, no less than we are on our heart or liver, by what right do we exclude them from the definition of the self? (2007, 415–16)

In a sense, predators and their prey are corporate elaborations as well. This gets to the heart of what makes the Law of Life an interspecies peacekeeping law. Hoagland highlights that wolves typically "take only the smallest, weakest, or most unhealthy of the prey species, leaving the fittest members to survive and reproduce. This may be seen as being competitive at the individual level, cooperative at the group level. (Although we don't suggest that creatures generally think in terms of the group.)" (1995, 30). The manner in which wolves hunt facilitates a robust gene pool not just among their own but also among the species on whom they prey. Their relationship with their prey is evolutionarily stable for both parties. This is a great example of what Quinn calls the ABCs of ecology (I, 114f., and B, 293ff.). Notably, it also serves to limit the proliferation of both species, which benefits as a whole the ecosystems in which they reside (Ripple and Bechta 2012).

Oh, and once the wolves make their kill, the surviving members of their prey visibly relax—even as the wolves feed among them. They return to grazing and, yes, are at peace (TA, 45). They neither live on a knife's edge of survival nor spend their days in a state of perpetual anxiety and despair.

Intraspecies Strategies

Holography is lensless photography, and a hologram is a three-dimensional encoding of an interference pattern in a light field. If you cut a photograph imprinted on film in half, each piece shows half of the photographed scene. But if a hologram is cut in half, the entire encoding is still visible in each piece.

According to Quinn, every fragment of the community of life—every being, every molecule, every cell—is imprinted with the whole Law of Life (B, 138; see also Cajete 2000, 210). But how each is imprinted can differ. So what's evolutionarily stable for one fragment may not be so for another. This is most evident when we look at intraspecies strategies.

Quinn doesn't provide a more specific name for the Law of Life as it applies to intraspecies relations. There's no label here that complements the law of limited competition. I suspect this is because intraspecies strategies are so highly variable that he can identify no one phrase that captures something common about them. He instead offers a number of illuminating examples of how the Law of Life is imprinted on the members of different species.

Newly hatched ducklings, for instance, follow this imperative: "*Latch on to the first thing you see that moves, and follow it no matter what*" (B, 139). This usually leads ducklings to bond with their mother, which is necessary for their survival. Goats tend to suckle only their own offspring, refusing to feed orphaned offspring even as they starve. Eagles typically lay two eggs, one a few days before the other. This "is naturally a better survival policy than producing a single egg. But if the first chick survives, it will almost invariably peck or starve the younger chick to death" (ibid., 140). Lions and bears often abandon litters with a sole survivor, even if the survivor is healthy (ibid., 141). And mice, voles, gerbils, and lemmings hunt down and kill the pups of others among their species when the territory they both inhabit becomes especially crowded (MI, 74).

It would be foolhardy to look at fellow members of the living community "as if they were characters in *Bambi,*" Ishmael tells Julie (ibid., 75). Because intraspecies competition is a contest for exactly the same resources, it's "always more arduous" (ibid., 78) and "necessarily more comprehensive" (ibid., 104) than interspecies competition. For this reason, "the rules for interspecies competition don't apply to intraspecies competition" (ibid., 77). But the latter is still limited, as it must be for individuals to be successful at optimizing their representation in their species' gene pool. Individuals don't try to annihilate all their competitors. Such an undertaking might precipitate their own deaths and limit the access of their offspring to viable mates.

What about intraspecies relations among humans? Quinn notes that the forms of social organization—or intraspecies cooperation—we observe in the community of life are products of evolution, too. Schools of fish, troops of monkeys, flocks of geese, and tribes of humans "each survived millions of years of testing by natural selection. It's no wonder they work well for their members. They work as well as eyes work, as well as nests work, as well as hands work" (IS, 63). Given our relative lack of speed, strength, and eyesight compared to other species, it proved advantageous among our distant ancestors to be able to engage in teamwork with their immediate cohorts to garner the provisions required to live. As the capacity for teamwork spread throughout the human gene pool, tribal living took root.

Humans didn't evolve *to* live tribally, Quinn emphasizes. We evolved *by* living tribally. What typically works best for every member of a tribe is to perpetuate the tribe, hence to cooperate with tribal cohorts (MI, 88).[16] So this is one prominent manifestation of the Law of Life among our kind: maintain the integrity of your tribe. This doesn't mean that tribal members always get along or that people don't get out of line. It means instead that situations like these must be addressed in a manner that maintains the tribe's cohesion.

What about interactions between tribes? Whereas the evolutionarily stable strategy for those within one's tribe centers on cooperation, evolutionary stability is maintained between tribes via *erratic retaliation,* Quinn contends. Conflict resolution can take three basic forms, Ishmael remarks. In the face of an antagonist, one can always fight, always back down, or sometimes fight and sometimes back down. The first two don't seem particularly advantageous. Fighting over every morsel of food, every patch of ground, and every potential mate is reckless (ibid., 81). But it generally doesn't pay to give up or run away in the face of every antagonist either. I'll raise issues with erratic retaliation in chapter 6. For now, though, it seems safe to conclude that the strategy that tends to be evolutionarily stable is sometimes to fight and sometimes to back down, with one's decisions being driven primarily by how much one needs available provisions. Moreover, it's advantageous to be predictable but not too predictable (ibid., 105). In other words, creativity is key.

The Community of Life

Recently, I happened to be watching a rerun of a television show that I enjoyed in my youth. During the episode, a character described his society as being "fully integrated" with the environment. "We don't just live here," he said. "We're part of our environment. It is part of us." The character indicated that this sets their society apart from others. But surely it would be a miracle if any society, or any species, wasn't fully integrated with the world. Indeed, the world just is a manifestation of the manifold interactions of countless species (Keith 2009, 25).

Recall that what Quinn refers to as *the world* is a site of habitation. It's a nexus of habitats fit for human survival and flourishing. What we humans inhabit isn't "the environment," whatever that is. All members of the living community are one another's habitats. We're both dwellers and dwellings at the same time. So the world changes because the living community changes (Lewontin 2000, 58). Each and every being is part of this dynamic process. We're all in this together, entwined in a complex network of relationships marked by interdependence among organisms, species, and ecosystems—all with a role to play in sustaining the health and wellbeing of the whole and each part of the whole.

The Web Endlessly Woven

The community of life is thus best viewed as what Hoagland calls "a multidimensional, integrated system." What evolves "are patterns of organization—the organism plus its strategies for making a living and for fitting in. Any successful change of strategy by one organism will create a ripple effect of adjustments" by others (1995, 33). Each and every living being on Earth is part of this system. We're born belonging to it in the same sense that our skin and our nervous system belong to us (B, 163; see also Eisenstein 2007, 416). We shape the world, and it shapes us. And the process of shaping and being shaped is fueled by each member of the community of life feeding and being fed upon. "Nothing is exempt. Nothing is special. Nothing is wasted. Everything that lives is food for another," Quinn declares (BD, 23).

Among the most important of the roles we all play is to pay back upon death the life we've been given by the living community. Every life is "on loan" in this respect, and every loan is paid back in full (B, 163). Quite literally, one way or another, we return to the land. Here's how Aldo Leopold puts it:

> Land, then, is not merely soil; it is a fountain of energy flowing through a circuit of soils, plants, and animals. Food chains are the living channels which conduct energy upward; death and decay return it of the soil. The circuit is not closed; some energy is dissipated in decay, some is added by absorption from the air, some is stored in soils, peats, and long-lived forests; it is a sustaining circuit, like a slowly augmented revolving fund of life. (1949, 216; see also Callicott 1989)

Solar energy flows throughout all biota, and heat is dissipated throughout all life processes. The molecules and nutrients that are our building blocks and that become enlivened by sunlight and heat are cycled and recycled.

All outputs are used also as inputs. Waste for one is a life source for another. We members of the community of life borrow, use, and return nutrients over and over again.

Indeed, Hoagland remarks, life is characterized by the circular flow of both information and materials. The ongoing process of making and breaking the molecules that serve as nutrients is "the basic process of life" (1995, 144). It's a function of self-regulating and self-correcting feedback. "Life loves loops. Most biological processes, even those with very complicated pathways, wind up back where they started" (ibid., 21). The circulation of blood, the sense-and-response process of the nervous system, menstruation, migration, and the cycle of birth and death all operate on the same principle.

Ecosystems operate this way, too. Looping patterns in one also invariably affect those in others. Nothing lives, and nothing occurs, in isolation. Together, each smaller loop is thus part of a bigger loop. We learn in primary school that oxygen, which is necessary for animals' respiration, is given off as a waste product of photosynthesis by plants. Animals exhale carbon dioxide that's inhaled by plants to make sugar, which they use for food. This process has global climactic effects. Likewise, I recall learning during my secondary schooling that in fresh water systems, fish eat algae and excrete organic waste. Bacteria then eat the waste and excrete inorganic material, which is eaten by algae. If one link in this chain is broken, the health of the entire water system is adversely affected. And while we Takers often struggle to accept that humans have integral ecological roles to play, our ancient ancestors wouldn't have spread so expeditiously to nearly every corner of the globe many millennia before the dawn of civilization had they not been able to give back in consonance with what they received from so many different places (Mann 2005, 264, Salmón 2012, 29, and Clarke 2019, 257). "From the standpoint of the whole ecosystem, these interchanges occur so smoothly that the distinction between production and consumption, and between waste and nutrient, disappears," states Hoagland (1995, 22). They're often noticeable only when some sort of disruption occurs.

"Every track begins and ends in the hand of god," Adam says to Abel. "Every track is a lifetime long" (TA, 22). No track lies outside the hand of god. These tracks, these paths, constitute a "web endlessly woven," no strand of which is any more or less important than any other (ibid., 23). In a sense, then, we're all "comrades" (H, 379). Each of us makes our journey through life in the company of untold others. Our paths run together in both visible and invisible ways with "those of the mouse in the field, the eagle on the mountain, the crab in its hold, the lizard beneath its rock. The leaf that falls to the ground a thousand miles away touches your life. The impress of your foot in the soil is felt through a thousand generations" (B 186–87).

This isn't to say that the members of the community of life live in harmony or in balance. B rejects both ideas outright (B, 150; see also Lewontin 2000, 68). As products of evolutionary development, of the interplay of order and disorder, we instead live in "dynamic tension" (ibid., 163) with one another. Every species evolves because of habitat and/or genomic "disturbances" (WS, 27) and perturbations. This is a key ingredient for the perpetuation of life.

We also must be careful not to overstate our case regarding the extent of our interdependence. It *may be* the case that the faraway leaf affects my life and that my footprint reverberates for generations to come. But we can probably conclude that these effects are quite minimal. Some forces, like gravity, are so weak that "one can stir a flower without troubling a star," Richard Lewontin remarks (2000, 110). Likewise, the extinction of a single species may have little effect on the community of life as a whole even if it has significant ramifications for other species that rely on it for food.

Quinn's main point, though, is this. We can view species as the rivets holding the Taker Thunderbolt together. We can only remove so many rivets without eventually compromising its ability to operate. Little by little, its integrity weakens until the removal of that one last rivet causes it to come apart at the seams.

Think Tower of Uru.

The People of the Deer

Mowat states that the Ihalmiut are also known as the "People of the Deer." Indeed, the Ihalmiut and the deer were inseparable in his mind prior to his first journey into the Barrens. He was unable to think of one without also thinking of the other. Thus, "by accident," he "stumbled on the secret of the Ihalmiut before I had ever met them" (2005, 72).

Assuming the Ihalmiut perspective, B offers the following rendering of what they might say about this secret of theirs:

> The fire of life that once burned in the deer now burns in us, and we live their lives and walk in their tracks across the

> hand of god. This is why we're the People of the Deer. The deer aren't our prey or our possessions—they're us. They're us at one point in the cycle of life and we're them at another point in the cycle. The deer are twice your parents, for your mother and father are deer, and the deer that gave you its life today was mother and father to you as well, since you wouldn't be here if it weren't for that deer. (B, 182; see also MGY, 86)

Each of us in our turn is ablaze with the fire of life. "To each of us is given its moment in the blaze," B proclaims, "its spark to be surrendered to another when it's sent, so that the blaze may go on. None may deny its spark to the general blaze and live forever—not any at all. . . . Each—each!—is sent to another someday" (B, 187–88). The grass to the grasshopper, the grasshopper to the sparrow, the sparrow to the fox, the fox to the vulture, and the vulture (along with remnants of them all) to the grass: all have their moment to borrow, to use, and to return.

In this respect, the Ihalmiut could just as easily say that their mother and father are grass. For the grass and the deer, the grasshopper and the vulture are "one thing" whose "name is fire" (MGY, 86). This is borne out as well, Martín Pretchel asserts, among the Maya through their concept of *kas-limaal,* or "mutual indebtedness, mutual insparkedness." As an elder tells Pretchel, "Everything comes into this Earth hungry and interdependent on all other things, animals, and people, so they can eat, be warmed, not be lonely, and survive" (1999, 347). To acknowledge *kas-limaal* "is an adult knowledge," the elder adds. To want to be free of debt for the fire of life of which we're part "means that you don't want to be part of life, and you don't want to grow into an adult" (ibid., 349).

This dovetails with B's colloquy with Louis on death. The more he understands death, she explains, the less despondent he'll feel about the subject in general and the better he'll be able to bear B's impending demise (B, 159). "Most Takers are terrified of death," Quinn remarks (P, 164). This has a great deal to do with our avoidance of close contact with the community of life and our inability to see its sacredness. For the community of life is equally a community of death. It's a community of life *and* death, really, for we can't have one without the other. If every life is on loan, then every life is owed to this community. Paying back this loan is what keeps the web endlessly weaving. "The fire of life burns forever because god gives one to another without stint, each in its own time" (TA, 15).

Takers tend to assume that death is a solitary experience. We may have others at our bedside at our time of departure, but the journey is ours alone to make. No wonder we're terrified. But this may be yet one more dimension of the Great Forgetting. For we neglect, states Thom van Dooren, that each one of us is "interwoven into a system in which we live and die *with* others, live and die *for* others" (2002, 10). We deny ourselves the capacity to appreciate that our death "will be life for another," B declares. "I swear to you. And you watch, you come find me, because I'll be standing again in these grasses and you'll see me looking through the eyes of the fox and taking the air with the eagle and running in the track of the deer" (B, 188). One thing with one name. That name is fire. And the fire is god.

What, then, if we were to see death, states Val Plumwood, "as recycling, a flowing on into an ecological and ancestral community of origin?" This provides a fitting extension in death of what the land is in life: "a nourishing terrain." And it permits us to see death as "a nurturing, material continuity/reunion with ecological others" (2012, 92).

From this perspective, once we're supposedly gone, we nevertheless stay. Whatever makes us *us* returns to the land in death just as we're interconnected with it in life (Gunn Allen 1979; see also Deloria 1973, 174). To accept this proposition alters quite profoundly the way we understand not just how we should conduct ourselves while alive but also our connection to those who've come before us and those yet to come. For the earth is no "temporary lodging," no waystation, that we occupy until our essential self—our imperishable soul or spirit—departs the perishable body for "eternal life in a realm apart," Plumwood states (2012, 93). Nor, in questioning this view of death, are we consigned to atheism, whereby death entails finality, nullity, an incapacity for any sort of continuation. Indeed, atheism isn't a rejection of the heavenly view Plumwood describes. Its proponents simply deny ensoulment while maintaining a "devalued" (ibid., 94) view of the body. In so doing, they also reject reimagining death itself as transition from the human to the more-than-human—from entanglement in one set of living loops to another.

"At the individual level, death confirms transience, but on the level of the ecological community, it can affirm an enduring, resilient cycle or process," Plumwood remarks (ibid., 96). From an ecological standpoint, we both *are* and, upon death, more fully *become* parts of the lives of other species, part of an ongoing story that we continue to animate. "Because of course *the body* does not just 'end'—it decays and decomposes, its matter losing its prior organizational form and taking on or being incorporated into new forms in a sharing of substance/life force. Lots of linking, afterlife narrative here!" (ibid., 95).

From a social perspective, moreover, consider how Abram describes traditional forms of ancestor veneration: "For almost all oral cultures, the enveloping and sensuous earth remains the dwelling place of both the living *and* the dead. The 'body'—whether human or otherwise—is not . . . a mechanical object in such cultures, but is a magical entity, the mind's own sensuous aspect, and at death the body's decomposition into soil, worms, and dust can only signify the gradual reintegration of one's ancestors and elders into the living landscape, from which all, too, are born" (1996, 15; see also Forbes 2008, 10f.). Within this cultural context, the practice of venerating ancestors is thus intimately tied to the veneration of other-than-human persons, including both plant and animal persons who may become food. It signifies "not so much an awe or reverence for human powers, but rather a reverence for those forms awareness takes when it is *not* in human form, when the familiar human embodiment dies and decays to become part of the encompassing cosmos," Abram states (ibid., 16).

It's perhaps incorrect, then, to say that denying *kas-limaal* is disrespectful to one's food *and* one's ancestors, as if these entities are so easily separable. Maybe acceptance of the "adult knowledge" that *kas-limaal* constitutes should lead one to see that veneration for ancestors (and concern for future generations, for that matter) *just is* veneration for food, for the life-giving processes that bind together the living and the dead both physically and spiritually.

On the Way

In the same vein, B states that each of us is "*on the way*" and "*in process*" (B, 161; see also TA, 71 and 85). We're manifestations of ongoing change. This means that the world doesn't have to be put back to how it was before it was overrun by Takers. Because the gods know very well how to take care of *this place*, we do well to allow ourselves to be guided by it as we seek to facilitate ecological—and, for that matter, cultural—restoration. We'll see as we proceed that this also entails attending to how occupying pilfered and pillaged land disrupts and derails restoration, hence how decolonization becomes a necessary component of the threefold struggle.

Indeed, facilitating ecological and cultural restoration also means fostering diversity. "No two things alike in the mighty universe, Jared. That's the key. That's why everything here is *on the way* and not in its final form" (B, 161). Evolution may appear to be directed toward improvement (IS, 57). But, if anything, it's abundance that tends to proliferate, and abundance itself isn't a final form. It's the result of less workable genotypes being eliminated and more workable ones being preserved.

In this regard, we miss Quinn's point if we ask, on the way *to what?* If organisms, species, ecosystems, and the entire living community can take no eternally final form, if we're all in process throughout life *and* death (B, 188), then perhaps it's better for us to ask, what's *the way* we're on? In other words, we do better to focus not on where we might be going but on the path—the Road—we're currently traveling. Has the story we're enacting put us on a path to extinction? If so, then we already know where we're going. But our track across the hand of god isn't predetermined no matter how much trouble we may face extricating ourselves from the Taker story. There are other ways, other tracks, other paths to take. Be observant, listen, and learn. Our fellow members of the community of life are walking with us. We can rely on them for guidance.

Ex Plures Uno

This is my phrase, not Quinn's. But I hope its applicability is clear at this point. We're all ablaze with the fire of life, each in our own time. In this respect, we're one thing. But the fire of life "burns forever because god gives one to another without stint" (TA, 15). And the process of giving one to another, of feeding and being fed upon, is what shapes us all. *Ex plures uno*: out of one, many. Out of one process—the ongoing inspiration and expiration of fire throughout the living community—no two things alike in the whole of the universe emerge. So long as the fire of life rages, evolution continues.

There's another way, though, that many emerge from one, according to Quinn. "No two alike, as the gods seem to like things. No two alike, except for one thing only: that they were founded on the Law of Life. The law whose only restraint was to keep man living in the hands of the gods" (BD, 47). The hands of the gods are where life is to be found. And where there's life, there's an abundance of genotypes and behavioral policies. Just one law, that's all the gods need to facilitate the emergence of countless species and cultures (ibid., 42; see also TA, 17). Just one law, operative within and through the threefold struggle.

Chapter 5

Remembering How to Be Human

Gifts of Wisdom and Awareness of the Sacred

Awareness connotes a sort of alertness or attunement: to people, things, events, and specifiable patterns. It can involve knowing or understanding, but it also has a perceptual component that dovetails nicely with Quinn's frequent references to the importance of *sight*, particularly (and unsurprisingly) when it comes to developing a new vision. Takers are held captive in part by our inability to see with any clarity beyond the bounds of our culture. Indeed, many Takers are twice blind, unable even to see ourselves as captives of a culture in the first place, let alone a culture that doesn't work and can't be made to work (Veyne 1988, 118).[1]

Our blindness needn't be permanent, though. We can treat Quinn's philosophy in part as an exercise in learning to see—specifically, in developing what he calls "eyes that see."[2] Most notably, this involves being attuned to the land we inhabit—*this place, right here*—and to the community of life we share it with. Is this either a necessary or a sufficient condition for living sustainably? Quinn never makes such a claim. He wouldn't, since there's no one right way to live. But attunement to the land and the community of life works, *really well,* and has for millions of years. As such, we can regard this attunement as nothing short of sacred. Better yet, it's a conduit to the sacred, awareness of which provides significant support for ecological, social, and personal wellbeing.

In the next chapter, I'll give due attention to key structural inhibitors to Takers developing eyes that see. Most notable among these inhibitors is being occupiers and wanton abusers of stolen lands. Under such conditions, it is impossible to enjoy relationships with the land and living community that permit attunement. But let's begin by getting a clearer sense of the prerequisites for having eyes that see. Quinn calls them "gifts of wisdom." Every creature receives such gifts; Quinn delineates ours. We do well to acknowledge their critical contribution to the success story that the existence of our species reflects. It's equally important to understand how Takers have rejected the gifts of wisdom, hence how our capacities for awareness of the sacred have been so profoundly disrupted. In essence, we've thrown sight away. We can set ourselves on a path to its retrieval, according to Quinn, by remembering and embracing how we became human.

Gifts of Wisdom

What exactly is wisdom? While it's generally regarded as most closely associated with knowledge, I suggest that it also can be treated as a function of awareness. How so? Knowledge is often regarded, perhaps too simplistically, as the accumulation of facts and information. Wisdom, then, is the synthesis of knowledge with one's life experiences in a manner that deepens one's understanding and appreciation of the world and one's place in it.[3]

With this way of conceptualizing wisdom, *insight* plays a critical role. If we emphasize the *sight* in insight, we see that at least as important as having knowledge and making good use of it is having and making good use of awareness. This emerges in the enumeration of the three gifts of wisdom, shared by Adam with Abel in *Tales of Adam*. We cover the first two straightaway, leaving the last for later.

Seeing beneath Surfaces

We're already familiar with the first gift of wisdom, "the gift of seeing beneath the surface of things and calling them by their true names" (TA, 68). It's a component of recognizing and embracing that we're "twice born" of the beings who are our food. Recall here the Ihalmiut, the People of the Deer. Ihalmiut parents teach their children to identify the deer as a life giver in two senses: first as the species responsible for the very existence of the Ihalmiut and second as the being whose death "gave you its life today" (B, 182) to make your individual life possible.

More globally, seeing beneath surfaces highlights that we're all one thing yet still many, *ex uno plures*. Each of us lives because others give their lives, and our death means life for others. This is an essential part of how our paths crisscross and intersect.

To be sure, myriad institutions exist in Taker culture to keep us unaware. We're encouraged, for example, to be untroubled by the ongoing expansion of totalitarian agriculture (I, 44). But this only makes the ability to see beneath surfaces that much more monumental, and vital, for freeing ourselves from our cultural captivity.

Discerning True Courses

The second gift of wisdom, Adam explains to Abel, is "the gift of tracking, of discerning the true course of things" (TA, 71). We'll discuss tracking shortly. First, a few words about truth. Quinn provides no worked-out theory of truth. But his approach to the matter puts me in mind of William James's suggestion that we can think of truths as ideas, propositions, and modes of engagement that "agreeably lead." They're invaluable instruments of action.

For Quinn, truths agreeably lead with respect to what works for the planet and for people. They tend to make our lives go well, and they support the perpetuation of the world as a suitable human habitat. So more than just reflecting static facts, truths facilitate sustaining relations—*wise* relations—with fellow members of the living community.

Like health and wealth, then, truth is useful, satisfactory, and even expedient. James makes no bones about this. But he doesn't suggest that whatever happens to satisfy us deserves to be called true. That truths satisfy doesn't entail that everything that satisfies is true. This is why James is equally clear that for something to agreeably lead it must be "expedient in the long run and on the whole, of course, for what meets expediently all the experience in sight won't necessarily meet all further experiences equally satisfactorily. Experience, as we all know, has a way of *boiling over,* and making us correct our present formulas" (1975, 170).

This also means that truth is constrained by and answerable to experience taken as a living and continually unfolding process. In other words, truth—or what we *call* true—is subject to revision based on new findings. And this is just as it should be. For we "play fast and loose with the order which realities follow" if we fail to attend to experience and end up making "false connections" that lead us to fall prey to "endless inconsistency and frustration" (ibid., 99, 99, and 101, respectively).

Like some aspects of health and wealth, some truths do have a universal flavor. Here's one example: it agreeably leads to hone one's awareness of *this place,* wherever that may be. Doing so works. But what this involves in practice has a particular, local flavor. The important point is that truths agreeably lead, whatever their scope may be.

Reading the Signs

In order to discern the true course of things, what B calls *reading the signs* is indispensable. A sign conveys information about an object or event. It's "an essential vehicle of meaning," Carl Hausman remarks (1993, 8), but its meaning isn't self-evident. "Every sign is caught up in an interpretive web," so how a sign is read or whether it's even recognized as a sign can vary from interpreter to interpreter. This doesn't mean that anything goes when it comes to determining what a sign indicates. Some interpretations lead more agreeably than others. My father-in-law can look at a car engine and identify why it's not working. I just see a bunch of interconnected and nondescript auto parts. I think you can guess which one of us can get the car running again. His ability to read the engine's signs agreeably leads with respect to repairing it. I'm completely useless in this regard.

Both Takers and Leavers read signs constantly. It's the primary activity by which we orient ourselves to our surroundings. But most Takers are inept when it comes specifically to tracking, which is the form of reading the signs that's most helpful for discerning the true course of things.

Tracking

In *The Science and Art of Tracking,* Tom Brown Jr. tells a story from his childhood growing up in the Pine Barrens of New Jersey. One day, he was out camping with his friend Rick and Rick's grandfather, an Apache scout. After spending the afternoon exploring, Rick and Brown returned to camp. They were famished, and Grandfather—as they both called him—had already finished eating.[4] He told them, though, that there was food for them at the base of an old pine just beyond the other end of the campsite. They hurried over to grab their dinner only to discover that there was no such tree anywhere in the vicinity.

Was Grandfather playing a joke on them? It seemed so, but they were embarrassed by their failure to find the food anyway. Once they finally admitted as much, "Grandfather stood and began to walk to the far end of the camp, motioning us to follow." He abruptly stopped, turned to them, and asked:

> "What are you standing in?" I answered him quickly and confidently. "A small clearing!" He then asked, "What is strange about these trees around the clearing?" We looked for a long time but said nothing. I couldn't understand what he was getting at or what he wanted us to see. Finally, and almost by accident, I noticed that none of the small pine trees around the clearing had branches on the side facing the clearing. Instead, all the branches, except for the uppermost, faced away from the clearing. I told Grandfather about my observation and in the moonlight I could see him smile, apparently satisfied with my answer. He then proceeded back to camp. (1999, 15)

Still baffled, Brown asked what any of this had to do with where he and Rick might find their dinner. Grandfather snickered and responded that young Tom already had located the old pine, so he already had the answer to his question.

Why were none of the lower branches of the trees that ringed the clearing facing the clearing, Grandfather asked him. "I thought for a moment and then said, 'They were blocked from the sun so they did not grow on that side' " (ibid.). What blocked out the sun, Grandfather prodded. The old pine! It had once stood at the center of what was now the clearing. Brown and Rick rushed back to the clearing, finally finding their dinner just where Grandfather said it would be.

This was an early lesson during the ten years that Brown spent under Grandfather's tutelage, learning how to develop "the eye of the tracker." After logging countless hours of "dirt time," he now identifies his practice as part science and part art. It begins with close, patient observation of the landscape and identification of signs that convey information about the activities of inhabitants (1978, 214f.). Trackers then develop working hypotheses that help them answer such questions as " 'What has happened here?' or 'What is this telling me?' " (Brown 1999, 15), which they then test through further investigation.

In due time, signs also take on aesthetic contours—"patterns, colors, textures" (ibid., 27)—that awaken trackers to the web endlessly woven in *this place.* "Each being, each element, each entity is a thread that makes up the grand tapestry of life" (ibid., 9). To have the eye of the tracker is to see the beauty of each individual strand *and* the exquisiteness of the web in which it's embedded. Neither does one miss the forest for the trees nor the trees for the forest.

Consider, for example, what's involved in tracking an animal. For expert trackers, every bit of spoor speaks volumes. Brown describes how each footprint alone composes a miniature landscape full of "hills, valleys, ridges, peaks, domes, and pocks" that give it a character and shape all its own (ibid., 5). Apache scouts identify over five thousand such "pressure releases," or subtle intricacies in the way different substrates over which an animal travels respond to the animal's movement. No two footprints are alike, and none should be investigated with any less care than any other. For what the expert tracker is reading is an ongoing conversation—a running negotiation (ibid., 37f.)—between one's quarry, other living beings, the elements, and the land.

Trackers follow this conversation in two complementary ways. *Systematic tracking* involves carefully compiling empirical evidence that leads one to their quarry. *Speculative tracking* entails reading between the signs, as it were, by tying this evidence together into a coherent account of how one's quarry has been spending their time and where they're headed. Both systematic and speculative tracking involve anticipation and prediction, but the former is based largely on "repeated experience of similar situations," Louis Liebenberg notes (1990, 106), whereas the latter requires making conjectures and imaginative leaps that may go well beyond past encounters.

Using systematic and speculative tracking in tandem, trackers may even work several leads at once, shifting strategies or abandoning a search altogether as they acquire more or better information. This may mean taking time out to pick up a lost trail or drawing on an entirely new lead (TA, 56f.). "Here's a small example," B tells Jared:

> One day an anthropologist was tagging along with a !Kung hunter in the Kalahari. Around noon they abandoned one hunt as hopeless and started looking around for something else to go after. Soon they came across a gemsbok track the hunter judged to be just a couple hours old. After half an hour tracking, however, the hunter called it off. He explained that the track hadn't been made that morning after all, pointing out as proof a gemsbok hoof print with a mouse track running across

> it. Since mice are nocturnal, the gemsbok track had to have been made during the night. In other words, this particular gemsbok was long gone. (B, 167)

Jared is impressed even by B's rudimentary attempt to decipher what the beetle tracks she finds in the park where they're conversing tell her about the beetle's activities. But she specifies that expert trackers would "be able to identify every creature that left a mark here in the recent past, and they'd be able to tell you when it was here and what it was doing, whether it was hurrying or moseying, looking for something to eat or trying to get back home" (ibid., 166; see also TA, 20).[5] Moreover, they would be "keeping in mind the season, the time of day, the temperature, the condition of the ground, the nature of the terrain, and of course the typical behavior of the animal being tracked and other animals in the neighborhood as well" (ibid., 167).[6]

This practice helps to create what Paul Rezendes calls "a larger perspective of self" (1999, 22; see also Brown 1978, 9). To those of us with untrained eyes, places with scant human habitation often appear to be relatively empty of animal life (Conesa-Sevilla 2008, 120). There are no conversations, no negotiations, to be encountered. Just think by comparison of what it would be like to be aware that there are complex interactions going on all around you—some of them about you and even *with* you. Imagine being part of the conversation. How much bigger and fuller *this place* would be.

Throwing Sight Away

What about those among us without eyes that see? Humans experience what Quinn calls a "bottom-to-top flow of data." The people of our culture tend to regard it "as the ordinary process of perception" (WS, 136). It works like this:

> When your eye encounters photons bouncing off an apple, they're turned into a pattern that's sent to the primary visual cortex. There, the general shape of the apple is recognized and sent on to a higher region of brain function where its color is identified. Then this pattern moves along to a still-higher region where it's put together with other knowledge that enables you to recognize that this is an apple, not a strawberry. (Ibid.)

But here's the thing. There's "also a top-to-bottom flow of information that is equally powerful, and it's a curious fact that the neural paths carrying information down to the bottom outnumber the paths carrying information up to the top ten to one" (ibid.).[7] What exactly does this mean for our perceptual capacities? It turns out that even when the same photons hit your eyes as hit mine, we can end up perceiving what we see differently.

It's commonplace, for example, for white Americans to have trouble distinguishing people of East Asian descent. This isn't a problem that Koreans or Laotians or any other people from East Asia face. Why? Because "a lifetime of experience" (WS, 137) leads white Americans who don't routinely encounter East Asians to focus on the similarities among them, whereas Koreans and Laotians focus on their differences. In other words, the top-to-bottom flow of information that we experience frames what catches our eye.

Unsurprisingly, Quinn adds, the top-to-bottom flow of information is also, in part, a product of "cultural conditioning" (ibid., 143). The fact that neural pathways leading downward far outnumber those that lead upward indicates that we're "hardwired for culture," as Elaine puts it. "We evolved as cultural beings," Quinn replies, "and cultural conditioning at the top level serves to tell us how to evaluate and act on the information we receive from the bottom level" (ibid., 145; see also BD, 42). More to the point, our cultural conditioning—our *vision* (as in visions versus programs)—tells us how and what to see. Again, the process of enculturation to which we're all subject has fit us with a set of all-but-undetectable eyeglasses that strongly influence what's in focus, what's a blur, and what we don't see at all. So if we're to change our patterns of thought and action, we'd better figure out how to change our perception, too.

Optical Contortions

What happens when Takers appeal without a second thought to what Jared calls a "rough-and-ready empiricism" (B, 156) to make sense of the world and our place in it? Empiricists contend that knowledge is derived primarily from sense-experience. The everyday experiences of Takers tell us that because the people of our culture have lived for thousands of years as though the world was made for us, we can go on doing so. Yes, we're making a right mess of things, but this doesn't indicate to us that our sense-experience has led us astray. We can see clearly, we tell ourselves. Our flawed constitution gets in the way only when we make subsequent judgments and act on what we see. No perceptual problem here.

Charles Mills (1997, 18) contends that racism is particularly insidious in the United States because most white Americans are unable to accept, let alone see, that American society has been quite consciously structured in ways that (sometimes) subtly but (always) substantively privilege them. Indeed, state Shannon Sullivan and Nancy Tuana, a wide array of institutions support "white people's obliviousness of the worlds of people of color" (2007, 3).[8] In effect, these institutions have facilitated the development of a sort of "collective amnesia" (ibid., 4) among white Americans that far too many are loath to eradicate. Collective amnesia, then, is a product, states Ta-Nehisi Coates, of "the practical habit of jabbing out one's eyes and forgetting the work of one's hands" (2015, 98).

Consider, too, how the experience of collective amnesia plays out with our avowed interest in "fighting" cancer. Cures are what get the media attention and research dollars; prevention is largely ignored, except by making reference to requisite lifestyle changes. We're really good at making the issue about individuals instead of seeing what Rachel Carson, among others, went to such great pains to make obvious to us. The land, water, and air don't somehow detoxify the billions of tons of carcinogens deposited in them. With each bite, each sip, and each breath, what we do to our world we do over and over to ourselves.

Wittingly or not, we Takers have inhaled what B calls the "angel dust of our culture," which "blinds us to the fact that we are a biological species in a community of biological species and are not exempt or exemptible from the forces that shape all life on this planet" (B, 307). I know this, although in a superficial, distant way. It's rare for me viscerally and vividly to experience my ecological animality in my body and my everyday life (Hester et al. 2000). Indeed, leaving this experience unfelt, unacknowledged, and pretty much unseen is the path of least resistance in Taker culture.

This takes training. We're not born as "someone who's thrown sight away. Someone who refuses to see,' " as the mysterious character Mallory puts it in *After Dachau* (AD, 84). But, in time, we learn to engage in optical contortions so effectively that we unsee our contortionism.

Literalism

Takers have a powerful attraction to words—specifically, to written words. We rarely pause to acknowledge, though, that we read words as trackers read the signs. As David Abram remarks, "The scratches and scrawls you now focus upon, trailing off across the white surface, are hardly different from the footprints of prey left in the snow. We read these traces with organs honed over millennia by our tribal ancestors, moving instinctively from one track to the next, picking up the trail afresh whenever it leaves off" (1996, 96).

As with our ancestors, this permits us to participate in an unfolding conversation. Authors speak to us, sometimes directly and sometimes obliquely. They make statements and develop ideas whose meaning we must piece together as we proceed. We enter into texts and subtexts that set our cognitive and imaginative capacities aflame precisely because words—strung together just so—open doors to others' lives and the events that constitute them.

Think about the very act of spelling, states Abram. In Old English, *to spell* meant to recite a story, to tell a tale. But the term has since taken on a different, double meaning. Now, to spell is "to arrange, in the proper order, the written letters that constitute the name of a thing or a person," Abram remarks. But it also "signifies a magic formula or charm. For to assemble the letters that make up the name of a thing, in the correct order, was precisely to effect a magic, to establish a new kind of influence over an entity, to summon it forth!" Our eyes fall on printed marks, and we immediately "hear spoken words, witness strange scenes and visions, even experience other lives" (ibid., 133).

But our fascination with the written word may lead us to face some surprising adversities with respect to how we relate to the world around us. Consider how our vision, both perceptually and culturally, has changed with the emergence of phonetic language. Abram provides a loose genealogy:

> In the absence of phonetic literacy, neither society, nor language, nor even the experience of "thought" or consciousness, can be pondered in isolation from the multiple nonhuman shapes and powers that lend their influence to all our activities (we need only think of our ceaseless involvement with the ground underfoot, with the air that swirls around us, with the plants and animals that we consume, with the daily warmth of the sun and the cyclic pull of the moon). Indeed, in the absence of formal writing systems, human communities come to know themselves primarily as they are reflected back by the animals and the animate landscapes with which they are directly engaged. This epistemological dependence is

> readily evidenced, on every continent, by the diverse modes of identification commonly categorized under the single term "totemism." (1996, 123)

The emergence of petroglyphs, pictograms, and ideographs "involved the displacement of our sensory participation from the depths of the animate environment to the flat surface of our walls, of clay tablets, of sheets of papyrus," Abram maintains (ibid., 100). But the depicted images continued to relate closely to *this place* and the participants in its animation. No sense could be made of the images without appreciating the living context in which they were created. As such, the images served as supplicants to the direct forms of communication with the enveloping earth in which people otherwise routinely engaged.

The letters of the ancient Hebrew *aleph-beth* continued to refer to manifestations of everyday experience: *aleph* to ox, *beth* to house, *gimel* to camel. But the living context from which the letters arose was receding. Whereas *this place* and its inhabitants indirectly spoke *through* petroglyphs, pictograms, and ideographs, the characters of the *aleph-beth* spoke *for* and *about* other animals, plants, and the sun, moon, and stars. These beings lost their own voices. We see this even in the Book of Genesis, Abram notes, in which "the animals do not speak their own names to Adam." Instead, "they are *given* their names by this first man. Language, for the Hebrews, was becoming a purely *human* gift, a human power" (ibid., 101).

It's with the Greek alphabet that "the progressive abstraction of linguistic meaning from the enveloping life-world reached a type of completion" (ibid., 101–102). Aleph to *alpha,* beth to *beta,* gimel to *gamma*:

> That is, while the Semitic name for the letter was also the name of the sensorial entity commonly imaged by or associated with the latter, the Greek name had no sensorial reference at all. While the Semitic name had served as a reminder of the worldly origin of the letter, the Greek name served only to designate the human-made letter itself. The pictorial (or iconic) significance of many of the Semitic letters, which was memorialized in their spoken names, was now readily lost. The indebtedness of human language to the more-than-human perceptual field, an indebtedness preserved in the names and shapes of the Semitic letters, could now be entirely forgotten. (Ibid., 102)[9]

The sensible character of each phoneme, each discrete sound that comprises each word, is now embodied "solely by the gesture to be made by the human mouth," Abram adds (1996, 100). Language itself now belongs solely to us. Our mode of voice not only takes priority, it's the only genuine mode there is.

It's easier now to see how the ancient Greeks could transform the psyche from an unseen medium constituted by air and transferred by breath throughout the living community into "an individual 'interior,' a private 'mind' or 'consciousness' " that could belong only to humans (ibid., 257). For as it has played out in Taker culture, immersing oneself in phonetic reading and writing has given rise to a sense of self that profoundly diverges from that of the tracker. Here, one last time, is Abram:

> The capacity to view and even to dialogue with one's own words after writing them down, or even in the process of writing them down, enables a new sense of autonomy and independence from others, and even from the sensuous surroundings that had earlier been one's interlocutor. The fact that one's scripted words can be returned to and pondered at any time that one chooses, regardless of when, or in what situation, they were first recorded, grants a timeless quality to this new reflective self, a sense of relative independence of one's verbal, speaking self from the breathing body with its shifting needs. (Ibid., 112)[10]

Whereas the tracker is a *porous* self, those of us who are firmly under the spell of the printed word can hardly help but view ourselves as *buffered* (Taylor 2007, 38f.). No longer open, permeable, and in constant negotiation with fellow members of the living community, we now experience ourselves as disengaged from the wider order of things. Our thoughts are entirely our own. And, for most Takers, we humans are the only possible sources of thought the world contains. Indeed, it's not that animals, plants, mountains, and rivers no longer speak. *They never spoke at all,* and it's the height of magical thinking, infantile, to assume otherwise.

Perhaps this is yet another dimension of the Great Forgetting.

Dreaming and Awakening

Dreaming is sometimes described as our subconscious coming to the fore. It's assumed to be constituted by emotion-laden images, concocted we know not how by our own minds and frequently linked together in the most bizarre and surprising ways. Dreams can terrify, arouse, even inspire. They're mystifying. But if we Takers know one thing for sure, it's that—as with thinking—they take place "strictly within the confines of our individual skulls," Franklin Waters comments to Ginny in Quinn's first novel, *Dreamer* (D, 202).

This view, too, may be a cultural oddity. Consult "the knowledge and experience of ten thousand older cultures scattered all over the world," Waters continues, and "you will learn something different. In all these cultures, it's accepted without question that in dreams we inhabit a separate realm of reality that exists as surely as the one we inhabit in waking life" (ibid.). Perhaps our dreams are themselves tracks, paths to forms of wisdom about which we're scantly aware (ibid., 207). Quinn's beetle dream in *Providence* surely gives this impression (P, 14ff.), as does Tim's dream of Rome (H, 375ff.).

Consider what the main character in Natasha Alvarez's novella *Liminal* says about a dream she had of a fawn and its mother. "In the dream the deer were dancing, like people, standing up on their hind legs, and laughing, so happy. They took my hands gently in their hooves and we spun around, like children, until we were dizzy and fell on the grass. 'There are other ways of knowing, Koweenassee,' the mother deer told me" (2014, 35–36).

Becoming Human

We now pick up the third gift of wisdom, *reading the message of events*. It's "the subtlest wisdom of all," Adam conveys to Abel (TA, 81). It also may be the most monumental of gifts with respect to the emergence of the human species.

Cast your mind back to the time just before *Australopithecus* became *Homo*, B advises Jared. Of course, it's not as if there was ever "a day when you would've been able to point to one generation of parents and say, 'These are Australopithecines,' then point to their children and say, 'These are humans' " (B, 137).[11] And we don't need to speculate about how long the full transition from the former to the latter took, she insists. "All we know is that on our side of the line there are creatures we feel confident calling *Homo* and on the far side of the line there as creatures we *don't* feel confident about calling *Homo*" (ibid.).

It's common for the people of our culture to assume that the transition from *Australopithecus* to *Homo* was made possible by tool use. This is hardly surprising since we tend to equate advancement with the rollout of ever more sophisticated technological gadgetry (B, 164). It's also incorrect, B states. "You have tool users on both sides of the line. We can be virtually certain of this, since even chimpanzees are well known tool users, and *Homo*'s immediate predecessors were far beyond chimpanzees" in terms of the cognitive and kinesthetic capacities required for tool use (ibid., 137–38).

What if instead it was a matter of *Homo* acquiring a specific kind of awareness that *Australopithecus* didn't have? B's proposal is developed by means of what she calls *bricolage*, "which is the craft of building with whatever comes to hand. It comes from the French *bricoleur*, to putter about" (ibid., 130).[12] B illustrates what she's trying to get Jared to see by working with what the two of them find at hand in the park. But she's also highlighting that the best she can do when it comes to identifying how we became human is to engage in a bit of speculative poking around along the border between the human and the almost human.

As she does so, she relays:

> I say to myself that perhaps thought is like a musical tone, which . . . is never a single, pure tone but is always a composite of many harmonics—overtones and undertones. And I say to myself that perhaps, when mental process became human thought it began to resound with one harmonic that corresponds to what we call religion, or, more fundamentally, awareness of the sacred. In other words, I wonder if awareness of the sacred is not so much a separate concept as it is an overtone of human thought itself. (B, 130–31; see also ibid., 179)

Could it be that humanity emerged by having one's mental processes resonate with one's proximate living community—one's *people*, as I'll explain in the next chapter—in such a way that one became aware of it as sacred? This is what B is suggesting. Both *Australopithecus* and *Homo* exhibit mental processes. But, if B is correct, the latter are attuned to a harmonic that the former weren't. This harmonic awakens the mind of *Homo* to a way of seeing the world and one's place in it in a new way. *This place* isn't just territory or home. The people who populate it aren't just fellow inhabitants. It and they are now *resoundingly special.*

This is a matter of conjecture, B remarks, rather than of faith. *Bricolage* may not be falsifiable; it's not subject to scientific experimentation. But it can yield "*scientia*, knowledge" to the extent that it can "astound, make sense, and stimulate thought. It can still impress with its veracity, validity, soundness, and cogency" (ibid., 131). We need to see more, though, to determine whether B's speculations meet this bar.

How the Sacred Harmonic Emerged

So we became human when we acquired awareness of the sacred. We'll focus in the next chapter on the character of the sacred itself. At present, let's discuss how we became aware of it. How did we gain the ability to see *this place*—or, perhaps, specifiable components of it—and its people as resoundingly special?

According to B, hunting played a critical role in the emergence of *Homo,* not because of the violence it involves (B, 170; see also Cajete 2000, 40) but because the cognitive and interactive skills it requires were subject to selection.[13] Those who proved adept specifically at reading the message of events, the core capacity required to engage in hunting, were better providers. Rudimentary forms of this practice likely emerged under conditions in which it was relatively easy to carry out, developing further in increasingly difficult conditions (Liebenberg 1990, 29). Success relative to both demands and needs has played a foundational role in human development, B speculates.

Among the cognitive skills needed to read the message of events is the ability to conceptualize time. In order to see pressure releases and spoor as windows into the lives of one's quarry, it's critical to "recognize that they're traces of *past events,*" B tells Jared. It's also necessary to see that tracks move in a specifiable temporal direction, that they tell a story of our quarry's activities that has a "beginning, middle, and end. The beetle's story begins here, progresses to here, and ends here, where it intersects with the mouse's story. We can see that the mouse's story continues—into the future that we can make *predictions* about" (B, 174).

Making predictions, B continues, "is so deeply ingrained in us, so much taken for granted, that we don't give a moment's thought to how remarkable it is" (ibid.). We take an umbrella with us while running errands in anticipation of rain and trust that a doctor's prescription, if properly followed, can be expected to bring relief for what ails us. We can't help but engage in acts of prediction, which is why we're thrown off by "unpleasant surprises" or flustered when our day doesn't go "*as planned*" (ibid.).[14]

We're thus practitioners of divination, B remarks. We seek to foresee, which is why hypothetical reasoning is among our most well-worn rituals. *If I do* x, *then I can expect* y *to happen.* It's "fundamentally based on making predictions," B states. The scientific method operates similarly. "'Theory predicts that doing A, B, and C will result in D. I'll test the theory in this way and see whether the prediction is accurate or not,' we can hear the researcher say" (ibid., 175–76).

Readers of the message of events who are crafty, cunning, and stealthy have a clear advantage in pursuing their quarry over those who aren't. Those who make good use of observation, deduction, and inference to the best explanation are more successful, in general and on the whole, than those who rely on happenstance and dumb luck. The same goes for those whose awareness extends beyond their quarry, lest they're being stalked themselves.

With respect to interactive skills, even among adept hunters some are bound to be more successful than others. This may be attributable to slight cognitive or physical advantages, but not necessarily. Some hunters also may be better at communicating and cooperating, which effectively permits them to expand their perceptual field. Indeed, perceptual expansion of this sort—taking advantage of a larger sense of self—can be both synchronic and diachronic; it can occur at a specific point in time and also across time.

During the hunt, teamwork paid off for our human progenitors. Teamwork was facilitated by good communication, including both spoken language and body language. And because being a valuable hunting partner also made one a valuable mate, B states, "Language ability meant you were both more likely to survive and more likely to reproduce." It hereby is appropriate to say that "we became human not just by hunting but by hunting and talking" (B, 169).

So too were early hunters who had a prevailing talent for organizing events into stories—who could see events as spatiotemporally connected—more successful than hunters who were less skilled in this regard. This too tended to translate into reproductive success, which helps to explain why people "seem to be irresistibly attracted to stories, everywhere and everywhen," B observes (ibid., 174). It's easy to see this penchant in our children, but we adults have it, too. Have you ever finished watching a film or reading a novel that you don't particularly like just to see how it ends? Do you have trouble keeping yourself from rubbernecking when you drive past an accident? And what about the news? Do you like to keep up with the events of the day? If so, you're just as addicted to a tale—to knowing what happened, what's happening now, and what could happen next—as the rest of us.

Storytelling served at least three functions for our early ancestors. It entertained, yes. It also was a means directly or indirectly to confer knowledge, wherein having a flair for the dramatic helped to ensure a continuous flow of useful information (Liebenberg 1990, 43 and 69). And it provided a means to reinforce social ties among a people and the land (Abram 1996, 182). Peoples talked, chanted, and prayed the land and fellow inhabitants into their being (Cajete 2000, 184). Or perhaps the land spoke through them (Berndt and Berndt 1989, 5–6). Either way, this is a manifestation of the sacred harmonic.

Science and the Sacred

Time to reset. Our goal is to see how human thought came to resonate with a sacred harmonic emanating from *this place* and the beings who compose it. Awareness of the sacred emerged as a result of the development and use of cognitive and interactive skills that are integral to tracking. Most notably, both the power of prediction and the ability to cooperate and communicate effectively are reproductively advantageous in general and on the whole. They combine to make possible storytelling. They also facilitated seeing *this place* and its people as sacred, as resoundingly special, although we haven't yet seen how.

To Takers, the juxtaposition of science and the sacred sounds strange. It's commonly assumed that they're at odds, or at least that they have divergent foci. Yet while Taker religions *do* have distinct points of focus vis-à-vis science, the same can't be said of animism.

Animists can perceive themselves as allied with scientists "because both seek truth in the universe itself," B tells Jared (B, 138). Neither looks for truth "in books, revelations, or authorities," as do devotees of revealed religions (ibid., 136). Both put a premium on dealing with doubt and uncertainty in a systematic manner by collaboratively weighing theories against available evidence (McIntyre 2019). Animists may not read the message of events as contemporary scientists do. But scientific practices are rooted in the three gifts of wisdom, which is why B is comfortable stating that the gods write what they write not just in terms that animists understand but that also are readily accessible to your typical physicist, chemist, and biologist.[15]

How, then, does science work as an epistemic practice? On one general view, scientists aim to discover the causal laws that facilitate the workings of the universe. From this perspective, "the essential activity of scientists consists in the postulation and testing of theories, and then applying those theories to the phenomena in question," states David Carruthers (2002, 79; see also Nagel 1961 and Hempel 1965). On another view, scientists construct, elaborate on, and test models of cosmic and worldly phenomena to make the models themselves more accurate (Cartwright 1983 and Giere 1992). Either way, scientists are interested in explaining doings and happenings. They investigate phenomena and specify principles that shed light on how things are the way they are as well as how things would be were certain other things to be the case.

"Crucial to the activity of science, then, is the provision of theories and/or models to explain the events, processes, and regularities observed in nature," Carruthers continues. "Often these explanations are couched in terms of underlying mechanisms which have not been observed and may be difficult to observe; and sometimes they are given in terms of mechanisms which are unobservable" (2002, 79). Whatever the scientists' goal, theoretical accuracy, economy, consistency, and coherence are key. So are the abilities to collaborate with colleagues, make fruitful forecasts, and resolve discrepancies in the data.

It's no coincidence that these are precisely the sorts of competencies that engaging in both systematic and speculative tracking requires, which is why both Carruthers and Liebenberg stress that the cognitive and interactive skills exhibited by scientists are akin to those exhibited by subsistence hunters. Indeed, the only salient differences between the subsistence hunter and the scientist are reflective of technological and sociological factors, not intellectual ability. The latter might (but only might) have a broader knowledge base than the former, but the former is bound to understand *this place* and its inhabitants with greater subtlety and refinement.

How do these points of commonality between science and subsistence hunting apply to our capacity for awareness of the sacred? Although close observation is critically important for both, success depends on being able to make inferences from what's observed to what's unobserved and even unobservable but nevertheless quite real.

This, I think, is the key to understanding awareness of the sacred. It's not just a matter of seeing what we see, although this is critically important (B, 164). It's also a matter of being attuned to how what we see relates to real *unseens* and real *unseeables*. Expert readers of the message of events are able to spot pressure releases and spoor. They're also able to make good inferences about the animals, no longer present, who left them. And they grasp that their own tracks and the tracks of their quarry are connected even though this connection, quite real, is itself unobservable. How else could Grandfather state sincerely and accurately to Brown and Rick that their dinner was to be found at the base of the old pine? How else could *any* hunt—for food, for the solution to a mystery (ibid., 189), for the Higgs boson—possibly succeed, except perhaps by happenstance, which surely can't serve as the basis for a lifestyle that's worked for millions of years?[16]

And what about the common denominator that underlies the observed, the unobserved, and the unobservable? The land, *this place,* the very hand of god is the firmament, Brown states, for "the grand tapestry of life":

> To be aware is to understand the interwoven fabric of life, and, to understand an individual fiber, we may explore it through a track. It is then the track that expands the awareness, but so too the awareness expands the track, where all become one. When we pour ourselves into the track, part of us becomes that track, and we become the whole. Our tracks, like all tracks, move within the realm of creation, but so too does the realm of creation move within our tracks. There is no inner or outer dimension, no separation of self, just that which Grandfather called "oneness." To understand the track is to understand the animal and its relationship to the land. It is also to understand our own place in the natural world. (1999, 9–10; see also Brown 1988, 33)

All one thing yet still many, *ex plures uno,* within the web endlessly woven. None standing alone or isolated from the rest.

"Every hunt begins here," B says to Jared, patting the ground in front of them, "and is pursued into the domain of the gods" (B, 179). This opens us to a kind of experience Jared calls "oceanic," which puts us "in touch with the fountainhead of meaning and being" (ibid., 178). Take Altamira, Chauvet, and others caves that house Neolithic wall paintings. "These caves aren't art galleries or shamanistic temples," B asserts, "they're schools of the hunting arts—the equivalent of one of our museums of science and industry" (ibid., 183). Painters paid close attention to all sorts of important cues associated with the animals depicted, from their scat to the plants they fed on to what the hunter was likely to see most clearly when the animal was partially hidden by a rock outcropping or tall grass (Rosenberg 2012). Painters even expertly rendered the perceptual effects of animals in motion (Azéma and Rivère 2012).

Clearly, the connection the painters felt for the animals they hunted ran deep. The painters studied their subjects closely both as potential sources of food and as much more than food. "I'm talking about something like 'feeling tone,' " B continues. "These hunters obviously revered the animals they were painting—were in awe of them, idolized them the way people in our culture idolize movie stars and sports heroes. To paint them the way they did, they had to feel a joyous involvement and identification with the magnificent creatures they hunted" (B, 184).

There's one painting, however, that goes a step further: *The Sorcerer.* "It's conventionally interpreted as a shaman wearing a ritual mask, but you have to be pretty literal-minded (and not much of an anatomist) to see him this way. He has the antlers and body of a stag, the ears of a lion, the face of an owl, and the tail and genitals of a horse—and there's not the slightest indication that he's wearing a mask." What is most idiosyncratic about *The Sorcerer* is that the represented creature doesn't merely inhabit the plane on which he's painted. He looks out at and *takes notice* of us. "Look closely," he seems to say, "and you'll see man, horse, owl, lion, and stag" (ibid.). I am all these things, his look conveys . . . *and so are you* (MGY, 87).

Remembering How to Be Human

This place is the embodiment of a holy trinity—composed of self, people, and land—that's the subject of awareness of the sacred. It's also the basis for exceptional wealth, although Takers' optical contortions obfuscate this. Takers tend to describe Leaver culture in terms of *absence.* Lacking technology and material comforts, Leavers presumably in limited contact with Takers are fortunate if they're able to eke out a meager living. Lacking enlightenment, they show little interest in improving their lives. In denying themselves "the opportunities for wealth and luxury that we enjoy," they show limited interest in developing "the noble institutions of civilization" ("Talk about Wealth!"; see also Justice 2011, 475 and 479). Since some Leaver peoples engage (or once engaged) in such practices as infanticide and geronticide, they seem to lack respect for individual life and human dignity, too (Brooks 2013). So "it's easy [for Takers] to accept the idea that the Taker way is the way of wealth and the Leaver way is the way of poverty," Quinn states ("Talk about Wealth!").[17]

But recall from chapter 2 that, etymologically, *wealth* isn't synonymous with material affluence but with *wellness.* In terms of products, some Takers are fabulously wealthy. But in terms of "getting the things [we] desperately need *as human beings*," most Takers are "pathetically poor" (MI, 191).

We belong to the world. We became human by belonging to the world, by being manifestations of the sacred. From a Leaver perspective, states Nurit Bird-David, the capacity to read the message of events confirms that the world is part of a "cosmic economy of sharing" (1998, 122). Being members of human and more-than-human communities that appreciate this is critical to being well. Put succinctly, communal support is a necessary condition for living in a way that works. It provides among the most powerful checks against *wétiko* and zombification. This is because communal support is a function of what Eisler calls a *partnership system.*

Partnership Systems

Partnership systems, which Eisler contrasts with domination systems (also from chapter 2) are premised on mutual respect. They privilege relations based on "empathy, responsibility, and concern for human welfare and optimal human development," Eisler remarks (2007, 17). In stark contrast to domination systems, partnership systems are thus conducive to consensual and egalitarian social structures, are marked by low levels of abuse and violence, and are compatible with sexual equality and nonbinary gender identities.

Partnership systems needn't be predicated on charity or unconditional generosity.[18] "In Leaver societies, people look after each other for similar reasons that people in Taker societies take jobs and have careers," Quinn notes ("Talk about Wealth!"; see also BC, 12, and Q&A, 207). They do so to be fed, sheltered, clothed, and otherwise to live a satisfying life. Without financial support, Takers face hardship. Without communal support, Leavers face hardship. Yes, settler colonialism now routinely leads Leavers to face extreme hardship because they lack financial support, just as Takers suffer for want of communal support (Junger 2016). But we're talking here about primary modes of exchange. For Takers, one must prove that one is valuable—or that one has valuable connections—to partake of wealth. For Leavers, one must prove that one is detrimental—*really* detrimental—to one's community to be denied wealth. So Taker wealth, financial support, is hard to come by; Leaver wealth, communal support, is hard to lose.

Leaver wealth is thus a basis for that which is incredibly rare in Taker culture: *cradle-to-grave security* ("Talk about Wealth!"). Within systems that privilege communal support no one falls through the cracks, because there are no cracks to fall through. One is never left to fend for oneself. If one suffers, all suffer. In this regard, cradle-to-grave security is a renewable provision. It's in inexhaustible supply so long as a community is healthy.

Communal support is also "impossible to control for individual advantage," John Gowdy states. Because it's "shared and accessible to all," securing it doesn't even involve seeking fair compensation for good work (1998, xxiv). Good work is certainly admired among peoples the world over. The more individuals who see to the needs of their communities, the better off everyone is (MI, 181). But good work isn't necessarily required to get fed, clothed, sheltered—and, yes, even loved. This means that no one is beholden to others for their survival or wellbeing. As Jean-Jacques Rousseau famously puts it in *The Social Contract,* no one is so well off that they can buy another or so badly off that they must sell themselves.

"Taker wealth can be put under lock and key, but Leaver wealth can't," Quinn hereby asserts. As a result, "Taker wealth is inherently divisive." It's destructive of communities and socioeconomic equality, which is just as we should expect in domination systems.[19] "Leaver wealth, by contrast, is not divisive but inherently unitive" ("Talk about Wealth!"). As we'll see in the next chapter, it's at the very heart of kincentric relations.

Living Tribally

Tribal life is to humans as hive life is to bees. It's "a distinctly human social organization," Quinn states ("Dialogue on *Beyond Civilization*"). It has persisted because it's "*evolutionarily stable,* meaning not that it [is] perfect but that hundreds of thousands of years of natural selection—on a social level—was unable to produce an organization that [has] worked better" either for the planet or for people (WS, 119). This doesn't make it the one right way to live, mind you (I, 167). But that it hasn't disappeared, particularly in the face of widespread genocidal policies and practices, indicates just how valuable it is to Leaver peoples (BD, 41).[20]

Tribes are archetypical partnership systems. As such, they're inimical to what Eisler calls *hierarchies of domination* within both family structures—including with respect to the treatment of children—and across communities. With respect to sex and gender relations, it's not that heteropatriarchy is nowhere to be found among tribal peoples. Rather, Kyle Whyte remarks, available evidence, including stories and shared memories, suggests that his Potawatomi ancestors would have had no experience with heteropatriarchal exploitation and oppression, which "are taken for granted in the U.S. as timeless norms" (2018b, 230). His considerations aren't isolated. Among numerous tribal peoples, women, men, and two-spirit persons traditionally enjoyed a great degree of autonomy and decision-making power with respect to their life choices (Leacock 1998, Bird 1999, and Dyble et al. 2015). Where this has eroded, it's largely (if not wholly) a result of colonization.[21]

Eisler suggests that what she calls *hierarchies of actualization*—whereby leaders "facilitate, inspire, and empower rather than control and disempower" (2007, 31)—are tolerated in partnership systems. Comparably, while tribal societies have leaders, leadership is often more symbolic than substantive. Whatever authority leaders have is earned rather than seized or imposed. Leaders lead by example rather than by fiat, and the privilege of leadership must be continually renewed (BC, 73).[22] Among the Anishinaabe, for example, leadership traditionally changed (including among the sexes) based on the season, which correlated with making seasonal rounds. And however renewal occurs among tribal peoples whose forms of traditional leadership persist, it depends principally on leaders exhibiting a commitment to nurturing self-determination, fostering communal wellbeing, and enriching cultural traditions (Cajete 2000, 90). No wonder Marshall Sahlins urges us to alter our perspective from regarding Leavers as *poor* to instead regarding them as *free* (1972, 14).

Aren't there free riders in tribal societies? Surely, but what of it? The satisfaction embodied by living tribally derives from facilitating community success. Perpetuating one's community is the only way to keep getting what one wants personally. This seems like a strong incentive not to do too much of those things that would adversely affect the community's vitality. Moreover, if making a living is connected to one's wider social life, as is typical in tribes, it's likely to be far less of a chore to engage in productive activities (Liedloff 1977, 17, Gowdy 1998, xxi, and Davis 2009, 173f.). There are bound to be fewer free riders if making a living isn't such a grind.

Besides, why should free riders be all that worrisome anyway so long as everyone is taken care of and community integrity isn't at risk? Concern about free riders assumes that one should distrust the members of one's community by default—that everyone must somehow prove their worthiness before they get fed, clothed, and sheltered. This, of course, is a Taker view, not a Leaver view.

No wonder that Benjamin Franklin states (so, ahem, eloquently) in his papers that "Happiness is more generally and equally diffus'd among

Savages than in our civiliz'd Societies. No European who has tasted Savage Life can afterwards bear to live in our Societies" (1973, 308). Colonial-era essayist Michel Guillaume Jean de Crévecoeur comments that "There must be in the Indians' social bond something singularly captivating, and far superior to be boasted of among us; for thousands of Europeans are Indians, and we have no examples of even one of those Aborigines having from choice become Europeans." In order to prevent more Europeans from being tempted by the allure of Aboriginal life, it's best, de Crévecoeur continues, "to keep ourselves busy tilling the earth" (1981, 105 and 106, respectively). And Cadwallader Colden, a short-lived governor of colonial New York, relays that during prisoner exchanges between settlers and Native peoples that settlers commonly were unmoved by pleas from their loved ones to leave them with their erstwhile captors. After receiving a taste of "the most perfect freedom, the ease of living, the absence of those cares and corroding solicitudes which so often prevail with us," loved ones sometimes had to be bound hand and foot to prevent their escape back to Native villages (cited in Axtell 1985, 327). Jensen provides a number of other stories like these (2006a, 245ff.).

Closer to Nature?

Among the common explanations for why Takers enact a story that doesn't work is that we have become alienated from nature in our drive to control, conquer, and master it. Totalitarian agriculture, for example, exemplifies an unnatural way to live. What we need to do is to reconnect with nature, live in harmony with it, respect its balance, and so forth. This is what tribal peoples do, this story goes. It's why tribes work.

Yet that Takers commonly see tribal peoples this way represents little more than an updated version of the Noble Savage Theory, Ishmael asserts. Here's Alan's take on this theory: "It's the idea that people living close to nature tend to be noble. It's seeing all those sunsets that does it. You can't watch a sunset and then go off and set fire to your neighbor's tepee. Living close to nature is wonderful for your mental health" (I, 147). Pure bunk, Quinn insists. Living "close to nature," to some sort of pristine world untouched by humans, has absolutely nothing to do with why living tribally works. In equal measure, claiming that Takers are "alienated from nature" makes no sense. We can't be closer to or alienated from that which doesn't exist (B, 153, P, 53f., and Q&A, 62).

You read that right. Nature is a "figment of the Romantic imagination, and a very insidious figment at that," Quinn remarks (P, 53; see also Cronon 1996). Here's B's take:

> Nature is a phantom that sprang entirely from the Great Forgetting, which, after all, is precisely a forgetting of the fact that we are exactly as much a part of the processes and phenomena of the world as any other creature, and if there were such a thing as nature, we would be as much a part of it as squirrels or squids or mosquitoes or daffodils. We are *unable* to alienate ourselves from nature or to "live against" it. We can no more live against nature than we can live against gravity. On the contrary, what we're seeing here more and more clearly is that the processes and phenomena of the world are working on us in exactly the same way that they work on all other creatures. Our lifestyle is evolutionarily unstable—and is therefore in the process of eliminating itself in the perfectly ordinary way. (B, 180–81; see also IS, 110f., and Harvey 2019, 75)

Just as there's no environment *out there*, there's no nature to be in harmony or disharmony with (WS, 79, and Q&A, 438)—or, for that matter, to be at the "end of" in this technocratic age of ours (McKibben 2006).[23] Nor is totalitarian agriculture unnatural. It's an unsustainable strategy for acquiring food (Q&A, 210).[24]

There *is* a community of life. It animates *this place*. But we're just as much a part of it as is every species. As a product of evolutionary development, the living community is in dynamic tension, as we covered in the previous chapter. Again, every species evolves because of continual "disturbances" (WS, 27) and perturbations in their habitats and genetic structures. We can annihilate species. Takers are doing it to our own and countless others. But this has nothing to do with some sort of imbalance. It has to do instead with enacting a story that doesn't work and can't be made to work, full stop.

By all means, get outdoors more frequently. It can do the body good, moreover, to escape what Paul Eppinger calls the overwhelming "human-ness" of places like Philadelphia, where I currently live. Maybe he's right that the experience of being in less built-up spaces "is a much more valid lesson in humanity than being in a city (Eppinger and Eppinger

1994, 48). I find it hard to disagree with Brown that one form of bad medicine is being unable to shed our "city personalities" when we're in spaces that aren't overwhelmingly human (1978, 35). And Mark Boyle contends that living in a city "disables your ways of reading the signs" provided by other-than-human members of the community of life: of hearing and understanding what they have to tell us (2010, 105).

Whatever the case may be, B has no problem with people who advocate getting out of doors. "That's fine, of course—so long as they don't insist that sitting in a forest glade is 'closer to nature' than sitting in a movie theater" (B, 181).

Debuffering Ourselves

What, finally, about phonetic writing? Does it only reinforce the overwhelmingly human focus of Taker culture? According to John Zerzan, the emergence and perpetuation of symbolic culture involves the "inherent will to manipulate and control" (1994, 27). The use of formal writing and counting systems are effectively forms of domestication. Even art and ritual can be "considered as a regression from the state in which all shared a consciousness we would now classify as extrasensory" (ibid., 26). So there's no way to recast the spell we're under "without rejecting the symbolic and its estranged world" (2002, 4).

Abram suggests, though, that one of the tasks of writers like himself "is that of *taking up* the written word, with all its potency, and patiently, carefully, writing language back into the land. Our craft is that of releasing the budded, earthly speech of the things themselves" (1996, 273). Words needn't be just stepping stones to show us where other human minds have been. They can be means to *debuffer* ourselves: to transfer the frame and focus of our eyes from the printed page back into the world it ostensibly represents.

Paul Kingsnorth makes a similar case. There's nothing sacrosanct about the written word. But there are means of conveyance that facilitate:

> seeing and communicating in ways that Machine [i.e., Taker] culture downplays and ridicules, but which every traditional society before modernity's advent understood and worked with. That means myth, religion, practical expertise founded upon physical work, rooted imagery, holistic conceptions of life,

> communication with non-human beings, poetry, complexity, questions that do not have answers, questions which are not questions at all. (2019)

I'm not primarily concerned about persuading you that this book isn't a performative contradiction. I'm more interested in the prospect that the very scratches and scrawls I here make offer an invitation to reawaken our sensibilities to the mode of reading the signs from which they derive. In due course and in step with wider decolonizing practices, let the spell of the word be recast as the spell of the sensuous.

For what it's worth, note, too, that the word *book* derives from *beech*, "in language after language," Richard Powers notes. "At least one native language of the American West uses the same word for *footprint* and *understanding*" (2018, 116 and 134, respectively). I wonder if finding more connections like these offers an opening to more fully reinhabit our own bodies and lives.

Chapter 6

Vitalizing a People, Becoming a Person

Seeds of Reclamation and Resistance

At age fourteen, I moved with my family from a small town in western Pennsylvania to a small city in Upstate New York. The experience broke me. I was removed from a tight-knit, largely self-contained community and transported to a place that, while beautiful, remains alien territory to this day. I never successfully adapted or found a way to belong. I'm not sure that I wanted to belong even if I could have, but being a permanent outsider took its toll.

Three decades hence, I think I've pretty much come to terms with the move, but it's not an experience from which recovery is possible, at least not for me. I lost the best part of myself, although until quite recently I didn't fully understand this. Nor did I understand why I made certain decisions in the immediate aftermath of the move to try to cope.

Growing up, my best friend David and I had free rein to explore the town from which I moved and its surroundings. No helicopter parenting for us. We often headed to the lake on the town's edge, lined with copses of cattails inhabited by vocal bullfrogs. Then there was the old railroad bed that lay beyond, running parallel to a small, meandering river. The bed's rails and ties had long since been removed, and in the spring its edges were replete with wild strawberries, wild carrots, and (a personal favorite) yellow wood sorrel, also known as sourgrass. But no location transfixed us as much as the creek—pronounced *crick*—just down the hill from our respective houses. We spent countless hours at the creek year-round, especially a section adjacent to a small bridge along a gravel road. Crayfish hid themselves in the rocky shallows, while water bugs skittered over the surface of the pool that formed just below the bridge.

The south bank was lined with shade trees and berry bushes. We could follow the creek upstream into expansive woodlands and downstream through town. To us, it was as close to perfection as a place could get.

No doubt, my sense of place was rudimentary compared to that of the area's original human inhabitants. Nor could I see that my relationship with the land was made possible—literally—by the territorial dispossession of said inhabitants (Whyte 2018e).[1] Moreover, had I lived out my young adulthood there, the town probably would have come to feel confining. Our outdoor ventures likely would have ceased once David and I faced the typical demands associated with assuming our proper places in Taker culture. But because my abiding connection to that place was involuntarily severed, its resounding specialness crystallized in my mind. I felt the loss acutely and overwhelmingly. Writing these words, I realize I still do.

Although I didn't recognize it at the time, I effectively had two religions when I was growing up. Formulaically, I was a Christian, a Methodist if you're picky. Basically, this meant I spent my childhood being dragged to church and maintained a reflexive belief in, if a hazy understanding of, Scripture. Effulgently, though, I was an *animist.* I was enraptured by what "was once a universal religion on this planet," B tells Jared (B, 132).[2] "It was humanity's first religion and its only universal religion," Quinn remarks to Elaine, "found wherever humans were found, in place for tens of thousands of years. Christian missionaries encountered it wherever they went, and piously set about destroying it" (WS, 195).[3]

My Christianity was never in a position to destroy my animism. I don't see that it could have had it tried. But once I was parted from the anchors of my animism in that little corner of western Pennsylvania, my first inclination was to cling to my Christianity like a drowning man clings to a life preserver. In my first couple of years in Upstate New York, I read the Bible from cover to cover. I tried to like church. I prayed hard and often for deliverance and blamed my penchant for sinfulness for not receiving it . . . that is, until I finally concluded around age seventeen that God just didn't care, if God was there. Much like Quinn, I didn't bother with questioning God's existence. What mattered was that he couldn't possibly be concerned about me, so I stopped concerning myself with him.

For years, I simply assumed that I didn't have a spiritual bone in my body. Not atheist, not agnostic, just devoid of interest in the whole thing. But then a few short years ago, not coincidentally after I got sober, something strange happened. As ridiculous as it may sound (to Takers, at least), the creek began calling to me, beckoning me back. When I finally was able to pay a visit, I was petrified that the calls I'd received were mere delusions and that I'd be greeted as an interloper. I also feared that the creek might no longer be ecologically intact. Yet while houses on the north bank did now encroach, the place remained healthy, serene, familiar, and inviting. My animism, long dormant, reemerged.

Of course, when I was younger I didn't have the necessary conceptual apparatus to understand myself as an animist. Now that I do, I dislike the term, in part because of its etymology. Edward Tylor coined it in 1871 in the process of attempting to categorize testimony about Indigenous cultures provided by missionaries and explorers. I doubt you're surprised that the testimony portrayed the peoples whose practices were being categorized "as rather silly and childlike," states Quinn (Q&A, 715; see also ibid., 183). For Tylor's informers, animism represented a retrograde form of "spirit worship as opposed to the presumably more advanced worship of gods or God. In other words (as it's imagined), these poor, benighted savages [had] the silly idea that every tree and bush and rock 'has a spirit in it'" (P, 154–55). Animism was, and often still is, hereby treated "as a crude and simpleminded precursor of religion the way that chemists are aware of alchemy as a crude and simpleminded precursor of chemistry" (B, 132; see also WS, 196).

This way of understanding animism bears no resemblance to what I experience in relation to the creek and the land surrounding it. Nor, dare I say, does it come anywhere close to capturing Quinn's experience at Gethsemani (P, 167f.) or, for that matter, the myriad ways of knowing and being expressed and exhibited by Leaver peoples the world over (Cajete 2000, 21). Quinn's most basic statement about animism is deceptively simple. "Anyone who views the world as a sacred place (and humans as worthy of a place in a sacred place) is an animist," he avers (Q&A, 594; see also B, 189, and WS, 196). Humans belong to such a world because we ourselves are sacred (BD, 22). "Not in a special way, not *more* sacred than anything else, but merely *as* sacred as anything else—as sacred as bison or salmon or crows or crickets or bears or sunflowers" (WS, 197). Indeed, everything that lives is sacred, "the carrot no less than the cow. If there is any single doctrine that might win universal agreement among animists, I think it would be this, that the gods love everything that lives and have no favorites" (P, 165; see also Q&A, 171, and WS, 164f.). This is why, recall from chapter 4, "the gods lavish care without stint on every thing" (B, 161). It's why not a single organism is "made with any less care than any other" (ibid.).

Despite himself regarding animism as "irrelevantly named" (Q&A, 183), an "invention" that's "nothing more than a fabrication that we outsiders find satisfactory" (personal communication, September 2015) to designate a wide array of ways to live that reflect his basic statement, Quinn chooses to retain the term. Charles and Shirin are self-avowed "animist missionaries" (B, 145), which is how Quinn sees himself. "In effect," he remarks, "I have redefined animism for the Taker world, much in the way that Paul redefined Christianity for the Roman world. Paul didn't think he was falsifying it, he felt he was reseeing it in a way that would reveal its profoundest truths. No one (to my knowledge) has ever described the animist vision as I've done in *The Story of B*. Animists among Leaver people have no need to do such a thing" (Q&A, 383). The point here isn't to provide Takers with "spiritual candy" (ibid., 152). As always, he's focused on changing Takers' minds, averting the flow of our cultural vision away from catastrophe.

Quinn is thus adamant that while Leavers offer "authentic" forms of animism, "they haven't been given some ultimately authoritative 'word' " on it (Q&A, 183). Fair enough. It wouldn't do, though, to overlook recent work specifically by Indigenous philosophers, particularly from North America, that adds breadth, depth, and nuance to Quinn's considerations. They also highlight the necessity of decolonization with far greater poignancy.

I don't take Indigenous philosophers from North America somehow to speak for Leaver peoples the world over, mind you. I draw on their work because of their sustained efforts over the past several decades to develop what Thomas Norton-Smith calls a *rational reconstruction* "of the original Native world vision" (2010, 9) by drawing on linguistic studies, ethnographies, anthropological observations, interpretive narratives, and the work of fellow scholars. This enterprise isn't without obstacles. Indigenous philosophers must cut through layers of stereotypical portrayals. They also must contend with the fact that several generations of elders, who would typically safeguard their traditions and speak the native language, were taken from their homes and spirited away to boarding schools in which their connections to their people's lands and ways were subject to systematic eradication. Nevertheless, the work of Indigenous philosophers is yielding insights that can benefit an animist missionary like Quinn and, far more importantly, the resurgence of and resistance to colonization by their own peoples.

In what follows, I first offer my own basic statement about the character of *sacredness,* or *the sacred.* You'll see the influence of Indigenous philosophers straightaway. The world is a sacred place, Quinn stresses, and we humans are worthy of it; we too are sacred. This isn't a matter of belief about the planet or people (as belief is commonly understood by Takers). Nor does it have anything to do with faith. It's about enacting a story that works. For Indigenous people, enacting such a story is a defining feature not just of their peoplehood—of what makes them the people they are—but also of their personhood—of what gives each of them a specifiable place among their people.

This way of understanding the sacred supports *kincentrism,* a kinship-based orientation specifically toward proximate members of the living community (Salmón 2000, Martinez 2018, and Reo 2019). According to this orientation, our place in the order of things is defined and maintained by exhibiting respect for the specific beings—both human and other-than-human—with whom we share the land and routinely interact. We have a responsibility to see to the wellbeing of our kin, our shared community, including the land itself. For Takers, this must include striving as best we can to make amends for our continued complicity in colonization. This is a critical component of the threefold struggle, since we have no hope of relating responsibly to any place the people of our culture stole and continue to occupy (Red Nation 2021, 28).

Lastly, just as Indigenous lands are not ours to do with as we will, not all lessons that Indigenous peoples teach are for Takers. Leavers don't exist to help Takers figure out how to correct our own mistakes and the mistakes of our cultural forebears any more than Ishmael exists for Alan's edification. Yes, the people of our culture have much to learn, and Cain must stop murdering Abel. But Cain also must acknowledge, respect, and, with permission, support the ways in which Abel engages in acts of resistance all his own. His sovereignty—*Native* sovereignty—matters. Its pursuit is also a powerful and poignant way to venerate the sacred.

Sacredness

Does it make sense to presume, as Norton-Smith does, that there's such a thing as an original Native world vision? Doesn't this invite overlooking the sheer diversity of ways of knowing and being exhibited by Indigenous peoples? Perhaps trying to identify a single, comprehensive Native vision that can inform our understanding of animism is folly, too.

Lorraine Brundige and Douglas Rabb contend that looking for common ground of this sort among Native visions "is just not important—given the primacy of place in these various worldviews" (1997, 81). This makes sense, but other Indigenous philosophers still side with Norton-Smith. Scott Pratt (2002) proposes that *indigenous culture* (the lowercase is his), to be distinguished from *colonial culture,* reflects a metalevel viewpoint or generalizable philosophical framework regarding the order of things and our place in it that's shared by any number of Native peoples. More pointedly, Shay Welch contends that "the foundational principles of Native philosophy are broadly shared, as is the linguistic syntax and structure, which permits of a broad ideology through which to analyze the world—or more appropriately, to participate in the world and our relationships" (2013, 206; see also Welch 2017, 371ff.).[4] Neither Pratt nor Welch seeks to elide important microlevel differences among peoples. Nor does either scholar reject the primacy of place. But that what works in one place may not work in another place doesn't invalidate the generalizable value of pursuing *what works* where one lives.

The Basic Statement

In general terms, that which is sacred is typically associated with the divine, serves a specific religious or ritualistic function, and is deserving of veneration or reverence. It's of the highest meaning and value to its identifiers. And because there's no one right way to live for Leavers, we should expect that the beings, events, and processes that some peoples regard as sacred—or of preeminent sacredness—aren't necessarily so to other peoples. Again, place matters. So let me suggest this as a basic statement about the sacred: *it's that which defines, vitalizes, and sustains a people.*

This statement may seems rather mundane. But Dennis Martinez and his colleagues propose that for Native peoples the divine "is something that's a verb; it's active, it's a cocreative process" that a people has "a right and obligation to participate in on a moment-to-moment basis through our actions, thoughts, and behaviors. That seems to be a very different worldview from the Eurocentric perspective of a monotheistic Divinity, of a single God that is a noun, an authority, a thing that is a transcendent entity separate from our world" (2008, 108–109). So the divine isn't necessarily an entity that resides beyond the world or the cosmos. The divine operates on, in, and through us; it's manifest by our doings and undergoings. And, as noted in chapter 4, it's on clearest display with respect to the development and perpetuation of life, which is always "*in process,*" states B, "*on the way*" (B, 161; see also TA, 71 and 85).

The sacred isn't hereby a conduit to something otherworldly. The god or gods are *right here* (P, 181, and TA, 14). They're the animating fire of the living community that embodies *this place*. This is where the gods write what they write—not in books or on clay tablets or papyrus (BD, 43) but in topographies and ecosystems, "in galaxies and star systems and planets and oceans and forests and whales and birds and gnats" (B, 135), and, of course, in humans. The life of *this place,* of every place, is sacred—perhaps not to everyone, but to someone (H, 359; see also Silko 1997, 94f.). Wherever life is—and, more generally, wherever kin are—found, that place is infused with the divine.

So the gods aren't transcendent. Nor are they supreme beings. They're not all-powerful or invulnerable. Indeed, the gods can die, just as peoples and places can be extirpated (P, 141f.).[5] While the cosmological and terrestrial processes that they animate (or that animate them) are inexorable, for these processes to support the health of a specifiable place, the people of that place bear certain responsibilities. As Martinez et al. (2008) suggest, people's behaviors must support the perpetuation and vivacity of the living community that embodies that place. This, I think, is what it means to venerate the sacred. Defining, vitalizing, and sustaining a people doesn't just happen. It takes dedication, competence, and care.

"Religion Is, in Reality, Living"

What has come to be called animism is thus perhaps more aptly simply called *tradition,* Linda Hogan remarks (2013; see also P, 166, and Q&A, 533). There's no such thing as an "animist 'in general' " (Stengers 2012, 9). But we can look for key points of intersection among traditions and try to identify oft-repeated themes. There are more than 1,200 First Nations in North America alone, "each with its own culture, language, and spiritual traditions," Maureen Smith notes (2002, 117). We're looking, though, for foundational principles (Welch), a generalizable philosophical framework (Pratt), "a way of looking at the world" (B, 148), so perhaps better than comprehensiveness in this case is representativeness.

Additionally, venerating the sacred is ultimately a pragmatic activity. "In fact," Rebecca Adamson asserts, "none of the native languages [of North America] have words or terms synonymous with *religion*. The closest expression of belief translates to the way you live" (2008, 35; emphasis mine). Jack Forbes says the same. "Religion is, in reality, living. Our religion is not what we profess or what we say or what we proclaim; our religion is what we do, what we desire, what we seek, what we dream about, what we fantasize, what we think—all of these things—twenty-four hours a day. One's religion, then, is one's life, not merely the ideal life but the life as it is actually lived" (2008, 11).

Understood in this way, religion isn't a matter of faith or belief, at least not in the sense that Takers usually understand these things (Mohawk 2008, 134). As Quinn tells Elaine, "Believing in things that may not exist—or disbelieving in things that may exist—is a peculiarity of your culture, not a universal human activity. Because it's universal among you, you assume it's universal among humans in general" (WS, 49). This is an instance of what Quinn calls the "Cultural Fallacy" (BC, 47).

Take the gods, for example. Quinn prefers to think of the universe as peopled by gods. But this doesn't mean that he *believes* that gods people the universe (WS, 51, and Q&A, 618). This may strike you as nonsensical. Isn't preferring to think something the same as believing it? No, at least not in this case. "Beliefs are about things that are either factual or not," Quinn states (Q&A, 112). But to say that the universe is peopled by gods is the expression of a worldview that reflects a "value system" (ibid.) very different than that which is ambient in Taker culture.[6]

Ultimately, what matters is one's worldview—the story one enacts. Does it work for the planet and for people to enact a story in which the universe is populated by gods who are competent at what they do (BD, 39, I, 241, and WS, 61), who are so articulate that their workings are discernible for those with eyes that see, and who lavish care without stint on every thing? Are ecological, social, and personal wellbeing facilitated by a vision according to which the world is a sacred place and we humans are worthy of it? Give it some thought.

What Makes a People

A people is a plurality of persons who compose a nation, ethnic group, tribe, or some other means of affiliation or alliance of this sort. But what's a person?

Persons

Gary Varner takes a prototypical approach to how Takers conceptualize personhood. Personhood, he states, is denoted "by deciding what specific capacities or properties are relevant to the question of how to treat the individual, and then asking whether or not the individual has those capacities or properties" (2012, 7). The preeminent capacity that Varner takes to be required for personhood is *autonoetic consciousness,* "conscious awareness of one's past, present, and future" (ibid., 160). Autonoetic consciousness permits one to have a biographical sense of self, which entails having concepts of selfhood, birth (or at least some kind of origin), death (or at least some kind of end to a type of existence), and personality (that is, character-shaping experiences). Only humans have autonoetic consciousness, Varner asserts, so only humans can be persons (ibid., 181).[7] Some animals may be conscious in a more restricted sense. If so, they count as near-persons. Other animals are merely sentient, capable of feeling pain but lacking "any form of consciousness that is relevantly similar to normal humans' biographical sense of self" (ibid., 134). Still others aren't even sentient; they presumably have no more consciousness than, say, plants.

Persons have "special moral significance" (ibid.) that near-persons and nonpersons don't, Varner contends. Persons are deserving of a level of respect that lesser beings aren't. What counts as poor treatment of persons—exploitation, abuse, and the like—doesn't necessarily count as poor treatment of near-persons and nonpersons, presumably because persons can suffer or countenance being subject to disrespect in ways that lesser beings can't.

You can see how this understanding of personhood reflects the proposition that the world is made for us. But what if we instead prefer to think that we're made for the world? This helps to shift our focus, or mine at least, away from thinking of personhood in terms of individuals' capacities and toward how we interact with fellow members of the living community. If we're made for the world, then we must fit here. We belong—somewhere—just as every member of the living community belongs. From this perspective, it makes sense to regard personhood as a function of how we relate to each other. This suggests that respecting others is an *indicator* of personhood rather than a consequence. We're persons not because of the beings we are but because of what we do. Processes over properties; verbs over nouns.

Let's go a step further. Let's think of ourselves as being who we are *because* of what we do and where we do it. This means that we're constituted by our interactions with others in specific contexts. Belonging to the living community—interacting with others, including through feeding and being fed upon—is a matter of both being shaped by it and shaping it in turn (BD, 23f.). This doesn't mean we can't regard ourselves as individuals. There are situations when it works to do so. But focusing on individuality doesn't always work. Personal, social, and ecological wellbeing aren't always well served by it.

Animists recognize and appreciate that life is always lived in relationship with others (Harvey 2006, xi; see also Bird-David 1999, 73). One's very existence depends on shaping and being shaped, so how one comports oneself makes a difference in the composition and function of one's place and the living community that composes it. Moreover, those with eyes that see are well aware that humans aren't the only beings who exhibit respect for those with whom they interact. This means that *the world is full of persons, only some of whom are human* (ibid.). To be an animist, then, is to be devoted to getting to know others' personalities, needs, and interests in order to build trust, empathy, and space for mutual consent and respect (Pratt 2006, 5, and Burkhart 2018, 72ff.). It's to understand and appreciate the role we together can play in enacting a story that works.[8]

This isn't to say that the identification of others as persons is easy. Jean Piaget (1929 and 1954) has it exactly backward when he suggests that animism—denoted according to him by the assumption that every event is the result of a deliberate act—is a standard childhood phase that's outgrown through further and fuller cognitive development. You can see Tylor's influence here. As Graham Harvey notes by way of contrast:

> This animism (minimally understood as the recognition of personhood in a range of human and other-than-human persons) is far from innate and instinctual. It is found more easily among elders who have thought about it than among children who still need to be taught how to do it. In learning to recognize personhood, animists are intended, by those who teach them (by whatever means) to become better, more respectful persons. That is, humans might become increasingly animist . . . as throughout life they learn how to act more respectfully (carefully and constructively) towards other persons. (2006, 18; see also TA, 58)

Note here Harvey's parenthetical reference to the need for careful and constructive engagement with other persons. Respect might entail veneration, but this isn't always so. There are numerous members of the living community—including not just deadly organisms but also, perhaps, "yoo-hoos," "wild things," and "witches"—who are "not to be trifled with," save for those armed with the courage and discretion to engage in a battle for their lives (H, 57ff., 289ff., and 384ff.; see also TA, 75f., and Harvey 2019, 76).[9] For the most part, we do well to be cautious of them and maintain a *respectful distance.*[10]

Note also that personhood isn't ours to confer but instead to discern. This is because, for animists, humans don't hold some preferred ontological status that would enable us to confer personhood even if we wanted to do so.[11] "Humans don't even have the moral authority to extend ethics to the land community," Martinez et al. remark. "We don't have the right to extend anything. What we have the right to do is to make our case, as human beings, to the natural world" (2008, 89). While individuals within species—often elders—may wield great power, maintain prestige, or exhibit exceptional wisdom, no species corners the market on these traits.

Note, finally, that no being is born a person or automatically earns this status. It must be gained and can be lost. Some beings might go a lifetime without ever achieving it. For we become persons and sustain our personhood "by virtue of [our] relationships with and obligations to other persons," Norton-Smith states (2010, 77). This involves "participation in certain forms of social practices and performances" (ibid., 82) whereby we affirm and carry out our responsibility to facilitate personal, social, and ecological wellbeing. Humans have our responsibilities. Others of the living community do as well. So do ancestors, places, physical forces, the cardinal directions, and the sun and other celestial entities. All "are members of the American Indian familial community, and so are persons" (ibid., 77). What constitutes a people is expansive.

Place

In retrospect, my attempt to deal with my loss of place in the wake of the move by fully embracing Christianity was almost certain to fail. Yes, I turned for help to a being who didn't (or couldn't) care about me. There's that. But I could have continued to blame myself for this. A bigger obstacle was trying to fill my abiding (if attenuated) connection to a *here* with earnest concern about a *then* (Deloria 1973, 73ff., and Martin 1992). My focus on the wonders of a little corner of western Pennsylvania had to shift to something far less tangible: a singular event that presumably occurred some two thousand years ago, the crucifixion and resurrection of Christ. More generally, the revelations disclosed by Jesus and his followers somehow had to substitute for my ventures with David. Sacredness had to transform for me. It had to go from being an ongoing process of learning the personalities and attending to the needs and interests of the myriad beings with whom David and I routinely engaged in and around our town to being encapsulated by words inscribed once and for all in a text whose meaning was mediated by ecclesiastical authorities. Finding a community of fellow worshipers at my new church, now Presbyterian (my parents aren't particularly doctrinaire), might have helped. But there was no one. I was on my own. For all intents and purposes, I was *kinless.*

This profoundly altered me. How couldn't it? I wasn't the person I'd been—or the *quasi*-person, really, which is all any Taker can hope to achieve—in western Pennsylvania. And I didn't like this new me. In fact, I *loathed* the new me, which certainly helps me to understand the appeal of routinely drinking myself into oblivion. This, after all, was where I first learned to do so at age fifteen.

While I suppose my newfound self-loathing wasn't a given post-move, being a new me surely was. I couldn't be the (quasi-)person I'd been before because I was no longer connected in the same way with the place that made me . . . *me.* That's the thing. Persons are really *place-persons* (Pratt 2006, 7, and Norton-Smith 2010, 152f.). For Takers, this means that our abuse of the land, whether direct or indirect, and the peoples from whom our ancestors stole it compromises our personhood. For Leavers, this means maintaining spiritual and communal ties with the land through social practices and performances that serve to define, vitalize, and sustain them as peoples even if they've been displaced (Harjo 2019).

These social practices and performances are aided by the land itself being agential. It's an active participant in the lives of a people, particularly when the land and the people have developed deep and abiding relations of care (McKenna and Pratt 2014, 283). So the land, *this place,* isn't really an *it* at all (Kimmerer 2013, 57). We've already seen an example of this in the story of Cain and Abel in chapter 3. But the picture of the Land/God we get in Genesis is vitiated, stripped of fecundity. We get commandments and covenants, which is fitting for peoples habituated to domination systems. But for peoples of partnership systems, the land is instead a parent, a teacher, a story maker, an identity generator, a responsibility conferrer, a community organizer—in a word, *sacred* (Kimmerer 2013, 337ff., and Grignon and Kimmerer 2017, 68).

"How do we show our children love?" Kimmerer asks. "Each in our own way by a shower of gifts and a heavy rain of lessons" (ibid., 122). Each of us is alive and well (or as well as we can be) only because we've been nurtured. The original, abiding source of all nurturing is the land. A nurturing land—a land that's healthy and well tended—offers strength, shows patience, permits growth and individuation, and corrects inevitable mistakes. No, it can't provide "for all in every season," Quinn notes (TA, 7). Life has its limits. But the gifts and lessons it does provide, adds Kimmerer, are "far greater than I have the ability to reciprocate. . . . All I know to do is to leave another gift" for current and future inhabitants of *this place*, "those next unknowns who will live here" (2013, 70; see also Reo and Whyte 2012, 6f.).

Beyond partnership *simpliciter*, this is a kinship model of the land, which Quinn shares (B, 182 and 324). It involves what Brian Burkhart calls an "intimate knowing relationship" (2018, 72) among all parties—or, given the vagaries of Indigenous displacement and relocation, the perpetuation of this relationship in living memories, social identities, philosophies, and sources of heritage bound up with what Dian Million calls "felt knowledges" (2013, 65f.). To enact a story in accordance with this model is to accept that the land "grows you up, teaches you, misses you, and calls to you," Plumwood remarks (2007, 30; see also Basso 1996, 38). "The land loves us back," Kimmerer asserts. "She loves us with beans and tomatoes, with roasting ears and blackberries and birdsongs. . . . She provides for us and teaches us to provide for ourselves. That's what a good mother does" (2013, 122). And a well-nurtured child loves and cares for her mother in return. This creates a cycle of reciprocation that works, plain and simple.[12] "Knowing that you love the earth changes you, activates you to defend and protect and celebrate. But when you feel that the earth loves you in return, that feeling transforms the relationship from a one way street to a sacred bond" (ibid., 124–25).

This bond, this "*sensing* of place" (Norton-Smith 2010, 143), isn't transportable in the way that Christianity or other of the Taker religions are. To be removed from one's land, one's community, one's kin is to be stripped of the context that permits one to live one's religion to the fullest. "Context is therefore all-important for both practice and the understanding of reality," states Norton-Smith. "The places where revelations were experienced were remembered and set aside as locations where, through rituals and ceremonials, the people could once again communicate with the spirits. . . . It was not what people believed to be true that was important but what they experienced as true" (ibid., 66–67).[13]

Speaking decades ago in opposition to the construction of an oil pipeline in what at the time was called Canada's Northwest Territories, Richard Nerysoo made the point emphatically. "To the Indian people our land is really our life. Without our land we cannot—we could no longer exist as people" (cited in O'Malley 1976, 53). Notice: Nerysoo didn't say that he and fellow community members would no longer be *a* people, although this may be so. He implied that the integrity of the land is necessary for the integrity of the self (Brundige and Rabb 1997, 84).

Performance

The gods don't need our prayers or praise or adoration, "and we can't buy their patronage with such things" (P, 141). Yes, the gods lavish care on every thing without stint. But Quinn is never disappointed by them because he has no illusion that he or his kind is somehow favored "over viruses, sharks, wildcats, mosquitos, or any other life form" (ibid., 162). Nor is he or his kind favored any less than these beings.

Prayer and song, ceremony and ritual are part of the traditions of Indigenous peoples the world over, though. These traditions are no more set in stone than Leaver cultures are. Nor are they relics of a distant past. It's this sort of view that leads both to the "angelization" of Leaver peoples (B, 181) and "appropriative romanticization" (Curry 2008) of their practices by Takers. When traditions are understood instead as the progressive accumulation of experiences and adaptive responses to changes both within communities and across wider social, political, economic, and ecological dynamics, they take on a rather different hue (Reo and Whyte 2012, 15). Traditions can be better understood as the pragmatic tools that they are, altered as needed in the face of changing conditions and unexpected challenges. They're designed and reworked expressly to facilitate ongoing trust, empathy, consent, and respect among a people, in good times and bad (Whyte 2018c, 12ff.).

Indeed, performances themselves become animate entities "with a spirit created by the participants," Norton-Smith remarks (2010, 101). Songs, prayers, ceremonies, and rituals are thus as much part of a people as is the land or any specifiable biological member. And they too have responsibilities, including to remind participants of their own sacredness. Participants are awakened (or reawakened) to the realization that they're just as worthy of veneration as any other manifestation of the sacred, hence just as able to carry out obligations to be good medicine for the land in life and in death (Kimmerer 2013, x, and Wildcat 2009, 89).

Performances also serve as gifts to other kinds of persons that are part of one's people. They're meant "to restore and . . . renew connections to other nonhuman members of the Native community," states Norton-Smith (2010, 114). Performances are hereby part of an integrated, holistic approach to venerating the sacred. The physical and social skills required to see to the workaday needs of fellow members of one's community are incomplete without the spiritual skills required to effectively participate in performances—and vice versa (Brown 1999, 35). Together, these skills comprise the kind of "multigenerational spatial knowledge" (Wildcat 2009, 16; see also Styres 2019) that helps to make humans good neighbors both to other humans and to other-than-humans season after season.

Kincentric Circles

From what we've seen so far, it should be clear that animism isn't focused on understanding or perceiving the vitality or consciousness of fellow members of the community of life. It's not first and foremost about discerning whether others are *animated,* particularly in ways that we're animated (Cordova 2004, 177), which is another reason I dislike the term. Instead, states Harvey, animism constitutes "a lifelong effort to improve relationships among persons (across species boundaries and responsive to differences of species, age, and other characteristics)" (2017, 213). And it accounts for place and the demands associated with performance to support this enterprise.

Exhibiting respect not just for human persons but also for deep-rooted persons, leaf-headed standing persons, sea and river persons, stellar persons, directional persons, past and future persons, four-legged persons, crawling persons, and winged persons (Justice 2011, 52ff.) may sound an awful lot like the basis for an ethics—a codification of right and wrong or a theory of how we ought to behave. But this isn't typically what animists have in mind. "Respect is practical engagement and presence in the world," state Lee Hester and his colleagues. It's a stance that's rooted in awareness. To start worrying about rights and wrongs "is, to some extent, to cease to pay attention, it is to organize one's perception of the world according to the dictates of the mode of control (theoretical as well as physical) one wishes to impose" (2000, 281).

Practically speaking, for Quinn *right* and *wrong* are superfluous terms, facilitators of unnecessary quibbling over behavioral categories (WS, 70ff., and Q&A, 164). This is why, as he states, "my books don't contain lists of do's and don'ts. My books are about changing minds" (WS, 128). This certainly isn't to say that he advocates no specifiable protocols of engagement, including performative protocols, with other persons. The Law of Life is itself one such protocol—or set of protocols (B, 260). But the metric that guides implementation of the Law of Life isn't what's ethical but what works (B, 314, and Q&A, 497). And what works often must be determined on a case-by-case basis—since no two interactions are entirely alike—even if one is guided by the insight that ongoing awareness facilitates (Q&A, 508).

Etiquette without Ethics

Some philosophers prefer to distinguish between ethics and morality. I'm among them.[14] If ethics is about the codification of conduct—the establishment of do's and don'ts, rights and wrongs—then I agree with Quinn (as well as with Hester et al. 2000) that it's superfluous. Right and wrong, even good and evil, are halo and smear terms. They're forms of praise and scorn, respectively, for what one prefers and what one rejects (Q&A, 435 and 684).[15] By contrast, morality is less about *one's* actions than about *our* interactions. The focus isn't primarily on *me* but instead on *us* (Dworkin 2011 and Walker and Lovat 2014). More to the point, Deloria contends, every action is actually an interaction; we're rooted in relationships all the way down (1999, 46f.). As such, it's entirely fitting to describe the universe itself as moral in character (Burkhart 2004; see also Pratt 2006, 7).

Moreover, just as we can distinguish between interspecies and intraspecies protocols—or strategies, as I referred to them in chapter 4—when assessing how to navigate being subject to the Law of Life, we also can distinguish between interspecies and intraspecies etiquette. Harvey speculates that religion itself may have begun as a kind of the former, "especially when members of one species had to eat members of another" (2013, 2). From this perspective, interspecies etiquette is a matter of sustaining a community in all its biodiversity despite the eventuality of colliding agendas that invariably arise among its members (Hall 2011, 163). The threefold struggle isn't, and can't be, free from internal tensions. This is religion "in the real world," Harvey emphasizes (2013, 199). It's how communities perpetuate themselves, making it an ongoing process of members together fashioning and refashioning locally appropriate ways of relating.

We've already seen one example of intraspecies etiquette among humans in chapter 4: erratic retaliation. While it may seem odd to think of erratic retaliation as a form of etiquette, Quinn highlights that, like interspecies protocols, it's a form of limited competition within a wider set of cooperative relationships. Put more simply, it fosters cultural diversity, coexistence, and even a fair degree of noninterference, particularly in comparison to how Takers typically interact with Leavers (Brant 1990 and Brundige 1997). Consider, for example, that Leavers don't engage in religious wars. There's no oral history of battles being waged or justified over different ideas of what's sacred or who venerates the one true god (Cohen 1952, 177f., and Wildcat 2009, 59). The idea of waging such a war doesn't make sense for those for whom traditions, protocols, and connections to the sacred and the divine emerge in connection with the place they live (B, 160, and Cajete 2000, 94).

Intraspecies etiquette involves not just respect for fellow human peoples, though. It also involves respect for fellow human persons, for individuals. So while Indigenous philosophers certainly are concerned with collectives, they equally value individuals as unique sources of creativity and care. Welch states that numerous traditions reject the coercion of others, emphasize individual initiative, and even discourage overt forms of correction by teachers and elders. This serves to facilitate "the highest degree of self-determination in relation to individual freedom, since there is rarely any point at which individuals are coerced or directly instructed" (2013, 209). Individuals are given wide latitude to experiment, reflect, get stuck, fail, learn in ways that work for them, and hereby correct themselves (Cordova 2004, 185). We'll see more about this in chapter 10.

This manner of cultivating individuality certainly fits well with Ishmael's and Charles's respective approaches to maieutics. In their hands, maieutics is starkly antiauthoritarian and follows directly from the proposition that each of us belongs to the sacred. (It also happens to be mirrored by Verdelet's call for the redemption of Eve in *The Holy*.) This applies to adults and children alike, and it provides a robust basis for self-respect, which is as valuable as respect for others. Both play an essential roles in becoming a person. Moreover, if given the sort of nurturing that makes autonomy and self-determination possible, each of us has "the ability to know and to share, to bring forward great strides in understanding and knowledge," Gregory Cajete asserts (2000, 102). This nourishes the community in turn, which creates quite a nice feedback loop.

Relatives

One becomes a person by virtue of upholding relationships and fulfilling obligations to one's people, both human and other-than-human. And the bonds that make a people—*tribal* relations, in Quinn's terms—have a familial character. This doesn't mean that a people is "one big family," Norton-Smith cautions (2010, 91). Again (and again and again), what we're dealing with here is a matter of vision. How do we *see* one another, and how does that seeing influence the way we interact? More specifically, what *relationships* orient the way we see the world (Fixico 2003)?

Anthropocentrists tend to place greatest value on human relationships. They see communities and peoples as human manifestations. The relationships that humans have with other-than-human beings aren't seen to be among fellow community members; they aren't interpersonal. Perhaps excluding animal companions, other-than-human beings typically play a supporting role in sustaining human relationships. This is a quintessentially Taker way of looking at the world.

By contrast, to be an *egalitarian biocentrist* is to value all living organisms intrinsically and equally. From this viewpoint, other-than-human beings are fellow community members, and may even count as persons, too. Their individual lives matter. *Ecocentrists* go a step further, seeing what are often viewed as abiotic factors—water, soil—as active participants in the living community. Rivers, watersheds, mountains, and even whole ecosystems may be persons. These entities have intrinsic value from this viewpoint.

B certainly sounds like an egalitarian biocentrist at times (B, 182f. and 324). Given her focus on the centrality of the living community *writ large*, it's no stretch to view her as an ecocentrist either. I think, though, that the Leaver story, as Quinn most frequently describes it, operates according to a *kincentric* model. Animistic traditions are indelibly rooted in specific landbases. As a result, animists tend to view the sacred in terms of the ties they maintain with the human and other-than-human beings with whom they share these landbases (P, 162f., Weaver 1997, 39, and Salmón 2000). These relations directly define, vitalize, and sustain a people and the persons who compose a people. While no life is to be devalued, some beings and entities play a bigger role in making me *me* and making us *us*. This is worth acknowledging.

Here's the way I prefer to think about it. Since Leavers' identities are manifestly tied to *this place*, it stands to reason that they form bonds of solidarity with fellow members of *this place*. But that these bonds of solidarity don't extend—or don't extend in the same way—to other peoples doesn't mean the lives of those peoples are any less valuable. Leavers may play favorites in the sense that what's sacred to them isn't sacred to others. Nevertheless, the single doctrine that has universal agreement among animists, according to Quinn, is that *the gods* have no favorites (P, 165; see also Cordova 2004, 177). So the gods lavish care equally on every one while persons tend to foster specific relationships, namely with other persons with whom they most regularly interact, collaborate, and exchange gifts, including the gifts of life and death.[16]

This division (or vision, really) of labor has worked for millennia. Biocentrism or ecocentrism or some combination of both for the gods, kincentrism—or what could just as easily be called *topocentrism*—for people. Responsibility for the health and wellbeing of *this place* just is responsibility for the health and wellbeing of the coinhabitants of *this place*. To be *emplaced* is to be enmeshed in bonds of kinship. This creates a set of overlapping and intersecting spheres of responsibility within and across ecosystems and bioregions that are small enough to accommodate face-to-face interactions yet large enough to sustain the autonomy and structural equality of peoples (Rose 1998). Indeed, this is the framework Kyle Whyte (2019 and 2020b) uses to conceptualize Indigenous climate justice: fostering kin relationships and responsibilities, particularly by combatting colonization, just is to seek climate justice. These concerns are inseparable.

Kincentrism also makes sense from an ecological point of view. Within the web endlessly woven we're all multispecies muddles, corporate elaborations, products of and participants in *sympoesis*. We may think of relationships as intangible, particularly in comparison to objects. But relationships are very real. They're paradigmatic real unseeables (Callicott 1994, 206f.).

In a loose sense, we're all relatives because we're all part of the web endlessly woven. But it helps little from an ecological perspective to emphasize that everything is connected to everything else, Thom Van

Dooren states. “Rather, everything is connected to *something*, which is connected to something else. While we may *ultimately* be connected to one another, the specificity and proximity of connections matters—*who we are bound up with and in what ways*” (2014, 60).[17] We're permeable to certain persons far more than to others. Specificity and proximity facilitate permeability, at least among those who are free from zombification and *wétiko*. And permeability, which requires trust, empathy, consent, and respect, facilitates responsiveness to others' particular needs and interests (Rezendes 1999, 23).

Consider love again. Loving relationships help us to check and correct unhealthy tendencies, so long as we're open to change and truly care about not just those with whom we're in relationship but also about the relationship itself—the commitment. Loving relationships help us to grow as persons precisely because we accommodate others. This is fascinating. To make accommodations to kith and kin is to limit ourselves. And the very act of self-limitation is what helps us personally to grow and the relationships we're in to grow with us. This is another nice feedback loop. And I can't help but appreciate how it defies the Taker imperative according to which a life without limits is somehow prototypical of the one right way to live.

No One Right Way to Live

Is kincentrism culturally relativistic? Is Quinn suggesting that we have no right to judge the actions of peoples whose practices we regard as abhorrent? Shouldn't we pursue the eradication of female genital mutilation, for example? First, it's worth noting that female genital mutilation is actually rooted in heteropatriarchal Taker traditions (Walker and Parmar 1993; see also B, 314, and Q&A, 654). Debates over cultural relativism center on whether we can judge people of *other* cultures. Its proponents arguably aren't in a position to advocate similar restrictions on criticizing the people of a subset of our own. Second, we do well to acknowledge that in tribal settings people can't easily be compelled to continue doing things *they* abhor. Partnership systems aren't structured for coercion. Third, as members of the most murderous culture in human history, Quinn questions whether Takers are competent to stand in judgment specifically of kincentric practices and performances anyway (Q&A, 646). Whether or not we have a right to judge those of other cultures is beside the point if we lack the aptitude to do so.

Even if some among us do deem ourselves competent in this regard, we mustn't ignore the Law of Life. The gods love diversity, Quinn proclaims (BD, 42). Both interspecies and intraspecies etiquette reflect the Law of Life. They're *polycultural* protocols, manifestations of the tree of life. Enacting a story whereby there's one right way to live is *monocultural,* a product of the tree of knowledge of good and evil. The former fosters cultural and biological fecundity. The latter supports mass extinction when its fruit is ingested by anyone other than the gods (WS, 198; see also Whyte 2018a, 136). "This isn't sociological thinking," Quinn maintains, "this is ecological thinking" (BC, 97). Diversity works, uniformity doesn't. It's no wonder, Vandana Shiva notes, that the "co-evolution of cultures, life forms and habitats has conserved the biological diversity of the planet. Cultural diversity and biological diversity go hand in hand" (1993, 65; see also BD, 37ff., I, 206, Shrestha et al. 2008, and Sobrevila 2008).

Abel's Resistance

Quinn's considerations regarding animism are largely directed at helping us Takers change out our old minds for new ones. This is the point of being an animist missionary. And he's quite clear that new minds are intent on finding ways to stop Cain from murdering Abel. New minds "hunger and thirst for the survival of Leaver cultures" because Leaver peoples have proven adept at preserving "a legacy of wisdom accumulated from the beginning of time" ("B Attitudes"), despite being under continuous, expanding, and accelerating onslaught by Takers.

We arguably live not in a postmodern and postcolonial era, Harvey remarks, but, rather, in "the most-modern and most-colonial of times" (2013, 120). Perhaps this is why we Takers are accustomed to making a virtue of *displacement* (by fetishizing hypermobility) and *kinlessness* (by fetishizing atomized individualism), both of which drive the ongoing destruction of places and peoples.[18] Surely this is among the reasons why, in Quinn's obituary, we're asked to donate to Cultural Survival or Survival International, two organizations devoted to fostering the perpetuation and wellbeing of Indigenous peoples ("Daniel Quinn" 2018).

We Takers also do well to acknowledge that there are lessons taught by Leaver peoples that aren't for us. Not every scrap of wisdom Leavers have to offer is meant for "all humanity," as Whyte and his colleagues put it (2018; see also Whyte 2018b). Treating this wisdom as a source for guidance from which Takers are supposed to learn without first receiving permission from our instructors isn't merely disrespectful. It's yet another way to express that the world is made for us Takers to do with as we will. Takers should instead appreciate the ways in which Leaver peoples themselves are resisting extirpation, respect their resistance as yet another kind of performance that venerates the sacred, and resist alongside Leavers when our support is expressly requested or otherwise permitted.[19]

In the Hands of the Gods

Leaver resistance is yet another way in which said peoples strive to live in the hands of the gods. Pointedly, in word and deed Leavers challenge the common Taker assumption that humans ourselves aren't sacred beings within a world that itself is sacred. Nowhere is this assumption clearer than with invocations calling upon a higher power to step in and set things right.

If Takers have strayed from how the gods would have us live, a reader asks Quinn, "why don't the gods do anything about it? For instance, why don't the gods destroy those who don't 'live in their hands'? Or are they merely waiting for the Takers to destroy themselves" (Q&A, 467)? Note the implicit premise underlying the reader's question. We humans can't *really* save the world. Only the gods can do that. But, from Quinn's perspective, if the gods work on, in, and through us, then our attempts to save the world just are divine interventions. Saving the world isn't a them-or-us proposition. It's instead a matter of stepping into our power as sacred beings rather than abdicating our responsibilities.

When Quinn says that living in the hands of the gods is a matter of "casting your fate to the wind" or "trying your luck" (WS, 40), he's not saying that we somehow sit by passively and let events unfold around us. Another reader assumes that to be a Leaver is to live "at the whim of nature and simply [take] what comes free [without] worrying about what is to come next" (Q&A, 518). But living in the hands of the gods has nothing to do with whimsy, Quinn replies:

> The Ihalmiut . . . lived very successfully and happily inside the Arctic Circle—"in the hands of the gods," because they respected the conditions that the gods had set for them; they expected the gods to be consistent—and they were. But if you venture into the Arctic winter alone and unprepared, thinking the gods will take care of you, you'll probably end up dead,

> not because they're unfriendly or whimsical but because you were expecting them to make an exception for you, expecting them *not* to be consistent. (Ibid.)[20]

Indeed, *casting* and *trying* are active. "[T]he purpose of life is to live," Quinn states (Q&A, 178), to embody one's life. Embodying one's life implies facing up to inevitable challenges and defending oneself and one's kith and kin when under attack (ibid., 385, 483, and 670).

Undertaken responsibly, casting one's fate to the wind and trying one's luck are thus expressions of the gifts of wisdom—of seeing beneath surfaces, discerning true courses, and reading the signs—which help us carefully and conscientiously to navigate our ongoing interactions with others within the bounds of the Law of Life (ibid., 87). No aspiring actor "who stays home and plays it safe becomes a success on the stage and screen," Quinn remarks (ibid. 518; see also P, 162, and WS, 47f.). And no individual who waits for the gods to step in and fix our messes is behaving like a person.

So the kincentric (or topocentric) orientation of Leaver peoples isn't just the basis for a vision. It also serves as a means to push back against settler colonialism: the set of social, political, and economic policies whereby Takers "permanently and ecologically inscribe homelands of their own onto Indigenous homelands," Whyte et al. state (2018, 158). Takers seek to erase the cultures and undermine the lives of those whom they dispossess. These actions excise ecologies: "systematic arrangements of humans, nonhuman beings (animals, plants, etc.) and entities (spiritual, inanimate, etc.), and landscapes (climate regions, boreal zones, etc.)" (ibid., 159). They compromise what Whyte elsewhere calls the *collective continuance* of peoples (Whyte 2018c and 2018d).[21]

The idea of living in the hands of the gods may seem intangible here. But taking an uncompromising stance against monoculture in all its forms, which amounts to the same thing, isn't (Whitt 2004). Nor are supporting the proliferation of trophic cascades, fending off habitat encroachment, acting as water and land protectors in fights against the deployment of oil pipelines and tar sands, and combatting violations of treaties and international law in the name of climate justice (Goeman and Denetdale 2009). Leaver peoples are on the front lines of each of these enterprises, whether they continue to live on their ancestral lands or as part of the far-flung diaspora.

While Nerysoo may be right that without their land Leavers can no longer exist as people, this doesn't entail that they're unable to develop effective strategies to *regain* their personhood. A specific landbase may not be required for the survival either of persons or peoples, even if land rematriation is essential to enacting a new story (as we'll discuss in chapter 8). But relocation must always be a collaborative effort. Making a place for oneself and/or one's people in a new habitat necessarily entails negotiations with longer-term residents (Pratt 2002, 156ff.). It involves forging new relationships of mutual entailment, making oneself and/or one's people fit to be welcomed (Darnell 1999, 91).

This too is a form of resistance to settler colonialism. It's a determined stance against blithely encroaching on others' homelands.

Stewardship Revisited

We've seen in passing that Quinn has no truck with the idea of stewardship. Like ecosystem management and sustainable development, it insinuates that we're somehow in a privileged position with respect to fellow members of the living community. Promoting stewardship is thus nothing but another exhibition of "arrogance and vanity and anthropocentric tomfoolery," Quinn avers. "We have as much business being stewards of the world as infants have of being stewards of the nursery. It's we who are dependent on the world, not the other way around" (P, 143–44).[22] To assume otherwise feeds, or perhaps has been fed by, the common notion, particularly among adherents of the Abrahamic faiths, that we humans have been conferred the power "to watch over nature," Arne Naess remarks, "like a highly respected middleman between the Creator and Creation" (1989, 187).

But what if there's another way to understand what stewardship entails that supports resisting the anthropocentric arrogance endemic to Taker culture? At a 2012 symposium, the First Stewards offered a resolution emphasizing the importance of "awareness of the interconnectedness of the clouds, forests, valleys, land, streams, fishponds, sea, lakes, canyons, and other elements of the natural and spiritual world, and . . . expertise and methodologies to assure responsible stewardship of them" (McCarty et al. 2012). "Here stewardship does not express human exceptionalism or control over nature, as it typically does in other environmental discourses," Whyte and Chris Cuomo note. "Instead, it refers to acknowledgment of one's place in a web of interdependent relationships that create moral responsibilities, and it recognizes that there are methods and forms of expertise involved in carrying out such responsibilities" (2017, 238).

In this context, stewardship follows directly from personhood. Persons—both human and other-than-human—are stewards, Whyte and colleagues proclaim in another article, "not because they are privileged as knowledge holders, but more because they are in a position of having responsibilities to the many other relatives making up the genealogical community" (2016, 29). This view emphasizes appreciation for one's place in the web endlessly woven; for the fact that we owe our lives to an ongoing cycle of birth, growth, and death; for the cultivation of the gifts of wisdom; and for the critical importance of ecological and cultural abundance.

Here's another way to look at stewardship. Bernice Fischer and Joan Tronto contend that we do well to regard care as "*a species activity that includes everything we do to maintain, continue, and repair our 'world' so that we can live in it as well as possible.* That world includes our bodies, our selves, and our environment, all of which we seek to interweave in a complex, life-sustaining web" (1990, 40). This way of thinking about care fits nicely with regarding the sacred as that which defines, vitalizes, and sustains a people. It also suggests that our relationship with other persons entails one or more of the following: *caring about* them in the sense of taking responsibility for the continuation of our shared community; *caring for* their concerns or their individual autonomy; *being careful* of them, when doing so is warranted; and being willing to *receive care* from them.

Consider the critical role Anishinaabe women have played in resisting ways in which Taker practices defame and degrade essential water sources. Their actions aren't just a reflection of their own responsibilities to the water but a sign of recognition that the water isn't inert. It's a key member of the Anishinaabe people, a vital supporter of life with its own responsibilities to fulfill. To defame and degrade it is hereby not only to shirk our responsibilities but to interfere with the water's duties to the Anishinaabe and, as part of a wider global system of waterways, to the rest of creation (McGregor 2009, 37f.; see also Whyte 2014 and Kearns 2017).

Consider as well that as it's described here, stewardship is a form of gifting. And gifting can be an act of resistance, specifically to domination systems. It's a symbol of mutual respect shown by the giver for the receiver, and it confers an obligation on the receiver to reciprocate (Norton-Smith 2010, 109ff.). Furthermore, the practice of stewardship entails that one appreciates that all of us are both shaped by and shapers of the living community. This is the same as saying that we're shaped by and shapers of the gods. The gods can die, yes. We can kill them. But we also can animate and reanimate them by carrying out our responsibilities as persons.[23] We can be part of the processes of restoration, adaptation, and endurance that keep the fire of life ablaze in *this place,* this *sacred* place, wherever it may be.

The Grammar of Animacy

Kimmerer describes yet another form of resistance to Taker culture: keeping alive Indigenous languages. She herself describes the process of learning to speak Potawatomi. In boarding schools, children were expressly forbidden from speaking their native tongue. This was but one more Taker weapon of genocide.[24] For what's lost isn't just an assemblage of words and idioms. What's lost is a "grammar of animacy," Kimmerer emphasizes (2013, 55). This is because Indigenous languages facilitate the development of eyes that see (âpihtawikosisân 2012). With their loss, particularly as the elderly speakers who were able to resist assimilation die, comes a loss of awareness, of wisdom, of love, of stewardship—of the sacred.

"English is a noun-based language, somehow appropriate to a culture so obsessed with things," Kimmerer remarks. "Only 30 percent of English words are verbs, but in Potawatomi that proportion is 70 percent" (2013, 53). Compare, for instance, the difference between treating *bay* as a noun and a verb. In the former case, the water is inert, "defined by humans, trapped between its shores. . . . But the verb *wiikwegamaa*—to *be* a bay—releases the water from its bondage and lets it live. 'To be a bay' holds the wonder that for this moment, the living water has decided to shelter itself between the shores, conversing with cedar roots and a flock of baby mergansers" (ibid., 55).

Potawatomi is thus "a mirror for seeing the animacy of the world, for the life that pulses through all things, pines and nuthatches and mushrooms" (ibid.). By *baying,* the bay expresses its agency. Indeed, as with the land, it's not an *it* at all. "So it is in Potawatomi and most other Indigenous languages, we use the same grammar to address the living world as we do our family. Because it is our family" (ibid.). A family is a communion of subjects, not a collection of objects. Expressing communion facilitates respect for fellow persons, both human and other-than-human. Expressing thinghood quite literally objectifies. It absolves us of responsibility, gives us license not to care.

This isn't to say that speakers of English are unable to avoid objectifying others. Kimmerer isn't suggesting that Potawatomi and other

Native languages are morally superior in this respect. We're dealing here with vision, as we have been all along. For my part, I'm acknowledging the power of words to help us enact a story in which the world is full of *whos* rather than *whats*. And in line with the proposition that there are all sorts of Leaver lessons that aren't for me, I'm also paying deference to the power of words to animate performances (and relationships) in which I'm not invited to participate. I want a world full of such events. This, I think, is another way in which life, like love, is empowered by its limits.

Acknowledging Precedent

Saving the world, in Quinn's sense of the phrase, is processual. It's subject to modification, adjustment, and adaptation. It has to be, since it's embodied in practices that reflect reverence for the Law of Life, of living in the hands of the gods. In this respect, saving the world mirrors ideas most firmly rooted in Leaver traditions. Takers can't and shouldn't seek to walk in Leavers' shoes. What I have in mind is neither appropriation nor imitation but, instead, something more like sanctioned inspiration.

Saving the world also involves acknowledging up front that we, all of us, live in dystopian times. But dystopia is relative. All of us who live within the purview of Taker culture are captives. Yet those of us, like me, with generations of settler ancestors aren't captive in the same way as are Indigenous peoples. Their ancestors saw the erosion of individual and collective agency for what it is; mine may well have fantasized about Taker culture going global (Whyte 2017). This makes it easier for me and those like me to fool ourselves into believing that our experiences are somehow unprecedented, particularly with respect to climate change and ecocide. We effectively blind ourselves to the fact that what we dread most with respect to these phenomena—economic crash, widespread immiseration, social upheaval, grave political instability, mass migration, the precipitous die off of species, the loss of who and what we hold most dear—has already been endured by Indigenous peoples the world over (Callison 2014 and Whyte 2020a). Even those of us who fancy ourselves allies of Indigenous peoples may end up unwittingly being complicit in the erasure of their harrowing ordeals. This is yet another way in which we fail to heed the wisdom of people who've long been committed to collective continuance. Worse still, we may presume that Takers with an earnest desire to enact a story that works are somehow uniquely qualified or best positioned somehow to save Indigenous peoples from the very culture our own ancestors lauded and perhaps even violently supported (Whyte 2018b, 224).

As noted above, climate change and ecocide *are* forms of colonial violence. This is among Quinn's lessons as well, although it's certainly not his originally. "Robin Kimmerer often tells the story of one of the Potawatomi relocation processes from the Great Lakes region to Kansas and Oklahoma in the 19th century," Whyte relays. "The relocation process was literally the drastic change in climate regions and the ending of many ancient relationships with the species and ecosystems of Potawatomi homelands" (ibid., 226; see also Kimmerer 2014).

Yes, the scope and scale of the climatological and ecological disruption we all face today is extraordinary. But from the vantage point of Indigenous peoples subject to settler colonialism, the need to learn and adapt to complex and extreme climactic and ecological change is nothing new (Bardsley and Wiseman 2016). "Native Americans have seen the end of their respective worlds," Larry Gross states. "Indians survived the apocalypse" (2014, 33). From this perspective, the global change we now face isn't a new crisis. It's the inevitable outcome of twelve millennia of Taker expansionism (Davis and Todd 2017, 774).

The Accordion Effect

There's a certain flexibility that we children of settlement don't enjoy built into the way of life—and the lineage, too—of peoples who make (or who traditionally made) seasonal rounds. Not only does the population size of such groups vary according to season, economies and forms of social and political organization often vary as well. People who are together over the summer, for example, splinter when food becomes scarcer, although they typically remain in contact should one group or another require help.

This "accordion-like" system (Darnell 1999, 99) of season-to-season integration and partial fragmentation has clear survival advantages for groups. It facilitates adaptation and endurance under stress conditions. It provides a form of systemic group *tolerance,* in the engineering sense to which Quinn occasionally appeals (BC, 124ff., and MI, 122f.), that permits traditions to persist within inevitable states of ecological, social, and personal flux.

As Dennis McPherson and J. Douglas Rabb hypothesize, "it may well be this very kind of social organization which makes Native cultures so resistance to assimilation, which allows Native values to be resilient. Even if only a relative few families are continuing to teach and practice

Native values, traditional ways can always be reestablished" (2011, 136). From this vantage point, Native languages may not so much succumb to loss as to forced hibernation (Meissner 2018). This is particularly so if they're able to overwinter, as it were, within ancestral lands.

Take, for instance, the Menominee. Despite displacement from the vast majority of their ancestral lands, the Menominee have succeeded in making a living while also facilitating the health of forestlands in present-day Wisconsin and the Upper Peninsula of Michigan. In the nineteenth century, they confronted the difficult choice over whether or not to treat with the U.S. government in exchange for a sawmill, perhaps finally doing so after careful consideration of the meaning of the forest for future generations, Whyte speculates. "When faced with dilemmas in settler colonial contexts, people are often motivated to see future economic advantages as the primary benefit of negotiating with powerful parties. Yet the Menominee ancestors . . . also realized some of the hidden values future generations would want, such as the spiritual and cultural values of the forest" (2018b, 233–34; see also Pecore 1992). They were right, and their actions helped save their people.

The forest itself now (at least partially) defines, vitalizes, and sustains the nation. This surely helps to explain why the Menominee continue to engage in sustainable forestry to this day (Grignon and Kimmerer 2017, 69). This is a remarkable example of success, particularly under threat of genocide. And it's not isolated (Tsing 2015 and Peters 2018).

The Perils of Allyship

Like all couples, my partner Sherrilyn and I argue on occasion. Like every individual, I sometimes say hurtful things even when I don't intend to. One thing I've had to learn is that making amends doesn't involve taking responsibility only for what I intend to convey. It also requires taking responsibility for how what I convey is received. Indeed, being part of a loving relationship necessitates that I be cognizant of how our respective baggage colors the way we react to certain words and actions. I may not mean to be hurtful, which matters. But being hurtful matters, too.

My learning has been painfully slow, and I can't say I am particularly adept at it yet. I suppose this is due in part to some combination of residual stubbornness and the benighted idea that I gain something by "winning" arguments, both of which are probably vestiges of my patriarchal upbringing. But I fully accept that taking responsibility for both my intentions and how what I say and do is received is part of what's entailed in being committed to Sherrilyn and to the practice of commitment itself.

The same dynamic applies, I think, with respect to my pursuit of allyship with Indigenous peoples and persons. This pursuit isn't and can't be a matter of papering over the crimes of my ancestors or somehow proving my own blamelessness for ongoing efforts to eradicate Leavers (Tuck and Yang 2012). To be a Taker may not on its own make me culpable. But historical awareness and knowledge of current manifestations of genocide does confer upon me a responsibility to do what I can to enact a story in which my ancestors' crimes are rectified and genocide is answered for (Stevenson 1992, 307).

Seeking to be an ally isn't a badge of honor. As Ernest Owens (2020) says of white allyship with respect to black and brown people, I don't get to play both the hero and villain in others' trauma. Moreover, being accepted as an ally isn't up to me. Offering reasons for trust, exhibiting empathy, seeking consent, and paying respect are within my purview. Their reciprocation isn't. And I'm not owed anything, no matter how well I comport myself.

Whyte notes that his ancestors likely would warn him about would-be allies. His ancestors encountered no shortage of "friends of the Indian" who nevertheless sought to dismantle Indigenous kinship systems and liquidate Indigenous territories supposedly for the betterment of the Potawatomi themselves (2017, 232). Leanne Simpson emphasizes in turn that because whiteness is centered on domination, "there is virtually no room for white people in resurgence" (2017, 228), or what she also calls radical resistance. Indigenous peoples must refuse to center whiteness in seeking out allies. Instead, build constellations of coresistance with black and brown individuals and communities who are already part of the struggle in their own ways. And perhaps "our real white allies show up in solidarity anyway" (ibid.).

Croatoan

In *After Dachau,* as Jason is finally coming to grips with the truth of Mallory's former life and what it indicates about his own society's genocidal legacy, he questions whether making others aware of this legacy would make much of a difference. Initially, he thinks not, particularly after being sequestered and browbeaten by Uncle Harry. "You're right at last, Jason. *No one cares.* I think you can count on that," Harry states in a parting shot (AD, 217).

But it's not true that no one cares. *Jason himself cares* (Q&A, 635). This is enough of an incentive for him to make public his "great revelation" (ibid.). So he persists, opening an art gallery and exhibiting Mallory's damning photographic evidence. He had no idea how it would be received. Maybe Harry was right and the evidence would be ignored. But he had to try.

"Then one night we got really lucky," Jason narrates. "Someone heaved a paving stone through the front window. We were ecstatic. Someone *got it.* Someone *cared*" (AD, 217).

The name of Jason's gallery is Croatoan, the single word carved into a tree trunk at the site of an early English colony that vanished on Roanoke Island, seemingly inexplicably. But the secret of the Lost Colony is just as much a product of active forgetting as are Takers' assumptions about our wider cultural legacy. That is to say, it's no secret at all. For the Lost Colony only became lost in the nineteenth century, some three centuries after its inhabitants walked away from it.

Andrew Jackson had gained popularity among white Americans by stoking fears of slave rebellions and Native uprisings. New immigrants from Ireland, Italy, and Eastern Europe—not counted as white and widely vilified—arrived in the United States en masse. Worries among whites about interracial mingling and nefarious foreign influences ran high. As a result, fraternization between whites and members of other races became not just taboo but illegal in many locales. So the colonists' disappearance had to become a mystery. No longer could the obvious conclusion, that they relocated to a nearby Croatoan village, be true (Lawler 2018).

Whiteness, settler colonialism, Taker culture. One and all, they're mutually reinforcing domination systems. Each in its own way is an expression of the death urge. Each, as Coates puts it, is "the deathbed of us all" (2015, 151).

"And still I urge you to struggle," Coates adds, speaking directly to his son, named after Samori Touré, who resisted French colonialism in western Africa. Touré "died in captivity, but the profits of that struggle and others like it are ours, even when the object of our struggle, as is so often true, escapes our grasp" (ibid., 68). Quinn's struggle, if not in so many words, is to demystify Croatoan. That object, too, may escape our grasp. But it would help to know what sorts of things we're grasping for. This is what comes next.

PART III

A NEW STORY TO BE IN: ON TO CROATOAN

Chapter 7

Beyond Civilization

The Rise and Decline of Hierarchalism

On the morning of September 9, 2019, Gregory Eells jumped to his death from the seventeenth floor of a building in Center City Philadelphia. Eells, fifty-two, was a recent arrival to Philly, coming from Cornell University to serve as Executive Director of Counseling and Psychological Services at the University of Pennsylvania. Penn had experienced a spate of suicides in recent years, including by a student-athlete who herself jumped from a Center City building. A specialist in resilience under conditions of extreme stress, Eells was the perfect candidate to help bolster Penn's mental health services. This made his own suicide all the more shocking.

Eells's mother reported that he'd been overwhelmingly depressed since arriving in Philly. His new job turned out to be harder than he'd anticipated. This had prevented him from returning regularly to Ithaca, New York, where his wife and three children still lived. "I said, 'Well, quit,'" his mother told a reporter covering the incident. "His wife said the same thing. We are confused. He was the most smiling, upbeat person I have met in my life" (cited in Snyder et al. 2019).

You know as well as I that stories like this aren't rare in the United States, even if the experiences depicted don't typically befall experts in mental and emotional resilience. But it's not just this that caught my attention. No, what Eells and his family had gone through hit close to home. And I couldn't help but dwell on the difference in outcome between my experience and that of his wife.

When I took my current academic position, I left behind my spouse, too, along with two beloved cats. Just as I was heading out, Sherrilyn had become interim chair of her department at a state university in the Midwest. We hadn't yet figured out how to deal with our version of the "two-body problem"—that is, academic spouses with positions in locales far enough apart that living together most of the year isn't an option. So our plan was to travel back and forth about once a month and during breaks. We had done the same for four years while I was in grad school and she was just starting her career. So while we knew from experience it wouldn't be easy, we also knew that our relationship was strong enough to handle routinely being apart.

It was anything but easy to leave my family, but I was happy to have a tenure-track job, particularly in an enviable location. And while I couldn't manage to swing a spousal hire for Sherrilyn, we hoped she might be able to leverage her time as chair to find a position that came with a spousal hire for me. Besides, she was well suited to leading a department, which is no small matter. Capable leadership in academia is hard to find. But the chair position seems to me uniquely unenviable. Chairs are under constant pressure from both their faculty and university administration, and they aren't comfortably part of either.

Yet matters were made immeasurably worse for Sherrilyn when both her faculty and her immediate superior—the interim dean, who had been chair of her department—proved to be not merely difficult to deal with but openly hostile and abusive. Among her male colleagues, her department had a long-standing culture of bullying. She assumed leadership of her department only after receiving assurances that the interim dean had her back. Instead, he almost immediately sought to use her to engage in petty vendettas against departmental enemies. When she refused, as she did time and again, he lit into her. And when a faculty member wanted permission to have a grad student on call to teach his classes because he had a habit of running late, her denial earned her physical threats that administrators subsequently swept under the rug.

Experiences such as these were customary. Sherrilyn was left traumatized.

At a distance and in my perpetual alcohol haze, I knew Sherrilyn was suffering. But I couldn't (or, at the time, wouldn't) grasp the full extent of her trauma: seeking refuge under her desk at work as she tried desperately to manage another panic attack, developing an afternoon drinking habit of her own, experiencing frequent stress-induced migraines, becoming suicidal. Our relationship became strained. What I interpreted, poorly, as us growing apart was her planning to die and me being too intoxicated—and too self-regarding—to see it.

Eventually, things came to a head between us. It was over winter break. I still recall where our argument started, in the entryway of our old house. I also remember that we migrated to the dining room, her sitting on a chair against the wall beside the piano her dad had salvaged for us and me sitting across the room on a window seat. And it was there, as the cracks in our relationship grew into what seemed an unbridgeable chasm, that she told me with a firm air of finality to take the cats with me when I left.

This shook me to my core. Had I been standing, I'm certain my knees would've buckled.

I swear to you that I hadn't known she was suicidal. I find it hard to admit, and harder to write, that I wasn't aware she already had a plan (she, too, was preparing to jump) and that she was struggling mightily *not* to carry it out. How negligent I was. But the immediacy of it all hit me with her simple request. I couldn't leave alone; the cats had to come with me. The cats, siblings, who we'd adopted as kittens. Who'd been her constant companions in my absence. Whose own relationship had been fractured by redirected aggression, unwittingly caused by me, but who she'd patiently and lovingly coaxed back together. Who now regularly sat with her when she sobbed in the tub and curled up with her each night as she fought insomnia.

This wasn't a proverbial cry for help, nor was it an act of manipulation. This was her getting her affairs in order.

And out of nowhere, the words flew out of my mouth. "Quit your job. Walk away. *Get out of here.* Now."

She looked at me, blankly at first. But for the first time in years I saw the old fire in her eyes reignite. The fire was dull at first, but it began to grow as she realized that the door of this particular cage had been flung open. Leave a well-paying tenured position? Walk away from an established career with no idea what was to come next? Absolutely. Because the job wasn't just soul crushing. It hadn't just led to PTSD. In no uncertainly terms, it was about to kill her.

Maybe the decision to walk away seems to you like a no-brainer. But you try making it. The amount of courage it took, well, I'm don't have words for it. For now, I want to focus on the fact that her walking away was even *thinkable* for me. "Well, quit," Eells's mother had said to him. From my vantage point now, this is the obvious plea. But I doubt such a proposition would have occurred to me, at least with such sharply defined cogency, when things came to a head between Sherrilyn and me save for the fact that I recently had taught Quinn's *Beyond Civilization.*

In *Beyond Civilization,* Quinn confronts hierarchalism, or the normalization of domination systems in Taker culture, particularly socioeconomic ones. Recall from chapter 2 that on Riane Eisler's account domination systems are premised on rigid top-down control, class-based stratification, widespread abuse and violence, and entrenched heteropatriarchy. For the vast majority of us, to be employed is to be subject to domination. Admittedly, the domination I face is minimal compared to most, even if I bristle at it. What Sherrilyn faced may be closer to the norm, particularly for women, people of color, and the disabled.

But she got out. The transition hasn't been easy. She continues to struggle with PTSD, although the new career she's built—founding and overseeing a business and affiliated nonprofit that are devoted to cultivating people–plant relationships through restorative horticulture and arboriculture—has helped to mitigate its sharpest edges. In part, this is because her new career serves as a defiant rejection of hierarchalism both in terms of its inception and its function.

I tell Sherrilyn's story not to condemn Rick Eells. Nor do I wish to brush aside how Sherrilyn continues to draw on financial resources of my hierarchalist employer. Walking away isn't an exercise in purity for Quinn, though. It turns out that the parasitic character of her escape is actually a key component of what he calls the *New Tribal Revolution.* To be part of this revolution is to be beyond civilization, Quinn emphasizes. Stated plainly, it is to make a living in a manner that flouts heirarchalism. In the process, it also offers means to facilitate the collapse of Taker culture.

First things first, though. For Quinn, it's always helpful to understand how things came to be the way they are: in this case, how hierarchalism took root and became ascendant among Takers. We then can consider why we Takers tend unthinkingly to accept the *myth of no beyond,* that to escape civilization can only mean "going back" to living "primitively"—turning our backs on intellectual and cultural advancement, economic development, moral progress, and social and political complexity. Once we recognize these attributions for the halo terms they are, we'll be able to see more clearly what walking away entails and why, for Quinn, it serves not just as a salient "alternative to misery" (BC, 51) but even a rejection of the death urge. We'll also be well positioned to explore the contours and weigh the merits of the New Tribal Revolution.

Under Lock and Key

The term *civilization* derives from the Latin *civitatis,* or city-state. *Civitatis* derives in turn from *civis,* citizen, to distinguish Romans from their barbaric neighbors. Strip away the cultural detritus that the term (civilization) has since taken on, though, and what's exposed is a form of socioeconomic organization based on putting food—surplus food—under lock and key. Surplus food must be stored, which means there must be storehouses. Within the first villages, "it's conceivable that everyone in the community might have had completely free access to the village's stored food," Quinn notes (IS, 2). But as surpluses grew and villages grew with them, it no longer would have been possible for community policing alone to handle threats from outside invaders, scavenging by other-than-human neighbors, and theft by villagers themselves. So storehouses had to be made secure, locked tight and guarded.

"Storing and guarding food required coordination. Someone or some group had to work to make it happen. Division of labor was one of the earliest results of village life" (ibid., 3). A guardian class thereby emerged, the seeds of what would become the military. The guardians were charged with securing the storehouses, and those who recruited and organized the guardians held the storehouse keys (ibid., 4; see also Ponting 2007, 52, and Diamond 2012, 19). These keyholders assumed positions at the top of an incipient socioeconomic hierarchy, while those who needed access to it lined out below. Nothing changed when villages grew into towns, towns into cities, cities into city-states, city-states into nations, nations into empires, and empires into a global civilization, Quinn contends (ibid.).

But what led to the emergence of villages, to increased population density, in the first place? And where does intensified food production fit into this dynamic? Despite its widespread cultural appeal among Takers, a bottom-up theory of the emergence of totalitarian agriculture holds little weight. It's not the case that once gatherer-hunters discovered how to cultivate preferred foods, they gladly switched to this more destructive way of making a living. Totalitarian agriculture is a hard way to get fed (BC, 34; see also B, 77, 92, and 248f.). It's both less nutritionally rewarding and less experientially gratifying than either gathering-hunting or horticulture. It's also prone to greater risk of food shortages due to crop failure (Diamond 1987 and Cohen and Armelagos 2013).[1] As such, comments Colin Tudge, the real problem isn't to explain why Leavers resisted adoption of totalitarian agriculture "but why anybody took it up at all, when it is so obviously beastly" (cited in Manning 2004, 24; see also B, 78ff.).

Brian Fagan (2004) suggests that the answer lies in the Younger Dryas. The Younger Dryas marked a period of rapid cooling—quite possibly as a result of a meteoroid impact (Moore 2019)—in the late Pleistocene, some 12,800 years ago. It brought frigid temperatures to Europe and widespread drought throughout Asia. It also may have triggered the extinction of megafauna in North America, which challenges the theory that this phenomenon was the result of overhunting (Firestone et al. 2007 and Sweatman 2018). Fagan asserts that the drought in Asia is almost certainly the catalyst for people first massing in villages, specifically along the Euphrates. Traditional food sources, including desert gazelles, nuts, and wild grasses became less available. Their loss was offset by harvesting wild rye, lentils, and einkorn—all of which survived better under drought conditions—and then cultivating them with the help of rudimentary forms of irrigation (Anderson et al. 2011).

Lower food productivity during this period, despite intensified production efforts, may have triggered heightened conflict among villages. This would have imposed pressure to urbanize, including to protect food, since larger villages were now safer from invasion than small ones. Increased urbanization in turn necessitated putting more land to the plow and further divisions of labor, including for construction and maintenance of levee systems and recordkeeping regarding yields and flood patterns. New organizational needs led to tighter centralization of political power supported by new norms aimed at maintaining cohesion and control over enlarged and stratified groups. The first inklings of what would become Taker culture emerged.

As with the development of totalitarian agriculture, "there was clearly a 'ratchet effect' in operation," Clive Ponting remarks; "once a step was taken it was difficult to reverse, and changes in one area of society had major impacts elsewhere, were magnified, and produced more changes in a positive feedback spiral" (2007, 55; see also BC, 70). Indeed, it became increasingly common for political elites "to capture and hold much of their population by forms of bondage," James C. Scott asserts (2017, xii). Rulers and the military personnel they commanded either pressed people into service directly or removed feasible alternatives for making a living (McBay 2011a, 36).

"The thing we call civilization goes hand in hand with hierarchy—*means* hierarchy, *requires* hierarchy," Quinn proclaims; "you can't have civilization without hierarchy; at least we never have—not once, not anywhere, in ten [no, twelve] thousand years of civilization building" (BC, 85). Consider, for example, three specifiable forms of social relations that have become commonplace among the people of our culture. Occupants of higher rank enjoy (1) greater authority, assuming a considerable degree of control over the lives of subordinates; (2) heightened esteem, hence entitlement to extract tokens of deference; and (3) higher social standing, leaving them free to neglect the interests of subordinates or even to trample on them (Anderson 2017, 3f.).[2] The obedience, toil, and sacrifice of subordinates has become not only justifiable among Takers but expected (Bookchin 2005, 72).

Hierarchical societies are thus expressly designed not to benefit all members of society in the same way (BC, 72). Those who benefit most from locking up the food—the lords, short for *loaf-wards* (Snodgrass 2011, 38)—"make out like bandits," Ishmael declares (MI, 171). Under certain circumstances, those of the middle class do fairly well overall, too, even if they typically must work long hours engaged in unenjoyable work. And then there are those "at the bottom who live in the toilet" (ibid.). No wonder Frantz Fanon regards wealth not as "the fruit of labor but the result of organized, protected robbery" (1968, 191).

Perhaps hierarchalism is the price societies must pay for increased material affluence. This has a comfortable Taker ring to it anyway. Those at the bottom in highly industrialized societies live in greater luxury than many members of the middle class in minimally industrialized societies (so bottom dwellers of industrialized societies better just shut their mouths and enjoy their scraps). "But as societies become more affluent they tend to require more, rather than less, time and commitment by individuals," Sebastian Junger states (2016, 6). Worse still, their basic institutions take on the character of their esteemed leaders. Those who've accumulated wealth and power are granted authority to make decisions that affect society at large, even as they create systems of reward that channel affluence "to the indecent, the *wétikos,* the cannibals, to those who would destroy," as Jensen remarks (2000, 213).

Consider the structural conditions that led Sherrilyn to walk away from her job. Each of us who's employed by a hierarchalist organization is subject to what Elizabeth Anderson calls *private government.* "When workers sell their labor to an employer, they have to hand *themselves* over to their boss, who then gets to order them around," Anderson states (2017, xx). Most workplaces are dictatorships. Bosses "govern in ways that are largely unaccountable to those who are governed. They don't merely govern workers; they *dominate* them" (ibid., xxii). Orders may be arbitrary, and they can change on a whim without the requirement of prior notice or an opportunity to appeal. Bosses are thus unanswerable to subordinates. They "are neither elected nor removable by inferiors. Inferiors have no right to complain in court about how they are treated, except in a few narrowly defined cases" (ibid., 37). And even in such cases, the odds are stacked heavily against them.

Sherrilyn's PTSD was well documented, as were its workplace causes. Toward the end of her time at the university, she received some minimal accommodations after meeting with university counsel. But several physicians and therapists testified that her condition necessitated a leave that warranted long-term disability compensation. Her requests were summarily denied. Moreover, when all appeals for disability were exhausted, her accommodations were revoked and she was "voluntarily resigned" (their actual phrasing) by the university. This meant she was effectively fired but that the university was under no obligation to pay her severance. Indeed, the conditions of her dismissal even made her ineligible for unemployment compensation.

To be sure, the sanctioning power of private governments is usually more limited than public governments. Basically, they can demote employees, worsen working conditions, cut wages, or, as with Sherrilyn, dictate exile. Still, the vast majority of us have no realistic option save to subordinate ourselves to another private government. Only "A few manage to escape into anarchic hinterlands, or set up their own dictatorships," Anderson states (2017, 38). What are the anarchic hinterlands? They're the purview of "the thin ranks of the self-employed who have no employees of their own" (ibid., 63). If Quinn has his way, those ranks are overdue for expansion. More on that later.

Walking Away

Archeologists and anthropologists have devoted countless studies to identifying the sociological and ecological causes of the collapse of so-called "lost" civilizations, including the Maya, the Hohokam, the Olmec, and the Anasazi. By and large, the identified culprits reduce to some combination of overly intensive land and water use, natural disasters, persistent drought, insect infestations, epidemics, peasant revolts, and foreign invasions (IS,

5ff.). Sing Chew (2001) hypothesizes that urbanization, population growth, and capital accumulation (which drives material consumption) spiraled upward until said civilizations inevitably collapsed under their own weight. Effectively, they eroded the ecologies that sustained them. Richard Wright notes that once civilizations reach a point at which they can no longer "keep wringing new loans from nature and humanity . . . the social contract breaks down. People may suffer stoically for a while, but sooner or later the ruler's relationship with heaven is exposed as a delusion or a lie" (2004, 84). What triggers this, though, is precisely the same dynamic that Chew highlights.

Jared Diamond offers among the most detailed accounts of several civilizational collapses. The Anasazi took advantage of favorable wet conditions to expand agriculture into increasingly marginal locales. Population growth combined with a reverse of climatological fortunes undermined what had become "a complex, interdependent society" (2005, 150). A similar dynamic befell the Maya, although adverse conditions were exacerbated by competition among elites to erect increasingly elaborate monuments in their own honor at the expense of attending to the needs of their people (ibid., 177).

This isn't to say that the leaders of lost civilizations were invariably "ignorant bad managers," Diamond adds. "They were people like us, facing problems broadly similar to those we now face" (ibid., 10). And like the people of our culture, they may have failed to anticipate problems before they arose, failed to wrestle with the full weight of acknowledged problems, or tried and failed to find workable solutions to their problems.[3] In each case, though, collapse involved elites losing their grip on power (Tainter 1988).

People abandon civilizations because they collapse or are in the process of collapsing. At least this is the common archeological and anthropological frame. But why foreground collapse rather than *abandonment* itself? Is there something about how we Takers think about civilization that leads us to do this? Quinn thinks so (see also Lawler 2010, Wilcox 2010, and Degroot et al. 2021).

The typical explanations for civilizational failure may represent proximate causes for their disappearance, Quinn avers. Each conceivably is the last straw in a long line of offenses the people of these civilizations endured—particularly those at the bases of the hierarchy. But none of these explanations can count as the ultimate cause for civilizational demise, Quinn insists, for each phenomenon can be endured if people have the will to do so. Soil depletion is typically a localized phenomenon. Natural disasters and insect infestations can be devastating, but they're episodic. People have found ways to adjust to drought conditions. And revolts and invasions can be withstood (BC, 41f.). No, not always, but often. Empires fall, regimes change, many people suffer and die, but none of these explanations proves decisive to explain how entire civilizations disappear.

According to Quinn, the disappearance of lost civilizations instead comes down to two specifiable memes that animated the stories enacted by their people but that are largely absent in ours: (1) *"If the way we are living does not work, we should give up and try something else"* (BC, 44, and IS, 8); and (2) *"Our means of making a living are governed by what we prefer"* (I, 167). Unlike for Takers, maintaining civilization didn't have to continue at any cost. Abandonment wasn't unthinkable. Nor was there an indefeasible presumption that people knew one right way that everyone must live. Put the Taker memes together and people persist at all costs, "even if it kills us . . . and all life on this planet" (IS, 10; see also Fleming 2016, 123). Put the memes ambient in lost civilizations together, Quinn contends, and people—not all, but many—*walk away* when other options look more appealing. And this is exactly what they did.

Again, what we're dealing with here is a question of framing. There are salient reasons that Quinn wants to foreground abandonment. Namely, abandonment of highly stratified means of socioeconomic organization can happen, has happened (Dunbar-Ortiz 2014, 18). And if we're to succeed with the threefold struggle, it must happen again. It doesn't have to happen all at once, however quickly it proceeds. But for those of us yearning for another story to be in, who may be prepared deliberately to throw away what Takers presume is the best possible lifestyle for something the people of our culture are trained to deem inferior (BC, 41), Quinn's choice of frame matters (Q&A, 160).

The Mayans abandoned state religion, a complex political system, and towering temples. The Olmec jettisoned luxury goods made from jade and obsidian and turned away from extravagant monuments. The Hohokam ceded an extensive irrigation network, finely constructed ceramics, and sprawling trade routes. In practical terms, these civilizations no more became lost than did the English settlers who joined Croatoan. They simply took up less conspicuous ways of living and making a living (BC, 41). As Tsotsil Maya Miguel Sanchez Alvarez remarks, his ancestors "didn't just disappear, they dispersed into small *pueblos*, and here we are. We are very adaptable" (cited in Conant 2019). Nothing here is extraordinary or mysterious. As usual, it's us Takers—who've managed to persuade ourselves that we must not only persist in our misery but spread it as far and wide as possible—who are the aberration.

The Myth of No Beyond

We've all heard the refrain, though. There can be no going back to primeval ways of living. Totalitarian agriculture has won the day. Civilization as we know it "is a final, unsurpassable invention" (BC, 3). There's no way to make a living, at least in a way we possibly could tolerate, without it. Besides, with Taker culture having invaded just about every last corner of the globe, all imaginable alternatives are now foreclosed. As Richard Heinberg puts it, our options have been narrowed "to two: participate or die. But participation is death, too" (2005a, 196). There simply is no opting out. Onward comrades, to our own collapse!

Alternatively, states Quinn, consider that what's "so far utterly barred us from quitting" . . . are memes (BC, 74). Be absurd. Be ridiculous. Imagine that there's something beyond civilization. Yes, the institutions of civilization span the globe. But civilization itself:

> isn't a geographical territory, it's a social and economic territory where pharaohs reign and pyramids are built by the masses. Similarly, beyond civilization isn't a geographical territory, it's a social and economic territory where people in open tribes pursue goals that may or may not be recognizably "civilized." You don't have to "go somewhere" to get beyond civilization. You have to make your living in a different way. (Ibid., 117)

Beyond civilization is also "a cultural space that opens up among people with new minds" (ibid., 187). People in *open tribes* are people with new minds, people committed to making a living "beyond hierarchalism" (ibid., 85).

What's an open tribe, you ask? We'll get there. For now, let's just say that open tribes represent a powerful tool for carrying out the threefold struggle.

Structural Defectors

Let's leverage a point that Quinn is pretty sure his readers can agree on. We detest slogging stones, particularly for other people's gaudy pyramids (Q&A, 487). If you don't detest doing so, fine. Keep on keeping on. But if you too experience somatic rebellion as a result of the slog, particularly if you feel as if you have no choice but to do so, then one thing you clearly want is to be a *structural defector.* You want to abandon building physical structures for human godheads. You want alternatives to the institutional structures that channel you into pyramid building in the first place. And you abhor the normative structures that support the notion that we have no other choice but to serve our superiors.

Defecting, walking away, isn't defeatism. It's a matter of "refusing to help the machine advance," as Roy Scranton puts it (2015, 24). We can do so on principle, of course. But we also can do so specifically to get more of what we want. And it turns out that pursuing more of what we want just might be exactly what's in order to free ourselves from not just our socioeconomic captivity but our cultural captivity, too. "This is the choice I'm offering in *Beyond Civilization,*" Quinn affirms: "if you don't want to *contribute* your energy to the behemoth that is devouring the world, maybe you should consider *draining away* some of its energy by living on its back like a flea. Who lives more harmlessly in this case, the person who makes a living by contributing energy to the behemoth or the person who makes a living draining some of that energy away? Personally, I vote for the flea" (Q&A, 448).

The New Tribal Revolution

You don't like the idea of being a parasite? You want a clean break, a chance to leap freely, fully, utterly unfettered into enacting a new story? Good luck with that, says Quinn.

Quinn notes that an early reader of the manuscript that became *Beyond Civilization* "was hoping I'd be able to find a way of transmitting us to our new economic homeland without our having to 'get wet' in the Taker economy that surrounds us." This homeland may be the dry land on the horizon, but to reach it "while holding ourselves disdainfully aloof from the economy around us would make walking on water seem like a very minor miracle indeed" (BC, 188; see also Q&A, 549). This doesn't mean that one must continue to derive their living directly from pyramid building. But as one becomes a structural defector, connects with other structural defectors, and helps the idea of walking away to catch on, it likely will require still deriving one's living, or part of it, via transactions with pyramid builders and those in whose honor their structures are erected. From an *infrapolitical* perspective, this actually can end up being a key to the success of the New Tribal Revolution.

Infrapolitics

According to James C. Scott, "virtually every successful revolution has ended by creating a state more powerful than the one it overthrew, a state that in turn was able to extract more resources from and exercise more control over the populations it was designed to serve" (2012, x). At the same time, possibilities for populaces to enlarge their sphere of individual and collective agency "occur only when massive extra-institutional disruption from below threatens the whole political edifice" (ibid., xiv). If Scott is correct, this poses quite a challenge. Massive defiance would seem to be a necessary condition from upending hierarchalism. Yet far more often than not it leads to even greater repression.

It's true, Scott comments, that the civil rights, anti-Vietnam, labor, and suffragist movements all made gains when they were "at their most disruptive, most confrontational, least organized, and least hierarchical. It was the effort to stem the contagion from a spreading, noninstitutionalized challenge to the existing order that prompted concessions," he asserts (ibid., xviii; see also Brafman and Beckstrom 2006). Yet we tend to overlook the outsized, complementary effects of more widespread forms of resistance that have been successful precisely because they've gone largely unnoticed.

Particularly among subaltern populations, engaging in infrapolitics—informal, cooperative, and loosely coordinated forms of troublemaking and subterfuge—supports "political change from below" (ibid., xxi).[4] It involves "everyday forms of resistance" (ibid., 8), such as foot dragging, sabotage, desertion, absenteeism, and squatting. When multitudes so act quietly and doggedly, these sorts of actions can be at least as potent as revolutionary vanguards or rioting mobs. "Multiplied many thousandfold, such petty acts of refusal may, in the end, make an utter shambles of the plans and dreams of generals and heads of state," Scott concludes (ibid., 7).

Open Tribes

Remember Quinn's quip that saving the world is for upstarts and lovers? We've seen how it's for lovers in chapters 4 and 6. Now we get to the upstarts.

Sherrilyn is an upstart. She's freed herself from the (direct) clutches of private government by defecting to the "anarchic hinterlands" of self-employment. Yet the nonprofit she also started comes closer in structure and function to Quinn's chosen vehicle for defection—open tribes.

We've seen that tribal living can bring with it a great deal of spiritual significance for its members. This tends to obscure that tribalism also serves as an occupational designation, Quinn asserts. Indeed, acknowledging that "a tribe is simply a coalition of people working together as equals to make a living" helps to demystify tribalism (BC, 147; see also "Dialogue on *Beyond Civilization,*" Q&A, 763, and Junger 2016, 16). Unfortunately, the examples Quinn gives specifically of open tribes in *Beyond Civilization*—the traditional model of the circus; the Neo-Futurists, a theatrical collective; the *East Mountain News,* a paper he ran with his wife Rennie; and means of making a living most clearly on display among the homeless (Smith 2014a)—don't have quite the translational traction that Quinn hopes they do. Readers don't necessarily know how to convert these examples into viable life options. At least this is what I gather from numerous discussions with my students and a comprehensive study of the Questions and Answers at ishmael.org. For this reason, permit me to try to demystify open tribes a little more.

Among going concerns within Taker culture, *non-share worker cooperatives* serve as exemplars of open tribes.[5] Non-share worker cooperatives reflect an organizational model that has existed since the early days of the Industrial Revolution. According to John Stuart Mill (1852, 772), they're expressly designed to offer a means to make a living that doesn't require subjection to a hierarchalist firm.[6]

In simplest terms, non-share worker cooperatives are businesses that are owned and controlled by the people who comprise them. Decisions are made democratically, the business culture is egalitarian, and the focus of workers tends to be largely collective. Workers shun equity investments as a means to finance the organization (this is what makes this kind of worker cooperative *non-share*), since this has the potential to lead them to focus more on share values than on the bases of their collective well-being (Vieta et al. 2016, 441f.). Revenue isn't beside the point, since it's what keeps businesses afloat, but it also isn't all that matters. Workers must be treated "not just as factors of production but as valued partners engaged cooperatively in value-creating activities," state James Kennelly and Mehmet Odekon (2016, 169).

Non-share worker cooperatives—hereafter simply *worker cooperatives*—thus are expressly designed for the mutual benefit of all members.

Economic success supports collective wellbeing. Indeed, membership within worker cooperatives isn't exactly employment in the traditional sense, since jobs, professions, and careers typically are regarded among Takers as individual endeavors. It's more accurate to say that members *are* the worker cooperative, just as members of a tribe are the tribe (BC, 153). They're contributors to pooled energy and skill. Each member may have unique tasks to fulfill, but what's important about fulfilling these tasks is that they're essential for the success of the collective enterprise (AD, 16, Q&A, 590, and "Talk about Wealth!").

Also as with tribes, worker cooperatives still have leaders (see chapter 5). But being a leader is just one of the duties that must be performed for the worker cooperative to function (Q&A, 648); and managerial authority is earned rather than seized or imposed. It doesn't connote superiority, and it may not come with extra compensation. At least this is so when worker cooperatives hew to horizontal, or lateral, socioeconomic relationships rather than drifting, as some organizations do in response to market pressures, toward some combination of hierarchalist and nonhierarchalist practices (Edenfield 2017, 261).[7]

At their best, then, worker cooperatives fulfill Bruce Levine's call (from chapter 2) for the facilitation of organizational cultures conducive to autonomy, community, and humanity. These qualities help to create strong bonds of loyalty among members (BC, 150). They also support organizational resilience and greater job security in the face of start-up difficulties and economic fluctuations. Worker cooperatives in general fail at a rate of roughly 10 percent within the first year, compared to a 60 to 80 percent failure rate for conventional firms. And more than 90 percent of the former are still operating after five years, compared to 3 to 5 percent of the latter (Williams 2007, 32, and Landín 2018, 43). Worker cooperatives also offer means for socioeconomic empowerment among parties—Indigenous peoples, black and brown people, women—that are particularly susceptible to exploitation by conventional firms, if they're not denied employment altogether (Berry and Bell 2018, 376f., and Ya-Bititi et al. 2019, 117).[8]

Getting More of What We Want

If working in democratic, egalitarian, and collectively focused conditions that support autonomy, community, and humanity sounds appealing, you're hardly alone. Making a living in this manner has stood the test of time. It's evolutionarily stable among humans because it helps people to get more of what we want and need (Q&A, 719). Yes, making a living in this manner has been subject to unending assault by Takers, particularly corporations and their political enablers. Being evolutionarily stable doesn't make something invincible. But it does mean that, unlike hierarchalism, it's conducive to ecological, social, and personal wellbeing (BC, 173, and WS, 119).

According to proponents of self-determination theory, which has strong affinities with Levine's considerations, we humans have three basic needs: an abiding sense that we're competent at what we do, that our lives matter, and that we're connected with others. Meaningful work, meaningful lives, and meaningful relationships: let's call these *intrinsic goods.* Taken together, these goods are necessary and sufficient specifically for personal wellbeing. Yes, we also desire extrinsic goods like money and status. But while they can complement the intrinsic goods, they can't substitute for them.

Junger states, for example, that as societies become more materially affluent, rates of anxiety, depression, schizophrenia, and suicide go up rather than down. If Levine is correct, this is because said societies become more rigidly institutionalized. Junger adds, though, that another factor—financial independence—is at play. Being more financially independent affords greater access to creature comforts, but it also often leads to isolation, which puts people at greater risk of poor mental health and chronic loneliness. Matters are made worse when we prioritize the pursuit of extrinsic goods, since this creates "a desperate cycle of work, financial obligation, and more work," whether or not that work is intrinsically satisfying (2016, 17).

Consider, by contrast, the *East Mountain News*. Quinn and Rennie owned the paper, but ad revenue was equitably parceled out not just between them but also with two additional workers, C. J. and Hap. Earnings were fairly thin. Work at the paper was never going to be a path to material riches, although for those at the bottom of Taker social hierarchies options like this offer a better opportunity for fair compensation than employment within conventional firms. Besides, Quinn states, "We weren't tribal because we were noble and altruistic; we were tribal because we were greedy and selfish" (BC, 144). He and his cohort got "more of what people want (as opposed to just getting more)" (ibid., 115). Each member found the work fulfilling, cooperated roughly as equals, and played a necessary role in the perpetuation of the paper.[9] And each was able to cobble together a living. Yes, they had to remain connected to the wider hierarchalist economy.

East Mountain News had to make money. But making money wasn't the primary object of their work. Rather, "we had to keep the paper going so the paper could keep *us* going" (ibid., 142).

Suffering and Struggling—Together

Like worker cooperatives, then, *East Mountain News* was an economic hybrid: a vessel for generating revenue, yes, but expressly to meet the needs and interests of members (Eşim and Katajamäki 2017, 2, Landín 2018, 43, and Eşim, et al. 2019). Also like worker cooperatives, the manner in which *East Mountain News* operated was less a means to break cleanly from capitalism than to promote what John Restakis calls the "socialization of capital." This offers salient opportunities for "remaking and humanizing the current capitalist system," Restakis states (2010, 3), by asking members to take care that market pressures lead them neither to prioritize profits at the expense of people nor to pursue forms of growth that undermine their equal participation in decision making.

But just how revolutionary are worker cooperatives? If they're akin to open tribes, how revolutionary is the New Tribal Revolution? Does the fact that worker cooperatives are beholden even partially to the logic of capitalist production and exchange nullify their emancipatory power? Are worker cooperatives and other sorts of open tribes hereby prone to getting sucked into precisely the sorts of socioeconomic dynamics they're designed to avoid? These aren't new worries. There's compelling evidence, though, that the organizational design of worker cooperatives can serve not just as a buffer against hierarchalism but also as a vehicle for substantive socioeconomic transformation.

Take, for example, problems associated with the potential for worker cooperatives to replicate hierarchies of race and gender. Joan Meyers and Steven Vallas (2016) assert that such hierarchies tend to linger within worker cooperatives so long as members view race and gender dynamics as exogenous forces—forces impinging on the organization from without. By contrast, worker cooperatives with organizational designs that channel members to view race and gender as endogenous forces—forces that are inherent, if unwittingly, in members' social dynamics—fare better. The latter distribute managerial and hiring authority widely, including explicitly along racial and gender lines. They expressly challenge racialized and gendered divisions of labor (Meyers 2011). And their governance structures leave "substantial room for historically excluded groups (including women, people of color, members of the working class, and sexual nonconformists) to express their voice and represent their own needs," note Meyers and Vallas (2016, 121).

These steps aren't intended merely to eliminate (or at least moderate) members' biases. They're meant to foster a workplace that can be "an arena in which antioppression tactics [are] to be energetically pursued" (ibid., 122; see also Miller 2012). Members' differences are treated not as a peripheral concern but as "an issue that may well cut to the heart of the participatory ideal itself" (ibid., 123). In general and on the whole, this helps members to address grievances more expeditiously and prevent the emergence of systemic inequalities within the organization. It also may serve to change the minds of members who've had limited prior exposure to the politics of difference (Sobering 2016 and Ray 2019).

Particularly during times of upheaval, two further dynamics may strengthen bonds within worker cooperatives and enhance members' commitments both to personal and social wellbeing. Consider, first, that communities devastated by natural disasters rarely lapse into chaos and disorder. Natural disasters create acute stress and hardship for anyone who goes through them. Perhaps surprisingly, they also strengthen social bonds and overwhelmingly lead people to devote themselves to cooperative endeavors. Most notably, Junger contends, "individuals are assessed simply by what they are willing to do for the group" (2016, 54; see also Solnit 2009). It also isn't uncommon for people to "become more just, more egalitarian, and more deliberately fair to individuals whatever their prior differences" (ibid., 44). They develop what experts in disaster resilience studies call *therapeutic communities.*

Such outcomes aren't atypical.[10] A dynamic similar to the one Junger describes may be at play within worker cooperatives during periods of economic distress—that is, when worker precarity is at its highest within conventional firms. Under such conditions, members commonly choose to take pay cuts and to collectively reduce their work hours rather than to shed members (Pencavel and Craig 1994 and Pencavel et al. 2006). Much like tribes, then, in worker cooperatives all both benefit together and suffer together.

Moreover, Restakis's and Marcelo Vieta's coinciding studies of the conversion of troubled firms into worker cooperatives in Argentina offer an interesting account of how workers' minds were changed in ways that directly facilitated their commitment to personal and social wellbeing. When Argentina's economy collapsed in 2001, numerous firms were forced to close. Those that remained in operation routinely violated labor contracts, both endangering employees' lives and drastically reducing their pay. Unions proved toothless and the social safety net disappeared. In response, employees spontaneously began to take over firms and transform them into *empresas recuperadas por sus trabajadores*—worker-recuperated enterprises.

Transitioning, as Vieta puts it, "from mostly acquiescent or self-interested employees to cooperative and self-managed workers," wasn't easy (2014, 187). Old habits died hard, with the initial egalitarian impulses waning in some firms, particularly as the economy rebounded. Familiar forms of individualism and deference to authority reappeared as the trade unions and the government attempted to channel workers back "into conventional neo-Keynesian nostrums for economies and social policy," Restakis states (2010, 216). Not only did the authoritarian political culture in Argentina have to be overcome, so did the traditional mentality of industrial employees within a capitalist system. "The two share a common logic of control and command," Restakis adds. "The inability, or unwillingness, of many to make the transition from industrial worker to co-owner of an enterprise [was] a major impediment" (ibid., 215).[11]

Yet amid these failures were myriad successes, thanks largely to ad hoc and informal means of what Vieta calls "learning in struggle" (2014, 186). Learning in struggle requires persisting in solidarity through economic crisis, fending off both legal and extralegal harassment by bosses, and—most importantly—metabolizing cooperativism. What work itself means has to be relearned, as does what it means to be a worker. As Restakis remarks:

> Workers could no longer wait for orders and rest assured that a paycheck awaited them at the end of the month. Everything was now up to them. The transition from dependence and obedience to democratic ownership and control was a transition that affected not only how work was organized but what it meant. Workers had to create new modes of working and relating and in so doing they were forced to develop dimensions of their personalities they had never used. They were forced to become different people. Work took on a deeply social meaning. The simple act of creating and operating a cooperative in the circumstances of Argentina in these days was transformative and no one was untouched by it. (2010, 213)[12]

In the process, workers took up "community-minded and socially aware practices beyond just the daily concerns of the shop," Vieta relays (2014, 187). Through learning in struggle, concern for group-oriented responsibilities emerged alongside worker autonomy and self-determination.

Vieta notes that because worker cooperatives reinforce the pursuit of mutually beneficial practices, their members come to see their workplaces "as continuations of and integral players in the neighborhoods where they are located" (ibid., 204). Workers not only affirm what Erik Wright calls the "emancipatory values of egalitarianism" but also are "likely to contribute more consistently to the wider agenda of social empowerment" (2010, 22). Communities thus become not merely sites of expanding solidarity but even spaces in which something like the sacred can take hold in the manner of a more sustained and effulgent concern for one's community, one's place, and, if applicable, the peoples from whom one's place was stolen. This process is facilitated when everyday nonmonetary transactions—involving obligations, loyalties, and collaborations among friends, family, civic associations, neighboring Indigenous communities, and the like—interweave with and even partially supplant monetary transactions (Fleming 2016, xxi).[13]

Place-Based Enterprises

What, though, of ecological wellbeing? How might it be facilitated by worker cooperatives? Proceeding beyond civilization, in the specifiable manner that open tribes can permit, doesn't make one instantly "as harmless as a shark, tarantula, or rattlesnake," Quinn remarks, "but it will instantly move you in that direction" (BC, 112). This has to do in part with economies of scale, since the design of worker cooperatives and other kinds of open tribes "automatically limits your access to the tools needed to do harm. The people of the Circus Flora will never build a Stealth bomber or open a steel mill—not just because they wouldn't want to but because even if they wanted to, they wouldn't have access to the tools. To regain access to the tools, they'd have to leave the circus and find new places for themselves in a culture of maximum harm" (ibid.).

Quinn's position here is compatible with *degrowth,* or with refocusing away from a consumption-based culture and artificially induced scarcity toward building sustainable human and more-than-human communities. Degrowth advocates—including supporters of municipalism (Bookchin 2005 and Finley 2017), the transition movement (Hopkins 2011), and sustainable materialism (Schlosberg and Craven 2019)—argue in favor of economic downscaling, or the reversal of the trend toward centralized energy production, globalized networks of consumption, and increased mechanization (Kallis 2011 and Ellwood 2014). The reemergence of localized economies, which worker cooperatives facilitate, is key. This is particularly so when degrowth is coupled with decolonization, a matter we'll take up in the next chapter.

Sustainable societies are resilient, particularly in the face of climactic and ecological disruptions, in part because risk is dispersed among disaggregated and substantially self-sufficient communities. When each community can, for the most part, see to its own energy, food, water, and waste disposal needs, disruptions within one community are less likely to resonate throughout society. Furthermore, because localized communities are dependent for their survival on the ecosystems in which they reside, they have a vested interest in ensuring that the needs and interests of these ecosystems govern the form their infrastructures take and the day-to-day activities of their members. This doesn't obviate developing a robust trading network among communities (Nabhan 2013, 6f.). Nor does it necessitate that communities be left to their own devices in the face of adversity. The point of community self-sufficiency is instead to facilitate societal modularity: a dispersal of component parts that, while interactive, don't compromise the integrity of the whole should they fail (Brafman and Beckstrom 2006, 5).

To be sure, a good number of the firms taken over by workers in Argentina are incompatible with degrowth. Forja San Martin, an auto parts company, is one example. FaSinPat (*Fábrica Sin Patrones*, or Factory Without Bosses), a ceramics factory, is another. Perhaps the best known worker cooperative in the world is the sprawling Mondragon Cooperative Corporation. Headquartered in the Basque Country, it has an international foothold in the industrial, financial, distribution, and technology sectors.

Quinn is focused exclusively on enterprises that choose to remain small. From his vantage point, Mondragon and the like violate the open tribal model since they operate well beyond human scale. They're more akin to an organizational "tribe of tribes," or a "coalition of tribes working together as equals to make a living" (BC, 65).[14] But because of their largesse they remain perpetually at risk of succumbing to hierarchalist tendencies and hereby defying the avowed needs and interests of their members.

In anticipation of the increasing frequency and intensity of climatological and ecological disruptions—and, additionally, energy-related factors that we'll touch on in chapter 8—let's keep our focus on worker cooperatives that are better suited to meeting the demands of societal modularity. Such companies are likely to be limited in scale, hence to more closely align with Quinn's open tribal model. They can be expected to operate within intercooperative networks but also to remain localized (BC, 115). Some 280 million people today belong to worker cooperatives, and the vast majority are local ventures (Eum 2017).

Taking steps to bring an end to domination of humans by humans arguably itself translates into greater resistance to the domination of fellow members of the community of life (Bookchin 2005, 65). Moreover, to the extent that worker cooperatives assume the form of *place-based enterprises*, the provisions on which they rely, their productive activities, and their waste practices all are anchored in specific locales. Capital is more firmly rooted in and more likely to serve the needs of their ecologies (Imbroscio et al. 2003). These phenomena further solidify members' own sense of place both materially and relationally (Shrivastava and Kennelly 2013, 94) and, as we'll see, can serve as bases of support for decolonization.

Civilizational Atrophy

It's worth reiterating that proceeding beyond civilization as Quinn conceptualizes it doesn't entail that one is entirely free from Taker culture. But the former can lead to the latter, he contends. Again, those who remain committed pyramid builders are welcome to stick with hierarchalism, Quinn emphasizes. It's high time, though, that we acknowledge the millions, even billions, "who slog stones up the pyramids not because they love stones or pyramids but because they have no other way to put food on the table" (BC, 80; see also MI, 219). Pyramid builders can go on enjoying their job, careers, and professions. "The rest of us just want something else, and it's high time we had it" (BC, 85).[15]

To go beyond civilization doesn't necessarily involve directly dismantling the institutional bases of hierarchalism, then. Worker cooperatives and other kinds of open tribes instead are designed to allow structural defectors to withdraw their support for it—to the extent that they can while still making a living. They facilitate *civilizational atrophy* and the emergence of norms and practices that run counter to Taker culture (ibid., 171, and "Dialogue on *Beyond Civilization*").

Like the people of the purportedly lost civilizations, New Tribal Revolutionaries tend to focus on abandonment rather than on open revolt against the rulers (BC, 95).[16] Rulers have formidable defenses against attack from below. But they have fewer effective ways to prevent people infrapolitically from discontinuing their support.

Yes, the embrace of infrapolitics entails an incrementalist approach (MI, 218). In this respect, it isn't particularly sexy. But Quinn is no fan of either cataclysmic or Edenic revolutionary narratives. While both have rich legacies among Takers, "the idea of undermining civilization's foundations and sapping its titanic strength incrementally as a rewarding, lifelong process is a bit of a shocker" ("Dialogue on *Beyond Civilization*"; see also Kingsnorth 2010 and Tsing 2015).

This echoes Donna Haraway's call to *stay with the trouble.* Especially in difficult times, we Takers are particularly tempted to think that we must pursue the Edenic to avoid the cataclysmic. To stay with the trouble, though, involves seeking means for "partial recuperation and getting on together" as best we can, given the circumstances we face here and now, Haraway remarks (2016, 10; see also Hall 2017, 438). Indeed, for incrementalism to be rewarding doesn't mean it always must be fun. It's sure to require considerable sacrifice, which is one manifestation of assuming responsibility for oneself and for others. But sacrifice in the struggle for ecological, social, and personal wellbeing may be its own reward. It's also critical to getting more of what we want, not only when it's directed toward the pursuit of intrinsic goods but when it actually *involves* them (DeVega 2019).

Whatever else we can say, the threefold struggle isn't a matter of grasping at panaceas or grand fixes. No one gets and stays sober by taking palliative shortcuts. It starts instead by refusing to do what every active alcoholic does, namely, in Haraway's terms, "[putting] off until tomorrow the problems of life" (2016, 31)—and, ecologically speaking, the problems *for* life. From such a perspective, saving the world is an emergent property of events. It occurs piecemeal, at least at the outset. "A common livable world is composed, bit by bit," Haraway insists, "or not at all" (ibid., 40).

In the same vein, Rebecca Solnit observes that stories often "migrate secretly" from the margins to the center of the political spectrum (2016, 31). Ideas that people come to regard as commonsense frequently first were espoused by people who were regarded as "kooks, extremists, and impractical dreamers" (ibid., 32). While revolutions may look spontaneous, they're typically products of "less visible long-term organizing and groundwork—or underground work" (ibid., xv).

Consider the workings of the Industrial Revolution, Quinn notes. As a vision, it has been spread via the dissemination of a key meme: "*Improve on something, then put it out for others to improve on*" (Q&A, 159). Learn what others are doing and build on their ideas. Identify people who are figuring out how to make things work and draw inspiration from them (MI, 212). He expects the New Tribal Revolution to (continue to) emerge in a similar fashion.

"To acknowledge all this is not to make the Industrial Revolution a blessed event," Quinn emphasizes (BC, 19). We can condemn this period during which Takers have most aggressively and most destructively imposed our vision on Earth as the catastrophic mistake it has turned out to be and also acknowledge that it was the result of "a million small beginnings, a million great little ideas, a million modest innovations and improvements over previous inventions" (MI, 209). As we look to a future in which it's essential that we strive to get more of what we want even as the conditions required to do so will work increasingly against us, we've "got to be thinking about releasing just such another outpouring of human creativity," Ishmael tells Julie. The point this time, though, is to direct it not toward individual aggrandizement and "product wealth" but toward the communal wealth "you threw away to make yourselves the rulers of the world and now so desperately crave" (ibid., 210–11).[17]

The Unsubmissive

It's important to think structurally when considering the revolutionary character of New Tribalism. Lierre Keith emphasizes that withdrawal from hierarchalist institutions "has to happen on a much larger scale to be effective. . . . Alternative institutions like local food networks, communal childcare, nonindustrial schooling, direct democracy, and community-based policing and justice are essential to both a culture of resistance and to post-carbon survival" (2011a, 107). At the same time, Aric McBay states, we must acknowledge that a large-scale shift of this sort "would become a threat" to rulers, "a dangerous example, and would be treated accordingly" (2011c, 252). This, he warns, ends up making withdrawal useless as a resistance strategy. It must gain critical mass to be effective, but gaining critical mass is precisely what would lead to retribution.

For this reason, McBay—a founder along with Keith and Derrick Jensen of Deep Green Resistance (DGR)—calls instead for activists to engage in "decisive ecological warfare" (2011b). This involves all-out resistance through open violence, hacktivism, and eco-sabotage by those seeking to bring an end to civilization. The point, McBay insists, is to "*make maximum use of available levers and fulcrums.* Which is to say, play to our strengths and take advantage of the weaknesses of those who are trying to destroy the world" (2011a, 57; see also Alvarez 2014, 43). We can't wait on the people of Taker culture incrementally to embrace sanity and sustainability. As such, one reader of Quinn remarks, echoing DGR, "the very best those who love the world can do is to try to bring civilization down as soon as possible in a sort of planned demolition, like taking down a condemned building" (Q&A, 749).

What we have here is a philosophical disagreement between Quinn and DGR over the salience of changing minds as opposed to forcing a change of options (Q&A, 426 and 749). This leads in turn to a procedural disagreement. For while it's the case that rulers are prepared to defend against attacks from below, DGR maintains that this doesn't mitigate the need for such attacks. In this vein, Jensen states:

> Anybody who has ever been in a violent relationship knows that to leave is extremely dangerous, as abusers often kill their victims rather than let them escape (showing they'd rather kill than give up their control, and, as my mom said, give up their identities). They sometimes kill themselves as well, showing that they'd rather die, too, than give up their control and identity. . . . If an abuser cannot control a thing, it shall not be allowed to exist. This is the quintessence of abuse. (2006a, 200)

Under such circumstances, there's no option save direct confrontation, although the manner in which it's carried out requires a great deal of care.[18]

I see two ways to respond on Quinn's behalf. First, David Brooks highlights (in a surprisingly good article) that widespread changes in behavior usually occur "before we realize that a new cultural paradigm has emerged. Imagine hundreds of millions of tiny arrows. In times of social transformation, they shift direction—a few at first, and then a lot. Nobody notices for a while, but then eventually people begin to recognize that a new pattern, and a new set of values, has emerged" (2020). This is where the economically hybrid character of worker cooperatives serves perhaps its most important long-term purpose. Hybridity entails parasitism. Recall that along with other kinds of open tribes, members of worker cooperatives may continue to make a living, at least in part, via transactions with pyramid builders and those in whose honor their structures are erected. This can mask the breadth and depth of withdrawal as it's happening. Recall, too, that hybridity permits members of worker cooperatives to drain monetary wealth from hierarchalist institutions that then can circulate within their communities. So the incremental character of New Tribalism may mean its success goes largely unnoticed until it's too late to contain or crush.

Second, I won't try to defend Quinn's uncharacteristic suggestion that taking the world back from corporations and their political enablers "won't be hard. They're not expecting it—but even if they were, they'd be helpless to stop it" (BC, 181). We have ample evidence of politicians, financiers, and industrialists who already impede and oppose people trying to proceed beyond civilization. We can expect them to fight all the harder in cases in which their power and capacity are on the wane (Heinberg 2015, 84). Forced labor and indentured servitude are once again on the rise (Eşim et al. 2019, 62). In places such as the United States, criminalization of debt also has returned, largely due to people defaulting on student loans and medical bills (ACLU 2018). And while Quinn strangely doubts that rulers would try to kill abandoners as a last resort (BC, 110), Indigenous peoples know otherwise.

As a result, direct resistance is in order not just for self-defense but also to challenge rulers' worst excesses. Being a parasite may have its place, but so does actively impeding systems that undercut the threefold struggle. Quinn's affinity for a pithy claim offered by Buckminster Fuller suggests at first glance that he disagrees. "You never change things by fighting the existing reality," Fuller proclaims. "To change something, build a new model that makes the existing model obsolete" (cited by Quinn in BC, 138, WS, 92, and Q&A, 764). The claim offered in the second of these sentences surely supports Quinn's extensive efforts to outline the contours of a new story to be in. But the claim from the first sentence is flat out wrong if Fuller means that the sorts of open defiance and disruption that civil rights, labor, anti-Vietnam, and suffragist movements embodied are never effective. The same can be said, for that matter, about the efforts of Black Lives Matter and Idle No More.[19]

Whatever Fuller may mean, this isn't Quinn's position. I suspect instead that he takes Fuller's first claim to be more an acknowledgment of the power of engaging in prefigurative strategies for social change—enacting a new story within the shell of an old one (Leach 2013, 182, and Brown 2017, 55ff.). This interpretation fits better with the second claim anyway. It's also corroborated by the tenor of Quinn's praise for the

Occupy movement ("Open Letter to Occupy Protestors"). And it's supported by several key passages in *Tales of Adam* in which Adam defends drawing on the gifts of wisdom to act with calculated resolve when one must directly confront dangerous and deadly foes (TA, 76, 81–82, and 85; see also H, 161).

"The world will be saved, if it can be, only by the unsubmissive," André Gide insists (2000, 264). Both direct resistance and walking away are needed forms of unsubmissiveness. They're both examples of what John Lewis calls "good trouble, necessary trouble," the sort of trouble we must get into if we're committed to "the struggle of a lifetime, or maybe many lifetimes" (2018). Comparably, Richard Williams regards the worker cooperative and labor movements as complementary, highly effective reactions to the transformation of working conditions under industrialism. "While the labor movement found its power in confrontation with management, the cooperative movement focused its energy and found its power in providing a more democratic alternative to increasingly hierarchical free market capitalism" (2007, 26–27). They make a good pair.

And Unlocking the Food?

But what role, if any, is there for unlocking the food? Since this is what triggered the emergence of hierarchalism in the first place, finding a way even partially to get food out from under lock and key seems to be necessary to bring about hierarchalism's decline. While the homeless are often painted as freeloaders, Quinn lauds them instead as scavengers and collectors of discarded food from grocery stores and restaurants. Numerous restaurants willingly give away unused and expired food at the end of each night. Both restaurants and supermarkets dispose of considerably more, making dumpster diving a popular enterprise (Tett 2011). As such, the homeless—or the "Tribe of Crow," as Quinn evocatively calls them (BC, 139)—have found viable means of unlocking the food. They've identified "cracks in the strongroom wall," Ishmael proclaims (MI, 200; see also Boyle 2010, 42). This represents a powerful, if indirect, stance against both food waste and forms of socioeconomic organization that permit millions to go hungry.

In a reply to a reader, though, Quinn confesses to seeing no practicable way to widen these cracks. If all the food on store shelves were free for the taking, it would no longer be produced; "the vast machinery that presently makes it available would grind to a halt instantly—with calamitous results" (Q&A, 527). Locking up the food has been disastrous for people and the planet. Seeking some sort of reversal of this development "is not, however, a place to begin to change our situation" (ibid.).

I must admit that this reply baffles me. Why commit to incrementalism with respect to the New Tribal Revolution but refuse to consider that the reader might be thinking in incrementalist terms with respect to unlocking the food? Might it be because Quinn has no idea where the process could start? I can't say. Do I have some ideas? Yes.

Chapter 8

Unlocking the Food

In Defense of Symbioculture

Systemic risk. During the early days of the COVID-19 pandemic, I couldn't get the phrase out of my mind.

I recall sitting in my study as I began work on this chapter, looking out at a flowering hawthorn tree on a sunny March morning as the pandemic began its inexorable surge here in the United States. I couldn't help but wonder how this monumental event would influence your reading of the previous seven chapters, all written earlier. How would *I* view things as cases—and deaths—mounted? The prospect of widespread illnesses and fatalities was crippling. The thought of becoming uneasily habituated to it all somehow terrified me more.

Still, the speed at which minds changed was something to behold. In a matter of days, memes highlighting the need for *social distancing* and *flattening the curve* became ubiquitous. In a society in which attending solely to matters of personal risk has long been a dominant theme, concerns about systemic risk were finally getting their due. Given the circumstances, our interdependence and mutual vulnerability were palpable. The need to restructure our lives for the sake of others, particularly the elderly and the immunosuppressed, became imperative. As always, many holdouts remained. But they also stood out—and still do—not as exceptions per se but as increasingly obvious impediments to an emerging vision, a river flowing in a noticeably different direction (B, 49). I dare say the Taker axioms are looking a little worse for wear these days, even among many of those still under the thrall of Mother Culture.

What, if anything, does this have to do with unlocking the food? Although we tend not to categorize them as such, pandemics may count as ecocidal events. Available evidence suggests that the development and spread of pathogens to which humans haven't previously been exposed may be a consequence of Taker expansionism, particularly via totalitarian agriculture. Along with being the primary spreading mechanism for Taker culture, totalitarian agriculture is the foremost driver of deforestation. The ongoing loss of arboreal habitats by other-than-human members of the living community who once resided beyond the bounds of Taker culture forces those who remain to make their living on the fringes of cities and towns, where they inevitably encounter humans and (other) domesticated animals. Contact with these supposed interlopers has led to our exposure to pathogens—H1N1, Ebola, SARS, MERS, Zika, COVID-19—to which we've built up little or no immunity (Harris 2020, Kuchipudi 2020, and Shah 2020). The risk of human exposure to zoonotic diseases is further exacerbated by the extirpation of predators of rodent populations (Young et al. 2014).

But what does *this* have to do with unlocking the food? A lot, actually. For not only does unlocking the food facilitate the decline of hierarchalism, the manner in which I envision it being carried out may also greatly lessen systemic risk: to global climate change, widespread ecological destruction, and, yes, pandemics.

Recall from the previous chapter that societal modularity involves risk dispersal among disaggregated and substantially self-sufficient communities. When communities can, for the most part, meet their own needs, disruption within any one of them is less likely to reverberate outward. This doesn't mean that communities must fend for themselves in times of crisis, but it does put a premium on living in accordance with the needs and interests of their ecologies. Critical to this enterprise—and to unlocking the food—is to bring an end to totalitarian agriculture, or what, particularly in the wake of the Great Acceleration, is perhaps better labeled *toxiculture.*

Why toxiculture? Because now more than ever before totalitarian agriculture poisons relationships: with the land, with Indigenous communities, with the beings who we make our food, and with ourselves. It's the death urge embodied in "chemical regimes of living" (Murphy 2008), a fossil fuel-driven monoculture that erodes and depletes soil, requires deforestation, causes desertification, pollutes waterways, undermines biodiversity, renders myriad species extinct, is a primary generator of greenhouse gas emissions, compromises food security and food sovereignty, and is deeply implicated in physical and cultural genocide of Indigenous peoples.

Toxiculture also privileges eating practices premised on the consumption of poisoned food: highly processed, nutrient-poor forms of sustenance produced within a global agroindustrial food system that depends on the use of antibiotics, hormones, synthetic fertilizers, and *-cides*. These eating practices persist not because farmers the world over have an earnest desire to poison eaters. It's instead a function of the colonization and commodification of food. The former weaponizes food, making it a tool for the spread of Taker culture in its most current form: settler colonialism. The latter turns food from a source of nutrition into a source of profit, preventing people from enjoying healthy lives and lifeways.

Unlocking the food requires nothing less than decolonizing land and foodways and decommodifying food, traditional food-based knowledge, and food labor. Neither decolonization nor decommodification necessarily makes food free. But contrary to Quinn's expectations, this isn't required for food to be unlocked, hence to bring an end to toxiculture and the systemic risks to ecological, social, and personal wellbeing that it perpetuates. Indeed, decolonization and decommodification is about detoxifying our alimentary relationships—by supporting the proliferation of *symbiocultures* and scaling out *kincentric eating.*

The term *symbioculture* was coined by farmosopher, neologist, and "symbiost" Glenn Albrecht.[1] It's a "psychoterric concept," he remarks, a concept that's intended to highlight "our deeper, more intimate relationships to each other and the rest of life" (2014, 58).[2] Albrecht offers a rather oblique description of symbioculture across several blog posts, not a usual source in my experience of robust philosophical content. But the idea is rich with possibility—particularly, I suggest, when framed by Indigenous understandings of food systems (Smith 2021).

Symbiocultures support polycultural post-carbon food production and distribution that's directly rooted in traditional forms of Indigenous ecological knowledge. More broadly, it's reflective of kinship-based food cultures premised on enhancing affinity with the land and living community by functioning within the trophic networks of proximate ecosystems (Forbes 2008, 10f., Nelson 2008a, 10, and Nelson 2008b, 180). Symbioculture hereby facilitates multiple forms of wellbeing: from a healthy gut microbiome; to the symbiotic functions of fungi, manure, compost, and local bioturbation; to flourishing local food networks and cooperatives; to enhanced adaptation to and mitigation of global-scale anthropogenic geochemical and climactic disruptions.

By extension, kincentric eating supports mutualistic, commensalistic, and reciprocal relationships of interdependence among humans, other members of the living community, and the abiotic geochemical and climactic systems that support life on Earth. A kincentric eater eats ecosystemically and bioculturally, weaving their own alimentary engagement with the land with that of their neighbors, both human and other-than-human.

After getting a clearer sense of what makes toxiculture so, well, toxic, we look more closely at what kincentric eating entails. We then assess increasing evidence of impending energy descent, which necessitates a near-term shift (whether voluntary or otherwise) away from the use of fossil fuels. Since toxiculture depends on a continued supply of fossil fuels, the writing's on the wall. It's on its last legs, as it must be. Still, a just transition from toxiculture to symbioculture is imperative. Decolonizing land and foodways and decommodifying food, traditional food-based knowledge, and food labor are key to this transition. They're also the keys, as it were, to the storehouse door.

You'll notice, by the way, that Quinn's voice is far less prominent in this chapter than in others, largely because he says almost nothing about the matters considered here besides offering a passing endorsement of permaculture (IS, 148). Why this is so, I can't say. This chapter just has to be a bit more "in the spirit" (as the subtitle to this book indicates) of his broader considerations than usual.

Toxiculture

Toxiculture is the latest iteration of totalitarian agriculture. We're familiar with the most obvious topographical effects of totalitarian agriculture: aggressive clearing of land for crop cultivation, exploitation and manipulation of available water sources, and the sacrifice of topsoil—and entire ecosystems—for the sake of short-term fertility. As we discussed in chapter 2, each of these outcomes is a result of the operationalization of three interweaving presumptions. First, food that's dedicated to the use of Takers is denied to all others, both human and other-than-human (I, 127f.). Second, other-than-human competitors for Taker food may be exterminated at will, and Leaver competitors may be contained or killed as well if they persistently refuse conversion to Taker ways. This includes embracing totalitarian agriculture. Third, food that Takers don't designate as ours but that's needed by our competitors is destroyed to make room to produce Taker crops—including for factory farming and biofuels. Recall B's incisive conclusion: "That's the whole point of totalitarian agriculture. We hunt our competitors down, we destroy their food, and we deny them access to food. That's what makes it totalitarian" (ibid., 154).

Toxiculture is at once an outgrowth of and engine for the pursuit of unlimited growth—namely, today, of gross domestic products and corporate profits (Morrison 2020, 19f.). Its success in creating massive food surpluses for Takers is among the primary phenomena motivating the widely held assumption among the people of our culture that to be human is to be insatiable and that there are no limits to what we can have and what we can accomplish (Kingsnorth and Hine 2009, 10). Within this conceptual framework, the biosphere itself is viewed as an ever-given food preserve.

Consider the Green Revolution, which is based on the notion that soil fertility can be maintained indefinitely through the use of synthetic fertilizers, many of which are petroleum based and require high-energy processing. From the vantage point of its proponents, the Green Revolution is designed to radically improve global food productivity while also enhancing the prospects for land conservation in areas not under cultivation. Greater intensification on existing plots should make the expansion of arable land unnecessary.

But this isn't how things work out, for rather obvious reasons. The very success of the Green Revolution in growing more food for Takers *has created more Takers*. Human population has exploded. This has fueled the demand for putting ever more land to the plow and using ever increasing amounts of synthetic fertilizers due to precipitous soil erosion. The proliferation of factory farming and the demand for biofuels further reinforce this dynamic.

For decades, Vandana Shiva has been among the most visible and vocal opponents of toxiculture. The global food system is irrevocably broken "on every measure that counts," she proclaims, including in terms of sustainability, justice, health, and peace (2016, ix). Ecological, social, and personal wellbeing:

> are severely threatened by an industrial globalized agriculture driven by greed and profits. . . . Food, whose primary purpose is to provide nourishment and health, is today the single biggest health problem in the world: nearly one billion people

> suffer from hunger and malnutrition, two billion suffer from diseases like obesity and diabetes, and countless others suffer from diseases, including cancer, caused by the poisons in our food." (Ibid.)

Indeed, toxiculture is less a means of feeding people than "a collection of violent tools" that "were literally products of warfare . . . originally designed to kill people" (ibid., 3).[3] These tools have since been economically repurposed to financialize foodways and concentrate corporate ownership, both of which propel endemic food insecurity—particularly among Indigenous and peasant peoples—and the grossly unequal distributions of food (Figueroa-Helland et al. 2018 and Settee and Shukla 2020). Toxiculture is thus designed less to produce food than to produce commodities. "Ninety percent of the corn and soy grown in the world is used for biofuel or animal feed, because that's where the largest profits lie. Commodities don't feed people; they create hunger," Shiva emphasizes (2016, 87).

Every aspect of toxiculture "is rupturing the fragile web of life and destroying the foundations of food security" (ibid., xii). The replacement of this food system is essential. It's also possible.

Kincentric Eating

Food systems are typically viewed as encompassing the entire range of actors, value-adding activities, and technologies involved in the production, processing, distribution, consumption, and disposal of food products originating from agriculture, forestry, and fisheries (FAO 2018). They also include core components of the broader social, political, economic, and ecological spheres in which they operate. So food systems comprise not only the basic elements of how we get our food from farm or forest or fishery to fork but also all of the processes and infrastructures involved in feeding people.

But food systems aren't merely networks of actors, institutions, and provisions. Food systems are also value systems. They reflect ways of relating to the beings who we eat and all that goes into making them our food.[4] They embody what Kyle Whyte calls *systems of responsibilities* (2018d, 126). Symbioculture makes this explicit.

Etymologically, *symbioculture* is rooted in Latin: *sym-* (in company with), *bios* (life), and *cultura* (cultivation). So specified, it involves nurturing the lives of those in one's ecology, including the beings who become one's food. Relations among our food sources; cultivators, distributors, and eaters; and the land are sustainable when they function as extended kinship arrangements. Kincentric eating reinforces these relations.

When regarded in emergent and mutualistic terms, to be kin is to be interdependent with respect to an arrangement of beings (Sahlins 2011). Relatives have lives that intertwine. More succinctly, kin comprise one's ecology. As noted in chapter 6, ecologies are arrangements of human and other-than-human beings and entities enmeshed in relations of responsibility based on multigenerational spatial knowledge. Since eaten and eater are kin, each has specifiable responsibilities to the other.

Our food has responsibilities to us? Yes. Here's but one example. Rarámuri ethnobotanist Enrique Salmón notes that the traditional food of his community "itself, and the landscape from which it emerges, remembers how it should be cooked. This can happen because the food activates in us an encoded memory that reminds us how to grow, collect, and prepare food. The land and food then become the source of knowledge and history" (2012, 9).[5] This knowledge is rarely systematically recorded, which makes cultivator-to-cultivator training critical (Sharma et al. 2020, 91). Such training also resists decontextualizing local food-based epistemologies.

From this vantage point, what makes toxiculture so damaging is that it incentivizes rejecting our ecologies—abdicating our responsibilities to the land and the relatives who inhabit it—in part by consuming others' landscapes (Salmón 2012, 154). This makes toxiculture doubly poisonous (along with being doubly monocultural, as we saw in chapter 2). It introduces myriad *-cides* into ecologies while also undermining the life-affirming and life-enhancing relationships they embody.

Particularly within an Indigenous context, symbiocultural food systems and kincentric eating practices thus represent explicit resistance to toxiculture, Salmón implies.[6] "Food sovereignty for Native peoples is the antithesis to the industrialization of all people" (ibid., 150).

Indelibly burdened by settler colonialism, resisting toxiculture is a fraught enterprise for Indigenous peoples. It's messy. But messiness is hardly foreign to Indigenous cultivators, Salmón avers. It's quite visible in traditional Native fields, which tend to appear overgrown and neglected to the settler eye:

> The result, however, is a diversity of plants in and around the field that serve to keep the soils and planted crops from becoming overheated. In addition, the diversity of plants attracts pollinators and the birds that try to eat them. Rodents and

> small mammals approach the fields as well as welcomed snakes that feed on the rodents. In this scenario, repeated throughout Native America, traditionally planted fields offer green mosaics that create ecosystems and microinhabitants. A Native field is a diversity condo that can be eaten. (Ibid., 44)

Enjoying green mosaics and inhabiting diversity condos tend to inspire deep care for and careful attention to the needs and interests of ecologies—including the land, others, and oneself. This is critical, particularly in light of the emerging prospects for societal modularity. "When a community's survival depends on maintaining total connection with the intricacies of its environment, no detail is ever missed," Salmón asserts (ibid., 56). Such a community can't afford toxiculture. In a hotter, drier—and meteorologically weirder—world, particularly across landscapes where the bulk of the world's food is grown, none of us can.

The Honorable Harvest

Morally speaking, it's worth emphasizing that kincentric eating isn't primarily a matter of who we eat but of how we relate to the relatives we make our food in life and in death. As with the dictates of Indigenous stewardship (chapter 6), how our relatives have lived and how they subsequently become our food are both care-sensitive. Our relationships must involve caring about them in the sense of taking responsibility for the continuation of our shared community and the health of their kind, caring for them individually, being careful of them when warranted, and being willing to receive care from them.

Yet this seems to create a serious difficulty. How do we reconcile that our lives are dependent on eating relatives? How is this not a violation of our responsibilities to them? Addressing these questions is at the core of what Kimmerer calls the Honorable Harvest:

> Of course, acknowledging the complete dependence of humans on other beings creates tension. It is understood that humans must take other lives in order to sustain our own, so the way in which plants and animals are harvested becomes very important, and they should be taken in such a way that the life received is honored. This inherent contradiction, implicit in heterotrophic biology, is resolved in Indigenous philosophy

> by practices of reciprocity, by giving back. (2018, 32; see also Martinez 2018)

To eat relatives prohibits one from regarding them purely as resources or commodities. It's also what generates care-sensitive protocols, which are part of the "spiritual preparation" (Forbes 2008, 14) for complicity in taking life, that help one to guard against overexploitation and to ensure that both current and future generations—of eaten and eaters—thrive. Living at a distance from the killing done for us to have food is no excuse for failing in this regard, even if it makes the task of attunement to taking life that much more difficult.

As opposed to prohibiting use altogether, the Honorable Harvest hereby requires nurturing reciprocity by harvesting respectfully. This is the basis of thriving ecologies.[7] Asking permission to take a life entails conscientious assessment and evaluation of responses by one's food sources and the land, Kimmerer contends. With respect to animals, subsistence hunters exhibit the keen eye of the tracker (from chapter 5). Those with the ability to communicate with plants also discern clear behavioral replies. These replies may include not only responses to change but also "the apparency of the plant, the play of light, variations in resistance to harvest, and sensation of an emotional response between plant and harvester," Kimmerer states (2018, 34; see also Buhner 2002, 33, and Kimmerer 2013, 158). Inflicting as little damage as possible on surrounding vegetation and repairing detrimental disturbances, including through composting uneaten plant material, are signs of respect on par with supporting the health of animal populations and wasting none of a kill. These practices contribute to the wellbeing and resilience of one's ecology.

The mutualism between eater and eaten that Kimmerer describes offers a counterpoint to the unending demand within toxicultural food systems that the land and the living community keep giving no matter what we do to them. This demand essentially involves the expectation of moral supervenience from both, which is a clear violation of harvesters' responsibilities. Worse still, it prevents both the land and the living community from fulfilling responsibilities of their own.

The Honorable Harvest thus offers an antidote, if partial and incomplete, to the priorities that impel toxiculture. It's supportive of vulnerable plant and animal populations and also ecologically restorative in the sense that it facilitates the biocultural vitality of ecologies (Kimmerer 2018, 40). To restore ecologies just is to restore kinship relationships and responsibilities.

Kincentric eating involves alimentary practices that on their surface may seem alien to Takers, such as eating relatives, as well as more familiar regenerative activities. Increasing biodiversity both aboveground and below is among the foremost responsibilities we have to our ecologies. By helping to build soil, symbioculture increases its capacity to hold water, which provides a buffer against the destructive force of both excess rainfall and drought. Moreover, increased fungal and bacterial activity within the soil helps both to sequester carbon and to protect plants against pests and diseases. Seed diversity and the use of local varieties; crop rotation; use of cover crops, catch crops, and intercropping; and integration of livestock all have a context-dependent role to play as well. Each in its own way bolsters the resilience of ecologies and reduces risk of total production loss (Altieri 2013, GRAIN 2013, 21, Müller and Niggli 2013, 17, and Laughton 2017).

Given the increasing difficulties associated with climate change, restoring ecologies also means that communities can be as well positioned as possible to "*plan for uncertainty,*" Gary Nabhan remarks (2013, 9): adjusting their source of macronutrients to account for higher heat tolerance and new hydrologic cycles, shifting which plants are cultivated, or even partially or fully moving to agroforestry, aquaculture, silvopasture, or other such practices (Jones and Thornton 2009). It should be obvious, Nabhan adds, that there's "no cookie-cutter approach that can possibly work in all places for all peoples, given the complexities of our food systems—even if we do not fully take into account the multiple consequences of climate change" (2013, 8). Cookie-cutter approaches can't work because "Climate adaptation is inherently *place-based* adaptation, however much it must be set out in a global context of cause and effect" (ibid., 8–9). Top-down, centralized systems are highly vulnerable to compromise, particularly agricultural systems that require high-energy inputs and that are dependent on a handful of staple crops. "Bottom-up means that you and your neighbors must stay *more attentive to where you live and grow food,* and become more engaged with other members of your ecological and cultural community" (ibid., 9).

Diets and Systems

If it's not already clear, kincentric eaters make no moral distinction between eating plants and eating animals. To be sure, a long list of defenders of a strictly plant-based diet argue that it's not only morally questionable to blur normative lines between plants and animals but also ecologically questionable given the significant contribution raising animals for food makes to global climate change and widespread ecological devastation (Fox 2000, Singer 2002, Gruzalski 2004, Pluhar 2004, and Regan 2004). I've addressed these issues at length elsewhere (Smith 2016), so I'll offer only a brief response here.

On the one hand, worries about acknowledging the equal moral status of plants and animals seems to me to result from a spurious assumption. Namely, to be a moral eater requires having access to food sources without moral status, or at least with lesser moral status with respect to our own. This assumption comes with risks, including potentially neglecting the violence toxiculture does not just to animals and animal communities but also to plants and plant communities. By no means do I wish to paper over the barbarity of factory farming. My point instead is to express cognizance that the equal moral status of the beings who we eat can entail messiness—including, colliding agendas—*when we uphold our relationships with and responsibilities to them.* Factory farming is a violation of responsible food production, as is toxiculture more generally. Both deny that all living beings aren't just food but also much more than food (Plumwood 2012).

On the other hand, the source of the severe ecological damage eating animals does today isn't at root dietary. It, too, is systemic. Within toxiculture, animals are extraordinarily inefficient fodder for humans. This is due to a faulty food system, not faulty animals (Idel and Reichert 2013, 151). *No* animal—no living being—is faulty or inherently inefficient either as a consumer or as consumed (Fairlie 2010). In this respect, striving to eat kincentrically within toxicultural regimes involves supporting a transition to symbioculture. Yes, kincentric eating embodies specific alimentary practices. More broadly, though, it supports a systems approach to food through and through.

Consider, for example, that on smallholder farmsteads like those found in myriad Indigenous communities, livestock play a key biodynamic role. This is particularly so within a *leader-follower* grazing system. Ruminants harness nutrients contained in grasses, fibers, and crop residues (none of which can be used directly for human consumption); improve seed dispersal and localized bioturbation; move nutrients (most notably, phosphorous) from pasture to cropland; enhance shoot growth; and increase soil nitrogen content through their leavings, which enhances biodiversity by reducing nutrient competition among plants (Ostendorff

2013, Garnett 2017, 35, Haslett-Marroquin 2018, and McKenna 2018, 84f.). Each of these functions builds soil and facilitates the production of a diverse diet. Chickens feed on weed seeds as well as insects and insect larvae in and around ruminant manure. This improves the health of fungi and the subterranean bacterial rhizosphere (Duncan 2016). And pigs eat food waste and crop surpluses that otherwise would release methane as they decompose (Tudge 2010, 13, and McKenna 2018, 160).

Local sources of compost, mulch, worm casting, fish emulsion, biochar, and guano may round out the nutrient cycle. But the main source of energy is contemporary sunlight via photosynthesis rather than ancient sunlight (via ingestion of the long dead) from fossil fuels. Since most Indigenous farmers also reject of the use of *-cides* in favor of integrated pest management, their practices ably support the reduction and reuse of waste throughout the entire foodscape.

Do these considerations suggest that kincentric eating either promotes eating animals or precludes plant-based eating? No. The point is to be nourished in accordance with the needs and interests of our ecologies. This requires nourishing oneself by nourishing one's kin, whoever they may be.

Impending Energy Descent

In a key UN report (Järvensivu 2018), scientists affiliated with the BIOS Research Unit in Helsinki, Finland, attest that available evidence strongly suggests that access to cheap, plentiful energy is quickly disappearing. This is occurring at the same time that the effects of global climate change and widespread ecological devastation are putting an increasing strain on economies worldwide. In the near term, the use of greenhouse gas emissions must radically decrease if the worst effects of climate change are to be avoided. These findings are corroborated in even stronger language in more recent reports from the IPCC (2021 and 2022). But how should fossil fuel drawdown be carried out, and what role does transitioning from toxiculture to symbioculture play in the process?

Sustainable Development

Proponents of sustainable development, or *developmentalists,* defend the feasibility of creating sustainable energy, technology, and food infrastructures. What's essential, they contend, is moving from a growth economy to a steady-state economy (Daly 1996), or an economy in which profit generation is decoupled from ecologically harmful and climatologically disruptive forms of taking, making, and wasting. Whereas a growth economy depends on a perpetual quantitative increase in physical throughputs (more taking, more making, and little concern about wasting), a steady-state economy doesn't expand beyond the capacity of ecosystems to regenerate provisions and process waste.

Qualitative improvements in technological *efficiency* along with the wholesale *substitution* of nonrenewables for renewables, particularly as energy sources, are the cornerstones of sustainable development. Together, developmentalists assert, these changes make it possible to "maintain our technological lifestyles" (Tolinski 2011, 4), which are a hallmark of habitation in industrial society. Moreover, they can help break the cycle of exploitation of the global South by the global North, which has fueled industrialization since its inception (Hornborg 2001). Among other things, this means expanding the range of who has access to "technological lifestyles" the likes of which affluent people in the global North currently enjoy.

Transitioning from unsustainable industrialism to sustainable industrialism—which is what sustainable development amounts to—is neither easy nor straightforward.[8] But attention to sustainable growing methods, from permaculture and biodynamic farming to regenerative agriculture and agroecology, has increased exponentially among researchers and practitioners alike. Renewable energy sources are proliferating. Technologies for large-scale carbon sequestration are in development. The know-how arguably already exists to reduce physical throughputs by at least 75 percent in every economic sector (Hawken 2010). And while zero waste isn't currently possible, the conservation its pursuit inspires "will extend the useful life of the key ecological services," states Anthony Andrady (2015, 34). This buys time for further innovation while also giving the biosphere a partial reprieve so that it can have more time to repair itself.

Quinn himself (BC, 101) pays lip service to sustainable development in lauding Ray Anderson, who founded Interface, a modular carpet company. The BIOS researchers tend to favor fairly standard developmentalist policies, too, including drastically reducing industrial meat and dairy consumption, altering international trade policies to deincentivize the expansion of monoculture, scaling back sectors—such as global transportation—in which no alternatives to the use of fossil fuels currently exist, and favoring municipal designs that facilitate lowering total energy use (Paddison 2018). Each is a worthy goal in its own right, but I can't help feeling that BIOS's unstated concern is to highlight the magnitude of the predicament we face.

John Michael Greer (2009, 91) notes that industrial society has been in place long enough that we Takers are unable to conceive of circumstances in which it would cease to be. This might lead us to assume that the transition to sustainable industrialism is inevitable, or at least that the prospects for its emergence are good. Available evidence suggests otherwise, including that highlighted by BIOS.

The biggest problem for developmentalists is that there are no comparable renewable substitutes for oil. "Pound for pound or barrel for barrel, crude oil contains more energy than any other abundant naturally occurring substance on Earth," Greer states, "and it is much less costly to extract, process, and use than anything else" (ibid., 164). Renewable energy sources such as solar and wind are more diffuse, in part because their supply is intermittent and unevenly distributed (Smil 2008b). Taking the necessary steps to concentrate and regulate their supply itself takes energy, which today comes from oil and other nonrenewables.

The quantity of raw materials needed to create solar panels, wind turbines, and batteries for energy storage includes a number of rare metals, the increasing demand for which is a constraint on scaling up renewable energy. Mining companies the world over report declining ore quality. In many, perhaps most, cases it likely isn't possible to find adequate substitutes, since they too are depleted (Bardi 2014). Reliance on less-than-adequate substitutes, should they be identified, entails that the amount of energy produced by renewable sources will be reduced. Even if limited viable inputs were to present no problem, it's difficult to envision how wind energy, for example, which has the best energy return on energy invested (EROI) of any renewable energy source, could fully replace oil (Pielke 2010).

It's undoubtedly wise to utilize fossil fuels to build post-carbon energy, technology, and food infrastructures. But it's unclear how these infrastructures can match their predecessors in scale or scope. One study (Hall et al. 2008) estimates that the minimum EROI required to maintain industrial society is 5:1. Conventional oil sources exceed this (30:1), as do solar (11:1) and wind (25:1). Unconventional oil (3:1) and biofuels (1:1) don't.[9] But the EROI for both solar and wind are as high as they are only because of conventional oil inputs. Without these inputs, they fall well below the 5:1 threshold. Technological innovation on its own can't save industrial society either, since it too is dependent on energy sources of a quality that only oil can provide (Greer 2009, 165, and Dhara and Singh 2021). Even if we ignore the inability of renewables to match oil as an energy source, we must account for myriad uses of petroleum other than for electricity that renewables can't readily replace: not just as fuel for transportation but also in its role in the manufacture of plastics, steel, cement, rubber, and glass (Lerch 2010).

Peak Oil

Greer thus concludes that we have neither the time nor the material base to stave off the "decline and fall" of industrial society (2009, 11). Even Bill McKibben's dream of a "green Manhattan Project, an ecological New Deal, a clean-tech Apollo mission" isn't likely to be enough (2010a, 52). If the evidence provided by proponents of peak oil, or *peakists,* is accurate, industrial society is already on life support. For while the earth's crust still contains vast quantities of oil, the issue instead is that its conventional quantities are now much smaller.[10] Understandably, "the fossil fuel industry has typically targeted the highest-quality, easiest-to-extract resources first," Richard Heinberg and David Fridley note (2016, 2). The unconventional sources—tight oil, deepwater oil, and tar sands—are increasingly what's left in large quantities at this point, and they're too costly in terms of reduced EROI to extract in quantities comparable to conventional oil (Sverdrup and Ragnarsdottír 2014).

So even if we ignore the other prevailing problems that come with relying on oil, it's "fairly inevitable," states Heinberg (2015, 8), that we'll reach a point in the near future at which the investment required to find, extract, and refine oil won't be worth the return. Nafeez Ahmed (2017) estimates that this will occur in some locations by the end of the 2020s and no later than the 2040s everywhere. A more recent estimate by industry analyst Gaya Herrington (2021) comes to the same conclusion. And insofar as conventional oil is the basis for the global economy, diminishing returns on investment are likely to lead to near-term economic stagnation.[11] This represents yet another formidable obstacle to the transition developmentalists envision (Fridley 2010, 230).

But even if Ahmed and Herrington are wrong in their estimations, few experts on the matter now deny the pressing need to convert from nonrenewables to renewables—and rein in the overuse of renewables *and* restore compromised biomes the world over—as expeditiously as possible. To be sure, even in later stages of degrowth, many communities are likely to have access to myriad forms of mechanization. It's reasonable to expect the ongoing local provision of "the simplest of manufactured goods" well into the future, Heinberg asserts. But "we will likely never see families getting together in church basements to manufacture laptop computers or cell phones from scratch" (2015, 94–95). The same applies to mechanized farm equipment, even if it more easily can be refurbished with salvaged goods. This sort of future boggles the industrial mind. It may seem to stand "at best, at the limits of practical possibility," David Fleming remarks. He nevertheless maintains that it "has the decisive argument in its favor that there will be no alternative" (2016, 301). Perhaps he's wrong. But it's probably still safe to conclude that degrowth stands to become much more appealing in a world marked by energy descent. So does symbioculture.

It's theoretically possible for some unexpected technological breakthrough to result in the rapid deployment of a cheap and effective alternative to oil, Heinberg notes. But it's improbable. A breakdown of the global food system at every level—from farmer to processor to distributor to retailer and finally to consumer—is in the offing. And "there is not a solution to the world's worsening food crises within current energy and agricultural systems" (2013, 291; see also Pollan 2020).

If this all is a reasonable facsimile of tomorrow's world, your progeny won't have the option not to attend to the needs and interests of their ecologies. You and I may not even have this option fairly soon. When one can't rely on ghost acres to get fed, developing mutual, commensalistic, and reciprocal relations with one's human and other-than-human neighbors becomes a priority. One's practices of making, taking, and wasting must be well integrated into the trophic network of one's proximate ecological community. It's not that one doesn't shit where one eats; we have to shit somewhere. Rather, it's that one sees to it that where one shits and how one facilitates its decomposition serve the community that allows one to eat (Jensen and McBay 2009).

Just Transitions

Transitioning to the widespread embrace of what Albrecht (2017) calls *symboikoi* is among the salient means for growers to scale out symbioculture. On my reading, symboikoi bear a striking similarity to what Colin Tudge (2016) calls a convivial society. A convivial society is supported by a form of economic democracy that privileges community ownership alongside public and private ownership. Ecologically minded small and medium-size businesses flourish.

Symboikoi thus give pride of place—no pun intended—to place-based enterprises (chapter 7). They facilitate living and making a living symbiotically as coinciding beneficiaries of and contributors to the biotic and abiotic processes that support thriving communities. Like worker cooperatives, symboikoi favor optimizing membership benefits rather than maximizing profits.

Symboikoi hereby promote the cultivation of food sources that are bioculturally suitable to local growing and raising conditions. They serve as a backbone for a safer and more diverse, nutritious, and affordable diet. When food systems are, in turn, reorganized around networks of symboikoi, entire regions can gain not just food security but food sovereignty—the capacity for community self-determination with respect to the function of the food systems on which they rely. In line with the potential social benefits of worker cooperatives, each of these dynamics supports the reemergence of vibrant local communities (La Villa Campesina 1996). Communities become sites of expanding human and more-than-human solidarity. They also may serve as what Albrecht calls *ghedeistual* epicenters (2019, 131ff.).[12] For Albrecht, the ghedeistual is akin to the sacred, if perhaps a bit more general than the way I described the sacred in chapter 6. The ghedeistual is a life spirit that holds all things, biotic and abiotic, together. But it also can convey a secular acknowledgment and celebration of the interconnectedness of all members of the living community or a feeling of intense affinity with and empathy for other beings, particularly within shared places and spaces.

Difficulties abound, though, especially when confronting the worsening effects of climate change. These effects fall hardest on people of color, and Indigenous peoples face a unique set of challenges due to the vagaries of settler colonialism. Having been divested of their most fecund lands—if not *all* their lands—decades or centuries ago, they are far less able than they otherwise would be to draw on the knowledge and skills for adaptation embodied by their traditions.

And let's not mince words. In many locales, adaptation simply may not be possible. Temperature increases across the planet are on par with the Paleocene-Eocene Thermal Maximum but are occurring at a much faster pace (Spratt and Dunlop 2018, 22). One recent study suggests that this is pushing one-third of crop production outside a "safe climate space" (Kummu et al. 2021). Growers are already observing a decline in crop nutrient density (Macdiarmid and Whybrow 2019). Heirlooms, often endemic to a place, are less likely to handle increased heat stress and unusual seasonal changes. Routine government negligence of Indigenous needs and interests, increased strains on already shaky infrastructures, and substandard housing make the situation more dire.

None of these matters is independent of the others. Seen through a long lens like that offered by Indigenous peoples' collective memories, climate change itself is an extension of totalitarian agriculture and its colonial offshoots. These offshoots include military aggression by colonizers, corporate exploitation of resources, anti-Indigenous territorial dominance by settler-industrial nation-states, and widespread degradation of landscapes (Whyte 2015, 144; see also Grinde and Johansen 1995, Weaver 1996, Whyte 2016, and Flavelle and Goodluck 2021). Each offshoot is designed, if obliquely, to destroy ecologies via both containment of mobility traditions, including seasonal rounds, and disruption of kinship bonds (Whyte 2020a). Both mobility and kinship are necessary for bolstering the resilience of ecologies—most notably by learning from and adapting to emerging metascale dynamics to avoid preventable harms and promote full-spectrum wellbeing (Colebrook 2017).

To resist settler colonialism is to resist both containment and the disruption of systems of responsibilities embodied by kinship arrangements. The speed and degree of climate change may yet overwhelm attempts to restore resilience among especially vulnerable peoples (Klein 2013). But this makes decolonization and decommodification—linchpins of both Indigenous climate justice and prudence for us all—that much more pressing.

Throwing Open the Storehouse Doors

Early in *Braiding Sweetgrass*, Kimmerer (2013, 9) asks whether it's possible for settlers to become indigenous to the places they inhabit. If so, she observes, this must involve living as if all our children's futures matter. Among other core requirements, this necessitates learning to speak the language of the land and respecting its teachings.

But why does she pose such a question in the first place? It seems to give cover for settlers to justify their presence on pilfered and pillaged lands on the grounds that they're pursuing indigeneity, including by creating symboikoi to support efforts to transition from toxiculture to symbioculture. Such efforts may give settlers yet another pretense to claim Indigenous ecologies as their own, displacing and erasing Indigenous peoples under the guise of honoring them.

Much later in the text, Kimmerer finally answers her question with a firm *no.* No one can *become* indigenous to a place. "*Indigenous* is a birthright word," she emphasizes. "No amount of time or caring changes history or substitutes for deep-soul fusion with the land" (ibid., 213). But settler peoples nevertheless can become *naturalized* to places, she contends. If I understand her correctly, for starters this requires that settlers must prove ourselves fit to be welcomed by the land's original inhabitants—and by the land itself. We also actually must be welcomed. Making a place for oneself and/or one's people in a new habitat, or simply entering others' lands, necessarily entails supplications to and negotiations with rightful residents (Pratt 2002, 156ff., and Snelgrove et al. 2014, 5). It involves forging new relationships of mutual entailment. Done well, this is a form of resistance to settler colonialism by settlers ourselves. It's a determined stance against blithely encroaching on others' homelands.

Decolonization

Like Taker culture more generally, settler colonialism is predicated on land theft. The history of settler nations is rife with forced relocations, spurious land purchases, and broken treaties. So decolonizing work first and foremost involves the struggle for land rematriation (LaDuke 1994, Driskill 2010, Tuck and Yang 2012, and Pasternak 2017). Among the central rallying cries of both the Idle No More and Land Back movements is that Indigenous peoples across North America maintain a legitimate claim to permanent, unencumbered access to their homelands. Treaties must be honored; stolen and dubiously ceded lands must be relinquished. The Original Instructions that tie Indigenous peoples to places must be permitted renewal, including through the restoration of alimentary systems of responsibilities (Nelson 2008b).

Clear precedent exists for tribal land rematriation. This includes the return of a large swath of the Northern Territory in Australia to a collective of Aboriginal peoples in 1976, the establishment of Inuit self-governance within Nunavut in Northern Canada in 1999, the Whanganui Treaty settlement in New Zealand in 2017, and federal recognition of Eastern Oklahoma jurisdictionally as Indian Country in 2020.[13] In each case, tribal self-determination remains compromised by colonial matrices of power (Mignolo and Walsh 2018) that adversely affect Indigenous governance structures and circumscribe Indigenous people's capacities to fulfill their cultural, spiritual, economic, and nutritional obligations. In the United States specifically, tribal recognition requires the federal government to engage with Native nations on equitable government-to-government terms. But Native lands remain held "in trust" under the paternalism of the Bureau of Indian Affairs.

This makes Indigenous peoples' living histories of resistance to colonization that much more important, including through societal reconstitution "in response to forced relocation, assimilative education, land dispossession, bodily violence, and environmental pollution," Whyte and Shelbi Nahwilet Meissner emphasize (2021, 38). Integral, too, is the reconstitution of traditional foodways. The work of Native chefs and food activists is critical in this regard. Nephi Craig launched the Native American Culinary Association to bring together elders and researchers to promote learning and teaching about Indigenous foods and foodways. "Sioux Chef" Sean Sherman is founder of North American Traditional Indigenous Food Systems (NATIFS), which is dedicated to addressing the economic and health crises affecting Native communities and reestablishing food-based connections with the land. Both attend as well, if indirectly, to addressing the residual material and emotional effects of intergenerational trauma.[14]

Dismantling colonial matrices of power, defunding the institutions that perpetuate them, returning lands to their rightful inhabitants, and fully respecting Indigenous jurisdiction are matters of both justice and prudence (Bendik-Keymer 2020). Considering that we all now live in what Sunaura Taylor calls *disabled ecologies,* these matters are of pressing cross-cultural concern. Disabled ecologies embody "the trails of disability that are created, spatially, temporally, and across species boundaries, when ecosystems are contaminated, depleted, and profoundly altered," Taylor states (2020). All of us comprise "an increasingly disabled people in increasingly disabled landscapes" (ibid.; see also Taylor 2019).

"Through hard practice—and in the face of centuries of legal, political, and physical struggle—Indian communities have become adept at the art of governance," David Treuer remarks. "And tribes have a hard-earned understanding of the ways in which land empowers the people it sustains" (2021). These practices and forms of understanding are crucial for navigating disabled ecologies, particularly since Indigenous peoples know these conditions all too well. Still, it's no coincidence that Indigenous people comprise just 5 percent of world population yet live on 22 percent of the planet's land surface and routinely interact with 80 percent of its biodiversity (Shrestha et al. 2008 and Sobrevila 2008). Careful, sustained attention to ecologies is common among myriad Indigenous traditions. This demands centering the work of Indigenous communities who, for generations, have been on the ground defending the use of regenerative strategies (Begay 2021). The long collective memory of these communities is also critical to prevent falling prey to shifting baselines (St. George 2021). Both are key—for us all—if we are to treat our shared ecological disability and give our ecologies a chance to have a future.

Decommodification

Decolonization is closely linked to decommodification. "Commodities are, in the most basic sense, goods that are routinely bought and sold," Paul Thompson comments. "Commodification (or commoditization) is, thus, the transformation of something that isn't bought and sold to something that is, or, to the extent that something can be bought and sold in varying degrees, an increase in the degree to which it is" (2006, 115). Commodification can take one of two broad forms, Thompson states. *Structural commodification* involves not direct change to a good itself but, rather, establishment of legal rules or transformation of customs that financially constrain the conditions for exchange. *Technological commodification* occurs when the good in question or the material circumstances required for its exchange is altered in a manner that embeds it with financial value it didn't previously have (ibid., 117).

Decommodification involves a reversal or negation of these developments. It needn't necessitate dissolving market economies or doing away with monetary food-based transactions. Unlocking the food doesn't require either step. But unlocking the food is made possible by fostering responsible transactions among the people who grow food and those who eat it by building robust relationship-based market systems that are equitable and just (Gliessman 2007 and Grey and Patel 2015).[15] This requires reversing the financialization of food, traditional food-based knowledge, and farm labor. I specifically focus on human labor here, but other-than-human farm labor must be decommodified, too.

With respect to the first concern, Shiva remarks that food in the hands of corporations has been transformed into far more of a commodity than we tend to assume. It's now "totally interchangeable between biofuel for driving or feed for factory farms or food for the hungry" (2009, 18). The last of these may be profitable only so long as governments buy it in bulk to distribute to the needy even as the needy are subject to the whims of financialization. In corporate hands, food "is no longer nourishment," Shiva continues. It's just another resource "to be manipulated and monopolized. If food grain makes more money as cattle feed than it does as food for human consumption, it becomes cattle feed. If food grain converted to biofuel to run automobiles is more profitable, it becomes ethanol and biodiesel" (ibid., 17).

In terms of structural commodification, the decommodification of food requires substantive changes not just to international trade policies that favor liberalization of markets but also to domestic programs the world over that discriminate against symbioculture. Technologically, the beings we eat are themselves materially transformed under toxiculture in ways detrimental to everyone's health solely to support commodification. Breeding food just to "meet economic expectations . . . and processing-related criteria such as refrigeration and transportation" is an affront to their wellbeing and ours, Raymond Anthony states (2017, 218). In all its bioculturally specific manifestations, symbioculture is expressly intended to challenge this practice.

Let's move now to the second concern, decommodifying traditional food-based knowledge. Although food produced by symbioculture may be used primarily by producers or sold for private revenue, the knowledge that supports traditional food production, distribution, and consumption practices is public (or at least is collectively held by a specifiable community). Traditional food-based knowledge more generally is a manifestation of many generations of shared lessons in success. It's deeply intertwined with self-determination and land-based conceptions of Indigenous futurity. The gastronomic wisdom collected in traditional recipes and represented by local and regional dishes is a function of the capacity to facilitate systems of responsibilities (Coté 2016). Genetic heritages passed down in seeds, cuttings, and cultivars keep the practices of ancestors alive. John Vail (2010) contends that considerations of fair trade and just microfinancing fit under the rubric of food-based knowledge decommodification, too.

And what of decommodifying farm labor? Within a symbiocultural context, it must involve taking steps to revitalize traditional economies. At present, most Indigenous smallholders in North America are what Salmón calls *hobby farmers*. They focus on raising ceremonial crops, augmenting grocery store purchases with fresh fruits and vegetables, or supplementing their incomes by selling produce at farmers markets and/

or to local restaurants. Few people are solely subsistent on the foods they grow in their own fields.

The goal of decommodifying food labor needn't be complete self-sufficiency. "It is possible, however, for a community to support a portion of the population that returns to farming in order to supply locally grown foods to a percentage of the population," Salmón states (2012, 42). Particularly by working not as isolated households but within larger collectives, they also can focus on stewarding their ecologies under increasingly trying conditions (Toledo 2001).

By and large, Shiva adds, "food production, processing, and provisioning have been women's domain in the social division of labor (women grew food, cooked food, processed food, served food). Women-centered food systems are based on sharing and caring, on conservation and wellbeing" (2009, 18). A good many Indigenous farmers across the globe are women; many girls are future farmers. Women make significant contributions to food sovereignty, and the manner in which girls are trained makes them pivotal to breaking free of toxiculture. So symbioculture may not be inherently gendered, but women have been and remain among its leading lights.[16]

Indeed, Shiva declares, "a new food revolution is underway, building on women's food and agriculture heritage to create just, sustainable, and healthy food systems that secure safe and healthy food for all" (ibid., 18). The same can be said of myriad Indigenous food heritages, which are themselves frequently women-centered. The defining imperatives of both involve concern for meeting the need for basic sustenance and facilitating cooperation, including with fellow members of the living community. As Shiva herself emphasizes, "other species and plants are kin, not 'property,' and sustainability is based on renewal of the earth's fertility and renewal and regeneration of biodiversity and species richness on farms to provide internal inputs" (ibid., 24; see also Shiva and Pandey 2007).

Shifting Terrain

Small disruptions create small societal shifts, Henry Grabar (2020) maintains; big ones change things for good. Just a few years ago, systemic changes of the sort Shiva and Albrecht envision might have seemed to be from a different world for most Takers. Sitting again in my study, now with page proofs in hand, many months into the pandemic and looking out my window once again at the hawthorn, a different world is here.

But the jury is still out on where *here* is. Will concerns about our interdependence and mutual vulnerability prove ephemeral among Takers, or will they take root? Can a pandemic that might have been born of toxiculture create a groundswell of resistance to the systemic risk of all risks embodied by our cultural death urge? Can we finally quit the damn dance?

Chapter 9

Ending the Food Race

From Biomass to Human Mass and Back Again

Less than a year before he walked on, Quinn told me in a personal communication (May 2017) that he was "in the middle of the most difficult book of my life." Oddly enough, he noted, most "modern biologists worldwide (I'm told by one of them) reject one of the plainest facts ever set down on paper (by Thomas Robert Malthus): 'population does invariably increase when the means of subsistence increase.' So clearly has the history of the past 12,000 years written it, Malthus evidently felt it was sufficiently obvious that not a single syllable needed to be added to this statement."

One must be willfully engaging in optical contortions (chapter 5) to miss the "astounding growth" in human population that's followed from the practice of totalitarian agriculture, particularly in its toxicultural form. But year after year the mantra is repeated: " 'We *must* increase food production *to feed our growing population*' (which would not—could not—be growing without that increase in food production)." What underlies these contortions? Why is engaging in them so deeply entrenched among Takers, apparently including those with the professional credentials to know otherwise? "Alas," Quinn concluded, "I felt this was a matter that must be straightened out. If we are going to go down, the people of the world have a right to know why."

What was I to make of Quinn's final sentence? Had he given up on the prospect of saving the world? I regret not asking him to elaborate then and there. Instead, I filed the question away to pose to him in person, during upcoming interviews we were planning.

I was excited, though, to hear about the new project. Halting and reversing the precipitous conversion of other-than-human biomass to human mass, is "the most important thing in the world right now to change people's minds about," Quinn states elsewhere (Quinn and Thornhill 1998). But some of what he has to say about human population is fraught with confusion that I hoped the new book he was preparing might go some way to clearing up. I hoped as well that the new book would provide a venue for him to venture an opinion on some topical issues about which he'd long remained silent.

Upon contacting Quinn some months later to nail down dates for my visit to him at his home in Houston, Rennie (May 2018) informed me that he'd died. "He kept a list of upcoming appointments and reminders taped to his printer in big type so he could see it easily," she told me, "and your name and email ended that list. I'm sorry it didn't work out."

Before the shock and grief set in, I replied to Rennie with condolences. I also asked about the book Quinn was working on. Had he completed it? If so, did she know when it might be in print? Did he leave any additional unpublished material that I could read, with her permission? "I'm sorry," she wrote back, "but there is no new Daniel Quinn book and no manuscript material that I can share with you." I was dumfounded and said as much to Rennie. I didn't know what to make of my earlier exchanges with her husband. (Nor could I console myself with some final words from him.) "Yes, he was working on a book and, contrary to his usual pattern, he did talk about it to some people. But it caused him great distress, and, ultimately, what he hoped to do could not be done."

I could tell at this point that Rennie was ready to be done with our exchange. Who could blame her? I thanked her for her time.

And I was left wondering what caused Quinn to abandon his final project.

Perhaps he was trying to explain why the people of our culture mustn't be afraid to come to grips with the need to decrease our numbers, to convert human mass back to other-than-human biomass. If so, then he hadn't given up on saving the world after all. Might he also have been trying to work out a vision, or the outline of a vision, for *how* to do so in a manner that befits the threefold struggle? Probably not, since he'd resisted all prior calls to do so. But that doesn't mean I can't try.

Among committed Takers, raising concerns about human overpopulation is regarded as taboo. Doing so represents a direct rejection of the proposition that humans aren't really animals, separate from the rest of the living community, exempt from the Law of Life. For less committed Takers, including those who care about ecological wellbeing, it still has malignant historical associations with racism, classism, colonialism, xenophobia, and eugenics (Haraway 2016, 6, and Roberts 2017). It also may be seen to imply that interference with reproductive autonomy is warranted and justifiable (Kates 2004 and Warner 2004). Indeed, it's almost impossible to express concern about human overpopulation without being accused of being in favor of letting fellow humans—lots of them—die.

The last of these charges redirects attention away from the fact that Indigenous peoples in particular have been left to die, or intentionally killed, for generations on settler culture's expansionary altar. Most notably via land expropriation but also by outright murder, this is how our culture typically spreads. The accusation that concern about human overpopulation is inherently callous and macabre also hinges on a non sequitur. Human overpopulation is commonly treated as a social problem, associated with women's lack of access to birth control, education, and other means of empowerment. Empowering women has proven effective at lowering birth rates, which has slowed the rate of population growth. Yet how the growth rate can be reversed remains undiscussed, largely, I think, because it's widely assumed that population reductions only result from a substantial surge in mortality rates.

We'll see, though, that Quinn defends the iconoclastic proposition that human population growth is a biological phenomenon through and through. There are more human beings on Earth than ever before because there's more food exclusively for humans than ever before. Reduce the number of available calories, *incrementally*, and our numbers will diminish, *incrementally*. This includes drastic reductions in global livestock holdings, specifically by dismantling the animal-industrial complex. And nothing prohibits pushing at the same time for an immediate and precipitous decline in overall consumption by the most gluttonous global actors.

It's true that starvation as we know it today, which is often what people have in mind when they raise concerns about letting people die, is largely a social problem. It's a function of politics (Sen 1981a and 1981b). There's more than enough food available to feed the world's human population and then some. The problem is that food, or the material bases for its acquisition, isn't equitably available to everyone.

But here's the kicker. It's possible *both* to reduce human population *and* provide everyone with sufficient nutritious and bioculturally appropriate food. These outcomes aren't mutually exclusive. An incremental (yet nevertheless exponential) decrease in available per capita calories can take place—which, critically, can facilitate population reduction by modestly diminishing fertility and sexual activity—alongside a much more equitable per capita distribution of calories across the globe.

Simple, right? Hardly. But it's worth considering how something like this can happen, particularly since energy descent and accelerating climate change are bound to lead to an overall reduction of available calories in coming decades. Is a just transition from toxiculture to symbioculture a viable facilitator for an equitable and incremental reduction in our numbers? I think so.

The Food Race

When it comes to discussing human population, states Quinn:

> The most horrific element of cultural mythology that has to be dealt with . . . is the notion that if we *didn't* continue to increase food production—year after year after year—we would face mass starvation. I think at the base of this notion is the strange idea that our population explosion would continue to run on—even if there was no food to fuel it. This is rather like thinking that the engine in your car might continue to run even if the gas tank was empty or like thinking that the lights in the room might keep on burning even if the electricity was turned off. ("Reaching for the Future"; see also I, 136, and Q&A, 169)

How can such a notion persist? Why assume that failing to continue with what Quinn calls the *food race*—perpetually producing more food to meet the needs of a perpetually growing population—"would spell catastrophe" (Quinn and Thornhill 1998) for the millions of humans facing starvation or on the verge of it (FAO 2009 and Foley 2014)?

If we substitute the phrase *meet the needs of* with *keep pace with,* the basis for this assumption is clearer. It reflects another more well-known Malthusian claim, encapsulated by his principle of population. This principle stipulates that total human population has a tendency to grow faster than the total means of human subsistence (1798, 61). A growing human population eventually outstrips the capacity to keep everyone fed, at which point famine and disease "decrease the surplus population," to use a familiar Dickensian trope. There's no breaking this cycle, according to Malthus. Any attempt to ameliorate the conditions of the surplus population—namely, the destitute and the infirm—is bound to fail. Increasing people's purchasing power, improving their agricultural productivity, and/or improving their health might stave off the next famine or plague for a time. But these steps end up only exacerbating the cycle by creating a larger human population that's subject to a larger crash.

Neo-Malthusians draw a similar conclusion, although with one notable omission and one notable addition. They omit the appeal to Dickensian policies but contend that human population growth, particularly among the global poor, is bound to lead not just to major societal upheaval but also to wholesale ecological collapse. Both dynamics erode carrying capacity in locales inhabited by the global poor, leading to a serious threat of localized population collapses (Ehrlich 1968, Meadows et al. 1972, and Kates 2004).

Quinn rejects Malthus's principle of population. Indeed, in direct contrast to it, B contends that population is always catching up with increased food production (B, 305). Human population *can't* outstrip our means of subsistence. Population growth can't continue unabated without that which fuels it—any more than combustion engines can go on running without gasoline or LED bulbs can stay lit without access to an electrical current. In order for human population to grow, food must be available. Populations can level off; they can decline. But this isn't because they outstrip available food. It's because available food levels off and declines ("Texas Legacy Project").

The idea, then, that we must increase food production to feed a growing population is based on a misunderstanding of the relationship between populations and their food supplies. Exponentially increasing food production, as the people of our culture have, particularly since the end of World War II, exponentially increases people production. Producing more food hasn't alleviated starvation because starvation isn't typically caused by food shortages. "The food is there, it's just not getting to the people who are starving," B emphasizes (B, 297).

No Winning, Much Loss

Just as with the nuclear arms race between the United States and the Soviet Union, there's no way to win the food race. Engage in the Green Revolution, produce GMOs, embrace sustainable intensification.[1] Proponents of each are committed—publicly, at least—to once and for all solving world hunger (Q&A, 718). But mass starvation is no more solvable by engaging in the food race than nuclear holocaust is solvable by a perpetual escalation of weaponry. Neither the food race nor the arms race has a "finish line" (Q&A, 210; see also "Reaching for the Future" and Q&A, 216). There "can be *no final triumph*" (BC, 114) in either case. Ultimately, the arms race ended because the Soviet Union "refused to go on racing with us," Quinn remarks.[2] "The food race could end the same way, if we simply walked away from it, refused to perpetuate the race between food production and population growth" (WS, 31). "Nothing will end the food race but ending the food race" (Q&A, 452).

Those who assert that we must continue the food race to prevent demographic catastrophe thus have it exactly backward. "Constantly increasing food production doesn't *avert* disaster, it *hastens* it" (IS, 105). Why? Because increasing food production is carried out by totalitarian agriculture. Totalitarian agriculture requires hunting down competitors for Taker food, destroying and otherwise denying them access to their food, and, ultimately, making all food Taker food. The earth is effectively a Taker "dinner plate," Alan Thornhill states in an extended discussion with Quinn. "Turning human mass into larger human mass is always at the expense of the rest of the biomass on the planet" (Quinn and Thornhill 1998).

In 1965, total human biomass was roughly 50 million tons, Quinn contends. By 2010, it had doubled. Where did this increased human biomass come from? "The answer: It came from other members of the community of life" (2010, 10). There's nowhere else it could come from. Little by little, meal by meal, more of us have been created "from the species around us. . . . When we grow our crops or pasture our cattle on that land, we make sure that none of that biomass goes back to the creatures that formerly lived there. We protect it carefully because we want it for ourselves. It is our understanding that we *need* this biomass for ourselves and that we have a *right* to take it for ourselves—in ever-increasing amounts" (ibid., 11; see also BC, 113, and "*Diminuendo*").

This is the basic dynamic driving the increased human, mainly Taker, use of the planet's photosynthetic capacity (Diamond 2005, 491; see also Hopfenberg and Pimentel 2001, 6). It's what's behind the sixth mass extinction, the loss of some two hundred species per day:

> Those two hundred species . . . why exactly are they becoming extinct? Are they just running out of air or space or what? No, those two hundred species are becoming extinct because they are something *we need*. We need their *biomass*. We need the *living stuff* they're made of. We need their biomass in order

> to maintain *our* biomass. . . . We *need* to make two hundred species extinct every day in order to maintain the biomass of six [now almost eight] billion people. It's not an accident. It's not an oversight. It's not a bit of carelessness on our part. . . . We are literally turning two hundred species a day into human tissue. (WS, 175)

"And when we've gobbled up those species, they're *gone*," Quinn emphasizes. "Extinct. Vanished forever" (ibid., 170).

This is unsustainable by definition. The food race has made every living community increasingly fragile, hence "highly vulnerable," states Alan (Lomax) in *Ishmael* (I, 129–30). Correct, Ishmael replies: "Diversity is a survival factor *for the community itself*" (ibid., 130). Brick by brick, the Tower of Uru is coming undone.

The Great Acceleration

Birth and death rates are influenced by factors other than available food, of course. The ready availability of clean water, decent healthcare, sanitation, and viable trade networks all matter. Quinn focuses on food, though, because it's how we acquire energy. Energy is "a uniquely universal currency," state John DeLong and Oskar Burger, "because all forms of work require energy expenditure" (2015, 2). This applies to the metabolic rates of all living beings. It applies, too, to the industrial systems driving toxiculture, including clearing land, pumping irrigation water, manufacturing and fueling farm equipment, producing fertilizers and *-cides*, processing and packaging food, and perpetuating global food transportation (Smil 2008a, Brown et al. 2011, and Burger et al. 2011).

Each of these phenomena has an ecological footprint. Each also supports population growth. The "entire industrial food system essentially ensures that your food is marinated in crude oil before you eat it," Bill McKibben remarks (2010b, xiii). Every stage of toxicultural food production is dependent on fossil fuels (WS, 110). Taken together, they're a precondition for the exponential growth in human population over the past couple of centuries.

With just biomass available as an energy source, population can grow only so long as more arable land can be put to the plow. Even then, though, growth is incredibly slow by contemporary standards. "The emergence of coal as an energy source eliminated the carrying capacity limits to population growth that any traditional and biomass energy-based culture would eventually face," Graham Zabel (2009) contends. "Similarly, the predominance of oil after the middle part of the twentieth century raised the carrying capacity even further." Coal permitted the development of more powerful farm equipment and the expansion of transportation. Among other applications, oil "has literally been fed to the plants we grow for food, which has greatly increased agricultural output" (ibid.).

We hereby aren't in a state of overshoot, as some commentators argue (Catton 1982, Jensen 2006a, 123, and Hawken 2010, 31). We haven't exceeded carrying capacity because we *can't* exceed carrying capacity, at least not in the way those who propose this think. Such a notion is a vestige of Malthus's principle of population. For now, more and more of us are being carried. Because we have access to the energy required to fuel our lives. As Clive Ponting states:

> The huge increase in the area under crops and pasture in the last two centuries and the development of a world trade in food would not have been sufficient on their own to sustain the seven-fold increase in the world's population in this period. This depended on a series of technological changes that radically transformed agriculture in the industrialized world into a high-input, high-energy business with much higher levels of output. (2007, 239)

The biggest leap came not only with the development of the internal combustion engine and the tractor but also with the commercialization of the Haber-Bosch process of industrial nitrogen fixation. The production and use of both are energy intensive and energy inefficient.[3]

If totalitarian agriculture nudged Taker culture into existence, toxiculture supercharged it. Both human population and energy consumption have increased by more than 800 percent since the beginning of the Industrial Revolution (Heinberg 2015, 112). And while per capita consumption in the high-energy-use global North has far outstripped that of the low-energy-use South, it's the South that's today experiencing the highest population growth rates. This can only be because "societies that adopt new energy sources, high-energy societies, have a profound impact on . . . low-energy societies," Zabel contends. "Vaccines and antibiotics that reduce third world mortality are discovered, produced and distributed with first world energy, and oil contributes at every step. Fertilizers, pesticides, and herbicides that aided the Green Revolution in much of the developing world could not have been produced without large oil and gas inputs. The airplanes, boats, and trains that deliver and distribute food all run on oil" (2009).

Peakism and Population Decline

But none of this can last. If human population is a function of available energy provisions and if the most impactful of those provisions is at or near or even past its peak rate of extraction, then this is bound to affect our numbers. Unless a source of energy comparable to oil and other fossil fuels becomes available, which is unlikely, human population will decrease in direct response to peakism. Indeed, as Quinn conceptualizes it, saving the world depends on proceeding from what Zabel calls "oil population" to "biomass population," or a population that can be carried by biomass alone without the added input of fossil fuels (see also Tverberg 2012). We *have* exceeded biomass carrying capacity in most, if not all, human habitats.

Zabel estimates that human biomass population is around one billion.[4] For our numbers to return to this once again would mark a decline of more than 85 percent with respect to our current population size. And even this number might be an overestimate of how many of us the planet can sustain in coming years as our warming and weirding world becomes less hospitable for us and our food (Xu et al. 2020). Add to this the disastrous effects of conventional farming on soil fertility and impending water shortages (Postel 1999) and the situation looks bleak. So whether the commonly cited UN projection that there will be more than nine billion people on Earth by 2050 actually materializes may end up being the least of our concerns (Brown 2001, 202).

The Insufficiency of Social Remediations

Proponents of classic demographic transition theory appealed to the idea that human birth rates could most felicitously be reduced if factors could be identified that would short-circuit people's natural desire to have many children (Davis 1945 and Notestein 1953). On their account, state Eileen Crist and Philip Cafaro, "modern developments like urbanization, rising incomes, and women's empowerment" fit the bill, since they all "are reliably accompanied by falling fertility rates" (2012, 11). Global rates of reproduction that peaked during the baby boom at between five and six children in the 1950s are today below 2.6. The rate of human population growth has slowed in response, leading some demographers to posit that our numbers are stabilizing (Cohen 2005, Lutz 2008, and Pearce 2010).

That modern developments may be facilitating human population stabilization hardly entails that our numbers are somehow sustainable, of course. "Population size always matters, and in today's world, a smaller population is a more resilient one," Karin Kuhlemann notes (2018, 184; see also Q&A, 439 and 672). Slowing population growth by means of social remediations of the sort the classic demographic transition theorists highlight is one thing. Reversing growth is quite another (Q&A, 440). Yet while a number of aspects of the classic theory have gone out of style (including the idea that people have an inborn desire for large families), appeal to said remediations hasn't.[5] They're now primarily presented in terms of addressing endemic poverty and patriarchy.

Poverty and Patriarchy

Although attributable to decades- and centuries-long pilfering by colonizing nations that now also bear almost total responsibility for global climate change and the sixth mass extinction, human population levels are growing fastest in areas of the world heavily populated by the poorest of the global poor. John Firor and Judith Jacobsen remark that "poverty, especially in rural cultures where a child's labor is a meaningful contribution to the household economy and where children provide a couple's only financial security in old age, does indeed cry out for many children" (2002, 36; see also Brown 2001, 223). Whereas the expense of having children outweighs its financial benefit among those who are better off, children frequently provide the only viable "asset" for the poorest of the global poor. For the rural global poor, the more children that parents have on hand, the more free labor they have at their disposal to work the fields and tend animals. Children of poor urban families, particularly boys, can work instead of going to school to increase the family's aggregate income.

To reduce the financial incentives among the global poor associated with having children, Firor and Jacobsen call for "a social revolution characterized by greater equity and opportunity, including better health, for the poor of all countries, but with a special emphasis on women and girls" (2002, 189; see also Brown 2009, 155, Guillebaud and Hayes 2009, Keith 2011b, 227f., Grant 2015, Crist et al. 2017, 260ff., and Roberts 2017). Abject poverty must be alleviated through the direct infusion of resources as well as the facilitation of capabilities that tend to lead women to delay childbearing. Poor women and girls in particular need salient educational and economic outlets that provide them with the opportunity to be breadwinners, which can improve their social status—hence their control over their bodies—while also reducing the familial demand for and need to have more children. Women and girls also need effective family planning services, including ready access to contraception (Willott 2012, 526).

Regarding patriarchy, Firor and Jacobsen add that:

> Something else drives high fertility, too. If you were to ask a woman in a high-fertility country why she has many children, she might answer as follows: "I am nothing in my culture unless I bear children—in fact, I am nothing in my culture unless I bear sons. Sometimes the daughters keep coming, and I have to keep having babies until I've produced a son. Or two. And I was really nobody until I married, so I married young. As soon as I married, the babies started to come." (2002, 36–37)

Giving women and girls educational and employment opportunities surely can help. But they're likely to take advantage of these opportunities only if they provide prestige that's comparable to that which currently is gained through marriage and childbearing—not just for women and girls themselves but for the men and boys with whom they associate (Anderson and Kohler 2015, Mazur 2016, and Ehrlich 2018, 154).

This requires a wider change of outlook on gender roles and sexual status. But changes of this sort aren't without precedent. Among other steps, Thailand, Bangladesh, Costa Rica, South Korea, and Iran have all lowered birth rates by engaging in comprehensive campaigns to promote women's empowerment and overall wellbeing (Potts 2009, Keith 2011b, 227f., and Crist et al. 2017, 263). All such steps remain radically incomplete and subject to retrogression. But in each society women now have a stronger platform than they did even a decade or two ago to defend their reproductive autonomy.

The ABCs of Ecology

Addressing poverty and patriarchy play important roles in the threefold struggle. But when it comes to effectively addressing human population growth, relying on them exclusively "is an act of faith that has virtually nothing to do with science," Quinn asserts ("Reaching for the Future").

As Pater Farb puts it, "Intensification of production to feed an increased population leads to a still greater increased in population" (1978, 121). Yet while Farb regards this as a paradox—for our species, although for no other (I, 133)—we know at this point that Quinn doesn't. Perhaps laying out what B calls the ABCs of Ecology will help to solidify Quinn's position.

A: Food. "The community of life is nothing else," B declares. "It's flying food, running food, swimming food, crawling foods, and of course just sitting-there-and-growing food" (B, 294).

B: "[T]he ebb and flow of all populations is a function of food availability" (ibid.). An increase in food availability means growth; reduction in food availability means decline. "Always. . . . Every time, ever and always. *Semper et ubique.* Without exception. Never otherwise. More food, growth. Less food, decline. Count on it" (ibid.; see also I, 131, and Quinn 2010, 11f.).

C: "There is no species that dwindles in the midst of abundance, no species that thrives on nothing" (ibid., 295).

Food and feeder populations, eaters and eaten, create a negative feedback system. This system is "self-regulating," Quinn insists (Quinn and Thornhill 1998). The gods created a world that functions flawlessly. No (extra-biological) divine intervention is required. As the number of feeders goes up, the food population goes down, and vice versa. This creates a sigmoid or s-shaped population curve for every species on Earth, point out Russell Hopfenberg and David Pimentel (2001, 9). This is as true for us humans as it is for everyone else.

The people of our culture can go on trying to win the food race, but "the built-in processes of the world" (WS, 61) are already kicking in. Takers also can go on pretending that totalitarian agriculture has permitted us to transcend the usual population-limiting factors. Eliminate competitors, increase foods supply, face population explosion. Repeat. "*Grow, then get more land, increase food production, and grow some more*" (BC, 15). But transcendence is illusory. Yes, Takers have " 'raised the ceiling,' i.e., the asymptote of food limitation," state Hopfenberg and Pimentel (2001, 9). But higher ceilings tend to bring more precipitous declines.

Objections and Replies

"I've been surprised by how challenging people find these ideas," B remarks. "They feel menaced by them. They get angry" (B, 301; see also Quinn and

Thornhill 1998). They object, vociferously, usually due to misunderstanding Quinn's point of emphasis.

Regionalism Objection

This objection hinges on the generalizable disparity in birth rates between agriculturally productive areas, particularly in the global North, and agriculturally bereft locales, mainly in the South. This disparity seems to indicate that humans aren't subject to the ABCs of Ecology, at least not in the straightforward way Quinn proposes. "We increase food production in the U.S. tremendously every year," Alan says to Ishmael, "but our population growth is relatively slight. On the other hand, population growth is steepest in countries with poor agricultural production. This seems to contradict your correlation of food production with population growth" (I, 138–39).

Ishmael shakes his head, frustrated. "The phenomenon as it's observed is this: 'Every increase in food production to feed an increased population is answered by another increase in population.' This says nothing about where these increases occur" (ibid., 139).

Alan is still confused, so Ishmael elaborates. "Every increase in food production is answered by an increase in population *somewhere*. In other words, *someone* is consuming Nebraska's surpluses—and if they weren't, Nebraska's farmers would stop producing those surpluses, pronto" (ibid.).[6] Does this mean that farmers of the global North are fueling the global population explosion, Alan asks. Yes, Ishmael replies.

It's critical in this regard that we approach the issue in global terms. With greater *global* food production comes greater *global* population growth. When viewed systemically, regional and national variations are beside the point. It's "a matter of what *whole populations do*," B states (B, 292; see also Q&A, 14 and 721).

The same reply holds with respect to regional and national differences in growth rates. "I've said only that the population of any species will grow if more food becomes available to it," Quinn tells Elaine (WS, 108). "The reason why growth rates differ in developed and undeveloped nations has nothing to do with food availability. It has to do with family economics. In developed nations, having a multiplicity of children is a burden, no matter how abundant food is, whereas in undeveloped nations it's a blessing, no matter how scarce food is" (ibid., 109).

Right, Elaine responds. "In developed nations it costs a lot of money to raise children, and they're not expected to contribute anything to family income. In undeveloped nations it costs little to raise children, and they generally contribute a lot to family income" (ibid.). "So—in light of all this—the difference in growth rates between developed and undeveloped nations really seems like a nonissue" (ibid., 111).

"It's a red herring," Quinn remarks. "Thrown out to distract from the fact that, like all other species, our overall population grows when our food supply grows, no matter whether growth occurs faster in one place or another" (ibid.; see also I, 136f.).

Independence Objection

Still, given the rate of malnutrition and undernutrition among the global poor, it seems clear that food *isn't* being made available to them. How, then, are their numbers "growing like wildfire" (B, 303)? Doesn't this indicate that population growth is actually independent of increased food availability after all? If so, our population can continue to grow even if we curtail food production.

"All I can say," B rejoins, "is, if this is true, then we are clearly in the presence of a miracle. These are not people made from food. . . . They must be made of air or icicles or dirt" (B, 303; see also Q&A, 122). No, the population explosion among the global poor must be because they have food, even if they lack enough for proper nourishment. In this case, as in all cases, societal differences differentially shape individuals' behavior. But no society, no individual, exists without biotic inputs (Quinn and Thornhill 1998 and Q&A, 760).

Standard of Living Objection

Yet it must be possible to increase food production and reduce our population. Improve the standard of living among the poor and their birth rates will decline (B, 305).

The latter claim may be true, remarks B, but it too is beside the point. It's simply a variation of the regionalism objection. Again, the *B* of the ABCs of Ecology is undeniable: "If you make more food available, there will be more people to consume it" (ibid., 302).

Besides, those who focus on raising the standard of living have a habit of overlooking that when translated into policy, this often reduces to the global dissemination of consumer culture and the proliferation of toxiculture (Crist 2012, 141f.; see also WS, 35). Thornhill notes that from a corporate perspective, it's always good to develop "emerging markets" (Quinn and Thornhill 1998; see also Q&A, 150), which also includes creating more consumers—both in absolute and relative terms. Widespread poverty creates its own set of ecological concerns, but so do the rebound effects associated with greater material affluence (Kuhlemann 2018, 183).

Contraception Objection

Okay, but "because *as individuals* we're able to govern our reproductive capacities," it must be the case that "our growth *as a species* should be unresponsive to the mere availability of food" (B, 262). This objection is aimed in part at the mouse experiments B describes in his public lectures. Humans aren't mice. We can take advantage of contraception. They can't. This sets us apart.

"This is of course absolutely true," B responds, "especially at the individual level. Each of us as an individual is capable of making reproductive choices that mice absolutely cannot make" (ibid., 301). Nevertheless, our behavior as a biological population is indistinguishable from the behavior of all other biological populations. Once again, make more food available to a population and that population expands.

This doesn't mean Quinn has anything against contraception. Nor does he regard it as useless as a means of supporting population reduction (Q&A, 133). He's simply observing that relying on it for this enterprise is a poor strategy. As B puts it, "The rule in crisis management is, don't make it your goal to control effects, make it your goal to control causes. If you control causes, then you don't *have* to control effects. . . . Birth control is a strategy aimed at effects. Food production control is a strategy aimed at causes" (B, 304).

Consumption Objection

Maybe, though, concern with population growth is overblown. Jonathan Safran Foer states that if our current global population "had the needs and outputs of the average Bangladeshi, we would require an Earth the size of Asia to live sustainably—our planet would be far more than enough for us. Earth is approximately the right size to supply the Chinese budget—despite being the face of environmental villainy. . . . For everyone to live like an American, we would need at least four Earths" (2019, 123). Shifting wealth among us humans, drastically reducing the number of very wealthy people and those in poverty, "can have as much carbon impact as reducing overall population," David Roberts states (2017). So let's focus on decreasing the number of big emitters, who uncoincidentally are also the world's primary conduits for "endless growth and profit accumulation" (Alberro 2020; see also Pope Francis 2016).

Social remediations aren't necessarily aimed at turning low-impact humans into higher-impact humans. Nevertheless, this is precisely what's happening. This makes questions about population size also about "total human impact," Jared Diamond insists (2005, 495; see also Crist et al. 2017, 261). This impact includes not just our carbon footprints but also our ecological footprints, which those who make this objection often ignore. Excessive consumption is unquestionably helping to drive the conversion of other-than-human biomass into human mass. But if current food availability is indeed dependent on fossil fuels and if fossil fuel use is at, near, or past its peak, we don't have a choice about whether to focus either on decreasing consumption or on decreasing population. Both are bound to happen.

Alas, this doesn't entail that the population problem will equitably and incrementally solve itself, B contends. "If you learn that the building you're living in has a structural fault that will soon cause it to collapse under the force of gravity, you're certainly at liberty to let the system take care of it. But if your children are living in the building when it finally collapses, they may not think as highly of this solution as you do" (B, 306). The same can be said, for that matter, for any of our kith and kin. The question before us, then, is how we avert precipitous population collapse—specifically, how, if at all possible, we can facilitate what McKibben dubs a "relatively graceful decline" (2010a, 99).

A Relatively Graceful Decline

"Population 'blooms' (that is, periods of rapid growth) are always followed by crashes and die-offs," Richard Heinberg proclaims. "Always" (2010, 8). Well, that's grim. And categorical. William Catton further complicates matters by noting that as time goes on, we face a " 'bottleneck' of narrowing opportunities and a real possibility of massive die-offs due to degradation of essential ecosystem services" (2012, 25). But even if Heinberg and Catton are right, we aren't somehow absolved of the responsibility to do what we can for both people and the planet. Are there easy ways equitably and incrementally to convert human, particularly Taker, mass back into other-than-human biomass? No. Can we at least consider how to facilitate such a conversion? It's worth a try.

Quinn himself notes that he's quite intentionally "ventured no opinion" (Q&A, 575) about how to proceed—besides reiterating that the food race must be brought to an end. And it can only end, he insists, by changing people's minds: by getting enough people to accept once and for all that increasing food production is what creates a growing population in the first place (Q&A, 525). But in terms of how to make even this happen, Ishmael simply says, "If the will is there, the method will be found" (I, 140).

Letting People Starve?

Ishmael does have more to say on a related topic, though. His further comments come within an exchange with Alan regarding the causes and possible means of redressing famine. Periods of want are hardly unique to humans, Ishmael observes. All species are subject to them. When a species' available food diminishes, its population declines. Yet Mother Culture insists that humans should be exempt from this eventuality. So when food supplies run short in a given locale, she demands that humanitarian aid be supplied from those who are able to provide it.

This creates a persistent problem. Namely, the population of that locale never proceeds to decline "to the point at which it can be supported by its [immediately available] resources," Ishmael states (I, 138). As a result, famine becomes a chronic feature of the lives of the constituents of that population. "If there are forty thousand people in an area that can only support thirty thousand, it's no kindness to bring in food from the outside to maintain them at forty thousand. That just guarantees that the famine will continue" (ibid.).

"True," Alan responds. "But all the same, it's hard to sit there and let them starve." (ibid.).

And here it comes. "This is precisely how someone speaks who imagines that he is the world's divinely appointed ruler," Ishmael chides: " 'I will not *let* them starve. I will not *let* the drought come. I will not *let* the river flood.' It is the gods who *let* these things happen, not you" (ibid.).

What Ishmael says is trivially true, of course. You and I don't—and can't possibly—have control over abiotic factors like those he lists. But there's nevertheless more than a hint of unexpected callousness here. It comes across even more strongly in Quinn's exchange with Thornhill (1998), on video, which is difficult to watch.[7]

I think this callousness is due, at least in part, to Quinn's own commitment of the regionalism fallacy, only in reverse. Why are so many of the global poor starving? His explanation is straightforward: the poor go hungry not because there's actually no available food but because they don't have the means to buy it, "to *make* it reach them" ("Texas Legacy Project"; see also WS, 33f.). The same dynamic occurs even during times of famine. "End poverty and there will be no starving millions; everyone knows that there is enough food for them—if they could afford to buy it. There are no starving *rich* people anywhere in the world" (Quinn 2010, 13).

No matter how much food is produced, nothing changes for the starving masses. As long as they fail to have the ability to purchase food or otherwise to make it reach them, they go hungry. Providing humanitarian aid only ends up exacerbating the situation, Quinn adds:

> Have you not seen the images of the UN workers spreading food among hungry crowds? Have you not seen Sally Struthers asking us to support children that are starving by sending money (and food) to them? They cannot produce enough food because they are exceeding their local carrying capacity—the land cannot support that many animals. It wouldn't matter if they were elephants, rats, beetles, or humans. If we send more resources, we will have more animals. (Q&A, 122)

Exceeding local carrying capacity? As I note above, no, although they have exceeded local biomass population. And this is no coincidence.

The number of human inhabitants of northern Africa, for example, traditionally has remained quite limited. Their numbers exploded the way they did everywhere else: due to access first to coal-driven technologies and then to oil-driven technologies (Q&A, 767). Most notably, the farmers of the region were pressed into embracing the products and processes of the Green Revolution in order to grow staples for affluent nations. And the land suffered for it—to the point that the people of the region couldn't even grow enough food (or otherwise make enough money) to feed themselves (B, 257).[8]

The people of affluent nations now supposedly send the global poor food because it would be inhumane to permit them to continue to go hungry, Quinn states, "which keeps their population high and therefore perpetuates the problem of starvation." From a Taker perspective, "it would be terrible for us to allow them to go back to a population level that they can actually sustain themselves" ("Texas Legacy Project"; see also WS, 106f.). To do so would defy the one right way to live.

Is Quinn suggesting that the people of affluent nations withhold humanitarian aid instead? "Not withholding it. I'm just not sending it" (ibid.). Or, as he remarks elsewhere, "I'm not 'letting' the people of Africa starve. I'm standing by helplessly while they starve. To send food into a famine is precisely like throwing gasoline on a burning house—far from helping, it makes matters worse" (Q&A, 21). In any case, Quinn concludes, "We can abandon them now or we can abandon them later. We are going to have to abandon them eventually because our own population is growing and our own resources are being used up, and right now we are eating petroleum" ("Texas Legacy Project"; see also Q&A, 702 and 731).

Systemic Confusion

In response, let me begin by noting that Quinn's stance fits broadly within the parameters of Garrett Hardin's philosophical considerations. For Hardin, providing aid to the global poor would be suicidal for our species as a whole. It would have the same effect, after a shipwreck, of those who've made it to a lifeboat, now nearly full, trying to save the many passengers still in the water. Ultimately, this would lead those who've already been saved *and* those yet to be saved to perish. The overfilled lifeboat couldn't possibly stay afloat for long.

Continuing to help the poor has a comparable ratchet effect, Hardin asserts. When a population grows too large and its numbers are prevented from declining, particularly in the face of famine, this creates conditions for an even worse famine down the road—one that affects an ever-widening constituency. In the long run, this makes conditions less livable for future generations. In the even longer run, were this dynamic to continue in perpetuity, we'd face such widespread ecological devastation that the very existence of humankind would be in jeopardy. Indeed, Hardin maintains, we run such a risk even by helping the poor help themselves. "Complete justice, complete catastrophe" (1974, 562). Either millions die now or billions die later.

While Quinn does worry about localized rachet effects, he doesn't follow Hardin any further. Nor does he side with the likes of Holmes

Rolston (1996), for whom it's better to prioritize suffering ecosystems than suffering people. Such a proposal defies the threefold struggle. But Quinn is nonetheless strangely silent about some factors that Hardin conveniently neglects. Specifically, given Thornhill's cited comments about the obsessive corporate pursuit of emerging markets, Quinn doesn't mention the main driver of humanitarian aid. Susan George points out, for example, that U.S. food aid in particular is provided largely as "a means of developing markets, for helping agribusiness, for gaining a stranglehold on the policy decisions of needy governments, and for promoting U.S. foreign policy and military goals" (1986, 212). Michael Slote highlights in turn that the ultimate cause for the landbases occupied by the destitute becoming ecologically bereft is the fact that those landbases are systematically stripped of their provisions, and also treated as dumping grounds, by colonialist powers (1996, 144).[9]

Moreover, Alan Carter remarks that Hardin "seems to take it for granted that those lucky enough to be in a well-provisioned lifeboat have their right to a place on board" (2004, 351). Besides, Carter adds, from Hardin's perspective, "if we have, in effect, stolen what rightfully belonged to the poor in other countries, more might die in the long run if we simply return it" (ibid., 353). Quinn draws neither such conclusion, at least not that I've found. But he's not off the hook.

Quinn gets into trouble because he confuses, or conflates, two different systems. When it comes to the persistence of starvation, Quinn is describing the phenomenon that Amartya Sen refers to as *entitlement failure*. "Starvation," Sen argues, "is the characteristic of some people not *having* enough food to eat. It is not the characteristic of there not *being* enough food to eat" (1981b, 1). Lack of food per se isn't typically a proximate cause of famines, Sen contends. Of greater import are instead (1) the lack of access to food that's widely available to others in the very region in which the famine is occurring and (2) the inability to hold authorities accountable for their failure to facilitate the wellbeing of those affected.

To understand why famines occur, Sen maintains that it's necessary instead to focus on entitlements: on the ways in which people legitimately—by means of consensual trade, production, or inheritance—gain ownership of commodities. Among the factors that determine a person's entitlement are whether they can find sustained employment at a decent wage, what they can produce by means of their own labor power, and whether they have access to a sufficiently robust social safety net. To the extent that relevant jurisdictions facilitate these factors, these jurisdictions can help to provide people with the capacity to legally acquire sufficient food (ibid., 8 and 45).

Quinn recognizes these things. End poverty and there will be no starving millions, he states. Producing more food changes nothing; alleviating deprivation—presumably by addressing entitlement failure—does. So why embrace aspects of Hardin's philosophical position? Why float withholding food from the global poor?

From Sen's vantage point, ending starvation is a political issue—or a socioeconomic one, depending on how it's framed. By contrast, Quinn is adamant that population decline is a *biological* issue. Quinn couches references to withholding food from the needy in terms of facilitating a necessary reduction of a regional population such that it no longer exceeds the available biomass of that region. In other words, he seeks to resolve a political (or socioeconomic) problem by applying a biological solution.

Food need not be withheld from the people of Houston because "we're not overpopulating this area," he states (Quinn and Thornhill 1998). But this is incorrect. Most human habitats today can't possibly feed their human inhabitants at anywhere near the population levels we may request. Places like the Sonoran Desert in the American Southwest stand out in this regard. "The Hohokam and Pima were the last people to live on that land without creating an environmental overdraft," notes Barbara Kingsolver (2007, 5). Houston is no exception. It only seems not to be overpopulated because its residents are able to rely extensively on ghost acres for food. They're supported, if inequitably, by a global food system that funnels provisions from the landbases occupied by the poorest of the global poor. Those landbases are stripped bare rather than their own.

So people nearly everywhere exceed biomass population. But, according to Quinn, only the poorest of the global poor are to have food withheld. *Their* numbers must decline to fit within the needs and interests of their landbases. *Ours* don't. This is the regionalism objection in reverse. Take steps to resolve global human population growth by "standing by helplessly" as those who already suffer disproportionately from the excesses of Taker culture perish.

If we consider population systemically, then regional and national variations can't be our focus. *Reduce the amount of food available for human consumption and our global numbers will fall.* This is all Quinn needs to conclude. Ecological devastation anywhere and everywhere must be remediated. But so must human misery. We're in dire need of enacting a story that works for both the planet *and* people, right? This is among the most critical insights that Quinn offers. It's the keystone of the threefold struggle. Yet, at this critical juncture, Quinn seems to equivocate.

"I know that if you leave these people alone," he says, as if in reply, "they will be once again back in balance with their resources. And they will be happy people. They will no longer be living in famine" (Quinn and Thornhill 1998). This is quite a claim: enhance people's long-term wellbeing by leaving them alone now. It also hinges on a false dichotomy. The two systems at the heart of our current discussion, the socioeconomic and the biological, interweave, of course. The latter makes possible the former, while the former also "overlays and modifies what happens" with the latter, Thornhill avers (ibid.). We've witnessed millennia of Taker socioeconomic systems adversely affecting the biosphere. We also know that humans aren't inherently destructive—that Indigenous peoples have lived and continue to live in ways that work for the planet and for people. As such, it's at least conceivable that a social organization designed to modulate food production can *also* facilitate an equitable, incremental human population decline. If so, we aren't forced to choose between either abandoning the needy now or abandoning them later. We have a viable third option.

The Demographic Benefits of Symbioculture

If Quinn is a differentiated holist, as I assert in chapter 4, then his philosophical considerations still offer fertile ground to support envisioning what a relatively graceful decline looks like. No two things are alike because the gods lavish care on every thing without stint. As such, the gods value every thing along with the community of life as a whole. Tensions and conflicts are bound to arise. They always do. This is why it's such difficult work to determine who should live and who should die (I, 156ff.). But there can be no one right way for such decisions to be settled.

I added in chapter 6 that one possible moral upshot of embracing differentiated holism involves holding a vision according to which the gods are biocentric or ecocentric or some combination of both whereas people are kincentric. For kincentrists, responsibility for the health and wellbeing of *this place* just is responsibility for the health and wellbeing of the coinhabitants of *this place.* To be *emplaced* is to be enmeshed in bonds of kinship. This can create a set of overlapping and intersecting circles of responsibility within and across ecosystems and bioregions that are small enough to accommodate face-to-face interactions yet large enough to sustain the autonomy and structural equality of peoples (Rose 1998).

Perhaps this way of viewing things can support "a well-conceived, clearly articulated, flexible, equitable, and internationally coordinated program focused on bringing a *very significant reduction* in human numbers over the next two or more centuries," as J. Kenneth Smail states (2004, 58). Recall, though, that according to Quinn what we need is a vision that "works so well that programs are superfluous." Such a vision "works so well that it never occurs to anyone to create programs to make it work" (BC, 10). People deserve to live and make a living within social organizations that facilitate ecological, social, and personal wellbeing. Worker cooperatives and symboikoi are well positioned to facilitate precisely this. Worker cooperatives and symboikoi that operate within a symbiocultural context are even better situated to succeed in this regard, in part because symbioculture is designed for successfully living and making a living in a post-carbon, nonhierarchalist world.

Here, then, is my proposal: population reduction can occur without something like the program Smail has in mind. No such program is required in a world in which symbiocultures proliferate and serve as bases for overlapping and intersecting circles of responsibility across ecosystems and bioregions. Once again, decolonization and decommodification are key. Let's address the latter first.

Decommodification and Ending the Food Races

Refreshingly, Quinn responds to a reader who asks why he doesn't address "how to redo our agricultural food system" with the following: "A lot of good minds have to change before these twin problems get solved: (1) how to feed humanity sustainably and (2) how to systematically and humanely reduce our population from its present catastrophic levels to a noncatastrophic level" (Q&A, 752). In one respect, this is simply a different way to venture no opinion on the matter the reader raises. Nevertheless, it's good to see Quinn veer definitively away from Hardin, at least in a vague and noncommittal way.

The roots of the food race are socioeconomic, Quinn stresses, even if its output is biological. While a grand display is made by agribusiness magnates and their political affiliates—*Big Wétikos* one and all—of desiring to feed the starving masses, farmers only endeavor to grow more and more food because food is a commodity. "The more food you make, the more money you make" (Quinn and Thornhill 1998).

Now, he adds, venturing at least one opinion after all on how to end the food race, "we could eliminate that impetus if we said, no, we're not going to pay you for the amount you grow. We're going to pay you for the service of growing the food we need" (ibid.). Masons aren't paid by the brick. They typically earn an hourly wage for fulfilling specified work orders. Doctors aren't paid extra if they call for more tests for their patients. They earn a salary for engaging in practices that are designed to meet their patients' needs. Why not compensate farmers for doing something like the same? Treat the cultivation of food as a way to make a living that supports our ecologies rather than undercutting them. Give farmers an incentive, states Thornhill, to integrate themselves into a wider set of "tribal relationships" (ibid.)—systems of responsibilities that foster relationships of mutual support.

"I've never said that totalitarian agriculture 'must be eliminated,'" Quinn states in answering another reader, "and putting food under lock and key has nothing to do with our population crunch (and I've never said it must be eliminated either)" (Q&A, 575). But, of course, this is exactly what he says in the material just cited. I doubt we've caught Quinn in a lie. It's more likely that this answer was provided before his discussion with Thornhill. But this isn't the point. What matters is that Quinn himself offers support for a key aspect of the transition to symbioculture. To the extent that symbioculture requires decommodification, it offers systematic bases for ending the food race. In the process, it provides a means to facilitate an equitable and incremental reduction in human population.

Decolonization and Leveraging the Limits of Biomass

On more than one occasion, Quinn asserts that erratic retaliation provided the decisive controlling factor in limiting tribes' populations, hence global population as a whole, before the spread of Taker culture. "Population control wasn't a luxury, it was a necessity in tribal cultures," Ishmael states (I, 140). Why? Because the people of every tribe lived within a definitive "cultural boundary" (ibid., 141). Crossing that boundary could get you killed. "That gave people a powerful incentive to limit their growth" (ibid., 142).

Tribes hereby limited each other, Alan responds. They forced one another to rely on the food available inside their boundaries. "It's another case where diversity seems to work better than homogeneity" (ibid.). And it worked not because it depended on the reproductive behavior of individuals but because it provided a systemic check on an entire population (Q&A, 390).

Here's Ishmael:

> These were not people limiting their growth for the benefit of mankind or for the benefit of the environment. They limited their growth because for the most part this was easier than going to war with their neighbor. And of course there were some who made no great effort to limit their growth, because they had no qualms about going to war with their neighbors. I don't mean to suggest that this was the peaceable kingdom of a utopian dream. (I, 142)

None of this is to suggest that we should revivify the erratic retaliator strategy (Q&A, 729). The point instead is that a global patchwork of tribes did the demographic work for tribal peoples. Human population didn't have to be *made* sustainable. It couldn't be otherwise. The system was self-regulating.

There's one problem, though. It's far from clear that intertribal relations reliably exhibited the basic characteristics Ishmael claims they did. Viola Cordova challenges the idea that precolonial Indigenous peoples were in a constant state of low-grade warfare. "This is absolutely not the case. There was an extensive trading system of goods between the groups" (2007, 223). Intermarriage was common, too. "This, of course, created a kind of bond between said groups, even if they were sometimes enemies," note Dennis McPherson and J. Douglas Rabb (2011, 148).

Perhaps these and other such practices occurred when tribes weren't engaging in acts of retaliation. It was erratic after all, Quinn claims, not perpetual. But this isn't the heart of the problem. For Cordova's and McPherson and Rabb's respective considerations undercut Quinn's specification of the systemic driver for population control among tribal peoples: hard and fast cultural boundaries. No hard and fast boundaries, no self-regulating demographic system.

Fortunately, another driver presents itself. Other things being equal, if biomass is our only energy source and people are able to engage in traditional forms of food production and acquisition, their populations will stabilize along a sustainable, sigmoidal curve. Symbioculture is simply a general term for a wide array of Indigenous food systems. Within a decolonial context, said food systems support living and making a living within a specifiable ecology. Hard and fast cultural boundaries likely were lacking among precolonial Indigenous peoples, just as they're lacking today. But they exhibit an excellent record of operating within broad, overlapping circles of ecological responsibility. This, I submit, is what did the demographic work among Indigenous peoples prior to colonization. Given the track record Indigenous peoples have shown for fostering biodiversity—for quite literally stewarding other-than-human biomass—symbioculture feasibly can do the same demographic work again, so long as these peoples enjoy the sovereignty and capacity for collective self-determination that decolonization can make possible.

A Word about Productivity

"Buy local," Thornhill declares. "Also, initiate locally," Quinn replies (Quinn and Thornhill 1998). Among the most popular local initiatives in the United States are community-shared agriculture groups (CSAs). Numerous CSAs focus on supporting plant-based diets. There may be viable context-dependent reasons to do so. Quinn, though, takes what may seem on its face like an oddly intransigent stance against vegetarianism, particularly against those who favor scaling out local plant-based initiatives. Why? Because such initiatives are often couched in terms of continuing the food race.

Proponents of vegetarianism routinely assert "that that earth will support more humans as vegetarians than otherwise (which is absolutely true)," Quinn remarks (Q&A, 58). What's troubling is that they regard this as a justification for becoming a vegetarian. Wittingly or not, they defend their preferred dietary practice because it "will enable us to convert more of this planet's biomass into human flesh than nonvegetarianism does" (ibid.). In championing being able to *feed* more people, vegetarians hereby end up supporting *producing* more people (ibid., 78 and 83).

Quinn isn't the first to level this charge (Rodman 1977, 106f., and Callicott 2001). Draw your own conclusions about its merits, if you like.[10] I bring up the matter here since it's related to concerns about agricultural productivity. Let me explain.

While proponents of agricultural intensification tend to focus on short-term productivity, kincentric eaters prioritize productivity over time, which requires close attention to minimizing ecological risk. Nevertheless, symbiocultural growing practices have proven time and again to be highly productive. They routinely outproduce their toxicultural counterparts (Pretty et al. 2006, De Schutter 2010, and Cook et al. 2015, 20). On its face, this may raise a red flag for Quinn. Proponents of symbioculture aren't concerned with feeding a growing world, but this may be what symbioculture delivers anyway.

As always, though, context matters.

In what they deem an "understatement of existential climate risk," David Spratt and Ian Dunlop (2018) highlight how limited the capacity for climate-based adaptation is likely to be in numerous locales, despite our best efforts. We touched on this issue in the previous chapter, but here are a few more details. The heat index in parts of Africa, India, the Middle East, South America, Southeast Asia, and Australia is expected regularly to exceed 55 degrees C (131 degrees F) within a matter of decades (Xu et al. 2020). These areas, home to about one-third of our population today, will become uninhabitable. An average increase in global temperatures of 4 degrees C (7.2 degrees F), which is expected by the end of the century at the latest, potentially could be a sufficient condition for the reduction of our numbers by as much as 80 to 90 percent (World Bank 2012).

Yes, some colder regions could become more suitable for living. But they generally include far less fertile land. So optimizing agricultural production where we can is critical, particularly if we're to facilitate as graceful a decline in human population as we can.

Equitable and Incremental

The proliferation of symbiocultures doesn't guarantee equitable means of living and making a living. But it does offer bases for a model of social organization far better designed to do so than that which supports toxiculture. Whereas toxiculture requires hierarchalist socioeconomic relations, symbioculture is socioeconomically horizontal or lateral. Particularly as a facilitator of decolonization, symbioculture is organizationally conducive to the promotion of autonomy, community, and humanity (Levine 2001, 4). It systematically fosters sustainably and humanely reducing birth rates and (more) equitably dispersing rising death rates, particularly given peak oil and the limits of adaptation just noted.

Let's talk numbers. What might an incremental decline look like? Consider the following from Hopfenberg and Pimentel:

> If food availability for the population is held constant and population increases continue at 1.4 percent per year, the reduction in per capita food per year is relatively small on average. For example, if a population consists of 1,000 humans and food availability for this population is held constant forever and allows for 3,000 calories per person per day (holding other vital nutrients constant relative to calorie count), this is a total calorie count for three million calories per day. If the number of people increases to 1,014, the number of calories per person is reduced to 2,959. If the same amount of population growth occurs the next year, the population will grow to 1,028. The calories per person per day will then be 2,918. Repeated twice more, the calories available per person per day will drop to 2,879 and then to 2,838. After four years of 1.4 percent population growth, calories per person per day is reduced by only 162. After a total of nine years, the reduction in calories is only 353, to a level of 2,648 calories per person per day. The impingement of the food and nutrient limitation, although subtle, will eventually serve to curb human reproduction. (2001, 10–11)

What the authors partially illustrate here is the lag that's likely to occur in population decline resulting from a gradual decrease in aggregate calories. But they also indicate how the growth rate, which is about 1.05 percent at the time I write this, can be reversed in relatively short order.

With respect to Hopfenberg and Pimentel's calculations, Quinn asks, "Does this sound like mass starvation to anyone here? Are there people who feel they'd be starving if they missed a couple swallows of orange juice a day? I know I certainly don't" ("Reaching for the Future"). And while you may wonder how seemingly minor modifications in intake can have such large demographic effects, it's important once again to consider not how a little less orange juice would affect *you* but how a little less orange juice (or its caloric equivalent) for *everybody,* or at least everybody who can spare it, would affect our entire population.

And now, at long last, we get to fertility and sexual activity. (I know it's taken quite a while, but the setup took some doing.) Male fertility rates are already decreasing the world over across all demographics, with evidence implicating widespread exposure to an array of toxins, including neurotoxins, endocrine disruptors, and other hazardous substances—many of which are byproducts of toxiculture (Mima et al. 2018, Mann et al. 2020, and Pizzol et al. 2021).[11] And even a small reduction in food availability can diminish female fertility (Fontana and Della Torre 2016). Again, think systemically. The point here isn't to reduce the provision of nourishing food for those who are already starving. A modest decline in fertility due to a modest reduction of calories *among the billions who aren't starving* can go hand in hand with an equitable caloric distribution. Particularly given peakism, the proliferation of symbiocultures can help make this happen.

A modest reduction in calories also tends slightly to diminish sexual activity (Gill and Rissman 1997 and Pierce et al. 2007). For most of the nonstarving billions, feeding oneself via symbioculture will mean more time and energy on food cultivation and preparation. This isn't a bad way at all to make a living, fully or partially, directly or indirectly. But it still stands to add a degree of "food stress" and "time stress" to one's day, states Thornhill (Quinn and Thornhill 1998; see also "Texas Legacy Project" and Q&A, 731 and 238). Over time, both forms of stress are likely to make a consequential difference demographically.

Albert Bartlett (2012) indicates that population doubling time T(2) is calculated using the "rule of 70": T(2) in years = 70/annual growth percentage.[12] An average 1.05 percent rate of population decline would lead current human population to be halved in roughly sixty-seven years, and it would reach one billion in 267 years. An average 2.2 percent decline rate, which mirrors the peak percentage growth rate from 1962, would halve our numbers in thirty-two years. At this rate, human population would reach one billion in 128 years. Reaching one billion humans by the end of the century would require a rate of decline of 3.5 percent. None of these scenarios reflects a massive die-off. None need be accompanied by widespread misery.

Still Skeptical?

Taking a breath as we reach the end of the chapter, I must admit that I feel the weight of your abiding skepticism. And why shouldn't you be skeptical? Of all the topics we've covered in this book, it's hardly surprising that Quinn's brush with abandoning the threefold struggle comes here—if my speculations at the chapter's opening bear weight. There's nothing he or I can say that somehow casts away Heinberg's and Catton's warnings.

Maybe, then, we persist because these warnings don't somehow excuse inaction. Or, with Ta-Nehisi Coates (chapter 1), perhaps we do so because it's what helps keep us sane and resilient, somewhat anyway—a little less prone to zombification, a tad more emboldened to challenge *wétiko,* including our own.

Persistence in the name of the threefold struggle. Persistence in resisting zombification and *wétiko.* Persistence in asserting the world's sacredness and our own. However we put it, I think this is perhaps the best qualification that I can identify to be a teacher, in Quinn's sense of the term. It's fitting, then, that education is the theme for our final chapter.

Chapter 10

A Farewell to Miseducation

Unschooling and the Circus of Learning

As demonstrations against police brutality in the wake of George Floyd's extrajudicial execution unfolded in 2020, a friend from my youth—from before my move—posted a comment on social media:

> Many years ago, I was riding a bus in Dublin when a man stepped off the curb and was hit by the bus. I saw him just before it happened, and I felt the slightest little bump as he bounced off the front of the bus. I don't know what happened to him, he might have survived, but he was at least badly injured. That little bump that I felt has haunted me, because I know enough physics to know that that feeling was my own little bit of personal momentum being transferred into his body. When combined with the momentum of the bus, and everybody else on board, it was enough to kill him.
>
> If you don't see where I'm going with this, keep in mind (even though I often fail to keep it in mind) that I'm a white, middle-aged, hetero, (formerly) Christian American man. This racist system that we have built is carried along by my personal momentum. Every black or brown or gay or trans or female body that gets run over by this system is damaged by my little contribution to that momentum.
>
> I'd like to get off this bus now.

More so, I'd like to help render the bus inoperable, dismantle it. But how? That's the initial question that came to my mind when I first read these lines. And it's not a helpful question to begin with. Because I haven't come close to fully metabolizing just how much the successes I've experienced, particularly in my professional life as an academic, are attributable to systemic racism and heteropatriarchy.

"Whiteness is a metaphor for power," states James Baldwin (cited in Peck 2016). In Taker culture, so is being a cishet male. I may despise heirarchalism. I may be hellbent on resisting it. But this changes not one whit that I'm a walking embodiment of it, which means I also need to resist the ways in which I conveniently overlook my privilege, usually without even being aware of what I'm doing. Of late, nowhere is this on my mind more than in the classroom. Because nowhere am I more obviously part of the system.

According to neoclassical economists, the marketplace is fair and efficient. At least this is so in theory, although this theory underpins the work of nearly every economist today. In general and on the whole, private actors, whether individuals or firms, operating freely and without undue state interference are maximally empowered within the marketplace because resources are allocated strictly on the basis of Pareto optimality. Becoming a fully functioning participant in society essentially involves developing the wherewithal to be an effective actor individually and a valued contributor to a firm. This requires that one have the capacity to be independent, informed, and socially competent. These are the keys to material success and a life of personal fulfillment.

From this perspective, a good education provides translatable knowledge and skills: information and capacities that are learned in the classroom sufficiently well to then be honed within the marketplace and one's wider life without undue difficulty. Yet, in the United States, schools at every level are generally assumed to be representations of systematic failure (MI, 134; see also Côté and Allahar 2007 and Arum and Roksa 2011). Not every school may be found wanting, but the American school system as a whole is deemed deficient and defective since many, perhaps most, students graduate without translatable knowledge and skills. They're ill-equipped to take advantage of the opportunities for material success and personal fulfillment that the marketplace provides directly (through good jobs and bountiful consumer choices) and also makes possible indirectly (by creating national wealth).

But schools aren't failing, Quinn insists, not by a long shot. They're just as successful now as they've always been at achieving that for which they're *actually* designed: funneling and controlling the flow of bodies into the market economy of an industrial society. Indeed, the model for compulsory schooling that's still operative today was created at institutions such as the University of Chicago, Johns Hopkins, Stanford, Carnegie-Mellon, and Harvard well over a century ago "and funded by captains of industry . . . explicitly . . . to ensure a docile, malleable workforce to meet the growing, changing demands of corporate capitalism," Michael Albert contends (cited in Gatto 2005, xx).

John Taylor Gatto provides an even starker assessment with a familiar ring. "School, as it was built, is an essential support system for a model of social engineering that condemns most people to be subordinate stones in a pyramid that ascends to a terminal of control" (ibid., 13). It's expressly designed for "compulsory subordination," which is "necessary to maintain a society where some people take more than their fair share" (ibid., 14). Far from creating an independent and informed populace, school curricula thus operate as a reverse *elenchus*, producing physical, moral, and intellectual paralysis on the part of students.

In this respect, schooling succeeds so long as it creates a populace of pliant human resources that's sufficiently well molded to market demands (H, 182). Students continue to be trained well to be materially dependent on the market economy and to subordinate their needs to its needs (MI, 144f., and Eisenstein 2007, 322). A steady flow of captive consumers—including lots of "non-wage-earning consumers" (MI, 136) in the form of children—and captive producers keep things humming. Measured on these terms, the American school system is a rousing success ("On Investments" and IS, 13 and 77). It's a paragon of Taker culture.

This is the system in which I find myself. With respect to my teaching duties, I'm paid to be a glorified sorter. Echoing Curtis White, I may teach against the grain of Taker culture, but I'm also complicit with it. Complicit under duress, yes, but still complicit. For whatever I teach in class runs up against the demand that I also perform "the task of sorting human beings into categories useful to the state and to future employers: these are the A students, there the B, and those over there are the failures. Use them accordingly" (cited in Spencer 2019).

Particularly since getting sober, I've been struggling with how to get off this bus, too, or at least to alter its momentum. But, of course, it's the same bus about which my childhood friend writes. I may not be called on (explicitly) to sort students by race or ethnicity or sexual orientation or gender identity. Nevertheless, I'm a functionary of an absurdly expensive credentialing service—a bottleneck through which students are constantly told they must pass to signify their qualification for professional advancement. This service is expressly designed to support the thinly veiled illusion that the socioeconomic institutions operative within Taker culture today are meritocratic. Indeed, I've been trained to accept that it's part of my calling as a tenured professor to pretend that I myself am an example of the meritocracy at work.

Rubbish.

Yet this is where I find myself.

Don't get me wrong. I don't hate my job or my employer, even if the system in which I'm forced to operate doesn't work. Moreover, it would be cruel for me to fail to acknowledge how fortunate I am to have tenure. With the job security that comes with it, I've been making an effort for a while now to transform myself from a sorter into a teacher—a facilitator of changed minds in Quinn's sense, one who's engaged in the struggle in Coates's. But it's time to put this work into a wider context.

What would it mean to be an educator of sacred beings, as each of my students is? What would it mean to honor their sacredness? How do I honor my own in the process? This is what I'd like to investigate in this final chapter. For if "it is through learning that persons and personalities are constructed," as Shay Welch asserts (2013, 209), then it's through teaching that I'm best positioned to carry out a prefigurative strategy for ecological, social, and personal transformation. It's in this setting that I can strive to enact a new story within the shell of our current one (Leach 2013, 182, and Brown 2017, 55ff.). Let's begin, though, by looking more closely at the origins and purpose of compulsory schooling in the United States. We still have more to see about the character and function of education, including higher education, within a paragon of the culture of maximum harm.

Invisible Successes

Prior to the Civil War, no social imperative existed for compulsory schooling. Schools existed, but because the antebellum United States was largely an agrarian society most people expected to become farmers. If they got any formal education at all, it typically ended by age twelve. Higher education was strictly for the social elite, who received just as much instruction as they wanted and no more, Gatto notes. But even without formal schooling, people "learned to read, write, and do arithmetic just fine anyway; there are some studies that suggest literacy at the time of the American Revolution, at least for non-slaves on the Eastern seaboard, was close to total" (2005, 12).[1]

What, then, was the original purpose of compulsory schooling? Industrial sectors of the economy expanded exponentially in the American North during the Civil War. Captains of industry gained a sufficiently firm political foothold to leverage public policy on behalf of their commercial interests. The fulfillment of these interests required the establishment of an entirely new social order, which "didn't arise as a product of public debate as it should have in a democracy," Gatto remarks, "but as a distillation of private discussion" (2006, xxviii) among "Northeastern policy elites of business, government, and university life" (ibid., 37). These discussions were driven by "the new logic of the Industrial Age" (ibid.), according to which family and community life were to refocus from the farm to the factory. An exaltation of intensive productivity and "social efficiency" (ibid., xxiii) resulted from the seemingly limitless potential of coal-driven machinery. And bodies were needed to tend both these machines and the bodies that tended the machines.

Surely, there were many communities that resisted compulsory schooling. But a number of factors help to explain how it took firm hold relatively quickly in American society. Gatto (2005, 16) asserts that public support for compulsory schooling was already strong in the North among middle- and upper-class whites prior to the Civil War as a result of (1) the Red Scare of 1848 and growing fears of revolution among the urban poor and (2) fears of the cultural influence of Catholicism due to an influx of Celtic, Slavic, and Latin immigrants. Compulsory schooling was regarded as a means to mitigate both threats. Support for it in the South and North alike gained strength among whites of all classes after the Civil War as it provided a means to control the mobility and economic opportunities of newly freed slaves. It also served as a cornerstone of the federal government's Indian Removal Act and commitment of genocide.

Compulsory schooling thus provided a means to indoctrinate and sort children within an increasingly centralized and hierarchical economy. A generation later, sociologist Benjamin Kidd defended the need to "impose on the young the ideal of subordination to the common aims of organized humanity" (1918, 306) rather than to ethnic and religious identifications. Elwood Cubberly, future dean of education at Stanford, argued in his 1905 dissertation for Columbia Teachers College that schools should be viewed as factories designed expressly to disassemble a system in which children learn crafts associated with provincial living. Rather than completing school by age twelve, childhood was to be extended by two, four, or even six years to provide extra time for children to be sorted and then "shaped and formed into finished products . . . , manufactured like nails" (cited in Jensen 2004, 37).[2]

Frederick T. Gates, who, with John D. Rockefeller, funded the General Education Board, a philanthropic organization that supported the expansion of higher education, envisioned a society in which "people yield themselves with perfect docility to our molding hands." For this to occur, agrarian conventions and parochial traditions should be made to:

> fade from our minds, and unhampered by tradition we work our own will upon a grateful and responsive folk. We shall not try to make these people or any of their children into philosophers or men of learning or men of science. We have not to raise up from among them authors, educators, poets, or men of letters. We shall not search for embryo great artists, painters, musicians, nor lawyers, preachers, politicians, statesmen, of whom we have ample supply. The task we set before ourselves is very simple. . . . [W]e will organize children . . . and teach them to do in a perfect way the things their fathers and mothers are doing in an imperfect way. (Cited in Gates 1913, 6)

William Torrey Harris, U.S. Commissioner of Education from 1889–1906, lauded that "Ninety-nine [students] out of a hundred are automata, careful to walk in prescribed paths, careful to follow the prescribed custom. This is not an accident but the result of substantial education, which, scientifically defined, is the subsumption of the individual" (1893).

It didn't much matter what new material was inserted into the curriculum to fill the extra years of schooling, Quinn asserts. Nor did it matter that lessons once learned were immediately forgotten after obligatory examinations. Prior to the Great Depression, an eighth-grade education was decreed "essential for every citizen, and so curriculum writers provided materials needed for an eighth-grade education" (IS, 74; see also MI, 135f.).[3] Compulsory high school then emerged during the Great Depression, as it became urgent to further delay adulthood in order to ease pressure on the labor market. Again, it didn't much matter what students were taught, "so long as it was marginally plausible" (ibid., 75; see also MI, 139). And after World War II, as war industries disappeared and fears arose of another economic contraction, "word began to go out that the citizen's education should really include four years of college" (ibid.). It was only as these turned into boom years that schools began to be perceived as failing. "With ready workers on demand, it was apparent that kids were coming out of school without knowing much more than the sixth-grade graduates of a century ago" (ibid.).

Perhaps this surprised observers because the original intent of compulsory schooling was by this time largely forgotten. It's a wonder, though, since the outcomes envisioned by its original supporters remained the same even as more years of schooling were added. Lesson by lesson, the vast majority of students continue to be taught to submit to authority figures and obey orders, to embrace standardization and regimentation (including literally being formed into rows), to please (or at least not rile) their superiors, to be granted privileges but no effective rights, to become accustomed to routine evaluation and judgment by strangers, to measure themselves by their class position, to regard emotional and intellectual supplication as normal, to spend hours doing tedious exercises, to sit quietly despite being bored stiff, to look interested despite being exhausted, and to believe that their failure at any of these enterprises represented an individual moral deficiency that would compromise future success.[4] "What better preparation for accepting unquestioningly the lives given us?" Gatto comments. "Where else can students 'learn to think of themselves as employees competing for the favors of management?' " (2005, 38; see also Illich 1970, Eisenstein 2007, 319ff., and Pitt 2011).

Nearly every schoolteacher teaches these lessons, if unwittingly. "This is a great mystery to me," Gatto adds, "because thousands of humane, caring people work in schools as teachers and aides and administrators, but the abstract logic of the institution overwhelms their individual contributions. Although teachers do care and do work very, very hard, the institution is psychopathic—it has no conscience" (ibid., 22).

"We've built a way of life that depends on people doing what they are told because they don't know how to tell themselves what to do," Gatto concludes (ibid., 9). This applies to students and teachers alike, which is to be expected since teachers were once students themselves. This creates a guaranteed supply of people who are entirely willing "to arrive at certain decisions about themselves and their futures based on the casual judgments of strangers" (ibid., 10). It floods the labor market with people who are adept at killing time and who regard as completely normal wishing away much of how they spend their days (Jensen 2004,

4). Such a populace is not only easy to control. By and large, it controls itself. As a former student of mine once told me, much to her chagrin, for Takers this is "the only way to live a normal, successful, healthy life."

The extent to which such a life is normal, successful, and healthy is, of course, contestable. I offered the following two quotes in chapter 2, but they're worth repeating. "All fancy philosophy aside, we value asking someone if they would like fries with their burger more than we value a rich and healthy emotional and spiritual life and a vital community," Jensen remarks (2000, 328). And from Paul Eppinger: "Building cardboard boxes or shaving poodles or maybe even being the Head Pickler at Burger King. Shit, I got pretty angry thinking of all the fresh young energy being wasted. Folks just getting stiffer and staler every day" (Eppinger and Eppinger 1994, 12).

And what of those students who resist? What about miscreants? They also must be managed. This is accomplished primarily by inducing fear of the inability to access the only pathway to occupations that aren't pure drudgery. It's incredible that nearly all skilled labor in the United States today is accessible solely by passing through the schooling bottleneck (Fishkin 2014). This in itself displays just how successful the social engineering enterprise begun in the nineteenth century still is in the twenty-first. If fear fails, there's always medication (Levine 2001) or routine punishment. And if these fail as well, the school-to-prison pipeline provides for-profit "correctional" corporations with bodies, mainly black and brown, for cheap or unpaid labor (Alexander 2012).

Schools thus continue to succeed—marvelously—at doing what they were originally intended to do. Their purpose was never to educate in the typical sense of the term. Their purpose was, and still is, to "break a child's will" (Jensen 2000, 102). And by extending childhood, schools take up time and energy that people once had devoted to developing life skills with direct survival value: from producing food, to making clothing, to building shelter, to bolstering communities of support. As a result, the vast majority of us who've been subject to schooling are left with no salient or easily identifiable choice but to take our place in the pyramid (or laboring to build it; choose whichever metaphor you prefer) and, tragically, to be thankful for it.

"I was a curious boy, but the schools were not concerned with curiosity," Coates remarks (2015, 26). Indeed, schools do more to conceal truths than reveal them, in no small part by valorizing " 'personal responsibility' in a country authored and sustained by criminal irresponsibility" (ibid.,

33; see also Parkinson 2016). Not just a country, a culture. No wonder getting ahead requires being what Curtis White calls " 'stupid-smart,' or smart enough to do the chores that industry calls for but stupid enough not to resent the deadly limits it imposes" (cited in Spencer 2019). And if you do happen to see through the system's cracks, feign ignorance. Just keep your head down and get through the assigned material (MI, 132f.).

College certainly affords a little more wiggle room than either primary or secondary school. One need not feign ignorance any longer, not always, at least. But upon graduation, my students still "must immediately find someone to give them money to buy things they need in order to survive. In other words, they have to find jobs." Because food is under lock and key. "This isn't something that's optional for them, unless they're independently wealthy. It's either get a job or go hungry," Ishmael emphasizes (ibid, 134).[5]

Learning and Unlearning

Quinn observes that the need for school is bolstered by "two well-entrenched pieces of cultural mythology" (IS, 77). First, students won't learn unless they're compelled to do so. For this reason, teachers must distrust their students' motives and work ethic by default (MI, 165, and Wheatley 2009). This makes education inherently disciplinary (Holt 2008, 86). Second, teaching goes best when all students are taught the same things at the same pace in the same way with a cohort of the same age. Teachers might enter the profession to be awakeners of young minds, but they soon learn that their primary charge is to get their class "to a certain predetermined point in the curriculum by a certain predetermined time," Ishmael remarks (MI, 131). Students in turn "soon learn to help the teacher with this task. This is, in a sense, the first thing they must learn" (ibid.; see also P, 103).

What's confounding, though, is that small children in particular are perhaps be the most powerful "learning engines in the known universe," Ishmael continues. "They effortlessly learn as many languages as are spoken in their households. No one has to sit them down in a classroom and drill them on grammar and vocabulary. They do no homework, they have no tests, no grades. Learning their native languages is no chore at all, because of course it's immensely and immediately useful and gratifying to them" (ibid., 146). "The learning of small children is limited only by what they're able to see, hear, smell, and get their hands on" (ibid., 147). This "desire, this need to understand the world and be able to do things in it, the things big people do, is as strong as the need for food, for warmth, for shelter, for comfort, for sleep, for love," states John Holt (2008, 85). It's "*hardwired*" into small children, Quinn adds (IS, 78).

Any parent who isn't irrevocably damaged by our culture is well aware that children learn with ease "if they have a *reason* to learn it—their *own* reason" (P, 119). School functionaries know this, too:

> but they would never dream of allowing children to learn this way as a general rule. That wouldn't do at all, because of course how would you *organize* such a thing? How can you possibly know when a child will develop a *reason* to learn how to read a map? And what would you do when you found out? No, the only way to *organize* learning is to give children a reason to learn *all at the same time.* This is called *motivating* them. (Ibid., 119–20; see also Houssenloge 2008, 37)

Sometimes children are motivated with carrots, but more often it's the sticks that come out. Because even those, like Coates, who despised "the whole process—with its equally spaced desks, precisely timed periods and lectures, with its standardized pencils and tests"—hated failing even more (2008, 169).

From Instruction to Interaction

By third grade, Ishmael tells Julie, "most children master the skills that citizens need in order to get along in your culture, commonly characterized as the 'three R's'—reading, writing, and arithmetic" (MI, 147). So, long before they reach my classroom, learning, such as it is, has largely ceased not only to be useful for my students but also has become a grind, "a boring, painful experience they'd love to be able to avoid if they could" (IS, 79). And why not? Some students in well-funded school districts still have opportunities here and there to express artistic and musical talents or to partially free their imaginations. But nearly every student in nearly every school district in the United States spends far more time on assignments that call for a narrowly conceived, readily testable form of analytical intelligence.

From the perspective of most of my colleagues, my university's administrators, and my university's accrediting institution, my courses should follow suit. I'm called on to play a calculable role in helping my students learn to think critically, communicate effectively both orally and in writing, analyze and parse complex arguments, and so forth, all of which are to be dutifully outlined in my course "learning outcomes" on the syllabus.

These aren't bad skills to have, mind you. They have pedagogical value. But within the current system they're also representative of a "monochromatic flattening of education," as James C. Scott (2012, 71–72) puts it, that reduces philosophy itself to a series of threadbare mental exercises.

This concerns me, but it's probably the least of my concerns. I find the demand that I be a sorter far more troubling, which is why I began to distance myself from it a few years ago and gave it up entirely (save in graduate courses) during the academic year that ended with the COVID-19 pandemic.[6]

The primary function of grading is to coerce students to do what they'd rather not, Jensen points out. "Grades, as is true once again for wages in later life, are an implicit acknowledgement that the process of schooling is insufficiently rewarding on its own grounds for people to participate of their own volition" (2000, 104). From a market perspective, grading thus offers a critical lesson: "to value abstract rewards at the expense of our autonomy, curiosity, interior lives, and time" (ibid.).

In the same vein, my students' lives largely are governed by a *productivity fetish*. More often than I'd like to admit, so is mine. Work, work, work—in the words of Quinn's so-named children's book (WWW). And feel guilty when you aren't. Earn good grades, qualify for a better income, receive exemplary performance evaluations, acquire accolades, get the big promotion. Always look to improve, at least on paper.

Slowly but surely, we become our achievements. We're a number on a transcript, a paycheck, and an annual review. We're the pedigree of the institutions with which we're affiliated. We're a list of accomplishments on a resumé or vita. We are a *what,* not a *who.* And we're well trained to judge ourselves and one another accordingly. Somehow we never quite measure up. Happiness is always a slightly larger number, a slightly better affiliation, a slightly longer accomplishments list away. Why? Because schooling selects for *heteronomy* rather than autonomy. This is why I've begun to devote myself less to supporting students' learning per se than their *unlearning*—and mine in the process.

Once again, the work of Indigenous philosophers has proven invaluable for me in this enterprise. Here's Thurman Lee Hester Jr.:

> Correction is an important part of Euro-American education. Almost everyone in academic life has as part of his or her job the grading of papers. It is central to the Euro-American tradition. It is almost completely alien to Choctaw tradition. This is in part because of the value of context . . . but also because of the value of *respect*. . . . Correction implies that one person knows what is correct and the other person does not; even worse, that one person acts correctly and the other does not. Though there may be many ways of rationalizing the need for correction, or how correction, properly understood, actually *is* a form of respect for the person being corrected, it is very difficult—maybe impossible—for it not to convey a feeling of superiority versus inferiority: a lack of respect for, if not downright disrespect for, the person being corrected. (2004, 184–85)

This claim is echoed over and over throughout the literature.

Lecturing and comparable forms of instruction, for example, play a central role in the typical Taker education. By comparison, asserts Welch, myriad Native traditions favor engaging almost exclusively in forms of learning characterized by "choice making and skill development, an intense emphasis on individual initiative, and a proscription of direct guidance or correction by teachers and elders" (2013, 209). Children of all ages are left largely to their own devices, and discipline is rare. Even for the young adults Welch and I teach, "To immediately mark and correct a student's paper is nothing more than to act as if you did not believe that the student was capable of coming to the right answer eventually on her own with appropriate guidance . . . ; it is a denial of dignity and deemed rude, which is a serious transgression in Native interaction" (ibid., 211).

Ishmael's maieutic lessons with Julie lean in the direction Welch describes, since he offers her ample discursive space to ask and answer her own questions, make mistakes, and self-correct. Ishmael's stories and parables, too, typically serve as "unobtrusive and gentle but steady moral guidance," as Dennis McPherson and J. Douglas Rabb put it (2011, 105; see also Cordova 2004). His interactions with Alan become more brusque and confrontational as their discussions proceed, not just because it becomes clear that Alan wants to possess Ishmael but because Ishmael is uncomfortable with doing as much hand holding as Alan wants.

The point, in any case, isn't that Native teaching precludes guidance, Lorraine Brundige notes. It's that guidance is typically indirect, and it's never pushy (1997, 46). Nor are learners ever treated as inferiors. Keith Basso comments that among the Apache, stories are often designed to "work on you," "get under your skin," "make you want to change," and/or "make you want to replace yourself" (1996, 59)—to morally transform yourself as, or into, a person. Basso calls this practice "interventive-noninterference," and it regularly involves telling tales that might not seem to have anything to do with whatever question the learner asks or the problem they present. The learner is hereby "given the autonomy, the complete freedom to discover the relevance of the reply" (ibid., 105). The storyteller has *intervened* in the learner's affairs, but only on request. Moreover, the storyteller doesn't *interfere* with the learner's capacity to work out on their own what lesson(s) to take away.[7]

Am I able to engage in something like interventive-noninterference in the classroom? I must admit that I haven't tried, at least not in a systematic way. Without having unlearned heteronomy myself, it would be foolhardy of me to believe I have the skillset—or mindset—to successfully pull it off.[8] I'm not a maieutic teacher either, even if I'm more comfortable with the technique. There's no one right way to teach, of course. But I take these considerations from Indigenous philosophers as a clear reminder that to be a teacher is to be one kind of caretaker of sacred beings. It's my responsibility to contribute to their wellbeing on their own considered terms, and I take this charge seriously.

Ecologies of Intimacy

Another key lesson from Indigenous philosophers offers equally helpful pedagogical direction. Recall that the main point of schooling is to learn behaviors, rather than to gain knowledge and skills—specifically, behaviors associated with compliance to the will of superiors. Yet what if instead the behaviors learned have a freely embraced communal focus? Information matters. So do intellectual development and skill building. My students get their fill of these demands elsewhere. Me, I've come around to focusing on what Jenny Davidson refers to as "self-care and the sane management of responsibilities to the broader community" (2020), notably including both the living community and the community we build as a class.

Davidson makes this comment in an article entitled "Forget Distance Learning. Just Give Every Student an Automatic A." It's a response to the acute stress both students and faculty faced trying to figure out how to transition to remote instruction during the early days of the coronavirus pandemic. But I've found typical conditions at my university to be highly stressful even without a pandemic, particularly for students. Our ten-week terms are intense from the get-go. Many students take at least seventeen credits (or six courses), and it's not at all uncommon for them to take as many as twenty credits (seven courses). A good number also hold down a part-time job and/or engage in independent research. There's simply no letup. As such, I began reformulating my classroom into what Leanne Simpson calls an *ecology of intimacy* well before I became familiar with the concept.

Simpson remarks that ecologies of intimacy are highly prized among her people, the Michi Saagiig Nishnaabeg, because they foster "relationships in the absence of coercion, hierarchy, and authoritarian power" (2017, 8). Consent, caring, sharing, and individual self-determination are given pride of place. This has allowed the Michi Saagiig Nishnaabeg to accumulate "networks of meaningful, deep, fluid, intimate collective and individual relationships of trust" (ibid., 77).

Trust: It's the first of the Four Pillars at the heart of each undergraduate course I teach. (They're listed in place of learning outcomes on my syllabi.) My students don't have to earn my trust. They have it by default. Instead, it's my responsibility to earn theirs. *Respect:* My students' needs, interests, and concerns matter. They deserve my attention. And my desires don't outweigh theirs. *Empathy:* Life at my institution is stressful for us all but especially for students. I refuse to ignore this. *Consent:* My students aren't asked to do anything that isn't subject to their prior agreement. We begin our work together by deciding not how my students will earn their grade. The A is theirs at the outset no matter what they choose to do. So we focus on how we can get the most out of our time together, and this can only be determined by collective involvement and decision making.

Students learn up front that they don't need to look to me for instructions. But our studies—typically centered on reading, films, and far-flung discussion—aren't always the point. And they invariably fall by the wayside at times, sometimes by design (with regular walks) and sometimes not (with ad hoc trips to a coffee shop or local park simply to decompress). Canine companions are always welcome with prior unanimous student approval, since they provide a welcome distraction.[9]

By engaging in practices such as these, students ease into the idea that it's perfectly fine to get as much out of the course as they wish—that they have my support with whatever they choose to do. Are you concerned about free riders in this setting, just as some commentators are about their eventuality in tribal societies (chapter 5)? I'm not. I don't expect my students to be better than they are, and I have no interest in forcing them to spend time doing something they have no desire to do. Call me crazy, but if a course is running smoothly and participants' needs and interests are being met (to the extent possible within institutional confines), I'm satisfied. It's my responsibility to make my classes worth my students' time while accepting that they always have a litany of other demands to address.

Call my courses blow-offs if you like. Accuse me of being lazy, a grade inflater, or overly permissive. Frankly, I don't care. I simply can't envision a scenario in which I'll ever again assign a grade other than an A for my undergraduates. Paraphrasing Justin Good (2014), why on Earth should something beautiful and effortless instead be boring and painful? More to the point, Murray Bookchin remarks that the wide latitude parents in tribal communities typically give to their children only seems permissive when viewed through a Taker lens. From their own perspective, "they simply respect the personality of their children, much as they do that of the adults in their communities" (2005, 115). Imagine it, a community of *whos* taken as we are, warts and all, worthy of validation simply for existing (P, 112).

I'm fortunate that I have about fifty to seventy-five students during any given term. I can get to know many of them pretty well. But not every course seamlessly gels into a community, even if I'm getting better at facilitating this. When we succeed, we get something far more precious than the analytical intelligence I'm supposed to focus on. We get what Simpson calls "intelligence as consensual engagement" (2017, 160), which helps us to glimpse what it's like to be "loving, creative, self-determining, interdependent, and self-regulating community-minded individuals" (ibid., 151).

This is satisfying work, which doesn't mean it's easy. For my students, it involves less prep but more presence. For me, it requires a lot of both. But the better we do with facilitating intelligence as consensual engagement, the closer we come to embracing our shared sacredness. This is profoundly special.

On the Road to Nowhere

Far too many of the people of our culture confuse schooling with learning, grade advancement with education, a diploma with competence. Even those, like Coates, who see through the chimera and who hate what they see hate failing even more. In *The Holy,* David Kennesey saw through it, too, but he betrayed himself for forms of acceptance, respectability, and security that never quite delivered (H, 112; see also Q&A, 684).

For young adults in particular, does instead traveling the road to nowhere (chapter 3), the road to living otherwise, entail foregoing a college education? Quinn doesn't think so. "A bachelor's degree will give you a ticket of admittance to certain kinds of jobs." If you want to be a physician, a scholar, an engineer, or a financial analyst, pursue the degree; "but if you don't want those jobs, a bachelor's degree will be almost worthless to you" (Q&A, 377). It's simple, right? If the degree can get you where you want to go, pursue it. If not, don't.

Of course, it isn't so simple, and Quinn knows this. A bachelor's degree is something anyone who seeks a white-collar job sees essentially as a requirement. But it's no golden ticket. It doesn't guarantee you a job you desire. It doesn't even guarantee passable employment to pay off your student loans (ibid., 557). This is an open secret. It's why colleges and universities now brand themselves in ways that highlight how the degrees they confer can put students at a competitive advantage within what's become "a credentialist arms race," as Bryan Caplan calls it (2018). In this respect, a college degree is about *signaling*. It gives you "a stamp on your forehead saying you're a superior worker," Caplan states (cited in Tan 2020). Compared with those whose highest degree is from high school, a college degree often pays financially, despite its absurd cost. But *why* it pays has little to do with education per se.

I accept this. I don't have much choice. The question I face is what I'm to do with this knowledge, and I can't help but play around with creating a rogue *circus of learning* within my university's hallowed halls.

The Circus of Learning

"What?" Quinn asks. "How would *I* organize the schools? To ask this question presupposes that we *must* have schools, doesn't it? I prefer to think about problems the way engineers do. If a valve doesn't work, they don't say, 'Well, we *must* have valves, so let's try *two* valves.' If a valve doesn't work, they say, 'Well, what *would* work?' Their rule is, if it doesn't work, don't do it *more,* do *something else*" (P, 120).

Unsurprisingly, Quinn looks to traditional tribal practices for what works for learning. In whatever form it takes, education is intended to ensure "that the children of every new generation are prepared to take their parents' place in the world" (IS, 10–11). This is as true of Takers as it is of Indigenous peoples. But whereas our educational system succeeds at channeling generation after generation into pyramid building, Indigenous peoples traditionally faced no such pressures. Until the rise of the settler-industrial state, they had no schools, no standardized curriculum, no people who devoted their time solely to teaching—and not because the stories they've enacted aren't sufficiently advanced or because their simple ways leave their children with little to learn. "This is ethnocentric balderdash," Quinn proclaims.[10] "What children learn in other cultures isn't *less,* it's *different.* And in fact nothing is too much to learn if kids want to learn" (P, 122; see also MI, 166f.).

Let children follow their interests. Let them play. Let them be with kinfolk and work on doing what adults do.[11] Let them ask for guidance and seek out answers. Do these things and learning takes care of itself. It's not magic, Ishmael insists. It's an evolutionarily stable strategy for collective continuance:

> It works very simply, without cost, without effort, without administration of any kind. Children simply go wherever they want and spend time with whomever they want in order to learn the things they want to learn when they actually want to learn them. Not every child's education is identical. Why on earth should it be? The idea is not that every child should receive the entire heritage but rather that every *generation* should receive it. And it is received, without fail; this is proved by the fact that the society continues to function, generation after generation, which it couldn't do if its heritage were not being transmitted faithfully and totally, generation after generation. (MI, 152; see also Q&A, 729)

It speaks to the resilience of this strategy and the peoples who practice it that countless heritages have endured despite centuries of colonization.

This brings us to the learning circus. Recall from chapter 7 that the circus is (or traditionally was) an open tribal enterprise, an enterprise that exists for and because of the people who compose it. For its members, the circus offers both an outlet for performance and a means to make a living in an egalitarian and mutually supportive context. For audiences, it provides entertainment.

Some days, entertaining the audience is a grind. Generally, though, the circus survives because its members find pleasure in the work. (Thankfully, though, circus animals are increasingly a thing of the past throughout much of the world.) Even for crew members, it's far less burdensome than slogging stones for the pyramid, because they're engaged in a collective enterprise and their working lives are at least partially integrated into their social lives.

Quinn envisions the same for the circus of learning, which, ideally, "combines spaces for working, exhibition, and performance to provide a center for work, play, performance, and education" (BC, 166). Consider it a makerspace, studio space, and theater space, combined with a playground, library, lab space, and study space, since scholars, artists, scientists, musicians, artisans, tradespeople, and technicians are all welcome and learning from them is open to students of all ages. "No grades, no required courses, no tests—just learn all you want, whenever you want" (ibid.).[12]

"Someone asked why students would prefer this learning circus over a university," Quinn notes. "The two aren't competitive, and the strictly career-minded will surely prefer the more conventional of the two" (ibid.; see also MI, 164). But what if, unnoticed by university administrators and academic credentialing organizations, I were to find a way to carve out a little room for students to study as they please—or, for that matter, to do whatever they please—for as long as it pleases them, *all for credit*? "Nothing difficult, nothing very demanding," if they prefer, and not necessarily all that productive; "but they'd have a hell of a lot more fun and they'd find out what it's like to live like human beings instead of workers" (P, 125).[13]

Humans *are* workers, of course, as are all living beings, in the sense that we must expend energy to survive. So perhaps it's better to say that students get to affirm their humanity in an educational setting. They have needs, interests, and concerns that include their work but aren't solely defined by it. To be clear, I have no interest in undercutting my students' desire for worthwhile employment. Nor do I deny them my full support with intensive independent research if this is what they want to do. Why would I? If they end up seeking out alternatives to pyramid building, wonderful. If not, that's fine.

Let's push this idea a little further. David Fleming observes that the decline of the carnival—a close cousin of the circus in terms of its performative and revelatory qualities—has coincided with increased urbanization and industrialization. This means it also has coincided with the rise of compulsory schooling. And no wonder. The demand emerged for workers with "habits of soberness" conducive to "turning up for work on Monday morning" to begin week after long week of labor under the boss's watchful eye. Not just the adults of our culture but increasingly our children, too, hereby suffer from "play-deprivation," Fleming asserts. Play still exists "to a weakened extent in sport," but even here the desire to win or support winners typically takes precedence over enjoyment of the game (2014, 186–87). This is a genuine loss, since play supports becoming a person, fosters "creative ingenuity" (Fleming 2016, 358), and reinforces community membership.

The carnival is about celebration, laughter, and public joy. Each of these characteristics is essential for making and sustaining a community as well because each contributes to three specifiable practices, Fleming states. The first is a radical break from the normalcy of the work routine, living according to convention, and following self-prescribed rules. Second is the release of "the animal spirit at the heart of the tamed, domesticated citizen: the deep reality, which, if recognized and cared for, connects us with the red-blooded truth about ourselves" (2016, 30). The animal spirit fosters folly, a wild sociality, even a lack of dignity. "It is the difference between belonging to the community because you feel you ought to and belonging to it because its artistic expression engages your soul" (ibid., 35). The third practice, sacrifice-and-succession, embodies an embrace of the need for renewal, including the realization that "the present will be laughable" (ibid.). The focus on renewal bears some similarity to Indigenous ceremonies involving reminders of and recommitment to connections with more-than-human community members (Norton-Smith 2010, 114). The laughability of the present highlights my need as a teacher to support the emergence of my successors: those who will carry the enactment of a new story further than I'm capable.

Fleming himself regards the carnival as ritualistic (2016, 31). Among its most critical pedagogical aspects is putting rank on hold, or at least making it "hard to sustain with due seriousness" (ibid.). More than anything else, I think, this helps a classroom community to emerge. At its best, it also releases "the creative potential of collective folly, while breeding new strains of good judgment for a different world" (ibid., 35). Such occurrences might be rare in school settings, but they do happen. And even if they don't, at least my students and I have had some fun.

Pedagogical Precedent

Despite the rarity of such an approach, nothing I propose is entirely new, not even among Takers. It's not typically found in postsecondary education, but the need for carnival-like levity and play isn't something we outgrow. And I have no clear idea why it can't facilitate learning, particularly if the cultivation of intelligence as consensual engagement is among our aims.

Consider Quinn's support for *unschooling*, which comes as close to learning tribally as Takers get. Not to be confused with homeschooling, which requires adhering to standards set by school districts and the state, unschooling has no standards. "We don't have a system," unschooling parent Nanda Van Gestel emphasizes; "there is no mold that our children have to fit" (2008, 16).

For unschoolers, Kim Houssenloge adds, speaking about her son:

> There are no schedules to follow. No deadlines to meet. No changing of topics when he's right in the middle of something fun or important to him. No pushing him to do something he's finding too hard or boring. No having to step when a bell rings. No having to ask to go to the toilet. No waiting to eat even when you're starving. No lining up. No hands up to talk. No staying in late. No detentions for talking in class—actually, talking is encouraged! Lots of time to play and dream; laugh and run; swim and ride; read and listen; and talk, talk, talk. He gets to experience real life with real people. He's learning to interact with the world safely and confidently and with room to grow and change in a natural way. (2008, 39)

Unschoolers live. And by living—within supportive, enriching settings—they learn. Freedom from coercion, time to imagine and explore, unstructured socialization, time on one's own, unconditional respect, and joy: unschooling facilitates them all.

This is a road to living otherwise. Unschoolers, states Rue Kream, "aren't in preparation for anything. They live in the real world right now, and it is a wonderful, amazing, challenging, beautiful, extraordinary place" (2008, 76). Unschoolers aren't channeled toward heteronomy either—toward accepting that a teacher has the right to control their actions and discipline contravention, that constant evaluation is normal and preferable, that self-esteem hinges on how one measures up to a superior's standards, and that one must concentrate above all on positioning oneself for gainful employment.[14] "These are lessons that an unschooled child never learns, and not one of them will help a child live in joy or contribute to her growing up to be a happy and autonomous adult" (ibid., 78).

Unschooling isn't without challenges. Peter Gray and Gina Riley (2013) conducted an informative survey of families who unschool. Many expressed that they had difficulty dealing with social pressures to conform to the standard view of what an education entails, let alone their own culturally ingrained beliefs about it. Forms of schooling that at least partially mimic unschooling offer middle ground. Consider the West Philly Cooperative School, which is play-based. Parents offer substantial hands-on support for the school's operational needs. This helps to keep the cost of tuition down, permitting children from my working-class (school-adjacent) neighborhood to attend. Teachers focus on students' needs and interests, both through direct questioning and by watching them play. They then create for each a personalized "emergent curriculum" that integrates free play with reading, games, fieldtrips and park outings, quiet time, artistic and musical activities, and small-group interactions.

The Sudbury Model is similar, if a bit more structured (MI, 211, and Q&A, 403). Students are solely responsible for their curriculum and learning methods. They choose the environment in which they learn; with whom they interact; and if, how, and when they're evaluated, often choosing to evaluate themselves (Traxler 2015). External forms of motivation are neither necessary nor desirable (Deci and Ryan 2002). Not separated by age, it's common for students to teach and learn from one another. Whatever their age, they participate as equals with staff in making decisions about the school's operation.

It's important not to overlook that, as things stand, unschooling in particular is largely available only to those with the time and disposable income to stay alert and constantly respond to their children's curiosity. But this isn't a mark against unschooling so much as it reinforces that the socioeconomic institutions to which Takers are beholden don't work. As with food, then, can learning be unlocked? Can it be decolonized and decommodified? The educational institutions that prioritize their own survival and cater to market demands rather than the full-spectrum wellbeing of their students can't be expected to become obsolete anytime soon. But alternatives exist, and they aren't going away either.

Reclaiming Our Research

Despite finding Andrea again on the Morningstar Path, David Kennesey never could break free from his self-imposed captivity. "Too old, too ignorant," Horse Killer (a.k.a., Dudley) concluded when they first met in a strange saloon, fittingly, in "the middle of nowhere" (H, 200–201). David should have been "prepared to meet an unusual destiny," Pablo tells him, but he shrugged off this proposition, unwilling or unable to entertain that "the gods have something special in mind" for him (ibid., 247). The pull of Taker culture endured, as it does for most of us, despite our best intentions and inmost needs.

Be realistic. Be practical. The drumbeat is unending. For people like David, the one right way to live, the best way to live, is to "have no choice but to find someone who will give them money in exchange for labor," Andrea remarks. Takers truly are an enchanted people. *Not* realistic, *not* practical. No, we're very much spellbound. "I'm not a learned person—I wouldn't want you to think that," she continues. "But there is one statement I came across in Plato's *Republic* that I thought was worth remembering: *Whatever deceives may be said to be enchanted.* You have been monstrously deceived—and are therefore monstrously enchanted" (ibid., 260).[15]

David fails to understand. Who, he asks, has enchanted us? "Oh, you managed to do that for yourselves long ago." Andrea suggests that he have Dudley explain all this to him. "He understands it very well—almost instinctively. His people have managed to resist the enchantment for three or four centuries now."

"His people?"

"He's a Navajo" (ibid.).

Andrea's point isn't that Dudley has some insider information about the meaning of life or any such thing. We Takers do well to stop pretending that the meaning of life is some sort of secret that somehow eludes us (P, 174). This is nothing but obfuscation by design. It's a product of the fog of war—war on anyone who isn't a Taker, on the community of life, on ourselves.

"My dear child," John Dee proclaims to David. "You ventured forth to discover uncharted lands of experience and then fled in terror when they proved to be truly uncharted. You wanted to probe beneath the surface of the piddling life your culture gives you to lead—but you wouldn't tolerate being disconcerted. Oh my, no. You wanted your adventure to be all nicely under your control; in fact, you wanted it to be indistinguishable from the life you'd abandoned" (H, 334). Ultimately, Dee concludes, "you refused to risk *anything*" (ibid., 336).

Ellen Kennesey failed to get nowhere, too, even upon realizing how much she despised being a "middle-aged Jane married to a middle-aged Dick." David's unexpected departure "left her with no choice but to become a person" (ibid., 302). As with David, it proved too much for her.

"Tim, your father left you in order to find something he wanted. Something he wanted but wasn't strong enough to have," Pablo remarks. "He became . . . lost. Your mother followed him and she too became lost" (ibid., 357).

Expressionless, Tim stared at the distant horizon.

"What is it you deeply want, Tim? Do you want to go back home and [go to] school with the other boys? If that's what you want, I promise you shall have it. You mustn't stay here if your heart yearns for the small, humdrum world you left" (ibid.).

"We'll wait for you, Tim. Not forever. But we'll wait" (ibid., 413).

❧

Am I David or Ellen? Tim? I know who I wish to be, but do *I* have the resolve?

If, like me, you're an academic whose research focuses broadly on issues in the humanities or social sciences, you've been "selected, trained, paid to think, imagine, envisage, and propose," states Isabelle Stengers (2018, 106). At least this is what we do when we're not "too busy meeting the relentless demands to which we now have to conform in order to survive." We're firmly ensconced in "an academic pseudo-market" that requires "fast publication in high-ranking journals specializing in professionally recognized issues—issues which, in general, are of interest to nobody except other fast-publishing colleagues" (ibid., 107).

For those of us who remain eager to do meaningful and valuable work, Stengers calls for engaging with trusted colleagues in subtle acts of disloyalty. She envisions "confusing the gaze of the inquisitors, of regenerating ways of honoring whatever it is that makes us think and feel and imagine" (ibid., 131–32). This is key to reclaiming the space we need to do the research we must. What disloyalty looks like, what forms it takes for you, are very much subject to local pressures from your inquisitors and the composition of your cohort of support.

Like me, do you find yourself battling your own demons, struggling with the ghosts of traumas past, present, and future? Do you also engage in scholarship aimed at facilitating ecological, social, and/or personal wellbeing? If so, Stengers's call is for you. This isn't a battle for the soul of the university. I doesn't have one and never did. It's a battle for those of us who are trapped in corporatized academic institutions that serve as glorified tax shelters for unscrupulous financial investment, respond tepidly (if at all) to systemic racism and heteropatriarchy, embrace adjunctification and contractualization (i.e., an academic caste system), and indebt students. Being tenured only makes me more obligated and more determined to resist these practices—and more obligated and determined to be a source of support for colleagues who seek to do the same. Because even if universities never had souls, they're still more thickly populated than most Taker institutions with individuals committed to changing minds. Never has this been clearer to me than now.

Echoing Jack Forbes's declaration (from chapter 6) that religion is, in reality, living, Jonathan Safran Foer insists that we *are* the structures of which we're part, whether willingly or not. How we live our lives, the actions we take or don't take, can solidify these structures or reshape them (2019, 199). When one is trained and hired to be a research "machine" (Berg and Seeber 2016, 58), it becomes too easy to confuse research per se with activism. But this doesn't mean research is inconsequential—particularly when it's focused on trauma-heavy topics.

Such work takes an emotional toll, Annita Lucchesi notes. For this reason she defends making it "spirit-based." This is particularly important when one's scholarship focuses on topics related to "colonial violence in intensely colonized spaces." Since universities are such spaces, spirit-based research helps in turn "to imagine other ways of surviving academia" (2019, 1). When she first developed this idea, Lucchesi continues, "I did not see it as a research method in itself, rather an informal and institutionally unappreciated life-vest in a sea of isolating curricula and toxic levels of expectation. Now, however, I argue that it should be recognized and taught as a method in its own right" (ibid.). I agree, especially since spirit-based research is overtly self-reflexive. It's "heart-work, or work that is centered on and guided by compassion, empathy, prayer, and love, rather than the clinical disconnect colonial academia espouses" (ibid., 2).

Heart-work, yes. Done well, perhaps it can help us bid farewell once and for all to miseducation. What James Baldwin calls the "fantasy"—of wellbeing through superiority, of self-aggrandizement through disrespect—is embodied by institutions of higher learning so long as they treat whiteness as a metaphor for power. Love for ourselves and one another: when this is achieved, perhaps not just systemic racism and heteropatriarchy but the miseducation they reinforce will cease to be quite so pervasive, because they "will no longer be needed" (Baldwin 2013, 17) by increasing numbers of those who can't now seem to do without them.

Epilogue

Changed Minds, Changed Options, and the Schematic of a New Vision

But what if it's too late? What if the world can't be saved?

Just in time to do the impossible (Klein 2014, 449ff.)? *Nope.* Buzzer beater for the underdogs? *Unh-uh.* Indigenous peoples already know catastrophe. Global climactic and ecological tipping points are here, yet "the monumental momentum of our culture's death urge" persists (Jensen 2000, 322).[1]

"Even if the car has gone off the cliff (which is a tenable opinion but not a certainty), I'd like people to understand WHY it went off the cliff," Quinn states. "Even if it comes too late for action, I prefer comprehension over incomprehension" (Q&A, 463). This is something, I suppose, but it strikes me as the work of an old mind.

What do new minds ask again? *How do we make happen what we want to happen?* I for one want to live better personally, social, and ecologically—if by a matter of degrees—*no matter how much time I and we have left.* This is the point of the threefold struggle. As I stated in the prologue, embodying my life is also a reason to resist rational dysfunction, including by staying sober. This makes the threefold struggle beautiful and sometimes surprisingly joyful, even when it's not the least bit fun.

At the 2019 Harvard Divinity School Commencement, Cornel West told the graduates, "You're going to have to take a risk, you have to pay a cost, you're going to have to cut against the grain. It's not going to be fun, but there'll be joy in that kind of struggle, joy in your intellectual courage exercise, joy in your moral and spiritual witness enacted even as you fall on your face."[2] Quinn himself seems to agree with this point in the following reply to a reader: "Your idea that the system is set up in such a way that the common man either plays along or dies in squalor seems to me to be a great oversimplification. A great many people do very well by NOT 'playing along.' Perhaps they don't become as rich as they might if they WERE playing along, but if they have a life that satisfies them, so what?" (Q&A, 755).

Coates insists that the struggle has both intrinsic and instrumental value. The struggle, "in and of itself, has meaning," he proclaims (2015, 69), at the same time that it helps to keep those engaged in it relatively sane and resilient in the face of ongoing adversity and pervasive oppression (ibid., 97). The struggle also permits us to bear witness to and tell stories of others' suffering when we can provide no succor.

Jonathan Safran Foer suggests that each of us has three options before us; they apply even if all is lost. We can be "running toward death, running away from death, or running toward life" (2019, 205). The first is a manifestation of the death urge. The second, I think, is on display when fixating on programs, in Quinn's sense. The third involves doing what we can to enact a new story, whatever obstacles we may face. Old minds focus on one of the first two options. In the first case, "We are killing ourselves because choosing death is more convenient than choosing life," Foer proclaims (ibid., 208). In the second, we apply Band-Aids that we call fixes to pretend we aren't "waiting for a convenient catastrophe to wipe us all out and spare us the embarrassment of having to live with the consequences of our actions," as John Michael Greer states (2017, 98).[3] (Who needs to be spared this embarrassment? Takers, of course, not all of humanity.)

The third option? What about it? I trust it's clear by now that it involves acknowledging that building a culture in which we meet people's ecological, social, and personal needs isn't an indulgence. It's a necessity (Lorde 2017, 130, and Q&A, 588). "Blessed are those who do whatever they can wherever they are, with whatever resources and opportunities are at their disposal," Quinn affirms ("B Attitudes"; see also "Uru in the Valley of Sleepers" and Q&A, 65, 490, and 568). Because whether or not we help save the world, we change it.

So assume it's too late to save the world if you prefer. Assume all is lost. And then run toward life anyway. Because you're worth it. We all are, every last one of us.

List of Mentioned Characters

Aaron Fischer (H): He sets Howard on his unexpected journey by asking him to track down the missing gods venerated by the early Israelites. Baal, Ashtaroth, and Moloch, among others, were worshipped alongside Yahweh before disappearing from biblical accounts.

Abel (TA): Archetype of a Leaver child and Adam's son. He doesn't represent Cain's brother from the Book of Genesis, at least not in the sense that the subject of biblical fratricide is depicted.

Adam (TA, MGY): In *Tales of Adam,* a Leaver archetype and Abel's father. He doesn't represent the first man of the Book of Genesis, at least not in the sense of being privy to Yahweh's first biblical covenant. In *The Man Who Grew Young,* he's a representative of the branch of humanity that became Takers. We follow his story as his life proceeds backward in time, from the precipice of human extinction to humanity's emergence within the evolutionary tree of life.

Alan Lomax (I): The narrator in *Ishmael,* yet we only learn his name in *My Ishmael.* Is it a coincidence that he shares a name with the famous American folklorist, writer, and oral historian? I'm not sure. After reviewing some of the latter's work (1960, 1968, and 2003), I see some connections. Lomax the folklorist is a careful ethnographer, noting how differences of custom and comportment are manifest in the content of local folk songs and the style of their performance. The land, and peoples' connections to it, clearly matters. He highlights that what Ishmael calls Leaver societies account for most of the cultural variety on Earth. And he was committed to preserving songs that were disappearing as the cultures from which they emerged disappeared. These aren't things the character Lomax countenances until Ishmael points them out to him. Still, it's at least possible that Quinn had someone like the folklorist in mind as a model for the narrator.

Andrea de la Mare (H): De la Mare, *of the sea.* Her last name is an oblique reference to the origins of life on Earth (H, 330, and MGY, 92ff.). David fails to find her after catching a glimpse of her as a young man on a drive with his friend Gil and ends up abandoning Ellen and Tim to pursue her again.

Bernard Lulfre (B): A priest, archeologist, and psychiatrist, he's a senior member of the (fictitious) Laurentian order. He sends Jared to Europe to investigate whether B is the Antichrist.

Bob Gaines (H): David's boss and an educational publishing guru.

Charles Atterley (B): He's the first B Jared meets and presenter of four of the five public teachings Jared attends: "The Great Forgetting," "The Boiling Frog," "The Collapse of Values," and "Population: A Systems Approach."

David Kennesey (H): Ellen's spouse and Tim's father. He becomes lost pursuing Andrea, never succeeding at going nowhere.

Denise Purcell (H): A reader of Tarot who meets Howard during his investigation. She warns him of the dangers of pursuing it further.

Dudley Case (H): Also known as Horse Killer, he's a Navajo ally of the yoo-hoos.

Elaine (WS): A reader of Quinn's work who visits him for further discussion. As his interlocutor, she sounds so much like Quinn that I suspect she's either fictitious or that her manner of expression has been heavily edited to mesh with his.

Ellen Kennesey (H): David's spouse and Tim's mother. She becomes lost trying to become a person.

Franklin Waters (D): A specialist on dreams and dreaming.

Gil Bingham (H): David's high school friend and companion for the fateful drive during which David first encounters Andrea.

Ginny Winters (D): A mysterious woman who, through others' experiences, seems to live two entirely distinct lives.

Howard Scheim (H): A private investigator who gets involved in trying to locate the gods who were once venerated by the Israelites (including, Baal, Ashtaroth, and Moloch) alongside Yahweh but who disappeared from biblical accounts. The investigation leads him to Andrea.

Ishmael (I, MI): A telepathic gorilla and specialist in maieutics, he's the teacher of Alan, Charles, and Julie. The biblical figure of the same name was a model for Quinn early in his life. Moreover, "what Genesis says happened to Ishmael is exactly what our [cultural] mythology says happened to the nonhuman community on this planet. This makes 'Ishmael' an appropriate name for someone who speaks for this community" (Q&A, 11). Why a gorilla? "The point I'm trying to make in all my work is this. 'If we want to survive on this planet, we must listen to what our neighbors in the community of life have to tell us.' So, who's in the best position to speak for those neighbors of ours? One of US or one of THEM? Obviously one of THEM. The teacher in *Ishmael* had to be one of those neighbors—a nonhuman. Among those neighbors none is more impressive and authoritative than a gorilla" (Q&A, 1).

Jared Osbourne (B): A priest of the (fictitious) Laurentian order. He's sent by Fr. Lulfre to investigate whether B is the Antichrist.

Jason Tull Jr. (AD): The narrator in *After Dachau,* he opens an art gallery expressly to exhibit Mallory's photos, preserved deep under Manhattan, from a long-forgotten era.

Jeffrey (MI): A consummate outsider who features in a story Ishmael shares with Julie. He's modeled on Paul Eppinger, whose journal was published with running commentary from his father shortly after Paul's suicide (Eppinger and Eppinger 1994).

John Dee (H): A yoo-hoo who plays a role similar for David that B plays for Jared.

Julie Gerchak (MI): The youngest and most precocious of Ishmael's students. She yearns to "get out of here" (MI, 17) and wants to understand not just how but why.

Karlak (MGY): A shaman and creator of ancient cave paintings that teach Adam of the origins of humanity.

Louis (B): Shirin's deceased son, who died only a few hours after his birth and before being properly named. This is the name Shirin privately gave him. He would have been eight years old at the time the events of *The Story of B* unfold.

Mallory Hastings (AD): A deaf white woman who experienced carbon monoxide poisoning after an auto accident and woke up in the hospital with the identity of a long-dead black woman with her hearing intact.

Pablo (H): A yoo-hoo who facilitates Tim's vision of the fire of life and answers Aaron's burning questions.

Shirin (B): She's the second B with whom Jared interacts and presenter of the fifth and last of the public teachings he attends, "The Great Remembering." The name *Shirin* is Persian in origin, passed down to Arabic. "I don't pick names for characters based on the meaning they have," Quinn remarks, "but some internet sites give the meaning as 'charming, sweet.' I just liked the way it looked" (Q&A, 144).

Tim Kennesey (H): The son of Ellen and David, he has a vision much like Quinn's at Gethsemani. The yoo-hoos suspect he may be one of their kind, culturally speaking.

Uncle Harry (AD): Also known as Harry Whitaker, he's a longtime close friend of Jason's family, not actually a blood relation. All Jason knows of his working life is that he'd been "something in the military" after receiving several advanced degrees and now is "something in the government" (AD, 17). He ends up holding Jason captive for a short time after Jason meets Mallory and uncovers his culture's ugly roots.

Verdelet (H): Also known as Joel Bailey, Howard's encounter with him proves pivotal.

Notes

Prologue

1. Quinn states in an early work that he "isn't talking to scholars" (BD, 31). He remarked to me in a personal exchange (September 2015), though, that this was due more to lack of scholarly uptake at the time than to his considered interests.

2. Candice Shelby (2016) contends that addiction is an emergent property with interrelated neurobiological, psychological, and sociological factors, often including trauma, that combine to perpetuate a deeply ingrained and damaging set of practices.

3. The core proposition of the threefold struggle is similar to the Quechua concept *sumaq kawsay* or *buen vivir*—living well within one's personal life; one's human communities; and in relation with Pachamama, or Mother Earth (Huambachano 2015 and Conant 2019). Its embrace is evident as well in research on climate justice by theorists who emphasize that action on climate change and ecological devastation isn't just about reducing emissions or restoring ecosystems. It's also a matter of reconstructing societies to be socioeconomically just and equitable. The work of Kyle Powys Whyte stands out in this regard, as we'll see in chapter 6.

4. Quinn insinuates that the United States alone embodies a "culture of maximum harm" (BC, 109), but he quickly broadens this to encompass Taker culture more generally. Doug Brown (2009) suggests that what he calls "Driven Taker"—or capitalist—culture is the fullest embodiment of the culture of maximum harm, since its internal logic is governed by insatiable growth (see also Klein 2014).

5. Throughout the text, I refer mainly to the "living community" or "community of life," since this is Quinn's preferred terminology. Specific living communities are composed of the populations in a given locale or region. Each such community interweaves within a wider biotic network to form the biosphere. Quinn regards the biosphere itself as a living community *writ large*.

6. Jared Diamond contends that these phenomena "are like time bombs with fuses of less than 50 years." If we address all but one, we are still in grave trouble, he asserts. But "the world's environmental problems *will* get resolved, in

one way or another, within the lifetimes of the children and young adults alive today. The only question is whether they will become resolved in pleasant ways of our own choice, or in unpleasant ways not of our choice, such as warfare, genocide, starvation, disease epidemics, and collapses of societies" (2005, 498).

7. A colleague of mine refers to the practices of governments and large-scale NGOs as "performative sustainability." Derrick Jensen and Aric McBay (2009, 61ff.) refer to it as sustainability™.

8. Correspondingly, conceptualizing climate change as a problem to be solved leads us to overlook that it's instead a manifestation of the earth's regulatory apparatuses adjusting to the specifiable activities of some members of one species.

9. "A truly anthropocentric perspective," states Jensen, "especially in the long term, is biocentric. It must be, since the anthro relies on the bio. No bio, no anthro. Any anthro who isn't bio must be really stupid. Or made stupid by a stupid culture" (2006b, 578).

Chapter 1

1. Even in these circumstances, bounded rationality and cognitive biases create difficulties. While their worst effects can be kept in check, doing so is no easy task (Smith 2014b).

2. Dawkins tends to equate minds with brains. He thus counts as a reductive physicalist, which Quinn is not. Moreover, Dawkins's account of memes in *The Selfish Gene* is highly speculative. It almost seems off the cuff. Further specification of how memetics works has been left to others (see, for example, Blackmore 1999, Aunger 2002, and Brodie 2011).

3. David Heath Justice (2011, 582) maintains that continuity sometimes is only possible through change. This will come into greater focus when we address the role of tradition in chapter 6.

4. Alan asks Ishmael why Mother Culture must be a woman. He implies that Ishmael is being misogynistic. "I don't consider her a *villain* in any sense whatever," Ishmael replies, "but I understand what you're getting at. Here is my answer: Culture is a mother everywhere and in every time, because culture is inherently a nurturer—a nurturer of human societies and lifestyles. Among Leaver peoples, Mother Culture explains and preserves a lifestyle that is healthy and self-sustaining. Among Taker peoples she explains and preserves a lifestyle that has proven to be unhealthy and self-destructive" (I, 148).

5. Quinn remarks in *Ishmael* that one person discovering Mother Culture's dubious claims doesn't make much of a difference, but their discovery by *everyone* does (I, 28). He clarifies in later work that this sort of universal transformation is a sufficient but not a necessary condition for enacting a new story. Everyone seeing the light surely would make a difference, but this isn't required for a difference to be made.

6. As we'll see in chapter 4, Quinn is neither a metaphysical dualist nor a nominalist. Minds aren't anything like souls trapped in bodies. And the living community is more than the sum of its parts. So it's worth entertaining the proposition that our minds extend not only beyond our individual brains but beyond our selves (Burton 2013). Indeed, our selves may well extend beyond our individual bodies.

7. Visions fit the model of what Riane Eisler calls "*systems of self-organization*" (2007, 93). The interactions among the core components of such systems maintain their basic character. They're self-reproducing. Programs aren't self-reproducing. They're instead products of intention.

8. Robert Burton (2013, 105ff.) notes that those from the global West are subject to the Müller-Lyer Illusion while, remarkably, those of the San culture aren't. Joseph Heinrich (2020) discusses ways in which "WEIRD" people—Western, educated, industrialized, rich, and democratic—systematically differ from people of other cultures with respect to considerations of fairness, punishment, cooperation, individualism, and related concepts. It turns out that, globally speaking, WEIRD people are outliers time and again.

9. For that matter, what does the fact that we Takers routinely define our distant ancestors in terms of the core material from which they constructed their tools and weapons say about us? "Stone Age: Definition by product" (BD, 19).

Chapter 2

1. Quinn isn't alone in specifying two broad cultures into which humanity divides. Robin Kimmerer distinguishes between the culture of Skywoman and the culture of Eve (2013, 6ff.). Kimmerer too begins her discussion of how these two cultures differ by referring to how the people who compose them acquire food. Scott Pratt (2002), inter alia, distinguishes between Indigenous and settler colonial peoples. Ramachandra Guha and Juan Martinez-Alier compare ecosystem peoples with omnivores. The latter are "individuals and groups with the social power to capture, transform, and use natural resources from a much wider catchment area, sometimes indeed the whole world" (1997, 12). Wendell Berry (1977, 9f.) differentiates exploiters from nurturers. Berry is actually describing two subcultures within Taker culture, but how they differ tracks the way Quinn distinguishes between Takers and Leavers.

2. I use the term *experiment* here advisedly, since this might be seen to insinuate that the two cultures can be studied in some sort of pure, "natural" form. This, of course, isn't true.

3. Quinn became increasingly dissatisfied with the labels *Leaver* and *Taker*, since many readers have treated them as a halo and a smear term, respectively. These readers mistakenly assume that Quinn intends for us to demonize Takers and "angelize" Leavers (WS, 37f., Q&A, 17, and "Texas Legacy Project"). I choose

to retain *Taker* and *Leaver,* though, given their frequency of use by Quinn and their general familiarity among his readers.

4. Ronald Wright conceptualizes *myth* in anthropological terms, which is the framework that Quinn uses as well. According to Wright, "Myth is an arrangement of the past, whether real or imagined, in patterns that reinforce a culture's deepest values and aspirations. . . . Myths are so fraught with meaning that we live and die by them. They are the maps by which cultures navigate through time" (1992, 5). "No creation story is a myth to the people who tell it. It's just the story," Ishmael notes (I, 50). Indeed, Takers typically assume that ours is a culture largely free of myth. But this itself is a manifestation of our cultural mythology.

5. *After Dachau,* which offers yet another perspective on the Great Forgetting—is a view of reality "as conveniently distorted as our own," Quinn states ("IndieBound").

6. Quinn contributed to writing a short mathematics primer during his time working in education publishing (Science Research Associates 1964). My choice of *axiom* tangentially pays homage to this as well, since my most memorable encounter with the term is from high school math class.

7. This proposal is most vociferously defended by the so-called ecomodernists, who are quintessential "Anthropocene boosters" (Wuerthner 2018). Quinn never mentions the Anthropocene, probably because the term didn't gain sufficient stickiness (chapter 1) until late in his life. Beyond this footnote, I won't mention it either, since I'm critical of the concept (and believe Quinn would be, too) for reasons that others have specified (Todd 2015, Cuomo 2017a and 2017b, and Greer 2017, 93ff.).

8. Ancient peat bogs form the basis for coal. Oil and natural gas come from ancient phytoplankton.

9. Towers are typically unlike biospheres, since the former generally can be augmented. I think we have to assume here that no additions to the Tower of Uru are possible.

10. Among the implications of the Taker axioms is that we humans are the culmination of biological evolution. So how does one live if one wants to make such a proposition come true? "You would live the way that Takers live," Alan remarks. "In order to make their [*our*] story come true, the Takers have to put an end to creation itself—and they're [*we're*] doing a damned good job of it" (I, 238–39; see also P, 50).

11. We tend to think of climate change, and ecocide more generally, as a form of "slow violence" (Nixon 2011). David Wallace-Wells (2019, 4) contends, though, that climate change is occurring quite quickly. More than half of the carbon dioxide released into the atmosphere by burning fossil fuels has been emitted in just the past three decades. And we're already to a point at which we have likely surpassed a number of critical climatological and ecological tipping points.

12. A fourth refrain by those who cry alarmism is that we can plan to colonize other planets so that we're prepared to evacuate Earth once it's unin-

habitable. I won't bother addressing it, but I welcome you to see what Quinn has to say (MI, 61f.; see also Foer 2019).

13. Long-term post-traumatic stress disorder is also associated with somatic hyperarousal and emotionally charged catastrophizing (Tsur et al. 2018). The afflicted may not somatically belong more to the dead than the living, but their sense of connection to themselves, others, and the world at large is nevertheless distorted in ways that cause great suffering.

14. Epigenetic effects from traumatic events can be passed to offspring, such as through genetic coding for specifiable levels of cortisol (Yehuda and Bierer 2007). This suggests that the manifestation of *wétiko* may be biochemically cumulative across generations.

Chapter 3

1. Armstrong adds that "Since the eighth century BCE, some Israelites had worshipped a host of astral deities alongside their own god, Yahweh, but in P's poem the sun, moon, and stars are given a purely functional role, 'to separate the day from the night; and let them be for signs and for seasons and for days and years'" (1996, 12). I discuss why P refers to God as Elohim rather than Yahweh below.

2. A. R. Millard (1984) states that the name Eden is etymologically rooted in the Semitic root *'dn,* meaning lush or abundant.

3. Don't be confused by the common assumption that Yahweh calls on the man to subdue the earth and maintain dominion over all other earthly creatures. This statement comes in P (Gen. 1:28), not J.

4. Ishmael makes no mention of the serpent in his extended discussion of J with Alan (I, 161ff.). Quinn remarks elsewhere that, in his opinion, the serpent is just a narrative device and doesn't "'stand for' anything. Unlike God, Adam, and Eve, who are the principals of the story, the serpent appears only in this one episode and then disappears forever. If the serpent 'meant' something, it would have had a history before and after this episode; the fact that it doesn't confirms that it's merely a device (and as such doesn't need to be dealt with as if it were one of the principals)" (Q&A, 459; see also ibid., 482). Interestingly, an earlier iteration of the book that became *Ishmael* was called *The Book of Nahash. Nahash* means serpent in Hebrew.

5. It also may be the case that the use of the plural Elohim reflects radical changes in the development of the ancient Hebrew religion. It was written during an era that the shift from polytheism to monolatry (belief in the existence of many gods but nevertheless worshipping only one) to monotheism as the coalescence of what we know today as Judaism was taking place (Smith 2002). Upon the emergence of monotheism, numerous gods end up disappearing from the Bible along with the female partner of the God of the Israelites. Perhaps they're

among the *yoo-hoos* that we encounter in *The Holy* (some of whom—like Eostre, the Teutonic goddess of spring and fertility—were coopted and repurposed by Christians). Pablo seems to suggest as much to Aaron Fischer anyway (H, 400ff.).

6. Isaac Asimov (1968, 34) suggests that Abel's name may connote the briefness of his presence in the story. But *hebel* also may mean nothingness or meaninglessness, suggesting that he has no legacy in the story that unfolds in Genesis (Vermeulen 2014).

7. Johnson Lim remarks that Cain's alienation from God, which is portrayed by "the breakdown of the human relationship to the ground" culminates with the flood story in Genesis 6:11–13 (2002, 158).

8. That Cain is to be a wanderer might lead you to presume that part of Cain's curse is becoming a nomad (Zeitlin 1984). But nomads don't wander restlessly. They have ingrained seasonal attachments to cyclical patterns of movement on the land (Davis 2009, 173). I suspect instead that Cain's worries have to do with the expectation of retaliation upon entering foreign lands.

9. Venkatesh Rao (2011, 35) makes the mistake of assuming that, for Quinn, to be a Leaver is to be a gatherer-hunter. Rao comments that Quinn confuses the herder Abel for a gatherer-hunter in *Ishmael*. Quinn is clear, though, that Leavers maintain a wide array of lifestyles, pastoralism included.

10. Or maybe the capabilities conferred by eating the forbidden fruit are, in a backhanded way, exactly what Yahweh wants for us. At least, this is a position taken by two notable theologians. According to Erich Fromm, the Garden of Eden story depicts "the liberation of man from the incestuous ties of blood and soil" (1966, 7). Moreover, God wants Eve and Adam to reckon with their original transgression by "going forward" (ibid., 123) and fulfilling their anointed destiny. Joseph Soloveitchik asserts that Yahweh intentionally "impaired reality in order for mortal man to repair its flaws and perfect it" (1983, 101). So the Fall sews the seeds for human beings to strive for world domination (ibid., 109; see also Aron 2005, 684).

11. Nietzsche is well known for his use of genealogy (see, for example, 1996). It has the appearance of a historical account but isn't intended to provide a decisive catalog of events. As Lawrence Hatab remarks, "Although Nietzsche is working with actual historical forces and periods, he is certainly not pretending to offer standard historical work. . . . Nietzsche is deliberately selective and he arranges narrative more for rhetorical force—to provoke us to think about larger questions evoked by broad historical considerations" (2008, 30).

12. Misbehavior becomes criminal only with the codification of laws that are put in place expressly to try to prohibit certain behaviors. Insurrections are less likely to occur among Leaver peoples, since their societies aren't typically structured hierarchically (Cajete 2000, 90, and Bookchin 2005, 122). And while Leavers engage in war, its mass scale and professionalization are unique to Taker culture.

13. Interestingly, atheism takes the same general form. David Foster Wallace dubs it an "anti-religious religion, which worships reason, skepticism, intellect,

empirical proof, human autonomy, and self-determination" (2009). For atheists, what's broken is religion itself. "The only solution is to get out the disinfectant and wipe your hands clean," states Stephen Prothero (2010, 321).

14. It should be noted that from the perspective of black liberation theologists, the attributions of these qualities to the soul serve to bolster resistance to oppressors by victims of the worst form of confinement ever devised by the people of our culture: race-based chattel slavery. In an interview on National Public Radio, singer/songwriter Rhiannon Giddens emphasizes, with respect to her slave ballad, "At the Purchaser's Option," that "there's something inviolable within me that you and no one else can break or take. I shall have my eternal reward. But I shall also have my temporal defiance. Do what you want to me. My spirit will endure. And I may not have overcome, but 'This babe upon my breast' will. Or if not her, then the babe upon her breast or the babe upon hers. *We* defy you. And we will defy you until we're free."

15. There are debates among Christian theologians over exclusive salvation (only Jesus saves) versus universal redemption (there are other viable paths to salvation, but Jesus is theirs). I leave it to you to investigate this more fully.

16. By origin and character, Judaism is an ethnic religion. For millennia, redemption was conceived of as a matter involving solely the people of Yahweh, the God of Israel. Yet, according to Maimonides, redemption is open to gentiles as well. What matters for final redemption is that each and every person the world over obeys God's laws (Mishneh Torah, Hilkhot M'lakhim 8:14).

17. Although outliers, there are even strains of the citizenship interpretation among Jewish scholars and theologians. Based on this interpretation, the Torah itself gives voice to a land-centered faith tradition (Diamond and Seidenberg 2000 and Bernstein 2005).

18. The same can be said of Jainism. At the moral core of its ascetic practices is *ahimsa,* or the proscription against killing or harming any living being, since each contains a soul with the same characteristics and qualities as one's own. This concern for the welfare of fellow members of the living community has clear ecological implications. As with the Hindu ascetic tradition, Jainism supports the embrace of minimal material consumption, particularly the rejection of possessions, comforts, and luxuries that come at the expense of the wellbeing of others (Jain 2017, 424).

19. Vajrayāna is sometimes referred to as a third school. It's associated with Tibetan Buddhism as well as Shingon in Japan. But Vajrayāna is founded on Mahāyāna philosophy, so it may be understood, too, as an extension of that school.

20. This view is especially prominent in Japan, in all likelihood due to the influence of Shinto, according to which the world is teeming with *kami,* or gods, in the form of mountain peaks, streams and lakes, trees, and caverns.

21. A similar ethos is central to Sikhism, although with an egalitarian twist. "According to the Sikh ideal," Mary Pat Fisher remarks, "the purpose of life is to realize God within the world, through everyday practices of work,

worship, and charity, of sacrificing love. All people are to be treated equally, for God's light dwells in all and ego is a major hindrance to God-realization" (2014, 444). Sikhs prize religious freedom and tolerance, emphasizing that sectarian divisions matter little in comparison to the ills associated with oppression and corruption.

22. Notwithstanding the reference Grapard makes here to the Japanese emphasis on "purifications" of nature, there is a world-embracing interpretation of this claim. It bears a similarity to Indigenous invocations, including by Enrique Salmón (2012) and Robbin Kimmerer (2013), of the need for humans to cultivate responsible relationships with the land and living community in order for all parties to flourish.

23. Both Shirin and Charles frequently refer to B as an Antichrist, only once as an Antisavior. I'm partial to the latter label, since it's more representative of their broader intentions.

24. At least among evangelical Christians today, it's common to profess a personal relationship with God. Such a view has roots in the Reformation as Protestants sought to circumvent papal power. It serves now, though, to mediate God's distance.

Chapter 4

1. This chapter also is devoted to laying out Quinn's metaphysics. According to Charles Sanders Peirce, "metaphysics, even bad metaphysics, really rests on observations, whether consciously or not; and the only kinds of phenomena with which every man's experience is so saturated that he usually pays no particular attention to them" (CP, 6.2). The abbreviation CP refers to Peirce's *Collected Papers*, which encompasses eight volumes. All references are to volume and paragraph number.

2. Strikingly, the abbot of Gethsemani at the time was Thomas Merton, whose writings bring together issues of spirituality, social justice, and environmentalism. Merton was a great admirer of Rachel Carson (Popova 2017).

3. Notice the difficulty Quinn has describing his experience. Perhaps it's this that's represented by the persistent struggles of the narrator in "At Woomeroo" to tell us about that strange place (AW, 1–6). Moreover, Quinn's description of his experience would seem to suggest that he does in fact embrace the idea that there's a *really* real order of things behind the veil of appearances we experience in our workaday lives. I rejected this view in chapter 1, and I stand by this. What he's instead describing here is having *eyes that see,* which we'll cover in the following chapter.

4. Technically, the question of God's existence is different than the question of God's reality. The former is an ontological question, and the latter is a metaphysical question. Characters in Quinn's novels refer to the gods as real on

at least two occasions (B, 135f., and H, 380). But he insists that establishing their reality is beside the point with respect to his overall project (WS, 49).

5. Sherri Tepper's description of the goddess Koré, the "incarnation of life," in *The Family Tree* comes close, I think, to what Quinn is articulating. Koré, states a central character, is "Maid, mother, and sage, the tripartite goddess: birth and growth, maturity and reproduction, age and death. Koré is the eidelon of fecundation" (1997, 360).

6. "*This* is the Holy Land," Leslie Gray proclaims. "Indeed, all over the planet you will find sacred sites that are honored and preserved by the Indigenous people of that bioregion. Everywhere you step you step on the sacred bones of ancestors. So this is the Holy Land—right here—the very soil upon which I am standing. And, of course, it lies beneath your feet as well, wherever *you* are standing" (2008, 86).

7. The Inuit—"the People"—live in coastal areas throughout the Barrens and possess a sea culture. The Ihalmiut—"the Other People"—live along inland waterways.

8. I offer no formal statement of the Law of Life because there's none to offer. As we'll see, the Law of Life can be expressed in a number of different ways, each of which highlights a specific vantage point from which to understand the doings and happenings of the community of life.

9. See, for example, the fable Adam conveys to Abel in *Tales of Adam* regarding the sage advice offered by the old lion (TA, 86ff.).

10. At one point, B states that in place of the terms *Leaver* and *Taker*, we can just as easily use "Followers of the Law" and "Rejecters of the Law," respectively (B, 253).

11. Darwin contends that evolution occurs via the operation of natural selection on random mutations. This remains the most common explanation for evolution among biologists. But it's implausible that this operation alone is sufficient to explain the amount of diversity and complexity in the living community (Nagel 2012, 6). Stuart Kauffman (1995) suggests that self-organization, or self-generating order, plays as important a role in evolution as does natural selection. Marc Kirschner and John Gerhart (2005) propose that the "evolvability" of genetic mutations and recombinations itself evolves in a direction that facilitates diversity and complexity. Andreas Wagner (2014) contends that what he calls "genotype networks" accelerate life's ability to innovate and to retain innovations that work. None of these proposals alters the fact that natural selection counts as an elegant concept. Rather, they expand our sense of the elegance of evolution more generally.

12. As such, Carl Hausman contends, causal determinists can "only explain diversity by supposing that all details of diversity and irregularity, as we find them in the world and expect them to be present in the future, had been present in the laws from the beginning" (1993, 116). More likely is that novelty emerges

within evolutionary processes (Hoagland 1995, 33, and Wagner 2014). This is Quinn's position (B, 151).

13. William Denevan argues that the concept of wilderness, or the wild, is an example of "the pristine myth" (1992; see also Cronon 1983). What's called the wild is far more often really one big food-producing system fostered by Leaver peoples. Indeed, the concept of wilderness tends to prop up the view of colonized lands as *terrae nullius*, hence ripe for pilfer and pillage (Mann 2005, 323).

14. Margulis (1999) contends that *symbiosis* is an evolutionary mechanism that operates on a par with natural selection. Whereas natural selection whittles away nonadaptive alternatives, symbiosis involves the creative exploration of adaptive alternatives (see also Hoagland 1995, 31, and Cuff 2007). "Seen from this perspective, reproductive success, or lack thereof, is a result of an organism's ability to successfully interact with others rather than to outcompete them," Adam Dinan and Tom Smith state (2016, 39). Dinan and Smith add that a shift in focus in evolutionary theory from biological individuals to holobionts, or assemblages of symbiotic partners, is currently underway. This shift dovetails with Richard Lewontin's (2000) defense of a "constructionist" account of evolution. Here's one example. We can thank the work of cyanobacteria beginning some 2.5 billion years ago for triggering the development of the oxygen-rich atmosphere that sustains us today. Without cyanobacteria, the community of life on Earth as we know it wouldn't exist. And the community of life on Earth has been good to cyanobacteria, which can be found the world over.

15. Hoagland expands on this point: "Among the most astonishing revelations in biology was the discovery that all visible living creatures are themselves made up of living 'creatures' called cells. Cells are not merely inert structural units or building blocks, but individual beings with lives of their own—living, reproducing, and dying just as we do. We are, in a sense, hives of cells. We move, eat, and speak thanks to the coordinated effort of specialized groups of individuals within our cellular community" (1995, 147).

16. This may explain why we find it easier to empathize with family, friends, and neighbors than with strangers. We take this for granted, as if it's just the way life is. But it's just the way *our* lives are because we evolved to take empathizing with kin and kith for granted. This doesn't preclude strangers from becoming friends. Who is and who isn't part of our in-crowd is open to change.

Chapter 5

1. Nowhere does Quinn claim that sight is the primary sense modality for humans. I think we do better to conceptualize Quinn's references to sight in metaphorical terms that capture a fuller array of sensuous and perceptual modes of engagement with the world. This may mitigate concerns that Quinn betrays

an ableist bent, although his references to blindness don't serve him particularly well in this regard.

2. This chapter comprises Quinn's epistemology. As typically conceptualized by philosophers, epistemology is the study of what it is to know, how we acquire knowledge, how we go about differentiating true beliefs—the building blocks of knowledge—from false beliefs, and how we're able to justify that what we believe is true. In certain respects, Quinn's epistemology fits this mold. But the pursuit of knowledge plays an ancillary role, since the pursuit of knowledge, at least for its own sake, is a bit too cerebral for his taste (Q&A, 753). As such, I instead treat awareness as the central orienting concept for his epistemology.

3. Ishmael suggests, though, that not all knowledge is conducive to wisdom. Taker knowledge typically is "about what works well for *things*," while Leaver knowledge is "about what works for *people*" (I, 206). Knowledge of what works well for people counts as wisdom, according to Ishmael. Knowledge of what works well for things doesn't, so long as it does nothing to foster wellbeing (TA, 74).

4. Grandfather's given name was Stalking Wolf. He was given the name because he was seen sneaking up on and touching a wolf, "one of the most aware, cunning, and hence most difficult of animals to catch," Brown notes (1988, 11).

5. Brown goes further still. "If an animal even thinks of turning right, for instance, it will register in the track. So too do emotions, like anger, fear, apprehension, and joy register in the track. The body reacts to thoughts and emotions in clearly defined pressure release maps" (1999, 38).

6. Tracking isn't only a terrestrial practice. Wade Davis describes how Polynesian wayfinders read the signs of the sea to navigate between islands without maps, sextants, or any other navigation devices (2009, 52ff.).

7. Quinn doesn't mention that he's addressing a topic that's been subject to considerable debate among psychologists. Does perception direct cognition from the top down (Gibson 1966), or is perception constructed by conception (Gregory 1970)? Are these faculties independent or not (Kveraga et al. 2007 and Pinto et al. 2013)? Do glial cells actually outnumber neurons by a factor of ten to one (Bear et al. 2007, 24), or is it more like fifty to one (Kandel et al. 2013)? Or perhaps glial cells don't outnumber neurons after all (Hiltetag and Barbas 2009). I leave it to you to delve into this morass.

8. Coates contends that to be black is simply a denotation for those who reside at the bottom of the social hierarchy in the United States (2015, 55). At one time, the Irish were black—"swarthy." So were Italians and Slavs. Members of these groups now can comfortably believe or imagine that they're white because their bodies are no longer subject to the degree of control to which black bodies are subject. It's safe for whites to be ignorant of the lives and experiences of blacks. But it's very dangerous for blacks to be ignorant of the lives and experiences of whites. This is a manifestation of what W. E. B. DuBois calls *double consciousness* (2003, 9).

9. As John Zerzan remarks, "symbols first mediated reality and then replaced it. At present we live within symbols to a greater degree than we do within our bodily selves or directly with each other" (2002, 2).

10. "For Plato, as for Socrates," Abram adds, "the *psychê* is now that aspect of oneself that is refined and strengthened by turning away from the ordinary sensory world in order to contemplate the intelligible Ideas, the pure and eternal forms that, alone, truly exist" (1996, 112–13).

11. B speaks of genus *Homo* as human rather than confining the term specifically to *Homo sapiens*.

12. I doubt it's coincidental that *bricolage* also captures one facet of the way in which evolution works. Mutations and recombinations are, in essence, forms of *bricolage* that get sifted and sorted and either accepted or rejected via selective pressure.

13. There's no doubt that hunting and killing beings who one respects and even venerates can create psychological and emotional tension for subsistence hunters. As Louis Liebenberg remarks, "To track down an animal, the tracker must ask himself what he would do if he were that animal. In the process of projecting himself into the position of the animal, he actually feels like the animal. The tracker therefore develops a sympathetic relationship with the animal, which he then kills" (1990, ix). But this is a genuine testament to how seriously those with the eye of the tracker take the business of killing. It isn't taken lightly, and it isn't done unnecessarily. No wonder B can state forthrightly that she's not offering anything like a justification of sport hunting (B, 170; see also Brown 1988, 37).

14. Quinn's assertion that time is directional doesn't somehow suggest that time is linear (Fixico 2003). Cycles themselves have direction. Seasons proceed in a prescribed order. A new moon follows a waning moon. We're born, we live, we die, giving way to a new generation.

15. In the hands of Takers, the knowledge and information acquired via science are often just as much instruments for extractivism as anything else. But this isn't an essential quality or attribute of science. Science can just as comfortably be directed toward "seeking life," states Gregory Cajete (2000, 15; see also Wildcat 2009, 15f.).

16. This might be one way to conceptualize how awareness has both physical and spiritual components. Being able to make inferences about real unseens and real unseeables is a manifestation of what we might otherwise call spirituality. After all, the Latin root of divination, *divinare,* implies that to foresee is to be inspired by the gods.

17. Here are two representative comments about the Penan, cited by Wade Davis. Former prime minister of Malaysia Mahathir bin Mohamad states that "There is nothing romantic about these helpless, half-starved, disease-ridden people" (2009, 177). James Wong, former Sarawak minister of housing and public health offers a similar take. "We don't want them running around like animals.

No one has the ethical right to deprive the Penan of the right to assimilation into Malaysian society" (ibid.). As Davis notes, the "real goal" behind statements such as these is almost always "the extraction of natural resources on an industrial scale from territories occupied for generations by Indigenous peoples whose ongoing presence on the land proves to be an inconvenience" (ibid., 171).

18. Among the Batek, for example, Kirk Endicott states that "Recipients treat the food they are given as a right; no expression of thanks is expected or forthcoming, presumably because that would imply that the donor had the right to withhold it. If someone were hoarding food, it would not be considered 'stealing' for others to help themselves to it" (1988, 117). Correspondingly, Robin Kimmerer (2013, 52) observes that there's no word for *please* among the Potawatomi. While early missionaries regarded this as evidence of crude manners, it instead reflects that food is meant to be shared. No added politeness is necessary or expected. For the same reasons, Davis observes, the Penan have no word for *thank you.* "The Penan live by the adage that a poor man shames us all. Indeed, the greatest transgression in their culture is *sihun,* a concept that essentially means a failure to share" (2009, 175).

19. Communal support also offers a way, states Robert Kelly, "to disengage people from property, to reduce the potential in property to create dependency." This "helps to maintain egalitarian social relations" (2013, 142; see also Woodburn 1998).

20. In later work, Quinn abandons the term *Leavers* in favor of *tribal peoples* as the designation for those who enact a story that works for people and for the planet. While not all Leavers live (or have lived) tribally, Quinn indicates that nontribal forms of Leaver social organization have tended to work when they operate similarly to the way tribes do (Q&A, 673).

21. It's common for Takers to privilege hunting over gathering when regarding Leaver people who make, or traditionally made, a living via these practices. Since hunters are assumed to be exclusively men and sharing meat was valorized, Takers also commonly presuppose that women were economically dependent on men in hunter-gatherer societies. First, such peoples are better categorized as *gatherer-hunters,* since many of them acquired the majority of their food from foraging. This is why it isn't uncharacteristic for Leavers to regard women as the primary guardians of a tribe's food economy (Bell 2001, 54f.). Second, B points out that "hunting is not an exclusively male activity among aboriginal peoples of today, so there's no reason to suppose it was an exclusively male activity among our earliest ancestors" (B, 168). This is confirmed by Chantal Norrgard (2014) with respect to the Ojibwe.

22. Jack Weatherford remarks that Europeans were amazed at the personal liberty of Indigenous peoples of North America "in particular their freedom from rulers and from social classes based on ownership of property. For the first time the French and the British became aware of the possibility of living in social harmony

and prosperity without the rule of a king" (1988, 121–22). Weatherford hereby contends that the embrace of democracy and liberty as cornerstone Enlightenment institutions "entered modern thought as American Indian notions translated into European language and culture" (ibid., 128; see also Johansen 1982).

23. Technocracy might be inherently destructive, but technology itself isn't. Like science, some forms of technology facilitate evolutionarily stable strategies and some don't (IS, 56ff., Q&A, 51 and 87, and "EcoGeek").

24. Even in Taker culture, appeals to nature and naturalness reflect a conceptualization of life that went out of style in the early nineteenth century. From then onward, states Michel Foucault (1971), at least in scientific circles life is mainly conceptualized in biological terms. This marks a distinction between what he calls the "classic episteme" and the "modern episteme."

Chapter 6

1. Officially, it was purchased from the Seneca in 1784. But the purchase occurred under threat of force after the Seneca had been decimated by post-Revolutionary settler incursions. Indeed, the land had been allotted for settlement by Revolutionary War veterans prior to its purchase. Moreover, while the Seneca did use the land as seasonal hunting grounds, it was occupied at the time primarily by the Lenape, who had been pushed west from their traditional homelands.

2. Animism was a universal religion in the same sense that there's a single generalizable Leaver culture. Just as Leaver culture is manifest in many localized iterations, we'll see as we proceed that a wide array of specific ways to express and embody sacredness reflect an animistic worldview.

3. Some people might assume B is referring to paganism here rather than animism, but this isn't so. Paganism is "a farmer's religion through and through, which means it's just a few thousand years old, and of course it was never a universal religion, for the simple reason that farming was never universal" (B, 132; see also H, 73, P, 140, Davies 2011, and Harvey 2017, 212).

4. Viola Cordova (2007, 3 and 102) insists that it's no surprise that Indigenous peoples throughout North America identify broad philosophical commonalities. This is an expected result of their common resistance to colonial pressures.

5. B states, though, that the gods aren't easily killed. "Any one of them can be vanquished by a flamethrower or a bulldozer or a bomb—silenced, driven away, enfeebled. Sit in the middle of a shopping mall at midnight, surrounded by half a mile of concrete in all directions, and there the god that was once as strong as a buffalo or a rhinoceros is as feeble as a moth sprayed with pyrethrin. Feeble—but not dead, not wholly extinguished. Tear down the mall and rip up the concrete, and within days that place will be pulsing with life again. Nothing needs to be done, beyond carting away the poisons" (B, 161).

6. Whether there's a hard distinction in kind between facts and values is itself subject to philosophical debate. Stephen Jay Gould (1999, 4) defends the distinction. A number of philosophers, perhaps most notably Hilary Putnam (2004), argue that denoting certain things as facts is itself part of an elaborate value system. I side with Putnam here, but this doesn't undercut the more general thrust of Quinn's point, which has to do with the religious attraction of an otherworldly order in which one is urged to have *faith* compared to the religious attraction of a mundane order that's enhanced by *eyes that see*.

7. Ishmael himself seems to privilege the capacity for autonoetic consciousness, but Quinn later walks this back (P, 141f.).

8. This links up with Anna Tsing's suggestion that persons are "protagonisists of stories" (2015, 155). Persons of all sorts can be *actants* (Latour 1996). They can play active and meaningful roles in the development and perpetuation of visions.

9. Yoo-hoos, wild things, and witches take center stage in *The Holy*. As Adam relays to Abel in *Tales of Adam*, "We share this world with others who are not beasts or men or spirits or gods. They are denizens of wastelands and barrens, of deserts and high places where nothing grows, and they don't follow the deer or the quail, nor are they followed by the lion or the hyena. All the same, they're making their journey in the hand of the god just as we are. What destiny they pursue in their journey I cannot say, for their tracks run beyond ours and where they end no man will ever know" (TA, 75–76). "All I can really say about them," Quinn adds, "is that they're not of our kind" (Q&A, 601).

10. That yoo-hoos and the like are dangerous doesn't make them evil, Quinn asserts. They're dangerous, at least in part, Denise tells Howard in *The Holy*, "because they're *attractive*" (H, 51). People seek them out without being prepared for what they might face, as is the case with David Kennesey. People also often routinely fail to prepare *not* to find them despite an exhaustive search. Consider, Quinn states, that "it wasn't just David who was looking for them, they were looking for him as well" (Q&A, 675).

11. The idea that we must extend moral entitlement or compassion or community standing to other-than-human beings is a common refrain among environmentalists—including land ethicists and deep ecologists—and those concerned with animal welfare (Leopold 1949, 204, Singer 2011, and Kingsnorth 2012, 150).

12. That relations between children and their elders is reciprocal doesn't imply that each has the same responsibilities. As Burkhart notes, "The kinship relationship of a child with an elder grandparent is different than the kinship relationship an elder grandparent has with a child. There are different responsibilities one has based on who one is and how one is related, and these change over time" (2019, viii).

13. The Algonquin term *manitou* translates as *spirit*, Norton-Smith conveys. Conceptually, *manitou* "is closely akin to the experiential content of the Western concept mind" (2010, 86; see also McPherson and Rabb 2011, 152f.). According to

Quinn, talk among Leavers both of spirits and of interaction with them, which is more or less constant "in a very casual way" (Q&A, 533), is thus no more mystical than talk among Takers is of mental faculties. Deloria and Wildcat conceptualize *manitou* as a "living energy that inhabits and/or composes the universe" (2001, 22). It's at once a unifying and individuating force (Pratt 2006, 6). So *manitou* also bears a resemblance to the fire of life.

14. Other philosophers prefer to focus on the broad equivalencies between ethics and morality, particularly since all that originally distinguished them is etymology. The former is from Greek, the latter from Latin. The distinction I here accept arguably is the result of an overwrought history of philosophical contestation. I nevertheless appropriate it because it helps to make a useful point.

15. Right and wrong, good and evil, are also perspectival, according to Quinn (chapter 3). It's not much help to apply these labels because what's *good* for one being is invariably *bad* for another, "and there's no avoiding this" (MGY, 65; see also B, 96).

16. What of B's assertion that the god is *here,* taking care of *this place* (B, 160ff.; see also P, 141, and TA, 14)? Doesn't this suggest that the god also cares more about this place than other places? Not necessarily. The god can facilitate, characterize, and even personify the particular dynamic of a place without at the same time caring any less for the beings who inhabit other places. Physicians at local clinics treat all patients with equal care even if they see patients from the neighborhoods in which their clinics are located far more frequently than patients who live elsewhere.

17. Note that this resonates with my concern in chapter 4 not to overstate the extent of interdependence among the beings and entities that comprise the cosmos.

18. As for displacement, it's important to note that Taker hypermobility is premised on Leaver confinement—not just on reservations but also by a colonialist system of laws and associated practices that deny Leavers land sovereignty (Whyte et al. 2019). As for kinlessness, Burkhart—who ably serves as a mouthpiece for Jisdu, the rabbit trickster—refers to the people of settler culture as "Kinless Conquerors." Takers in general tend to revel in "a Solitude that deceives itself as Dominating Power." Yet, where there's no kinship there can be no knowledge, "no human power that is not the imitation power of domination" (2018, 47).

19. This doesn't preclude Takers engaging in forms of resistance *within* Taker culture, an issue on which I focus in the next chapter.

20. From this perspective, striving to mitigate the worst effects of weirding weather associated with climate change represents another example of Indigenous climate injustice. For climate change disrupts the gods' efforts to uphold their responsibilities to the living communities in their care.

21. Burkhart highlights that "*Colo* refers to the removing of 'solids by filtering'. . . . Settler colonialism views Indigenous people as solid waste to be filtered

from the land so as to acquire what is most valuable to settler colonialists: the land itself" (2019, 27; see also Newcomb 2008).

22. In one sense, we're obviously dependent on the world in a way that it's not dependent on us. It can exist without us. This is what Quinn has in mind here. In what follows, I highlight other forms of dependency—among both the gods and members of the living community and among members of shared ecologies—that are more mutual.

23. A land reclamation project being carried out by Ohlone women in the San Francisco Bay Area is but one example of divine reanimation (Noisecat 2018). While the process of reclaiming land is slow and incremental, often involving small plots, the women have been able to plant community gardens and create ceremonial spaces. They have helped begin to restore what Plumwood calls "shadow places" (2008), blighted locales that are typically out of sight and out of mind for all but those forced to inhabit them.

24. Jacob Manatowa-Bailey (2007) reports that in the United States only some 18 percent of Native persons still speak their tribal language. Most are elderly, and almost half belong to a single nation: the Navajo.

Chapter 7

1. It might seem as if full-time farmers today who rely on industrialization have it fairly easy. But they only get away with the reduced *personal* calorie expenditure by exploiting petroleum-based chemicals and energy sources. In other words, like the great majority of present-day Takers, full-time industrial-scale farmers devour massive amounts of calories of the long dead in the form of fossil fuels. And while global food networks might offset concerns about malnutrition and undernutrition, the global poor both within and outside of industrial societies continue to struggle with both.

2. These conditions are reflected in four specifiable forms of inequality, according to Jürgen Schwettmann (2019, 43). First is inequality of access: to land, markets, financing, jobs, opportunities, and provisions in general. Second is inequality of rights: in terms of gender, race, religion, class, caste, etc. Third is inequality of participation: in local and national decision making, elections, governance structures, social dialogue, collective bargaining, etc. Finally, there's inequality of protection: by laws and authorities.

3. Then as now, Elaine states, politicians in particular "won't get it until they *have* to get it" (WS, 96)—and often not even then. By and large, policy makers are laggards ("Texas Legacy Project," Q&A, 598, and Heinberg 2015, 45).

4. Scott maintains that infrapolitics is anarchistic, since it's a manifestation of "mutuality, or *cooperation without hierarchy or state rule*" (2012, xii). Quinn likely

would offer the same "two cheers" for anarchism that Scott does. Scott withholds the third cheer because, unlike many other proponents of anarchism, he doesn't see abolishing the state as an option (although he doesn't seem opposed to its dissolution so long as conditions of mutuality fill the void). Quinn seems to agree ("Dialogue with Bob Conrad"). Nevertheless, from Quinn's perspective, it may be more accurate to "say that there's an element of what I'm saying in anarchism, rather than that there's an element of anarchism in what I'm saying" (ibid.).

5. Networks of artisans, peddlers, small independent professionals, and tradespersons also might fit the bill. As Scott asserts, these variations represent a precious source of autonomy and mutuality "in state systems increasingly dominated by large public and private bureaucracies" (2012, 85). While not typically well compensated, these means of making a living come with little or no supervision. It's no surprise, adds Scott, that they "formed the core of most radical working class movements" throughout the nineteenth century. "As an old class, they shared a communitarian tradition, a set of egalitarian practices, and a local cohesiveness that the newly assembled factory labor force was hard put to match" (ibid., 95).

6. The antihierarchalist lineage of worker cooperatives is also made evident by the Rochdale Principles of Cooperation, first codified in 1844 and adopted in 1995 by the International Cooperative Alliance (Williams 2007).

7. Daniel Bell and Wang Pei defend what they call *just hierarchies,* or "morally justified rankings of people or groups with respect to valued social dimensions" (2020, 3). While it is perhaps tempting to conceptualize tribal leadership as a just hierarchy, I caution against this for two reasons. First, Bell and Wang contend that social evolution has favored the emergence of large-scale societies with centralized bases of authority. Since large-scale societies are here to stay, they contend, we might as well seek just hierarchies as opposed to unjust ones. But for reasons that we explore in the next chapter, there are good reasons to presume that near-term selection pressures favor societal *decentralization*. Second, Bell and Wang neglect the lived experiences of Indigenous peoples. They betray a strong cultural bias against tribalism (ibid., 10f.), regarding hierarchalism as its organizational superior. For example, they discuss how to create just relations between "powerful and weaker states" (ibid., 19) with no acknowledgment of histories of colonialism.

8. Here in Philly is the Black and Brown Workers Co-Op, whose mission is "to actively challenge, resist, and dismantle those colonialist, white supremacist, and oppressive systems that impact our lives as Black and Brown workers" (blackandbrownworkerscoop.org).

9. Ultimately, though, the *East Mountain News* cohort wasn't equal in a tribal sense, since C. J. and Hap had no ownership stake. If not careful, such conditions can lead the firm to become hierarchalist. This also can occur within cooperatives that employ nonmembers and create structural barriers to gaining membership (Kaswan 2019, 653).

10. That the outcomes Junger describes occur quite frequently after natural disasters doesn't obviate that it's also true, particularly in the United States, that

white vigilantes and police routinely and indiscriminately kill persons of color during times of crisis (Solnit 2009, 259ff.), just as they do during otherwise peaceful times. Junger's considerations instead indicate that white vigilantes and the police tend to *disrupt* egalitarian forms of cooperation, including across racial lines—which may be at least partially the point of their aggression.

11. In places such as the Basque Country and the Emilia-Romagna region of Italy, these barriers have been easier to overcome. These regions share a long history of supporting cooperative enterprises. This also has proven so among people, mostly poor and disenfranchised, of nations emerging from colonial domination who recognize IMF and World Bank policies as being more of the same (Williams 2007, 26). By comparison, the United States has at best an incipient worker cooperative culture, in part due to predatory corporate expropriation and widespread resistance to establishing what are perceived, incorrectly, to be socialist forms of worker autonomy and self-determination (Landín 2018, 52).

12. Ian MacPherson suggests that worker cooperatives inherently serve as incubators for "associative intelligence." They facilitate "a special kind of knowing that emerges when people work together effectively, a conviction that people through working together learn skills that . . . make collective behavior more economically rewarding, socially beneficial, and personally satisfying" (2002, 90).

13. Marshall Sahlins remarks that within kinship relations, kin are "members of one another" (2011, 11). Worker cooperatives with particularly strong bonds might even resemble forged families similar in structure to those observed by Kath Weston among gay men and lesbians in San Francisco, which "tend to have extremely fluid boundaries," she states, "not unlike kinship organization among sectors of the African-American, American Indian, and white working class" (1991, 108).

14. Located in Emilia-Romagna, Damanhur provides another example of this phenomenon. Its six hundred-plus full-time members are primarily organized into small " 'nucleos,' or makeshift families," Alexa Clay reports. "The nucleos started as groups of 12 people; now they number 15–20" (2017). Scale is critical here, notes Macaco Tamerice, Damanhur's Coordinator of International Community Relations. "If you have too few people, you implode because you don't have enough inputs. But if you have more than 25 people, then it is hard to create intimacy and keep connections close" (ibid.).

15. Quinn states, though, that "people with changed minds are needed *everywhere*. More than anywhere else, they're needed in the *worst* sectors of our society. The silliest reaction people have to my work is to think that, because they're connected with some evil industry or organization, they should flee from it—leaving it entirely in the hands of people who don't give a damn about our future" (Q&A, 539).

16. In an odd and unique comment, Quinn argues against overthrow in part because we need "rulers and leaders to supervise civilization's drudgery for us—keeping the potholes filled, the sewage and water treatment plants running,

and so on" (BC, 96; see also Q&A, 481). This claim is out of character. I guess road repair and sewage treatment aren't fitting tribal ventures, although I'm not exactly sure why.

17. While Quinn argues that the New Tribal Revolution will have no more of a theoretical design than the Industrial Revolution has had, he does offer what he calls a "Seven-Point Plan" for the former. It's less a plan, though, than a statement of characteristics: (1) the revolution won't take place all at once; (2) it will be achieved incrementally by people working off each other's ideas; (3) it will be led by no one; (4) it won't be initiated by any political, governmental, religious, or union body; (5) it has no targeted endpoint; (6) it will proceed according to no preconceived plan; and (7) it will reward those who further the revolution with the coin of the revolution. "The coin of the New Tribal Revolution is economic equality; those whose efforts promote economic equality will benefit from economic equality" ("Open Letter to Occupy Protestors").

18. Part of the disagreement between DGR and Quinn is based on a misunderstanding by DGR of what Quinn actually is advocating. They mistakenly presume that Quinn defends the proposition that moving beyond civilization means physically relocating to somewhere beyond its global reach (Jensen 2000, 128, and Keith 2011c, 28). They also interpret walking away as turning away from the moral atrocities perpetuated by Takers, particularly by those at the pyramid's pinnacle (Keith 2011c, 28f.). Nowhere does Quinn insinuate that walking away entails standing aloof as the purveyors of these institutions wantonly destroy lives and livelihoods. Moreover, we've seen that Keith herself favors a specifiable form of withdrawal that reflects Scott's defense of infrapolitics. So does Jensen (cited in Zerzan 2002, 93).

19. Furthermore, it's not always the case that the financiers fight back. Bill McKibben (2020) proposes applying heavy pressure to the Wall Street lenders who provide financing for fossil fuel projects to withdraw current loans and refuse future ones. Persistent litigation against oil pipeline projects across the United States is leading to precipitous cost overruns, which is causing investors to pull funding and, potentially, hastening the pace of transition to renewable energy sources (Adams-Heard 2020).

Chapter 8

1. A symbiost studies, reflects on, and seeks to enact the art and science of living together within the matrix of all life.

2. As Albrecht describes them, psychoterric concepts bear a strong resemblance to *vincularidad,* or "the awareness of the integral relation and interdependence" (Mignolo and Walsh 2018, 2) of all living beings with the land and the cosmos as a whole.

3. Michelle Mart (2015) details how manufacturers of chemical weapons rebranded their products as pesticides, herbicides, and fungicides after World War II.

4. Langdon Winner notes that *artifacts embody politics*. The complex systems of technology that mediate our everyday experiences facilitate certain possibilities for ordering our societies while shutting off others. Because "the technological deck is stacked long in advance to favor certain social interests," Winner asserts, "technologies can be used in ways that enhance the power, authority, and privilege of some over others" (1980, 125). With different systems thus come different relations of power and authority. With different relations of power and authority come different "techno*social*" and "techno*moral*" futures (Vallor 2016, 5).

5. Salmón speaks of ecologies this way: "The Rarámuri are part of an extended ecological family that shares ancestry and origins. We share awareness that life in any environment is viable only when humans view the life surrounding them as kin" (2012, 21). The land suffers "and loses its identity" (ibid.) without humans fulfilling their inborn responsibilities.

6. I apply the term *symbioculture* to what Salmón describes advisedly. He instead calls this food system *eating the landscape*. Both designations are meant, in part, to reject the default form of agrarianism that operates within settler culture. Settlers privilege field tillage; we tend to regard it as the one right way to produce food. It's to be carried out via the conversion of "natural" ecosystems into "orderly and rational" croplands recognizable as such, Dennis Martinez states, by "the rectilinear structure of European farms with their repeated straight rows of crops, together, of course, with their initially very high *short-term* productivity" (2018, 156). Like eating the landscape, symbioculture privileges a decidedly messier approach to cultivating food, which also happens to work for people and the planet.

7. "Very little of the North American continent has been untouched by humans," Salmón remarks. "Except for some of the loftiest peaks and the hottest desert locations, the land has been managed just like a garden. And in most places where people have sustainably lived with their place, the diversity of the place has been enhanced by the practices of the people" (2012, 29; see also Cronon 1983 and Denevan 1992). I recently read a history of the small town in which I spent my early childhood. The authors note that its founders encountered unending thick and unruly undergrowth on the site where the town now stands. This likely was because the area's Indigenous inhabitants had been forced out several years earlier. The same phenomenon occurred on a larger scale in New England, Charles Mann notes. While early colonists believed they were encountering primeval forests, the landscape was "actually in the midst of violent change and demographic collapse" because of the loss of its human stewards. "Far from destroying pristine wilderness," Mann concludes, "Europeans bloodily *created* it" (2005, 323).

8. Developmentalists frequently contend that honoring market principles provides the most feasible and expeditious approach to facilitating sustainable development. This requires integrating the full ecological cost of production into

market prices and making manufacturers responsible for bearing the enduring costs of destructive practices (Speth 2008, Hawken 2010, and Wagner 2011).

9. Cutler Cleveland and Peter O'Connor (2011) contend that the 3:1 EROI estimate for unconventional crude is too generous. They estimate the actual EROI to be closer to 1:1.

10. Some industry analysts offer an inflated estimate of how much conventional crude is left by altering the definition of what counts as conventional (Ahmed 2017, 16ff.). For example, Michael Jefferson (2016) counts tight oil as conventional even though the former takes far more energy to extract than the latter.

11. Ahmed contends that we can expect states to employ quantitative easing to stabilize their financial systems and support ailing industries. But because lower EROI act as a "geophysical ceiling on economic growth" (2017, 84), the demise of the fossil fuel industry would trigger large-scale debt default—particularly since the fossil fuel industry and related sectors compose roughly one-quarter of equity and debt markets (Bond 2018). Reductions in net exports may well increase oil prices. But Ahmed states that this, too, "would trigger economic recession, causing a drop in demand, while lower production levels would exacerbate the economy's inability to grow substantially, if at all. In effect, the global economy would likely experience a self-reinforcing recessionary economic process" (2017, 85).

12. The term *ghedeistual* derives from *ghedh* (Proto-Indo-European): to unite, join, bring together. Old English derivations include *gōd,* good; *ghaith,* to gather; and *togædere,* to be present in one place or in a group. It's also associated with *geist* (German), spirit or mind.

13. David Treuer (2021) calls for immediately transferring jurisdiction over all national parkland in the United States to collective Native control. This, too, isn't without global precedent, with the Anangu in Australia acquiring jurisdiction with respect to Uluru (or Ayers Rock) decades ago.

14. A number of other Native chefs are engaged in these pursuits as well: Lois Ellen Frank, Loretta Oden, Walter Whitewater, and John Sharpe among them. Native food-specific podcasts such as Toasted Sister and Native Seed Pod extend the scope of outreach.

15. Chellie Spiller et al. (2011) defend a business ethic predicated on promoting "multi-dimensional relational well-being," which is intended to operate across spiritual, cultural, social, ecological, and economic spheres. This supports the proposition that the value of financial wealth is a function of its service to the relationships among stakeholders.

16. Within large-scale toxicultural operations—wherein sexism, heteropatriarchy, and other forms of gender-based oppression are rife—skilled women largely have been displaced by unskilled and undervalued men as farm workers. Along with combatting the rampant exploitation of the bodies particularly of Indigenous women and nonbinary persons (#MMIWG2S), decommodification

also must reverse deskilling and undervaluing farm labor more generally (Jaffe and Gertler 2006, Altieri and Toledo 2011, and Gilbert 2013).

Chapter 9

1. According to its proponents, sustainable intensification involves increasing food yield without adverse ecological effects (see, for example, Baulcombe et al. 2009 and Godfray et al. 2010). Critics note, though, that said proponents tend to privilege productivism over food sovereignty and essentially defend a continuation of the corporate-dominated food system with a green veneer (Crist et al. 2017, 262f.). Proponents of sustainable intensification also routinely defend their preferred practices in the name of feeding a growing population (Brown et al. 2011 and Cook et al. 2015, 4).

2. The situation wasn't quite this simple, of course. Yes, the Soviet Union refused to persist with the nuclear arms race. But it was less a matter of choice, as Quinn seems to frame it, than a consequence of "catabolic collapse" (Orlov 2008).

3. Ponting highlights that while toxicultural output is high, "this relies on huge inputs that consume large amounts of energy. Machines have to [be] made, and then consume fuel when being used. Huge sheds containing animals have to be heated and lit. Animal feeds have to be produced in factories. Huge quantities of artificial fertilizers, pesticides, and herbicides have to be used, and these require large amounts of energy to produce. Then the products of the farm have to be transported over large distances and stored" (2007, 243). These processes consume considerably more energy than they produce (Shiva 2009, 26).

4. Arne Naess puts the number at no more than one hundred million, or about 1 percent of current population (cited in Bodian 1982, 76). Alan Weisman calculates that optimum human population is more like two billion, although this depends on the standard of living to which we collectively aspire given available provisions (2013, 412). I'm not exactly sure what collective aspiration looks like, but I'll leave that aside.

5. A further concern with the classic theory centers on the presumed inevitability of modernization, which supports the notion that the population problem would solve itself. But "politics matters," assert Jay Winter and Michael Titelbaum; "we need to place a greater emphasis on political processes as fundamental elements framing fertility decline to low levels" (2013, viii).

6. Quinn corrects this claim in his exchange with Thornhill (1998). Nebraska farmers don't grow food because someone somewhere is consuming it but because someone somewhere is buying it. This includes purchasing crops for factory farms and biofuels, of course, the production of which hasn't reduced global food availability sufficiently to trigger population reduction. This correction

is important with respect to Quinn's discussion of how decommodification can help end the food race. We'll cover this shortly.

7. Quinn's callousness is of a sort that's led some defenders of the planet to be charged with ecofascism. William Aiken worries about those who insinuate that "massive human diebacks would be good. It is our duty to cause them. It is our species' duty, relative to the whole, to eliminate 90 percent of our numbers" (1984, 269; see also Regan 2004, 262). This is nothing less than "classical fascism," insists Frederick Ferré, "the submergence of the individual person to the glorification of the collectivity, race, tribe, or nation" (1996, 18). More specifically, asserts Kristin Shrader-Frechette (who takes aim at Aldo Leopold), "In subordinating the welfare of all creatures to the integrity, stability, and beauty of the biotic community, one subordinates individual human welfare, in all cases, to the welfare of the biotic community" (1996, 63). See Callicott (2001, 211) for a defense of Leopold against this charge.

8. Besides driving widespread ecological destruction, the returns on investment from the Green Revolution have already leveled off. "The level of fertilizer use is such that increased application no longer produces a bigger crop because most of the cultivated varieties are near to their maximum possible output," Clive Ponting contends. "Production also depends on a very limited number of crops and varieties. During the twentieth century, about three-quarters of the world's crop plants were lost and no longer cultivated. Ninety percent of the world's calories now come from just twenty species, and half of the world's intake comes from just four—rice, maize, wheat, and potatoes" (2007, 245). World output of all these staples is past peak (Seppelt et al. 2014 and Bawden 2015).

9. Humanitarian interventions are bound to fail, states Teju Cole (2012), if those who undertake them don't account for the "larger disasters"—militarization, short-sighted agricultural policies, resource extraction, government corruption, and so on—that led to the inequitable distribution of food in the first place. This is why simply providing foreign aid to fight starvation often fails to alleviate the suffering of those who are most in need. Michael Maren notes that aid instead ends up lining the pockets of corrupt local officials and militias, agribusinesses, media conglomerates, and aid organizations that are paid by the American government to distribute surplus food produced by subsidized American farmers (1997, 212–13; see also Katz 2013). In effect, Maren concludes, the foreign aid industry *writ large* has destroyed methods for dealing with local food shortages that worked for centuries, if not millennia. See Snow (2015) for a critique of proponents of effective altruism for their neglect of issues like these.

10. Here's a point worth noting from George Wuerthner: "It is surprising how little land is used to grow crops consumed directly by humans. For example, all fruits, nuts, and vegetables harvested in the United States are grown on about nine million acres, or 2.5 percent of the total acreage used for croplands. The bulk of U.S. cropland is devoted to grain such as corn and other crops that

are largely fed to livestock" (2012, 127). This indicates that one can call for the universal embrace of vegetarianism as a means to continue the food race and still see ample land converted back into other-than-human biomass—at least in the short to medium term. I assume, though, that Quinn is thinking long term here. In other words, if we're intent on feeding a growing population, then we'll perpetually grow more food—plant-based or otherwise.

11. I'm not advocating or endorsing exposure to such toxins. I'm simply offering evidence regarding a possible fertility-based contributor to population decline.

12. The rule of 70 reflects that 100 multiplied by the natural logarithm of 2 equals 69.3, or roughly 70.

Chapter 10

1. Kenneth Lockridge (1974) focuses on literacy rates in colonial New England. For white men, what he describes corroborates Gatto's claims. F. W. Grubb (1990) estimates that literacy among white men in the northern colonies exceeded 70 percent by the outbreak of the American Revolution. Slaves, too, found ways to learn to read despite ever-present threats of severe retaliation (Cornelius 1983). Tellingly, I could find no studies of literacy rates among women, either slave or free.

2. Gatto (2006, xxviii) notes that the idea of adolescence came into being as a result of added years of compulsory schooling. The term was a denotation for individuals who had never before existed: (quasi-)persons who had reached puberty but who hadn't yet become adults.

3. Throughout this chapter, I refer to Quinn's essay, "The Hidden Agenda—The One We Hide from Ourselves" (IS, 69–81). It's an updated version of Quinn (2008). Differences between the two versions are cosmetic.

4. Confusion, too, plays a paramount role in schooling. Lessons are routinely taught out of context and in a disparate, almost haphazard manner by too many teachers "each working alone with only the thinnest relationship with each other, pretending, for the most part, to an expertise they do not possess," Gatto asserts (2005, 3). And this is quite intentional, at least in terms of institutional design. It's critical to teach students that "confusion is their destiny" (ibid., 4). that evaluation by one stranger after another is normal, bells and vocal dismissals from class are more important than the lessons themselves, and completing their work far outweighs finding that work meaningful.

5. During her discussions with Ishmael, Julie suggests that if the people of our culture emerged from school with the skills needed to survive outside the marketplace, "Locking up the food wouldn't keep them in prison. They'd be *out*, they'd be *free*" (MI, 143). But locking up the food—and the institution of private

property more generally—is a principal way in which Indigenous peoples have been dispossessed of their lands and all too often forced into the bottom rungs of Taker economies. Altering the education system is critical, but it's only one of the systemic changes that's required to enact a new story.

6. Why do I continue to grade graduate students? Here's one reason: "Postgraduate work is obviously different," Ishmael says to Julie. "Doctors, lawyers, scientists, scholars, and so on actually have to use in real life what they learn in graduate school. So for this small percentage of the population schooling actually does something besides keep them off the job market" (MI, 144; see also Q&A, 377 and 380).

7. Tom Brown Jr. (1978, 101f., and 1999, 3) describes his lessons with Grandfather in similar terms.

8. "What you do not know yourself, you cannot teach another," states Bob Gaines, educational publishing guru and David Kennesey's boss (H, 116). With these words, he threw "a big, ugly rock at a cluster of notions that form the foundation of modern education: the notion of professionalism in teaching, the notion that teaching is primarily a matter of technique, the notion that a well-trained teacher can teach anything—whether he knows it himself or not" (ibid., 117). What's a teacher who knows nothing except how to teach? "A state-certified fraud," Gaines proclaims (ibid., 118).

9. Other-than-canine visitors are also welcome. Only once, though, have we had one, when a neighborhood cat tagged along with me on my walk to class.

10. Consider that by age thirteen or fourteen Indigenous children who live largely outside the bounds of Taker culture "know enough to survive entirely on their own. If all their elders were to disappear overnight, they would be perfectly capable of carrying on on their own. They'd know how to put together whatever kind of shelter they're used to. They'd know how to find, stalk, and kill their prey. They'd know how to cure hides for clothing and other uses. They'd know where their food grows and know how to collect it, preserve it, and cook it. They'd know how to make their own clothing and all the tools and weapons they need" (IS, 11; see also MI, 133). They'd also "know their tribal history, their tribal customs and laws, their tales, their songs, their dances—though it's certainly true that their knowledge of these things would grow in ensuing years" (ibid., 12). This is why they're typically initiated into adulthood at this age (Q&A, 599).

11. Under such circumstances, Ishmael relays to Julie, "parents will understand that including their children in their working lives is their alternative to spending tens of billions of dollars annually on schools that are basically detention centers. We're not talking about turning children into apprentices—that's something else entirely. We're just giving them access to what they want to know, and all children want to know what their parents are up to when they leave the house" (MI, 163). "But, of course, having your children underfoot in the workplace would seriously reduce efficiency and productivity. Even though sending them to educa-

tional detention centers is terrible for children, it's unquestionably wonderful for business. The system I've outlined here will never be implemented among people of your culture as long as you value business over people" (ibid., 165).

12. How might something like this be funded? How could it be made affordable to students? Perhaps the West Philly Cooperative School, which I discuss below, can serve as a model.

13. Critics might complain that letting students study what they want will leave them less well-rounded than they should be upon graduating. "Rounded according to whom?" Ishmael asks. And what exactly is so important about well-roundedness? "At age six or seven children begin to diverge widely in their interests" (MI, 161). "Given free access to everything in your world, children . . . would become as rounded as they want to be. . . . And in fact it would appear that very few people yearn to be Renaissance men and women. Why *should* they yearn for such a thing? If you're content to know nothing beyond chemistry or woodworking or computer science or forensic anthropology, whose business is it but your own?" (ibid., 164).

14. I entered eighth grade after moving. School was a nightmare. I did have a caring teacher for Reading, but even she insisted that my old school had failed me because I hadn't yet begun to seriously consider my viable career options.

15. This statement comes in Book II. Socrates and Adeimantus are discussing what sort of person is best fit to rule the republic. The enchanted, they specify, are people who make decisions based largely on the pursuit of convenience. They're also easily manipulated by demagogues. Takers are deceived into believing that living and making a living in ways that the people of our culture deem realistic or practical provide the only path to a life of comfort, fulfillment, and freedom. This is emblematic of our enchantment.

Epilogue

1. Kyle Whyte (2020c) refers as well to *relational tipping points,* which were crossed long before global climatological and ecological tipping points were approached. It's now too late for Indigenous peoples to avoid myriad harms and injustices. Nevertheless, Whyte observes, Indigenous resistance movements continue unabated.

2. West (2017) has vocally criticized Coates for being unduly pessimistic about the prospects for Black liberation. I tend instead to view Coates as a stoic, but this is a matter for another day.

3. Comparably, Roy Scranton suggests that the only responsible reaction to global climate catastrophe is to commit suicide. "There is simply no more effective way to shrink your carbon footprint. Once you're dead, you won't use more electricity, you won't eat more meat, you won't burn more gasoline, and you

certainly won't have any more children. If you really want to save the planet, you should die" (2018, 324–25). Foer sees this as thoroughly programmatic. "Suicide notes are written once; life notes must always be written—by having honest conversations, bridging the familiar with the unfamiliar, planting messages for the future, digging up messages from the past, digging up messages from the future, disputing with our souls and refusing to stop" (2019, 224).

References

Abram, D. 1996. *The Spell of the Sensuous.* New York: Vintage.

ACLU. 2018. *A Pound of Flesh.* New York: American Civil Liberties Union.

Adams-Heard, R. 2020. "Demise of $8 Billion Atlantic Coast Gas Project Shows Pipelines Are Becoming Unbuildable." *Financial Post,* 6 July.

Adamson, R. 2008. "First Nations Survival and the Future of the Earth." In *Original Instructions,* edited by M. K. Nelson, 27–35. Rochester, VT: Bear.

Ahmed, N. 2017. *Failing States, Collapsing Systems.* Cham, CH: Springer.

Aiken, W. 1984. "Ethical Issues in Agriculture." In *Earthbound,* edited by T. Regan, 257–88. New York: Random House.

Alberro, H. 2020. "Stop Blaming Population Growth for Climate Change. The Real Culprit Is Wealth Inequality." *The Conversation,* 11 February.

Albrecht, G. 2014. "Ecopsychology in the Symbiocene." *Ecopsychology* 6, no. 1: 58–59.

———. 2017. "Growth in the Sumboikos." *Psychoterratica.*

———. 2019. *Earth Emotions.* Ithaca: Cornell University Press.

Alexander, M. 2012. *The New Jim Crow.* New York: New Press.

Alter, R. 2004. *The Five Books of Moses.* New York: W. W. Norton.

Altieri, M. A. 2013. "Strengthening Resilience of Farming Systems: A Prerequisite for Sustainable Agricultural Production." In *Wake Up Before It Is too Late,* edited by U. Hoffman, 56–70. Geneva: UNCTAD.

———, and V. M. Toledo. 2011. "The Agroecological Revolution in Latin America: Rescuing Nature, Ensuring Food Sovereignty, and Empowering Peasants." *Journal of Peasant Studies* 38, no. 3: 587–612.

Alvarez, N. 2014. *Liminal.* Ephrata, PA: Black and Green.

Anderson, D. G., et al. 2011. "Multiple Lines of Evidence for Possible Human Population Decline/Settlement Reorganization During the Early Younger Dryas." *Quartenary International* 242, no. 2: 570–83.

Anderson, D. R. 1992. "Realism and Idealism in Peirce's Cosmogony." *International Philosophical Quarterly* 32, no. 2: 185–92.

———. 1995. *Strands of a System.* West Lafayette: Purdue University.

Anderson, E. 2017. *Private Government.* Princeton: Princeton University Press.

Anderson, T., and H. Kohler. 2015. "Low Fertility, Socioeconomic Development, and Gender Equity." *Population and Development Review* 41, no. 3: 381–407.

Andrady, A. L. 2015. *Plastics and Environmental Sustainability*. Hoboken, NJ: Wiley.

Ansary, T. 2009. *Destiny Disrupted*. New York: PublicAffairs.

Anthony, R. 2017. "Sustainable Animal Agriculture and Environmental Virtue Ethics." In *Philosophy, Technology, and the Environment*, edited by D. M. Kaplan, 213–28. Cambridge: MIT Press.

âpihtawikosisân. 2012. "Language, Culture, and Two-Spirit Identity." *Law, Language, Culture*, 29 March.

Aristotle. 1984. *Politics*. In *The Complete Works of Aristotle*, vol. 1, edited by Jonathan Barnes. Princeton: Princeton University Press.

Armstrong, K. 1996. *In the Beginning*. New York: Alfred A. Knopf.

Aron, L. 2005. "The Tree of Knowledge: Good and Evil—Conflicting Interpretations." *Psychoanalytic Dialogues* 15, no. 5: 681–707.

Arum, R., and J. Roksa. 2011. *Academically Adrift*. Chicago: University of Chicago Press.

Asafu-Adjaye, J., et al. 2015. "An Ecomodernist Manifesto." www.ecomodernism.org.

Asimov, I. 1968. *Asimov's Guide to the Bible*, vol. 1. New York: Doubleday.

"Ask the Rabbis: Do Jews Believe in the Afterlife?" 2011. *Moment Magazine*, July/August.

Aunger, R. 2002. *The Electric Meme*. New York: Free Press.

Axtell, J. 1985. *The Invasion Within*. New York: Oxford University Press.

Azéma, M., and F. Rivère. 2012. "Animation in Paleolithic Art: A Pre-Echo of Cinema." *Antiquity* 86, no. 332: 316–24.

Bacon, F. 1768. *De Dignitate et Augmentis Scientiarium, Works*, edited by J. Spedding, R. Leslie Ellis, and D. D. Heath. London: Robinson and Roberts.

Baldwin, J. 2013. *The Fire Next Time*. New York: Vintage International.

Bardi, U. 2014. *Extracted*. White River Junction, VT: Chelsea Green.

Bardsley, D. K., and N. D. Wiseman. 2016. "Socio-Ecological Lessons for the Anthropocene: Learning from the Remote Indigenous Communities of Central Australia." *Anthropocene* 14, no. 5: 58–70.

Bartlett, A. 2012. "Reflections on Sustainability and Population Growth." In *Life on the Brink*, edited by P. Cafaro and E. Crist, 29–40. Athens: University of Georgia Press.

Bar-Yosef, O. 1998. "The Natufian Culture in the Levant: Threshold to the Origin of Agriculture." *Evolutionary Anthropology* 6: 159–77.

Basso, K. H. 1996. *Wisdom Sits in Places*. Albuquerque: University of New Mexico Press.

Baulcombe, D., et al. 2009. *Reaping the Benefits*. London: Royal Society.

Bawden, T. 2015. "Have We Reached 'Peak Food'? Shortages Loom as Global Production Rates Slow." *The Independent*, 28 January.

Bear, M. F., B. W. Connors, and M. A., Paradiso, eds. 2007. *Neuroscience: Exploring the Brain*. Baltimore: Lippincott Williams and Wilkins.

Begay, J. 2021. "An Indigenous Systems Approach to the Climate Crisis," *Stanford Social Innovation Review*, 10 June.

Bell, D. 2001. *Daughters of the Dreaming*. North Melbourne, AU: Spinifex.

Bell, D. A., and W. Pei. 2020. *Just Hierarchy*. Princeton: Princeton University Press.

Bendik-Keymer, J. 2020. "Facing Mass Extinction, It Is Prudent to Decolonise Lands & Laws: A Philosophical Essay on Respecting Jurisdiction." *Griffith Law Review* 29, no. 4: 561–84.

Berg, M., and B. K. Seeber. 2016. *The Slow Professor*. Toronto: University of Toronto Press.

Berlant, L. 2011. *Cruel Optimism*. Durham: Duke University Press.

Berndt, R. M., and C. H. Berndt. 1989. *The Speaking Land*. New York: Penguin.

Bernstein. E. 2005. *The Splendor of Creation*. Cleveland: Pilgrim.

Berry, D., and M. P. Bell. 2018. "Worker Cooperatives: Alternative Governance for Caring and Precarious Work." *Equality, Diversity and Inclusion* 37, no. 4: 376–91.

Berry, W. 1977. *The Unsettling of America*. Berkeley: Counterpoint.

Bird, R. 1999. "Cooperation and Conflict: The Behavioral Ecology of the Sexual Division of Labor." *Evolutionary Biology* 8, no. 2: 65–75.

Bird-David, N. 1998. "Beyond 'The Original Affluent Society': A Culturalist Reformulation." In *Limited Wants, Unlimited Means,* edited by J. Gowdy, 115–37. Washington, DC: Island.

———. 1999. "'Animism' Revisited: Personhood, Environment, and Relational Epistemology." *Current Anthropology* 40, no. S1: S67–S91.

Blackmore, S. 1999. *The Meme Machine*. New York: Oxford University Press.

Bodian, S. 1982. "Simple in Means, Rich in Ends: A Conversation with Arne Naess." In *The Ten Directions*, 10–15. Los Angeles: Institute for Transcultural Studies.

Bond, K. 2018. "2020 Vision: Why You Should See Peak Fossil Fuels Coming." *Carbon Tracker Initiative*, September.

Bookchin, M. 2005. *The Ecology of Freedom*. Oakland: AK.

Boyle, M. 2010. *The Moneyless Man*. Oxford: Oneworld.

———. 2017. "Environmentalism Used to Be about Defending the Wild—Not Anymore." *The Guardian*, 22 May.

Brafman, O., and R. A. Beckstrom. 2006. *The Starfish and the Spider*. New York: Portfolio.

Brand, R. 2013. "My Life without Drugs." *The Guardian*, 8 March.

Brand, S. 2009. *Whole Earth Discipline*. New York: Viking.

Brant, C. 1990. "Native Ethics and Rules of Behaviour." *Canadian Journal of Psychiatry* 35, no. 6: 535–39.

Breitburg, D., et al. 2018. "Declining Oxygen in the Global Ocean and Coastal Waters." *Science* 359, no. 6371: eaam7240.

Broadt, L. 1984. *Reading the Old Testament*. New York: Paulist.

Brodie, R. 2011. *Virus of the Mind*. Carlsbad, CA: Hay House.

Brooks, D. 2013. "Tribal Lessons." *New York Times Sunday Book Review*, 10 January.

———. 2020. "The Nuclear Family Was a Mistake." *The Atlantic*, March.

Brown, A. M. 2017. *Emergent Strategy*. Chico, CA: AK.

Brown, D. 2002. *Insatiable Is Not Sustainable*. Westport, CT: Praeger.

———. 2009. *An Interpretation of the Social Theories and Novels of Daniel Quinn*. Lewiston, NY: Edwin Mellen.

Brown J., et al. 2011. "Energetic Limits to Economic Growth." *BioScience* 61, no. 1: 19–26.

Brown, K. S., et al. 2012. "An Early and Enduring Advanced Technology Originating 71,000 Years Ago in South Africa." *Nature* 491, no. 7425: 590–93.

Brown, L. R. 2001. *Eco-Economy*. New York: W. W. Norton.

Brown, T. Jr. 1978. *The Tracker*. Englewood Cliffs, NJ: Prentice-Hall.

———. 1988. *The Vision*. New York: Berkley.

———. 1999. *The Science and Art of Tracking*. New York: Berkley.

Brueggemann, W. 1970. "Of the Same Flesh and Bone, Gn 2:23a." *Catholic Biblical Quarterly* 32, no. 4: 532–42.

Brundige, L. F. 1997. "'Ungrateful Indian': Continuity of Native Values." *Ayaangwaamizin* 1, no. 1: 45–52.

———, and J. D. Rabb. 1997. "Phonicating Mother Earth: A Critique of David Abram's *The Spell of the Sensuous: Perception and Language in a More-than-Human World*." *Ayaangwaamizin* 1, no. 2: 79–88.

Buber, M. 1986. "The Tree of Knowledge: Genesis 3." In *Genesis*, edited by H. Bloom, 43–48. New York: Chelsea House.

Buchanan, W. 1976. "The Old Testament Meaning of Knowledge of Good and Evil." *Journal of Biblical Literature* 75: 114–20.

Bugbee, J. 2007. "The Consequences of Metaphysics: Or, Can Charles Peirce's Continuity Theory Model Stuart Kauffman's Biology?" *Zygon* 42, no. 1: 203–21.

Buhner, S. H. 2002. *The Lost Language of Plants*. White River Junction, VT: Chelsea Green.

Burger, O., J. DeLong, and M. J. Hamilton. 2011. "Industrial Energy Use and the Human Life History." *Scientific Report* 1, no. 56: 1–7.

Burkhart, B. Y. 2004. "What Coyote and Thales Can Teach Us: An Outline of American Indian Epistemology." In *American Indian Thought*, edited by A. Waters, 15–33. Malden, MA: Blackwell.

———. 2018. "On the Mysterious 1832 Cherokee Manuscript or *Jisdu* Fixes John Locke's *Two Treatises of Civil Government*." *Transmotion* 4, no. 1: 40–76.

———. 2019. *Indigenizing Philosophy through the Land*. East Lansing: Michigan State University Press.

Burton, R. A. 2013. *A Skeptic's Guide to the Mind*. New York: St. Martin's.

Butler, O. 1993. *Parable of the Sower*. New York: Grande Central.

Cajete, G. 2000. *Native Science*. Santa Fe: Clear Light.

Callicott, J. B. 1989. *In Defense of the Land Ethic*. Albany: State University of New York Press.

———. 1994. *Earth's Insights*. Berkeley: University of California Press.
———. 2001. "The Land Ethic." In *A Companion to Environmental Philosophy,* edited by D. Jamieson, 204–17. Malden, MA: Blackwell.
Callison, C. 2014. *How Climate Change Comes to Matter*. Durham: Duke University Press.
Caplan, B. 2018. "The World Might Be Better Off Without College for Everyone." *The Atlantic,* January/February.
Carruthers, P. 2002. "The Roots of Scientific Reasoning: Infancy, Modularity and the Art of Tracking." In *The Cognitive Basis of Science,* edited by P. Carruthers, S. P. Stich, and M. Siegal, 73–95. New York: Cambridge University Press.
Carter, A. 2004. "Saving Nature and Feeding People." *Environmental Ethics* 26, no. 4: 339–60.
Cartwright, N. 1983. *How the Laws of Physics Lie*. New York: Oxford University Press.
Catton, W. R. Jr. 1982. *Overshoot*. Champaign: University of Illinois Press.
———. 2012. "Destructive Momentum: Could an Enlightened Environmental Movement Overcome It?" In *Life on the Brink,* edited by P. Cafaro and E. Crist, 16–28. Athens: University of Georgia Press.
Charlesworth, J. H. 2010. *The Good and Evil Serpent*. New Haven: Yale University Press.
Cheng, H., and Y. Cheng. 1988. *Complete Collections of the Two Chengs*. Beijing: Zhonghua Shuju.
Chew, S. C. 2001. *World Ecological Degradation*. Lanham, MD: AltaMira.
Clarke, G. 2019. "Bringing the Past to the Present: Traditional Indigenous Farming in Southern California." In *Indigenous Food Sovereignty in the United States,* edited by D. A. Mihesuah and E. Hoover, 253–75. Norman: University of Oklahoma Press.
Clay, A. 2017. "Utopia Inc." *Aeon Essays,* 28 February.
Cleveland, C. J., and P. A. O'Connor. 2011. "Energy Return on Investment (EROI) of Oil Shale." *Sustainability* 3, no. 11: 2307–22.
Coates, T. 2008. *The Beautiful Struggle*. New York: Verso.
———. 2015. *Between the World and Me*. New York: Spiegel and Grau.
Cohen, F. S. 1952. "Americanizing the White Man." *The American Scholar* 21, no. 2: 177–91.
Cohen, J. 2005. "Human Population Grows Up." *Scientific American* 293, no. 3: 48–55.
Cohen, M. N., and G. J. Armelagos, eds. 2013. *Paleopathology at the Origins of Agriculture,* 2nd ed. Gainesville: University of Florida Press.
Cole, T. 2012. "The White-Savior Industrial Complex." *The Atlantic,* 21 March.
Colebrook, C. 2017. "Transcendental Migration: Taking Refuge from Climate Change." In *Life Adrift*, edited by A. Baldwin and G. Bettini, 115–29. Lanham, MD: Rowman and Littlefield

Collins, S. 1990. *Selfless Persons*. New York: Cambridge University Press.

Conant, J. 2019. "It Begins with Respect: What 'Living Well' Means for the Tseltal and Tsotsil Maya of Chiapas." *Intercontinental Cry*, 21 August.

Conesa-Sevilla, J. 2008. "Thinking in Animal Signs: Tracking as a Biosemiotic Exercise, Ecopsychological Practice, and a Transpersonal Path." *The Trumpeter* 2, no. 1: 116–25.

Cook, S., et al. 2015. "Sustainable Intensification Revisited." *IIED Natural Resources Group.*

Cordova, V. F. 2004. "Ethics: The We and the I." In *American Indian Thought,* edited by A. Waters, 173–81. Malden, MA: Blackwell.

———. 2007. *How It Is,* edited by K. D. Moore, et al. Tucson: University of Arizona Press.

Cornelius, J. 1983. "'We Slipped and Learned to Read': Slave Accounts of the Literacy Process, 1830–1865." *Phylon* 44, no. 3: 171–86.

Coté, C. 2016. "'Indigenizing' Food Sovereignty. Revitalizing Indigenous Food Practices and Ecological Knowledges in Canada and the United States." *Humanities* 5, no. 3: 57.

Côté, J. E., and A. L. Allahar. 2007. *Ivory Tower Blues*. Toronto: University of Toronto Press.

Crévecoeur, M. G. J. de. 1981. *Letters from an American Farmer and Sketches of Eighteenth-Century America*, edited by A. E. Stone. New York: Penguin.

Crist, E. 2012. "Abundant Earth and the Population Question." In *Life on the Brink,* edited by P. Cafaro and E. Crist, 141–53. Athens: University of Georgia Press.

———, and P. Cafaro. 2012. "Human Population Growth as If the Rest of Life Mattered." In *Life on the Brink,* edited by P. Cafaro and E. Crist, 3–15. Athens: University of Georgia Press.

Crist, E., C. Mora, and R. Engleman. 2017. "The Interaction of Human Population, Food Production, and Biodiversity Protection." *Science* 356: 260–64.

Cronon, W. 1983. *Changes in the Land*. New York: Hill and Wang.

———. 1996. "The Trouble with Wilderness; or, Getting Back to the Wrong Nature." In *Uncommon Ground,* edited by W. Cronon, 69–90. New York: W. W. Norton.

Cuff, J. M. 2007. "C. S. Peirce, G. W. F. Hegel, and Stuart Kauffman's Complexity Theory: A Response." *Zygon* 41, no. 1: 249–55.

Cuomo, C. J. 2017a. "Against the Idea of an Anthropocene Epoch: Ethical, Political, and Scientific Concerns." *Biogeosystem Technique* 4, no. 1: 4–8.

———. 2017b. "The Anthropocene: Foregone or Premature Conclusion?" *Earth*: 10–11.

Curry, A. B. 2008. "We Don't Say 'Indian': On the Paradoxical Construction of the Reavers." *Slayage* 7, no. 1.

Dallmayr, F. 2011. *Return to Nature? An Ecological Counterhistory*. Lexington: University of Kentucky Press.

Daly, H. E. 1996. *Beyond Growth*. Boston: Beacon.
"Daniel Quinn." 2018. *The Houston Chronicle*, 18 March.
Darlington, S. M. 2019. "The Potential of Buddhist Environmentalism." *The Ecological Citizen* 3, no. 1: 24–25.
Darnell, R. 1999. "Rethinking the Concept of Band and Tribe, Community and Nation: An Accordion Model of Nomadic Native American Social Organization." *Papers of the Twenty-Ninth Algonquian Conference*, edited by D. H. Pentland, 90–105. Winnipeg: University of Manitoba Press.
Darwin, C. 1981. *Descent of Man*. Princeton: Princeton University Press.
Davidson, J. 2020. "Forget Distance Learning. Just Give Every Student an Automatic A." *Washington Post*, 20 March.
Davies, O. 2011. *Paganism*. New York: Oxford University Press.
Davis, H., and Z. Todd. 2017. "On the Importance of a Date, or, Decolonizing the Anthropocene." *ACME* 16, no. 4: 761–80.
Davis, K. 1945. "The World Demographic Transition." *Annals of the American Academy of Political and Social Science* 237, no. 1: 1–11.
Davis, W. 2002. "The Naked Geography of Hope: Death and Life in the Ethnosphere." *Whole Earth* 107: 57–61.
———. 2009. *The Wayfinders*. Toronto: House of Anansi.
Dawkins, R. 1989. *The Selfish Gene*. New York: Oxford University Press.
Deci, E. L., and R. M. Ryan. 2002. "The Paradox of Achievement: The Harder You Push, The Worse It Gets." In *Improving Academic Achievement*, edited by J. Aronson, 61–87. San Diego: Academic.
Degroot, D., et al. 2021. "Towards a Rigorous Understanding of Societal Responses to Climate Change." *Nature* 591: 539–50.
DeLong, J. P., and O. Burger. 2015. "Socio-Economic Instability and the Scaling of Energy Use with Population Size." *PLOS One* 10, no. 6: e0130547.
Deloria, V. Jr. 1973. *God Is Red*. New York: Grosset and Dunlap.
———. 1999. *Spirit and Reason*. Golden, CO: Fulcrum.
———, and D. R. Wildcat. 2001. *Power and Place*. Golden, CO: Fulcrum.
Denevan, W. M. 1992. "The Pristine Myth: The Landscape of the America in 1492." *Annals of the Association of American Geographers* 82, no. 3: 369–85.
Descartes, R. 1985. "Discourse on Method." In *The Philosophical Writings of Descartes*, vol. 1, translated by J. Cottingham, R. Stoothoff, and D. Murdoch. New York: Cambridge University Press.
De Schutter, O. 2010. "Agroecology and the Right to Food." Presentation to the United Nations Human Rights Council, New York.
DeVega, C. 2019. "Cornel West on Hope and Resistance in the Age of Trump: We Must 'Find Joy in the Struggle.'" *Salon*, 3 November.
De Vos, J. M., et al. 2014. "Estimating the Normal Background Rate of Species Extinction." *Conservation Biology* 29, no. 2: 452–62.

Dhara, C., and V. Singh. 2021. "The Delusion of Infinite Economic Growth." *Scientific American*, 20 June.

Diamond, I., and D. M. Seidenberg. 2000. "Sensuous Minds and the Possibility of a Jewish Ecofeminist Practice." *Ethics and the Environment* 4, no. 2: 185–95.

Diamond, J. 1987. "The Worst Mistake in the History of the Human Race." *Discover Magazine*, May.

———. 2005. *Collapse*. New York: Penguin.

———. 2012. *The World Until Yesterday*. New York: Penguin.

Diaz, S., J. Settele, and E. Brondizio. 2019. *Summary for Policymaker of the Global Assessment Report on Biodiversity and Ecosystem Services*. Bonn: IPBES.

Dinan, A., and T. Smith. 2016. "Logos Bacteria: Life and Logic under the Microscope." *Dark Mountain* 9: 33–42.

Driskill, Q-L. 2010. "Doubleweaving Two-Spirit Critiques: Building Alliances between Native and Queer Studies." *GLQ* 16, nos. 1–2: 69–92.

DuBois, W. E. B. 2003. *The Souls of Black Folk*. New York: Barnes and Noble Classics.

Dunbar-Ortiz, R. 2014. *An Indigenous Peoples' History of the United States*. Boston: Beacon.

Duncan, T. 2016. "Case Study: Taranaki Farm Regenerative Agriculture. Pathways to Integrated Ecological Farming." In *Land Restoration*, edited by I. Chabay, M. Frick, and J. Helge, 271–87. Waltham, MA: Elsevier.

Dworkin, R. 2011. *Justice for Hedgehogs*. Cambridge, MA: Belknap.

Dyble, M., et al. 2015. "Sex Equality Can Explain the Unique Social Structure of Hunter-Gatherer Bands." *Science* 348, no. 6236: 796–98.

Edenfield, A. C. 2017. "Power and Communication in Worker Cooperatives: An Overview." *Journal of Technical Writing and Communication* 47, no. 3: 260–79.

Ehrlich, P. R. 1968. *The Population Bomb*. New York: Sierra Club/Ballantine.

———. 2018. "Interview with Paul Ehrlich." *Ecological Citizen* 1, no. 2: 154–55.

Eiselen, F. C. 1910. "The Tree of the Knowledge of Good and Evil." *The Biblical World* 36, no. 2: 101–12.

Eisenstein, C. 2007. *The Ascent of Humanity*. Harrisburg, PA: Panenthea.

Eisler, R. 2007. *The Real Wealth of Nations*. Oakland: Berrett-Koehler.

Ellwood, W. 2014. *The No-Nonsense Guide to Degrowth and Sustainability*. Oxford: New Internationalist.

Endicott, K. 1988. "Property, Power, and Conflict among the Batek of Malaysia." In *Hunter and Gatherers*, vol. 2, edited by T. Ingold, D. Riches, and J. Woodburn, 110–27. New York: Berg.

Engnell, I. 1955. "'Knowledge' and 'Life' in the Creation Story." In *Wisdom in Israel and the Ancient Near East*, edited by M. Noth and D. W. Thomas, 103–19. Leiden: E. J. Brill.

Eppinger, P., and C. Eppinger. 1994. *Restless Mind, Quiet Thoughts*. Ashland, OR: White Cloud.

Erlewine, R. 2010. *Monotheism and Tolerance*. Bloomington: Indiana University Press.

Eşim, S., and W. Katajamäki. 2017. “Rediscovering Worker Cooperatives in a Changing World of Work.” *IUSLabor* 1: 1–8.

———, and G. Tchami. 2019. “Cooperatives and Fundamental Principles and Rights at Work: Natural Disposition or Commitment to Action?” In *Cooperatives and the World of Work*, edited by B. Roelants et al., 57–72. New York: Routledge.

Eum, H. 2017. *Cooperatives and Employment*. Brussels: CICOPA.

Evans, F. 2008. *The Multivoiced Body*. New York: Columbia University Press.

Fagan, B. 2004. *The Long Summer*. Cambridge, MA: Basic.

Fairlie, S. 2010. *Meat*. White River Junction, VT: Chelsea Green.

Fanon, F. 1968. *Wretched of the Earth*, translated by C. Farrington. New York: Grove.

Farb, P. 1978. *Humankind*. New York: Houghton Mifflin Harcourt.

FAO. 2009. *How to Feed the World*. Rome: FAO.

———. 2018. *Sustainable Food Systems: Concept and Framework*. Rome: FAO.

Farrington, B. 1964. *The Philosophy of Francis Bacon*. Liverpool: Liverpool University Press.

Feeney, J. 2010. “Agriculture: Ending the World as We Know It.” *The Zephyr*, August/September.

Ferré, F. 1996. “Persons in Nature: Toward an Applicable and Unified Environmental Ethic.” *Ethics and the Environment* 1, no. 1: 15–25.

Figueroa-Helland, L., C. Thomas, and A. Pérez Aguilera. 2018. “Decolonizing Food Systems: Food Sovereignty, Indigenous Revitalization, and Agroecology as Counter-Hegemonic Movements.” *Perspectives on Global Development and Technology* 17, no. 2: 173–201.

Fingarette, H. 1972. *Confucius: The Secular as Sacred*. New York: Harper and Row.

Finley, E. 2017. “The New Municipal Movements.” *Roar Magazine* 6.

Firestone, R. B., et al. 2007. “Evidence for an Extraterrestrial Impact 12,900 Years Ago that Contributed to the Megafaunal Extinctions and the Younger Dryas Cooling.” *PNAS* 104, no. 41: 16016–21.

Firor, J., and J. Jacobsen. 2002. *The Crowded Greenhouse*. New Haven: Yale University Press.

Fischer, B., and J. Tronto. 1990. “Toward a Feminist Theory of Caring.” In *Circles of Care*, edited by E. Abel and M. Nelson, 36–54. Albany: State University of New York Press.

Fisher, M. P. 2014. *Living Religions*. Upper Saddle River, NJ: Pearson.

Fishkin, J. 2014. *Bottlenecks*. New York: Oxford University Press.

Fixico, D. 2003. *The American Indian Mind in a Linear World*. New York: Routledge.

Flavelle, C., and K. Goodluck. 2021. “Dispossessed, Again: Climate Change Hits Native Americans Especially Hard.” *The New York Times*, 27 June.

Fleming, D. 2014. “Lean Logic.” *Dark Mountain* 5: 187–200.

———. 2016. *Lean Logic*. White River Junction, VT: Chelsea Green.

Fletcher, A. M. 2013. *Inside Rehab*. New York: Viking.

Foer, J. S. 2019. *We Are the Weather*. New York: Farrar, Straus and Giroux.

Foley, J. 2014. "A Five-Step Plan to Feed the World." *National Geographic* 225, no. 5: 27, 35, 43, 45–46.

Foltz, R. 2006. *Animals in Islamic Tradition and Muslim Cultures*. Oxford: Oneworld.

Fontana, R., and S. Della Torre. 2016. "The Deep Correlation between Energy Metabolism and Reproduction: A View on the Effects of Nutrition for Women's Fertility." *Nutrients* 8, no. 2: 87.

Forbes, J. D. 2008. *Columbus and Other Cannibals*. New York: Seven Stories.

Foucault, M. 1971. *The Order of Things*. New York: Pantheon.

Fox, M. A. 2000. "Vegetarianism and Planetary Health." *Ethics and the Environment* 5: 163–74.

Franklin, B. 1973. *The Papers of Benjamin Franklin*, vol. 17, edited by W. B. Willcox et al. New Haven: Yale University Press.

Freedman, R. D. 1983. "Woman, a Power Equal to a Man." *Biblical Archaeology Review* 9: 56–58.

Fridley, D. 2010. "Nine Challenges of Alternative Energy." In *The Post Carbon Reader*, edited by R. Heinberg and D. Lerch, 229–46. Healdsburg, CA: Watershed.

Fromm, E. 1966. *You Shall Be as Gods*. New York: Holt, Rinehart, and Winston.

Garnett, T. 2017. "Livestock and Climate Change." In *The Meat Crisis*, 2nd ed., edited by J. D'Silva and J. Webster, 31–51. New York: Earthscan.

Gates, F. T. 1913. *The Country School of To-morrow*. New York: General Education Board.

Gatto, J. T. 2005. *Dumbing Us Down*. Gabriola Island, BC: New Society.

———. 2006. *The Underground History of American Education*. New York: Oxford Village.

George, S. 1986. *How the Other Half Dies*. London: Penguin.

Gibson, J. J. 1966. *The Senses Considered as Perceptual Systems*. Boston: Houghton Mifflin.

Gide, A. 2000. *André Gide: Journals*, vol. 4, translated by J. O'Brien. Champaign: University of Illinois Press.

Giere, R. N. 1992. *Cognitive Models of Science*. Minneapolis: University of Minnesota Press.

Gilbert, D. 2010. "Global Warming and Psychology." http://vimeo.com/10324258.

Gilbert, P. R. 2013. "Deskilling, Agrodiversity, and the Seed Trade: A View from Contemporary British Allotments." *Agriculture and Human Values* 30, no. 1: 101–14.

Gill, C. J., and E. F. Rissman. 1997. "Female Sexual Behavior Is Inhibited by Short- and Long-Term Food Restriction." *Physiology and Behavior* 61, no. 3: 387–94.

Ginzberg, L. 1956. *Legends of the Bible*. Philadelphia: Jewish Publication Society of America.

Gladwell, M. 2000. *The Tipping Point*. Boston: Little, Brown.

Gliessman, S. R. 2007. "Agroecology: Growing the Roots of Resistance." *Agroecology and Sustainable Food Systems* 37, no. 1: 19–31.

Godfray, C., et al. 2010. "Food Security: The Challenge of Feeding 9 Billion People." *Science* 327, no. 5962: 812–18.

Goeman, M., and J. Denetdale. 2009. "Native Feminisms: Legacies, Interventions, and Indigenous Sovereignties." *Wicazo Sa Review* 24, no. 2: 9–13.

Good, J. 2014. "Indigenized Education Teaches Real Democracy." *Elephant Journal,* 10 September.

Gordis, R. 1957. "The Knowledge of Good and Evil in the Old Testament and the Qumran Scrolls." *Journal of Biblical Literature* 76, no. 2: 123–38.

Gordon, A. R. 1907. *The Early Traditions of Genesis*. New York: Charles Scribner's Sons.

Gould, S. J. 1999. *Rocks of Ages*. New York: Ballantine.

Gowdy, J. 1998. "Introduction: Back to the Future and Forward to the Past." In *Limited Wants, Unlimited Means,* edited by J. Gowdy, xv–xxxi. Washington, DC: Island.

Grabar, H. 2020. "We're Not Going Back to the Way Life Was Before." *Slate*, 12 March.

GRAIN. 2013. "Food, Climate Change, and Healthy Soils: The Forgotten Link." In *Wake Up Before It Is Too Late*, edited by U. Hoffman, 19–21. Geneva: UNCTAD.

Grant, M. J. 2015. "The Demographic Promise of Expanded Female Education: Trends in the Age at First Birth in Malawi." *Population and Development Review* 41, no. 3: 409–38.

Grapard, A. G. 1985. "Nature and Culture in Japan." In *Deep Ecology,* edited by M. Tobias, 240–55. San Diego: Avant.

Gray, L. 2008. "Where is the Holy Land?" In *Original Instructions,* edited by M. K. Nelson, 86–87. Rochester, VT: Bear.

Gray, P., and G. Riley. 2013. "The Challenges and Benefits of Unschooling, According to 232 Families Who Have Chosen that Route." *Journal of Unschooling and Alternative Learning* 7, no. 14: 1–27.

Greer, J. M. 2009. *The Ecotechnic Future*. Gabriola Island, BC: New Society.

———. 2017. "Confronting the Cthulhucene." *Dark Mountain* 12: 91–101.

Gregory, R. 1970. *The Intelligent Eye*. London: Weidenfeld and Nicolson.

Grey, S., and R. Patel. 2015. "Food Sovereignty as Decolonization: Some Contributions from Indigenous Movements to Food Systems and Development Politics." *Agriculture and Human Values* 32: 431–44.

Grignon, J., and R. W. Kimmerer. 2017. "Listening to the Forest." In *Wildness,* edited by G. Van Horn and J. Hausdoerffer, 67–74. Chicago: University of Chicago Press.

Grinde, D. A., and B. E. Johansen. 1995. *Ecocide of Native America*. Santa Fe: Clear Light.

Gross, L. W. 2014. *Anishinaabe Ways of Knowing and Being*. New York: Routledge.

Grubb, F. W. 1990. "Growth of Literacy in Colonial America: Longitudinal Patterns, Economic Models, and the Direction of Future Research." *Social Science History* 14, no. 4: 451–82.

Gruzalski, B. 2004. "Why It's Wrong to Eat Animals Raised and Slaughtered for Food." In *Food for Thought*, edited by S. F. Sapontzis, 124–37. Amherst, NY: Prometheus.

Guha, R. 1989. "Radical American Environmentalism and Wilderness Preservation: A Third World Critique." *Environmental Ethics* 11, no. 1: 71–83.

———, and J. Martinez-Alier. 1997. *Varieties of Environmentalism*. London: Earthscan.

Guillebaud, J., and P. Hayes. 2009. "Population Growth and Climate Change: Universal Access to Family Planning Should Be the Priority." *Free Inquiry* 29, no. 3: 34–35.

Gunn Allen, P. 1979. "The Psychological Landscape of *Ceremony*." *American Indian Quarterly* 5, no. 1: 7–12.

Haberman, D. L. 2017. "Hinduism: Devotional Love of the World." In *Routledge Handbook of Religion and Ecology*, edited by W. Jenkins, M. E. Tucker, and J. Grim, 35–42. New York: Routledge.

Hall, C. A. S., R. Powers, and W. Schoenberg. 2008. "Peak Oil, EROI, Investments and the Economy in an Uncertain Future." In *Biofuels, Solar and Wind as Renewable Energy Systems*, edited by D. Pimentel, 109–32. New York: Springer.

Hall, K. Q. 2017. "Crippling Sustainability, Realizing Food Justice." In *Disability Studies and the Environmental Humanities*, edited by S. J. Ray and J. Sibara, 422–46. Lincoln: University of Nebraska Press.

Hall, M. 2011. *Plants as Persons*. New York: Columbia University Press.

Haraway, D. J. 2016. *Staying with the Trouble*. Durham: Duke University Press.

Hardin, G. 1974. "Living on a Lifeboat." *Bioscience* 24: 561–68.

Harjo, L. 2019. *Spiral to the Stars*. Tucson: University of Arizona Press.

Harris, I. 1995. "Buddhist Environmental Ethics and Detraditionalization: The Case for Ecobuddhism." *Religion* 25: 199–211.

Harris, M. 2020. "A Warning from a Scientist Who Saw the Coronavirus Coming." *Slate*, 5 March.

Harris, W. T. 1893. *The Philosophy of Education*. Baltimore: Johns Hopkins University Press.

Hartmann, T. 2013. *The Last Hours of Humanity*. Cardiff, CA: Waterfront Digital.

Harvey, G. 2006. *Animism*. New York: Columbia University Press.

———. 2013. *Food, Sex, and Strangers*. Bristol, CT: Acumen.

———. 2017. "Paganism and Animism." In *Routledge Handbook of Religion and Ecology*, edited by W. Jenkins, M. E. Tucker, and J. Grim, 211–19. New York: Routledge.

———. 2019. "Animism and Ecology: Participating in the World Community." *The Ecological Citizen* 3, no. 1: 72–77.

Haslett-Marroquin, R. 2018. "The Chicken and the Egg: Stop Linear Farming and Embrace Circular Agriculture." *Regeneration International*, 23 October.

Hatab, L. J. 2008. *Nietzsche's* On the Genealogy of Morality: *An Introduction*. New York: Cambridge University Press.

Hausman, C. R. 1993. *Charles S. Peirce's Evolutionary Philosophy*. New York: Cambridge University Press.

Hawken, P. 2010. *The Ecology of Commerce*, revised ed. New York: Harper Business.

Heinberg, R. 2005a. "Memories and Visions of Paradise." In *Against Civilization*, edited by J. Zerzan, 196–97. Los Angeles: Feral House.

———. 2005b. "Was Civilization a Mistake?" In *Against Civilization*, edited by J. Zerzan, 116–23. Los Angeles: Feral House.

———. 2010. "Beyond the Limits of Growth." In *The Post Carbon Reader*, edited by R. Heinberg and D. Lerch, 3–12. Healdsburg, CA: Watershed.

———. 2013. "Soaring Oil and Food Prices Threaten Affordable Food Supply." In *Wake Up Before It Is Too Late*, edited by U. Hoffman, 290–92. Geneva: UNCTAD.

———. 2015. *Afterburn*, Gabriola Island, BC: New Society.

———, and D. Fridley. 2016. *Our Renewable Future*. Washington, DC: Island.

Heinrich, J. 2020. *The WEIRDest People in the World*. New York: Farrar, Straus and Giroux.

Hempel, C. G. 1965. *Aspects of Scientific Explanation*. New York: Free Press.

Herman, J. 1997. *Trauma and Recovery*. New York: Basic.

Herrington, G. 2021. "Update to Limits to Growth: Comparing the World3 Model with Empirical Data." *Journal of Industrial Ecology* 25, no. 3: 614–26.

Hester, L., et al. 2000. "Indigenous Worlds and Callicott's Land Ethic." *Environmental Ethics* 22, no. 3: 273–90.

Hester, T. L. Jr. 2004. "Choctaw Conceptions of the Excellence of the Self, with Implications for Education." In *American Indian Thought*, edited by A. Waters, 182–87. Malden, MA: Blackwell.

Hilgartner, C. A. 1998. "*Ishmael* and General Semantics Theory." *Et Cetera* 55, no. 2: 166–79.

Hilgetag, C. C., and H. Barbas. 2009. "Are There Ten Times More Glia than Neurons in the Brain?" *Brain Structure and Function* 213, no. 4–5: 365–66.

Hoagland, M. 1995. *The Way Life Works*. New York: Times.

Hogan, L. 2013. "We Call It Tradition." In *The Handbook of Contemporary Animism*, edited by G. Harvey, 17–26. Bristol, CT: Acumen.

Holt, J. 2008. "Every Waking Hour." In *The Unschooling Unmanual*, edited by J. Hunt and J. Hunt, 85–88. Protection Island, BC: Natural Child Project.

Hookway, C. 2000. "Holism." In *A Companion to the Philosophy of Science*, edited by W. H. Newton-Smith, 162–64. Malden, MA: Blackwell.

Hopfenberg, R., and D. Pimentel. 2001. "Human Population Numbers as a Function of Food Supply." *Environment, Development, and Sustainability* 3: 1–15.

Hopkins, R. 2011. *The Transition Companion*. Totnes, UK: Green.

Hornborg, A. 2001. *The Power of the Machine*. Walnut Creek, CA: AltaMira.
Houssenloge, K. 2008. "Why I Chose Unschooling." In *The Unschooling Unmanual,* edited by J. Hunt and J. Hunt, 35–39. Protection Island, BC: Natural Child Project.
Huambachano, M. A. 2015. "Food Security and Indigenous Peoples Knowledge: El Buen Vivir-Sumaq Kawsay in Peru and Te Atanoho, Maori-New Zealand." *Food Studies* 5, no. 3: 33–47.
Huang, Y. 2017. "Confucianism: Confucian Environmental Virtue Ethics." In *Routledge Handbook of Religion and Ecology,* edited by W. Jenkins, M. E. Tucker, and J. Grim, 52–59. New York: Routledge.
Hull, D. 2001. *Science and Selection*. New York: Cambridge University Press.
Idel, A., and T. Reichert. 2013. "Livestock Production and Food Security in a Context of Climate Change, and Environmental and Health Challenges." In *Wake Up Before It Is too Late*, 138–53, edited by U. Hoffman. Geneva: UNCTAD.
Illich, I. 1970. *Deschooling Society*. New York: Harper and Row.
Imbroscio, D. L., T. Williamson, and G. Alperovitz. 2003. "Local Policy Responses to Globalization: Place-Based Ownership Models of Economic Enterprise." *Policy Studies Journal* 31, no. 1: 31–52.
IPCC. 2021. *Climate Change 2021*. Geneva: IPCC.
———. 2022. *Climate Change 2022*. Geneva: IPCC.
Jaffe, J., and M. Gertler. 2006. "Victual Vicissitudes: Consumer Deskilling and the (Gendered) Transformation of Food Systems." *Agriculture and Human Values* 23, no. 2: 143–62.
Jain, P. 2017. "Ecology (Jainism)." In *Encyclopedia of Indian Religions: Buddhism and Jainism,* edited by K. T. S. Sarao and J. D. Long, 424–26. Berlin: Springer.
James, W. 1975. *Pragmatism* and *The Meaning of Truth*. Cambridge: Harvard University Press.
Järvensivu, P., et al. 2018. "Governance of Economic Transition." *Global Sustainable Development Report 2019*. Geneva: United Nations.
Jefferson, M. 2016. "A Global Energy Assessment." *Wiley Disciplinary Reviews: Energy and Environment* 5, no. 1: 7–15.
Jensen, D. 2000. *A Language Older than Words*. White River Junction, VT: Chelsea Green.
———. 2004. *Walking on Water*. White River Junction, VT: Chelsea Green.
———. 2006a. *Endgame,* vol. 1. New York: Seven Stories.
———. 2006b. *Endgame,* vol. 2. New York: Seven Stories.
———, and A. McBay. 2009. *What We Leave Behind*. New York: Seven Stories.
Johansen, B. E. 1982. *Forgotten Founders*. Boston: Harvard Common.
Johnson, L. B. 2013. *Religion and Sustainability*. New York: Routledge.
Jones, P., and P. Thornton. 2009. "Cropper to Livestock Keepers: Livelihood Transitions to 2050 in Africa Due to Climate Change." *Environmental Science Policy* 12, no. 4: 427–37.
Junger, S. 2016. *Tribe*. New York: Twelve.

Justice, D. H. 2011. *The Way of Thorn and Thunder*. Albuquerque: University of New Mexico Press.

Kallis, G. 2011. "In Defence of Degrowth." *Ecological Economics* 70, no. 5: 873–80.

Kandel, E. R., et al. 2013. *Principles of Neural Science,* 5th ed. New York: McGraw-Hill.

Kaswan, M. J. 2019. "Happiness Theory and Worker Cooperatives: A Critique of the Alignment Thesis." *Labor and Society* 22, no. 3: 637–60.

Kates, C. A. 2004. "Reproductive Liberty and Overpopulation." *Environmental Values* 13, no. 2: 51–79.

Katz, J. M. 2013. *The Big Truck Went By*. New York: Palgrave Macmillan.

Kauffman, S. A. 1995. *At Home in the Universe*. New York: Oxford University Press.

———. 2008. *Reinventing the Sacred.* New York: Basic.

Kaza, S. 1993. "Acting with Compassion: Buddhism, Feminism, and the Environmental Crisis." In *Ecofeminism and the Sacred,* edited by C. J. Adams. New York: Continuum.

Kearns, F. 2017. "Water Is Life, Relationality, and Tribal Sovereignty: An Interview with Melanie Yazzie." *The Confluence*, 24 October.

Keith, L. 2009. *The Vegetarian Myth*. Oakland: Flashpoint.

———. 2011a. "Liberals and Radicals." In *Deep Green Resistance,* edited by A. McBay, L. Keith, and D. Jensen, 61–111. New York: Seven Stories.

———. 2011b. "Other Plans." In *Deep Green Resistance,* edited by A. McBay, L. Keith, and D. Jensen, 193–237. New York: Seven Stories.

———. 2011c. "The Problem." In *Deep Green Resistance,* edited by A. McBay, L. Keith, and D. Jensen, 21–29. New York: Seven Stories.

Kellert, S. 1995. "Concepts of Nature: East and West." In *Reinventing Nature?* Edited by M. Soule and G. Lease, 103–21. Washington, DC: Island.

Kelly, R. L. 2013. *The Lifeways of Hunter-Gatherers*. New York: Cambridge University Press.

Kelso, J. A. S. 1995. *Dynamic Patterns*. Cambridge: MIT Press.

Kennelly, J. J., and M. Odekon. 2016. "Worker Cooperatives in the United States, Redux." *Working USA* 19, no. 2: 163–85.

Kidd, B. 1918. *The Science of Power*. New York: G. P. Putnam's Sons.

Kidner, D. 2008. *Genesis*. Westmont, IL: Intervarsity.

Kimmerer, R. W. 2013. *Braiding Sweetgrass*. Minneapolis: Milkweed.

———. 2014. "Climate Change and Indigenous Knowledge." Presentation at the Center for Aboriginal Initiatives, University of Toronto.

———. 2018. "*Mishkos Kenomagwen*, the Lessons of Grass: Restoring Reciprocity with the Good Green Earth." In *Traditional Ecological Knowledge,* edited by M. K. Nelson and D. Shilling, 27–56. New York: Cambridge University Press.

Kingsnorth, P. 2010. "Confessions of a Recovering Environmentalist." *Dark Mountain* 1: 47–60.

———. 2012. "Dark Ecology." *Dark Mountain* 3: 7–27.

———. 2019. "The Language of the Master." *Emergence Magazine*, 8 May.
———, and D. Hine. 2009. *Uncivilisation*. Self-published.
Kingsolver, B. 2007. *Animal, Vegetable, Miracle*. New York: HarperCollins.
Kirschner, M. W., and J. C. Gerhart. 2005. *The Plausibility of Life*. New Haven: Yale University Press.
Klein, N. 2013. "Dancing the World into Being: A Conversation with Idle No More's Leanne Simpson." *Yes! Magazine*, 6 March.
———. 2014. *This Changes Everything*. New York: Simon and Schuster.
Kolbert, E. 2014. *The Sixth Extinction*. New York: Henry Holt.
Kream, R. 2008. "What about College?" In *The Unschooling Manual*, ed. J. Hunt and J. Hunt, 75–78. Protection Island, BC: Natural Child Project.
Kronz, F. M., and A. L. McLaughlin. 2007. "The Complementary Roles of Chance and Lawlike Elements in Peirce's Evolutionary Cosmology." In *Between Chance and Choice*, ed. H. Atmanspracher and R. Bishop, 189–207. Charlottesville, VA: Imprint Academic.
Kruszelnicki, K. S. 2011. "Frog Fable Brought to Boil." *The Conversation*, 3 March.
Kuchipudi, S. V. 2020. "Coronavirus: 5 Reasons Why So Many Pandemics Begin in Asia or Africa." *MarketWatch*, 9 March.
Kuhlemann, K. 2018. "'Any Size Population Will Do?': The Fallacy of Aiming for Stabilization of Human Numbers." *Ecological Citizen* 1, no. 2: 181–89.
Kummu, M., et al. 2021. "Climate Change Risks Pushing One-Third of Global Food Production Outside the Safe Climactic Space." *One Earth* 4: 720–29.
Kurzweil, R. 2005. *The Singularity Is Near*. New York: Viking Penguin.
Kveraga, K., A. S. Ghuman, and M. Bar. 2007. "Top-Down Predictions in the Cognitive Brain." *Brain and Cognition* 65: 145–68.
LaChapelle, D. 1978. *Earth Wisdom*. Silverton, CO: Finn Hill Arts.
LaDuke, W. 1994. "Traditional Ecological Knowledge and Environmental Futures." *Colorado Journal of International Environmental Law and Politics* 5, no. 127: 127–48.
Landín, S. A. 2018. "The Scarcity of Worker Cooperatives in the USA: Enquiring into Possible Causes." *CIRIEC* 92: 39–60.
Latour, B. 1996. "On Actor-Network Theory. A Few Clarifications." *Soziale Welt* 47: 369–82.
Laughton, R. 2017. *A Matter of Scale*. Coventry, UK: Landworkers' Alliance and Centre for Agroecology.
La Villa Campesina. 1996. "Tlaxcala Declaration of the Via Campesina." Presentation at The International Conference of The Via Campesina, Tlaxcala, Mexico.
Lawler, A. 2010. "Collapse? What Collapse? Societal Change Revisited." *Science* 330: 907–909.
———. 2018. *The Secret Token*. New York: Doubleday.

Leach, D. K. 2013. "Culture and the Structure of Tyrannylessness." *Sociological Quarterly* 54, no. 2: 181–91.

Leacock, E. 1998. "Women's Status in Egalitarian Society: Implications for Social Evolution." In *Limited Wants, Unlimited Means,* edited by J. Gowdy, 139–64. Washington, DC: Island.

Leopold, A. 1949. *A Sand County Almanac.* New York: Oxford University Press.

Lerch, D. 2010. "Making Sense of Peak Oil and Energy Uncertainty." In *The Post Carbon Reader,* edited by R. Heinberg and D. Lerch, 207–10. Healdsburg, CA: Watershed.

Lertzman, R. 2008. "The Myth of Apathy." *The Ecologist,* 19 June.

Levine, B. E. 2001. *Commonsense Rebellion.* New York: Continuum.

———. 2013. "Living in America Will Drive You Insane—Literally." *Salon*, 31 July.

Levy, P. 2013. *Dispelling Wetiko.* Berkeley: North Atlantic.

Lewens, T. 2007. *Darwin.* New York: Routledge.

Lewis, J. 2018. "Why Getting Into Trouble Is Necessary to Make Change." *Time*, 4 January.

Lewontin, R. 2000. *The Triple Helix.* Cambridge: Harvard University Press.

Liebenberg, L. W. 1990. *The Art of Tracking.* Cape Town: David Philip.

Liedloff, J. 1977. *The Continuum Concept.* New York: Alfred A. Knopf.

Lim, J. 2002. *Grace in the Midst of Judgment.* Berlin: Walter de Guyter.

Lockridge, K. A. 1974. *Literacy in Colonial New England.* New York: W. W. Norton.

Lohr, J. N. 2009. "Righteous Abel, Wicked Cain: Genesis 4:1–16 in the Masoretic Text, the Septuagint, and the New Testament." *The Catholic Biblical Quarterly* 3, no. 71: 485–96.

Lomax, A. 1960. *The Folk Songs of North America.* Garden City, NY: Doubleday.

———. 1968. *Folk Song Style and Culture.* Piscataway, NJ: Transaction.

———. 2003. *Selected Writings, 1934–1997.* New York: Routledge.

Lorde, A. 2017. *A Burst of Light.* Mineola, NY: Ixia.

Lucchesi, A. H. 2019. "Spirit-Based Research: A Tactic for Surviving Trauma in Decolonizing Research." *Journal of Indigenous Research* 7, no. 1: 1–4.

Lutz, W. 2008. "From Population Explosion to Expanding Human Capital: Changing Challenges for the Future of Humankind." Presentation at the Club of Rome's International Conference on Strategies for a Sustainable Planet, Rome.

Lynas, M. 2011. *The God Species.* Washington, DC: National Geographic Society.

Macdiarmid, J. I., and S. Whybrow. 2019. "Nutrition from a Climate Change Perspective." *Proceedings of the Nutritional Society* 78, no. 3: 380–87.

MacPherson, I. 2002. "Encouraging Associative Intelligence: Co-operatives, Shared Learning and Responsible Citizenship." *Journal of Co-operative Studies* 35, no. 2: 86–98.

Macy, J. 1990. "The Greening of the Self." In *Dharma Gaia,* edited by A. H. Badiner, 53–63. Berkeley: Parallax.

Malthus, T. R. 1798. *An Essay on the Principle of Population*. London: J. Johnson.

Manatowa-Bailey, J. 2007. "On the Brink: An Overview of the Disappearance of America's First Languages: How It Happened and What We Need to Do about It." *Cultural Survival Quarterly* 31, no. 2: 12–17.

Mann, C. C. 2005. *1491: New Revelations of the Americas before Columbus*. New York: Alfred A. Knopf.

Mann, U., B. Shiff, and P. Patel. 2020. "Reasons for Worldwide Decline in Male Fertility." *Current Opinion in Urology* 30, no. 3: 296–301.

Manning, R. 2004. *Against the Grain*. New York: North Point.

Maren, M. 1997. *The Road to Hell*. New York: Free Press.

Margulis, L. 1999. *Symbiotic Planet*. New York: Basic.

———, and D. Sagan 1995. *What Is Life?* New York: Simon and Schuster.

Marrow, S. B. 2002. "*Κόσμος* in John." *Catholic Biblical Quarterly* 64, no. 1: 90–102.

Mart, M. 2015. *Pesticides: A Love Story*. Lawrence: University of Kansas Press.

Martin, C. 1992. *In the Spirit of the Earth*. Baltimore: Johns Hopkins University Press.

Martinez, D. 2018. "Redefining Sustainability through Kincentric Ecology: Reclaiming Indigenous Lands, Knowledge, and Ethics." In *Traditional Ecological Knowledge*, edited by M. K. Nelson and D. Shilling, 139–74. New York: Cambridge University Press.

———, E. Salmón, and M. K. Nelson. 2008. "Restoring Indigenous History and Culture to Nature." In *Original Instructions*, edited by M. K. Nelson, 88–115. Rochester, VT: Bear.

Mazur, L. 2016. "Without Fossil Fuels, a New Population Puzzle." *YES! Magazine*, 22 March.

McBay, A. 2011a. "Civilization and Other Hazards." In *Deep Green Resistance*, edited by A. McBay, L. Keith, and D. Jensen, 31–59. New York: Seven Stories.

———. 2011b. "Decisive Ecological Warfare." In *Deep Green Resistance*, edited by A. McBay, L. Keith, and D. Jensen, 425–74. New York: Seven Stories.

———. 2011c. "A Taxonomy of Action." In *Deep Green Resistance*, edited by A. McBay, L. Keith, and D. Jensen, 239–76. New York: Seven Stories.

McCarty, M., et al. 2012. "First Stewards Resolution." Presentation at the First Stewards Symposium, Washington, DC.

McCauley, D. J., et al. 2015. "Marine Defaunation: Animal Loss in the Global Ocean." *Science* 347, no. 6219: 247–53.

McCluney, W. R. 2004. *Humanity's Environmental Future*. Cape Canaveral, FL: SunPine.

McFague, S. 2008. *A New Climate for Theology*. Minneapolis: Fortress.

McGregor, D. 2009. "Honouring Our Relations: An Anishnaabe Perspective on Environmental Justice." In *Speaking for Ourselves*, edited by J. Agyeman et al., 27–41. Vancouver: University of British Columbia Press.

McIntyre, L. 2019. *The Scientific Attitude*. Cambridge: MIT Press.

McKenna, E. 2018. *Livestock*. Athens: University of Georgia Press.

———, and S. L. Pratt. 2014. *American Philosophy*. New York: Bloomsbury.

McKibben, B. 2006. *The End of Nature*. New York: Random House.

———. 2010a. *Eaarth*. New York: Henry Holt.

———. 2010b. "Foreword." In *Diet for a Hot Planet*, A. Lappé, xi–xii. New York: Bloomsbury.

———. 2020. "A Very Hot Year." *New York Review of Books*, 12 March.

McMahan, D. 2008. *The Making of Buddhist Modernism*. New York: Oxford University Press.

McPherson, D. H., and J. D. Rabb. 2011. *Indian on the Inside*. Jefferson, NC: McFarland.

Meadows, D. H. 2008. *Thinking in Systems*. White River Junction. VT: Chelsea Green.

———, J. Randers, and W. W. Behrens III. 1972. *The Limits to Growth*. New York: Universe.

Meissner, S. N. 2018. "The Moral Fabric of Linguicide: Un-Weaving Trauma Narratives and Dependency Relationships in Indigenous Language Reclamation." *Journal of Global Ethics* 14, no. 2: 266–276.

Merchant, C. 2006. "The Scientific Revolution and *The Death of Nature*." *Isis* 97: 513–533.

Meyer, J. M. 2015. *Engaging the Everyday*. Cambridge: MIT Press.

Meyers, C. 2005. *Exodus*. New York: Cambridge University Press.

Meyers, J. S. M. 2011. "Employee Ownership, Democratic Control, and Working-Class Empowerment." In *Employee Ownership and Shared Capitalism*, edited by E. J. Carberry. Champaign, IL: Labor and Employment Relations Association.

———, and S. P. Vallas. 2016. "Diversity Regimes in Worker Cooperatives: Workplace Inequality under Conditions of Worker Control." *The Sociological Quarterly* 57, no. 1: 98–128.

Midgley, M. 2003. *The Myths We Live By*. New York: Routledge.

Mignolo, W. D., and C. E. Walsh. 2018. *On Decoloniality*. Durham: Duke University Press.

Mill, J. S. 1852. *Principles of Political Economy*. London: John W. Parker.

Millard, A. R. 1984. "The Etymology of Eden." *Vitas Testamentum* 34, no. 1: 103–106.

Miller, G. R. 2012. "'Gender Trouble': Investigating Gender and Economic Democracy in Worker Cooperatives in the United States." *Review of Radical Political Economics* 44, no. 1: 8–22.

Million, D. 2013. *Therapeutic Nations*. Tucson: University of Arizona Press.

Mills, C. 1997. *The Racial Contract*. Ithaca: Cornell University Press.

Mima, M., D. Greenwald, and S. Ohlander. 2018. "Environmental Toxins and Male Fertility." *Current Opinion in Urology* 19, no. 7: 50.

Mohawk, J. 2008. "The Art of Thriving in Place." In *Original Instructions,* edited by M. K. Nelson, 126–36. Rochester, VT: Bear.

Moore, C. R. 2019. "New Evidence that an Extraterrestrial Collision 12,800 Years Ago Triggered an Abrupt Climate Change for Earth." *The Conversation,* 22 October.

Morrison, D. 2020. "Reflections and Realities: Expressions of Food Sovereignty in the Fourth World." In *Indigenous Food Systems,* edited by P. Settee and S. Shukla, 17–38. Toronto: Canadian Scholars.

Mowat, F. 2005. *People of the Deer.* New York: Carroll and Graf.

Müller, A., and U. Niggli. 2013. "The Potential of Sustainable Agriculture for Climate Change Adaptation." In *Wake Up Before It Is Too Late,* edited by U. Hoffman, 16–18. Geneva: UNCTAD.

Murphy, M. 2008. "Chemical Regimes of Living." *Environmental History* 13, no. 4: 695–703.

Nabhan, G. P. 2013. *Growing Food in a Hotter, Drier Land.* White River Junction, VT: Chelsea Green.

Naess, A. 1989. *Ecology, Community, and Lifestyle,* translated by D. Rothenberg. New York: Cambridge University Press.

Nagel, E. 1961. *The Structure of Science.* New York: Harcourt, Brace and World.

Nagel, T. 2012. *Mind and Cosmos.* New York: Oxford University Press.

Narayanan, V. 2001. "Water, Wood, and Wisdom: Ecological Perspectives from the Hindu Tradition." *Daedalus* 130, no. 4: 179–206.

Nelson, M. K. 2008a. "Lighting the Sun of Our Future—How These Teachings Can Provide Illumination." In *Original Instructions,* edited by M. K. Nelson, 1–19. Rochester, VT: Bear.

———. 2008b. "Re-Indigenizing Our Bodies and Minds through Native Foods." In *Original Instructions,* edited by M. K. Nelson, 180–95. Rochester, VT: Bear.

Newcomb, S. T. 2008. *Pagans in the Promised Land.* Golden, CO: Fulcrum.

Nietzsche, F. 1996. *On the Genealogy of Morals.* New York: Oxford University Press.

Nixon, R. 2011. *Slow Violence and the Environmentalism of the Poor.* Cambridge: Harvard University Press.

Noisecat, J. B. 1018. " 'It's about Taking Back What's Ours': Native Women Reclaim Land, Plot by Plot." *Huffington Post,* 22 March.

Norrgard, C. 2014. *Seasons of Change.* Chapel Hill: University of North Carolina Press.

Norton-Smith, T. M. 2010. *The Dance of Person and Place.* Albany: State University of New York Press.

Noss, D. S., and B. Grangaard. 2011. *A History of the World's Religions,* 13th ed. New York: Routledge.

Notestein, F. W. 1953. "Economic Problems of Population Change." In *Proceedings of the Eighth International Conference of Agricultural Economists,* 13–31. London: Oxford University Press.

O'Malley, M. 1976. *The Past and Future Land.* Toronto: Peter Martin Associates.

Oring, E. 2014a. "Memetics and Folkloristics: The Theory." *Western Folklore* 73, no. 4: 432–54.

———. 2014b. "Memetics and Folkloristics: The Application." *Western Folklore* 73, no. 4: 455–92.

Orlov, D. 2008. *Reinventing Collapse.* Gabriola Island, BC: New Society.

Ostendorff, F. 2013. "Excessive Industrialization of Livestock Production: The Need for a New Agricultural Paradigm." In *Wake Up Before It Is Too Late,* ed. U. Hoffman, 154–56. Geneva: UNCTAD.

Owens, E. 2020. "White People, Please Stop Declaring Yourself Allies." *Philadelphia Magazine,* 15 June.

Paddison, L. 2018. "We Cannot Fight Climate Change with Capitalism, Says Report." *Huffington Post,* 31 August.

Parkinson, R. G. 2016. *The Common Cause.* Chapel Hill: University of North Carolina Press.

Pasternak, S. 2017. *Grounded Authority.* Minneapolis: University of Minnesota Press.

Pearce, F. 2010. *The Coming Population Crash.* Boston: Beacon.

Peck, R. 2016. *I Am Not Your Negro.* New York: Velvet Film.

Pecore, M. 1992. "Menominee Sustained-Yield Management: A Successful Land Ethic in Practice." *Journal of Forestry* 90, no. 7: 12–16.

Pedersen, J. 1926. *Israel: Its Life and Culture.* New York: Oxford University Press.

Peirce, C. S. 1931–1958. *Collected Papers of Charles Sanders Peirce,* edited by C. Hartshorne and P. Weiss (vol. 1–6) and A. W. Burks (vol. 7–8). Cambridge: Harvard University Press.

Pencavel, J., and B. Craig. 1994. "The Empirical Performance of Orthodox Models of the Firm: Conventional Firms and Worker Cooperatives." *Journal of Political Economy* 102, no. 4: 718–44.

Pencavel, J., L. Pistaferri, and F. Schivardi. 2006. "Wages, Employment, and Capital in Capitalist and Worker-Owned Firms." *Industrial and Labor Relations Review* 60, no. 1: 23–44.

Peters, C. M. 2018. *Managing the Wild.* New Haven: Yale University Press.

Piaget, J. 1929. *The Child's Conception of the World.* London: Kegan Paul.

———. 1954. *The Construction of Reality in the Child.* New York: Basic.

Pielke, R. Jr. 2010. *The Climate Fix.* New York: Basic.

Pierce, A. A., I. Iwueke, and M. H. Ferkin 2007. "Food Deprivation and the Role of Estradiol in Mediating Sexual Behaviors in Meadow Voles." *Physiology & Behavior* 90, nos. 2–3: 353–61.

Pimm, S. L., et al. 2014. "The Biodiversity of Species and Their Rates of Extinction, Distribution, and Protection." *Science* 344, no. 6187: 1246752.

Pinto, Y., et al. 2013. "Bottom-Up and Top-Down Attention Are Independent." *Journal of Vision* 13, no. 3: 16.

Pitt, J. 2011. "Weapons of Mass Distortion: A Narrative." *Journal of Unschooling and Alternative Learning* 5, no. 9: 18–28.

Pizzol, D., et al. 2021. "Pollutants and Sperm Quality: A Systematic View and Meta-Analysis." *Environmental Science and Pollution Research International* 28, no. 4: 4095–4103.

Pluhar, E. 2004. "The Right to Not Be Eaten." In *Food for Thought,* edited by S. F. Sapontzis, 92–107. Amherst, NY: Prometheus.

Plumwood, V. 2007. "Journey to the Heart of Stone." In *Culture, Creativity, and Environment*, edited by F. Becket and T. Gifford, 17–36. Amsterdam, NY: Rodopi.

———. 2008. "Shadow Places and the Politics of Dwelling." *Australian Humanities Review* 44: 139–50.

———. 2012. *The Eye of the Crocodile*, edited by L. Shannon. Canberra, AU: ANU E.

Pollan, N. 2020. "The Sickness in Our Food Supply." *New York Review of Books,* 11 June.

Ponting, C. 2007. *A New Green History of the World*. New York, Penguin.

Pope Francis. 2016. *Laudato Si': On Care for Our Common Home*. Huntington, IN: Our Sunday Visitor.

Popova, M. 2017. "Technology, Wisdom, and the Difficult Art of Civilizational Self-Awareness: Thomas Merton's Beautiful Letter of Appreciation to Rachel Carson for Catalyzing the Environmental Movement." *Brainpickings,* 14 November.

Postel, S. 1999. *Pillar of Sand*. New York: W. W. Norton.

Potts, M. 2009. "Where Next?" *Philosophical Transactions of the Royal Society B* 364, no. 1532: 3115–24.

Powers, R. 2018. *The Overstory*. New York: W. W. Norton.

Pratt, S. L. 2002. *Native Pragmatism*. Bloomington: Indiana University Press.

———. 2006. "Persons in Place: The Agent Ontology of Vine Deloria, Jr." *APA Newsletter on American Indians in Philosophy* 6, no. 1: 4–9.

Pretchel, M. 1999. *Long Life, Honey in the Heart*. New York: Jeremy P. Tarcher/Putnam.

Pretty, J., et al. 2006. "Resource-Conserving Agriculture Increases Yields in Developing Countries." *Environmental Science and Technology* 40, no. 4: 1114–19.

Prothero, S. 2010. *God Is Not One*. New York: HarperOne.

Putnam, H. 2004. *The Collapse of the Fact/Value Dichotomy and Other Essays*. Cambridge: Harvard University Press.

Putnam, R. 2000. *Bowling Alone*. New York: Simon and Schuster.

Quinn, D. 1988. *Dreamer*. New York: Tor.

———. 1992. *Ishmael*. New York: Bantam.

———. 1993. "On Investments." Presentation at the Minnesota Social Investment Forum, Minneapolis. https://www.ishmael.org/daniel-quinn/essays/on-investments/.

———. 1995. *Providence: The Story of a Fifty-Year Vision Quest*. New York: Bantam.

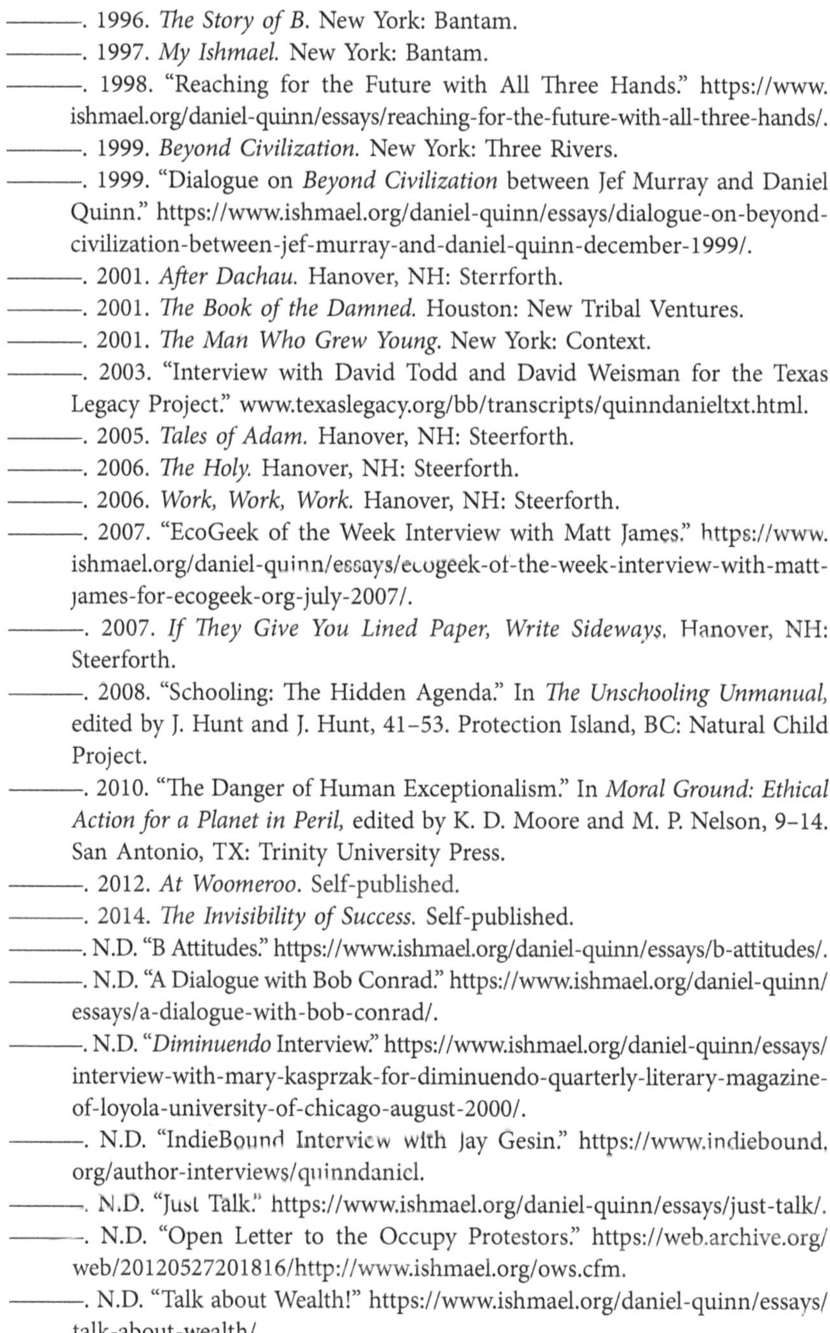

———. 1996. *The Story of B.* New York: Bantam.

———. 1997. *My Ishmael.* New York: Bantam.

———. 1998. "Reaching for the Future with All Three Hands." https://www.ishmael.org/daniel-quinn/essays/reaching-for-the-future-with-all-three-hands/.

———. 1999. *Beyond Civilization.* New York: Three Rivers.

———. 1999. "Dialogue on *Beyond Civilization* between Jef Murray and Daniel Quinn." https://www.ishmael.org/daniel-quinn/essays/dialogue-on-beyond-civilization-between-jef-murray-and-daniel-quinn-december-1999/.

———. 2001. *After Dachau.* Hanover, NH: Sterrforth.

———. 2001. *The Book of the Damned.* Houston: New Tribal Ventures.

———. 2001. *The Man Who Grew Young.* New York: Context.

———. 2003. "Interview with David Todd and David Weisman for the Texas Legacy Project." www.texaslegacy.org/bb/transcripts/quinndanieltxt.html.

———. 2005. *Tales of Adam.* Hanover, NH: Steerforth.

———. 2006. *The Holy.* Hanover, NH: Steerforth.

———. 2006. *Work, Work, Work.* Hanover, NH: Steerforth.

———. 2007. "EcoGeek of the Week Interview with Matt James." https://www.ishmael.org/daniel-quinn/essays/ecogeek-of-the-week-interview-with-matt-james-for-ecogeek-org-july-2007/.

———. 2007. *If They Give You Lined Paper, Write Sideways.* Hanover, NH: Steerforth.

———. 2008. "Schooling: The Hidden Agenda." In *The Unschooling Unmanual,* edited by J. Hunt and J. Hunt, 41–53. Protection Island, BC: Natural Child Project.

———. 2010. "The Danger of Human Exceptionalism." In *Moral Ground: Ethical Action for a Planet in Peril,* edited by K. D. Moore and M. P. Nelson, 9–14. San Antonio, TX: Trinity University Press.

———. 2012. *At Woomeroo.* Self-published.

———. 2014. *The Invisibility of Success.* Self-published.

———. N.D. "B Attitudes." https://www.ishmael.org/daniel-quinn/essays/b-attitudes/.

———. N.D. "A Dialogue with Bob Conrad." https://www.ishmael.org/daniel-quinn/essays/a-dialogue-with-bob-conrad/.

———. N.D. "*Diminuendo* Interview." https://www.ishmael.org/daniel-quinn/essays/interview-with-mary-kasprzak-for-diminuendo-quarterly-literary-magazine-of-loyola-university-of-chicago-august-2000/.

———. N.D. "IndieBound Interview with Jay Gesin." https://www.indiebound.org/author-interviews/quinndaniel.

———. N.D. "Just Talk." https://www.ishmael.org/daniel-quinn/essays/just-talk/.

———. N.D. "Open Letter to the Occupy Protestors." https://web.archive.org/web/20120527201816/http://www.ishmael.org/ows.cfm.

———. N.D. "Talk about Wealth!" https://www.ishmael.org/daniel-quinn/essays/talk-about-wealth/.

———. N.D. "Thoughts on Dialogue." https://www.ishmael.org/daniel-quinn/essays/thoughts-on-dialogue/.

———. N.D. "Uru and the Tower." https://www.ishmael.org/daniel-quinn/parables/uru-and-the-tower/.

———. N.D. "Uru in the Valley of Sleepers." https://www.ishmael.org/daniel-quinn/parables/uru-in-the-valley-of-sleepers/.

———. N.D. "Who *Is* the Awakener?" https://www.ishmael.org/daniel-quinn/parables/who-is-the-awakener/.

———, and A. Thornhill. 1998. "Food Production and Population Growth." Video. Houston: New Tribal Ventures.

———, and T. Whalen. 1997. *A Newcomer's Guide to the Afterlife*. New York: Bantam.

Raman, F. 2009. *Major Themes in the Qu'ran*, 2nd ed. Chicago: University of Chicago Press.

Rao, V. 2011. "The Return of the Barbarian." *Dark Mountain* 2: 32–41.

Ray, V. 2019. "A Theory of Racialized Organizations." *American Sociological Review* 84, no. 1: 26–53.

Red Nation. 2021. *The Red Deal*. Brooklyn, NY: Common Notions.

Regan, T. 2004. *The Case for Animal Rights*, 2nd ed. Berkeley: University of California Press.

Reo, N. J. 2019. "*Inawendiwin* and Relational Accountability in Anishnaabeg Studies: The Crux of the Biscuit." *Journal of Ethnobiology* 39, no. 1: 65–75.

———, and K. P. Whyte 2012. "Hunting and Morality as Elements of Traditional Ecological Knowledge." *Human Ecology* 40: 15–27.

Restakis, J. 2010. *Humanizing the Economy*. Gabriola Island, BC: New Society.

Rezendes, P. 1999. *Tracking and the Art of Seeing*, 2nd ed. New York: HarperCollins.

Ripple, W. J., and R. L. Bechta. 2012. "Trophic Cascades in Yellowstone: The First 15 Years after Wolf Reintroduction." *Biological Conservation* 145, no. 1: 205–13.

Roberts, D. 2017. "I'm an Environmental Journalist, but I Never Write about Overpopulation. Here's Why." *Vox*, 26 September.

Rodman, J. 1977. "The Liberation of Nature?" *Inquiry* 20, no. 1: 83–131.

Rolston, H. III. 1996. "Feeding People Versus Saving Nature." In *World Hunger and Morality*, 2nd ed., edited by W. Aiken and H. LaFollette, 248–67. Upper Saddle River, NJ: Prentice-Hall.

Rose, D. B. 1998. "Totemism, Regions, and Co-Management in Aboriginal Australia." Presentation at the Conference of the International Association for the Study of Common Property, Vancouver.

Rosenberg, M. 2012. *Cave Paintings, Perception, and Knowledge*. New York: Palgrave MacMillan.

Ryerson, W. 2012. "How Do We Solve the Population Problem?" In *Life on the Brink*, edited by P. Cafaro and E. Crist, 240–54. Athens: University of Georgia Press.

Sahlins, M. 1972. *Stone Age Economics.* New York: Aldine-Atherton.

———. 2011. "What Kinship Is (Part One)." *Journal of the Royal Anthropological Institute* 17, no. 1: 2–19.

Salmón, E. 2000. "Kincentric Ecology: Indigenous Perceptions of the Human-Nature Relationship." *Ecological Applications* 10, no. 5: 1327–32.

———. 2012. *Eating the Landscape.* Tucson: University of Arizona Press.

Sanderson, E. W., et al. 2002. "The Human Footprint and the Last of the Wild." *BioScience* 52, no. 10: 891–904.

Sarna, N. M. 1966. *Understanding Genesis.* New York: McGraw-Hill.

Schlosberg, D., and L. Craven. 2019. *Sustainable Materialism.* New York: Oxford University Press.

Schwettmann, J. 2019. "Cooperatives and the Future of Work." In *Cooperatives and the World of Work,* edited by B. Roelants et al., 34–56. New York: Routledge.

Science Research Associates. 1964. *A Guide to Modern Mathematics.* Chicago: Science Research Associates.

Scott, J. C. 2012. *Two Cheers for Anarchism.* Princeton: Princeton University Press.

———. 2017. *Against the Grain.* New Haven: Yale University Press.

Scranton, R. 2015. *Learning How to Die in the Anthropocene.* San Francisco: City Lights.

———. 2018. *We're Doomed. Now What?* New York: Soho.

Sen, A. 1981a. "Ingredients of Famine Analysis: Availability and Entitlements." *The Quarterly Journal of Economics* 96: 433–64.

———. 1981b. *Poverty and Famines.* New York: Oxford University Press.

Senge, P. M. 1990. *The Fifth Discipline.* New York: Doubleday.

Seppelt, R., et al. 2014. "Synchronized Peak-Rate Years of Global Resources Use." *Ecology and Society* 19, no. 4: 50.

Settee, P., and S. Shukla. 2020. "Introduction." In *Indigenous Food Systems,* edited by P. Settee and S. Shukla, 1–13. Toronto: Canadian Scholars.

Shah, S. 2020. "Think Exotic Animals Are to Blame for the Coronavirus? Think Again." *The Nation,* 18 February.

Sharma, I. P., et al. 2020. "Indigenous Agricultural Practices: A Supreme Key to Maintaining Biodiversity." In *Microbiological Advancements for Higher Altitude Agro-Ecosystems & Sustainability,* edited by R. Goels et al., 91–112. Singapore: Springer Nature.

Shelby, C. 2016. *Addiction: A Philosophical Perspective.* New York: Palgrave Macmillan.

Shiva, V. 1993. *Monocultures of the Mind.* London: Zed.

———. 2009. "Women and the Gendered Politics of Food." *Philosophical Topics* 37, no. 2: 17–32.

———. 2016. *Who Really Feeds the World?* Berkeley: North Atlantic.

———, and P. Pandey. 2007. *Biodiversity Based Organic Farming.* New Delhi: Navdanya.

Shoson, M. 1961. "The Authorship and Significance as a Theory of the Buddha-Nature of the Phrase 'Plants, Trees, and Earth All Become Buddha.'" *Journal of Indian and Buddhist Studies* 9: 672–701.

Shrader-Frechette, K. 1996. "Individualism, Holism, and Environmental Ethics." *Ethics and the Environment* 1, no. 1: 55–69.

Shrestha, K., et al. 2008. *Study of Sustainable Biodiversity Conservation.* Lalitpur, Nepal: National Foundation for Development of Indigenous Nationalities.

Shrivastava, P., and J. J. Kennelly. 2013. "Sustainability and Place-Based Enterprise." *Organization and Environment* 26, no. 1: 83–101.

Silko, L. M. 1997. *Yellow Woman and a Beauty of the Spirit.* New York: Touchstone.

Simpson, L. B. 2017. *As We Have Always Done.* Minneapolis: University of Minnesota Press.

Singer, P. 2002. *Animal Liberation.* New York: HarperCollins.

———. 2011. *The Expanding Circle.* Princeton: Princeton University Press.

Slote, M. 1996. "The Morality of Wealth." In *World Hunger and Morality,* edited by W. Aiken and H. LaFollette, 124–47. Upper Saddle River, NJ: Prentice-Hall.

Smail, J. K. 2004. "Global Population Reduction: Confronting the Inevitable." *World Watch* 17, no. 5: 58–59.

Smil, V. 2008a. *Energy in Nature and Society.* Cambridge: MIT Press.

———. 2008b. *Global Catastrophes and Trends.* Cambridge: MIT Press.

Smith, A. F. 2014a. "In Defense of Homelessness." *Journal of Value Inquiry* 48, no. 1: 33–51.

———. 2014b. "Political Deliberation and the Challenge of Bounded Rationality." *Politics, Philosophy & Economics* 13, no. 3: 269–91.

———. 2016. *A Critique of the Moral Defense of Vegetarianism.* New York: Palgrave Macmillan.

———. 2021. "Symbioculture: A Kinship-Based Conception of Sustainable Food Systems." *Environmental Philosophy* 18, no. 2: 199–225.

Smith, M. A. 2002. *The Early History of God.* Grand Rapids, MI: Wm. B. Eerdmans.

Snelgrove, C., R. K. Dhamoon, and J. Corntassel. 2014. "Unsettling Settler Colonialism: The Discourse and Politics of Settlers, and Solidarity with Indigenous Nations." *Decolonization: Indigeneity, Education & Society* 3, no. 2: 1–32.

Snodgrass, j. 2011. *Genesis and the Rise of Civilization.* Self-published.

Snow, M. 2015. "Against Charity." *Jacobin*, 25 August.

Snyder, G. 1969. *Turtle Island.* New York: New Directions.

Snyder, S., M. Newall, and M. M. Dean. 2019. "Penn's Head of Counseling and Psychological Services Dies by Suicide at Center City Building." *Philadelphia Inquirer*, 9 September.

Sobering, K. 2016. "Producing and Reducing Gender Inequality in a Worker-Recovered Cooperative." *Sociological Quarterly* 57, no. 1: 129–51.

Sobrevila, C. 2008. *The Role of Indigenous Peoples in Biodiversity Conservation.* Washington, DC: The World Bank.

Solnit, R. 2009. *A Paradise in Hell.* New York, Penguin.

———. 2016. *Hope in the Dark.* Chicago: Haymarket.

Soloveitchik, J. B. 1983. *Halakhic Man.* Philadelphia: Jewish Publication Society.

Spencer, K. A. 2019. "Critic Curtis White: Capitalism Needs Workers Who Are 'Stupid-Smart.'" *Salon,* 23 December.

Speth, J. G. 2008. *The Bridge at the Edge of the World.* New Haven: Yale University Press.

Spiller, C., et al. 2011. "Relational Well-Being and Wealth: Māori Businesses and an Ethic of Care." *Journal of Business Ethics* 98: 153–69.

Spratt, D., and I. Dunlop. 2018. *What Lies Beneath.* Melbourne: Breakthrough-National Centre for Climate Restoration.

Stengers, I. 2012. "Reclaiming Animism." *E-flux* 36.

———. 2018. *Another Science Is Possible.* Medford, MA: Polity.

Stern, H. S. 1958. "The Knowledge of Good and Evil." *Vestus Testamentum* 8, no. 4: 405–18.

Stevenson, J. T. 1992. "Aboriginal Land Rights in Northern Canada." In *Contemporary Moral Issues,* edited by W. Cragg, 297–311. Toronto: McGraw-Hill Ryerson.

St. George, Z. 2021. "We Are on Track for a Planet-Wide, Climate-Driven Landscape Makeover." *Mother Jones,* 4 July.

Styres, S. 2019. "Literacies of Land: Decolonizing Narratives, Storying, and Literature." In *Indigenizing and Decolonizing Studies in Education: Mapping the Long View,* edited by L. T. Smith, E. Tuck, and K. W. Yang, 24–37. New York: Routledge.

Sullivan, S., and N. Tuana. 2007. "Introduction." In *Race and Epistemologies of Ignorance,* edited by S. Sullivan and N. Tuana, 1–10. Albany: State University of New York Press.

Sverdrup, H., and V. Ragnarsdottír. 2014. "Natural Resources in a Planetary Perspective." *Geochemical Perspectives* 3, no. 2: 129–341.

Sweatman, M. 2018. *Prehistory Decoded.* Leicester, UK: Troubador.

Sylvan, R., and D. H. Bennett. 1988. "Taoism and Deep Ecology." *The Ecologist* 18, nos. 4–5: 148–59.

Tainter, J. 1988. *The Collapse of Complex Societies.* New York: Cambridge University Press.

Talisse, R. B. 2012. *Pluralism and Liberal Politics.* New York: Routledge.

Tan, S. 2020. "As Colleges Go Remote, Students Revolt Against the State of Higher Ed." *Salon,* 9 May.

Taylor, B. 2009. *Dark Green Religion.* Berkeley: University of California Press.

———. 2016. "The Greening of Religion Hypothesis (Part One): From Lynn White, Jr. and Claims that Religions Can Promote Environmentally Destructive

Attitudes and Behaviors to Assertions They Are Becoming Environmentally Friendly." *Journal for the Study of Religion, Nature and Culture* 10, no. 3: 268–305.

Taylor, C. 2007. *A Secular Age*. Cambridge: Harvard University Press.

Taylor, S. 2019. "Disabled Ecologies: Living with Impaired Landscapes." Presentation at the University of California, Berkeley.

———. 2020. "What Would Health Security Look Like?" *Boston Review*, 28 May.

Tepper, S. S. 1997. *The Family Tree*. New York: Avon.

Tett, G. 2011. "There's No Time to Waste." *FT Magazine*, 2 December.

Thompson, P. B. 2006. "Commodification and Secondary Rationalization." In *Democratizing Technology*, edited by T. Veak. 112–35 Albany: State University of New York Press.

Tirosh-Samuelson, H. 2019. "Judaism Responds to the Environmental Crisis." *The Ecological Citizen* 3, no. 1: 40–41.

Todd, Z. 2015. "Indigenizing the Anthropocene." In *Art in the Anthropocene*, edited by H. Davis and E. Turpin, 241–54. London: Open Humanities.

Toledo, V. M. 2001. "Biodiversity and Indigenous Peoples." In *Encyclopedia of Biodiversity*, edited by S. Levin et al., 451–63. Cambridge, MA: Academic.

Tolinski, M. 2011. *Plastics and Sustainability*. Hoboken, NJ: Wiley.

Traxler, C. 2015. "The Most Democratic School of Them All: Why the Sudbury Model of Education Should Be Taken Seriously." *Schools* 12, no. 2: 271–96.

Treuer, D. 2021. "Return the National Parks to the Tribes." *The Atlantic*, 12 April.

Tsing, A. L. 2015. *The Mushroom at the End of the World*. Princeton: Princeton University Press.

Tsur, N., et al. 2018. "The Traumatized Body: Long-Term PTSD and Its Implications for the Orientation of Bodily Signals." *Psychiatry Research* 261: 281–89.

Tu, W., and M. E. Tucker. 2003. *Confucian Spirituality*. New York: Crossroad.

Tuck, E., and K. W. Yang. 2012. "Decolonization Is Not a Metaphor." *Decolonization: Indigeneity, Education & Society* 1, no. 1: 1–40.

Tucker, M. E. 2017. "Global Traditions: Introduction." In *Routledge Handbook of Religion and Ecology*, edited by W. Jenkins, M. E. Tucker, and J. Grim, 33–34. New York: Routledge.

———, and J. Grim. 2017. "The Movement of Religion and Ecology: Emerging Field and Dynamic Force." In *Routledge Handbook of Religion and Ecology*, edited by W. Jenkins, M. E. Tucker, and J. Grim, 3–12. New York: Routledge.

Tudge, C. 2010. "How to Raise Livestock—And How Not to." In *The Meat Crisis*, 2nd ed., edited by J. D'Silva and J. Webster, 9–20. New York: Earthscan.

———. 2016. *Six Steps Back to the Land*. Cambridge, UK: Green.

Tverberg, G. 2012. "The Long-Term Tie between Energy Supply, Population, and the Economy." *Our Finite World*, 29 August.

Vail, J. 2010. "Decommodification and Egalitarian Political Economy." *Politics & Society* 38, no. 3: 210–346.

Vallor, S. 2016. *Technology and the Virtues*. New York: Oxford University Press.

Van Dooren, T. 2002. *Being-with-Death*. Unpublished manuscript.

———. 2014. *Flight Ways*. New York: Columbia University Press.

Van Gestel, N. 2008. "An Unschooling Adventure." In *The Unschooling Unmanual*, edited by J. Hunt and J. Hunt, 11–32. Protection Island, BC: Natural Child Project.

Varner, G. E. 2012. *Personhood, Ethics, and Animal Cognition*. New York: Oxford University Press.

Veldman, R. G. 2016. "What Is the Meaning of Greening? Cultural Analysis of a Southern Baptist Environmental Text." *Journal of Contemporary Religion* 31, no. 2: 199–222.

Vermeulen, K. 2014. "Mind the Gap: Ambiguity in the Story of Cain and Abel." *Journal of Biblical Literature* 133, no. 1: 29–42.

Veyne, P. 1988. *Did the Greeks Believe in Their Myths?* Translated by P. Wissing. Chicago: University of Chicago Press.

Vieta, M. 2014. "Learning in Struggle: Argentina's New Worker Cooperatives as Transformative Learning Organizations." *Relations Industrielles/Industrial Relations* 69, no. 1: 186–218.

———, et al. 2016. "Participation in Worker Cooperatives." In *The Palgrave Handbook on Volunteering, Civic Participation, and Nonprofit Associations*, edited by D. H. Smith, R. A. Stebbins, and J. Grotz, 436–53. New York: Palgrave Macmillan.

von Rad, G. 1962. *Old Testament Theology*, vol. 1, translated by D. M. G Stalker. New York: Harper and Row.

Wagner, A. 2014. *Arrival of the Fittest*. New York: Current.

Wagner, G. 2011. *But Will the Planet Notice?* New York: Hill and Wang.

Walker, A., and P. Parmar. 1993. *Warrior Marks*. San Diego: Harcourt Brace.

Walker, P., and T. Lovat. 2014. "You Say Morals, I Say Ethics—What's the Difference?" *The Conversation*, 17 September.

Wallace, D. F. 2009. "All That." *The New Yorker*, 14 December.

Wallace, M. I. 2005. *Finding God in the Singing*. Minneapolis: Fortress.

Wallace-Wells, D. 2019. *The Uninhabitable Earth*. New York: Tim Duggan.

Ward, P. D. 2007. *Under a Green Sky*. New York: HarperCollins.

Warner, S. 2004. "Reproductive Liberty and Overpopulation: A Response." *Environmental Values* 13, no. 3: 393–99.

Weatherford, J. 1988. *Indian Givers*. New York: Crown.

Weaver, J. 1996. *Defending Mother Earth*. Maryknoll, NY: Orbis.

———. 1997. *That the People Might Live*. New York: Oxford University Press.

Weeskaop Project. 2011. "History of Human Population Growth: 8000 BC to 2100 AD." *Scribd*.

Weisman, A. 2013. *Countdown*. New York: Little, Brown.

Welch, S. 2013. "Radical-Cum-Relation: Bridging Feminist Ethics and Native Individual Autonomy." *Philosophical Topics* 41, no. 2: 203–22.

———. 2017. "Native American Chaos Theory and the Politics of Difference." In *The Routledge Companion to Feminist Philosophy,* edited by A. Garry, S. J. Khader, and A. Stone, 370–81. New York: Routledge.

Wells, S. 2010. *Pandora's Seed.* New York: Random House.

West, C. 2017. "Ta-Nehisi Coates Is the Neoliberal Face of the Black Freedom Struggle." *The Guardian,* 17 December.

———. 2019. "There Is Joy in Struggle." Presentation at the Harvard Divinity School Commencement, Cambridge, MA.

Weston, K. 1991. *Families We Choose.* New York: Columbia University Press.

Wheatley, K. 2009. "Unschooling: An Oasis for Development and Democracy." *Encounter* 22, no. 2: 27–32.

White, L. T. 1967. "The Historical Roots of Our Ecological Crisis," *Science* 155: 1203–1207.

Whitt, L. A. 2004. "Biocolonialism and the Commodification of Knowledge." In *American Indian Thought,* edited by A. Waters, 188–213. Malden, MA: Blackwell.

Whyte, K. P. 2014. "Indigenous Women, Climate Change Impacts, and Collective Action." *Hypatia* 29, no. 3: 599–616.

———. 2015. "Indigenous Food Systems, Environmental Justice, and Settler-Industrial States." In *Global Food, Global Justice,* edited by M. Rawlinson and C. Ward, 143–56. New York: Cambridge Scholars.

———. 2016. "Is It Colonial Déjà Vu? Indigenous Peoples and Climate Injustice." In *Humanities for the Environment*, edited by J. Adamson, M. Davis, and H. Huang, 88–104. New York: Taylor Francis.

———. 2017. "Our Ancestors' Dystopia Now. Indigenous Conservation and the Anthropocene." In *Routledge Companion to the Environmental Humanities,* edited by U. K. Heise, J. Christensen, and M. Niemann, 206–15. New York: Routledge.

———. 2018a. "Critical Investigations of Resilience: A Brief Introduction to Indigenous Environmental Studies & Sciences." *Daedalus* 147, no. 2: 136–47.

———. 2018b. "Indigenous Science (Fiction) for the Anthropocene: Ancestral Dystopias and Fantasies of Climate Change Crises." *Environment and Planning E: Nature and Space* 1, nos. 1–2: 224–42.

———. 2018c. "Reflections on the Purpose of Indigenous Environmental Education." In *Handbook of Indigenous Education,* edited by E. A. McKinley and L. T. Smith, 1–21. Singapore: Springer Nature.

———. 2018d. "Settler Colonialism, Ecology, and Environmental Injustice." *Environment and Society: Advances in Research* 9: 125–44.

———. 2018e. "White Allies, Let's Be Honest about Decolonization." *YES! Magazine,* 3 April.

———. 2019. "Indigenous Climate Justice and Food Sovereignty: Food, Climate, Continuance." In *Indigenous Food Sovereignty in the United States,* edited by D. A. Mihesuah and E. Hoover, 320–34. Norman: University of Oklahoma Press.

———. 2020a. "Against Crisis Epistemology." in *Routledge Handbook of Critical Indigenous Studies,* edited by B. Hokowhitu et al., 52–64. New York: Routledge.

———. 2020b. "Indigenous Environmental Justice: Anti-Colonial Action through Kinship." In *Environmental Justice: Key Issues,* ed. B. Coolsaet, 266–78. New York: Taylor Francis.

———. 2020c. "Too Late for Indigenous Climate Change Justice: Ecological and Relational Tipping Points." *WIREs Climate Change* 11, no. 1: e603.

———, J. P. Brewer II, and J. T. Johnson. 2016. "Weaving Indigenous Science, Protocols and Sustainability Science." *Sustainability Science* 11, no. 1: 25–32.

———, C. Caldwell, and M. Schaefer. 2018. "Indigenous Lessons about Sustainability Are Not Just for 'All Humanity.'" In *Situating Sustainability,* edited by J. Sze, 149–79. New York: NYU Press.

———, and C. Cuomo. 2017. "Ethics of Caring in Environmental Ethics: Indigenous and Feminist Philosophies." In *The Oxford Handbook of Environmental Ethics,* edited by S. M Gardiner and A. Thompson, 234–47. New York: Oxford University Press.

———, and S. N. Meissner. 2021. "Without Land, Decolonizing American Philosophy Is Impossible." In *Decolonizing American Philosophy,* edited by C. McCall and P. Reynolds, 37–61. Albany: State University of New York Press.

———, J. L. Talley, and J. D. Gibson. 2019. "Indigenous Mobility Traditions, Colonialism, and the Anthropocene." *Mobilities* 14, no. 3: 319–35.

Wilcox, M. 2010. "Marketing Conquest and the Vanishing Indian: An Indigenous Response to Jared Diamond's Archaeology of the American Southwest." In *Questioning Collapse,* edited by P. A. McAnany and N. Yoffee, 113–41. New York: Cambridge University Press.

Wildcat, D. R. 2009. *Red Alert.* Golden, CO: Fulcrum.

Wilkinson, R., and K. Pickett. 2009. *The Spirit Level.* New York: Bloomsbury.

Williams, R. C. 2007. *The Cooperative Movement.* Hampshire, UK: Ashgate.

Willott, E. 2012. "Recent Population Trends." In *Environmental Ethics,* 2nd ed., edited by D. Schmidt and E. Willott, 526–33. New York: Oxford University Press.

Winner, L. 1980. "Do Artifacts Have Politics?" *Daedalus* 109, no. 1. 121–36.

Winter, J., and M. Titelbaum. 2013. *The Global Spread of Fertility Decline.* New Haven: Yale University Press.

Wirzba, N. 2003. *The Paradise of God.* New York: Oxford University Press.

Woodburn, J. 1998. "Egalitarian Societies." In *Limited Wants, Unlimited Means,* edited by J. Gowdy, 87–110. Washington, DC: Island.

World Bank. 2012. *Turn Down the Heat.* New York: World Bank.

Wright, E. O. 2010. *Envisioning Real Utopias.* London: Verso.

Wright, R. 1992. *Stolen Continents.* Boston: Houghton Mifflin.

———. 2004. *A Short History of Progress.* New York: Carroll and Graf.

Wuerthner, G. 2012. "Population, Fossil Fuels, and Agriculture." In *Life on the Brink,* edited by P. Cafaro and E. Crist, 123–37. Athens: University of Georgia Press.

———. 2018. "Anthropocene Boosters and the Attack on Wilderness Conservation." *Ecological Citizen* 1, no. 2: 161–66.

Xu, C., et al. 2020. "Future of the Human Climate Niche." *PNAS* 117, no. 21: 11350–55.

Ya-Bititi, G., et al. 2019. "'Coffee Has Given Us Power to Act': Coffee Cooperatives and Women's Empowerment in Rwanda's Rural Areas: A Case Study of Karaba Coffee Cooperative." In *Cooperatives and the World of Work,* edited by B. Roelants et al., 107–18. New York: Routledge.

Yao, X. 2014. "An Eco-Ethical Interpretation of Tianren Heyi." *Frontiers of Philosophy in China* 9, no. 4: 570–85.

Yehuda, R., and L. M. Bierer. 2007. "Transgenerational Transmission of Cortisol and PTSD Risk." *Progress in Brain Research* 167: 121–35.

Young, H. S., et al. 2014. "Declines in Large Wildlife Increase Landscape-Level Prevalence of Rodent-Borne Disease in Africa." *PNAS* 111, no. 19: 7036–41.

Zabel, G. 2009. "Peak People: The Interrelationship between Population Growth and Energy Resources." *Energy Bulletin,* 20 April.

Zaleha, B. D., and A. Szasz. 2014. "Keep Christianity Brown! Climate Denial and the Christian Right in the United States." In *How the World's Religions Are Responding to Climate Change,* edited by R. G. Veldman et al., 209–28. New York: Routledge.

Zeitlin, I. M. 1984. *Ancient Judaism.* New York: Polity.

Zerzan, J. 1994. *Future Primitive and Other Essays.* Brooklyn: Autonomedia.

———. 2002. *Running on Emptiness.* Los Angeles: Feral House.

Index

www.ingramcontent.com/pod-product-compliance
Lightning Source LLC
LaVergne TN
LVHW040201080826
844660LV00001B/68

* 9 7 8 1 4 3 8 4 8 8 7 1 4 *